Millennium Ed

GARDEN STATE

GOLF GUIDE

*Complete Coverage of
All New Jersey's
Public and Private
Golf Courses*

Esther Kaplan & Debra Wolf
Weathervane Press

GARDEN STATE GOLF GUIDE
Esther Kaplan & Debra Wolf

Published by Weathervane Press

ISBN 0-9645830-4-6

Printed in the United States of America

Library of Congress Cataloging in Publication Data

1. GARDEN STATE GOLF GUIDE - Title

2. Golf Guide

3. New Jersey

4. Kaplan, Esther

5. Wolf, Debra

Cover Design by Susan Steeg

Please note: The information in this book was provided by the personnel at the courses and country clubs. Every effort was made to provide accurate data. However, errors may have occurred, and the authors do not claim that every word is accurate and complete. Information regarding fees, reservation policies and access, is always subject to change without notice and should be verified before planning to play at any of these courses. There may have been changes since the time of the interviews

ACKNOWLEDGMENTS

We would like to acknowledge and thank the people who spent hours helping us put this golf guide together. In particular, Susan Steeg's graphic design talent helped us immeasurably. Her patience and expertise were essential in the production of this new edition. Ellis Wolf spent time editing the text utilizing his writing ability and his golfing experience. We could never have had so much information without the cooperation of the staff, pros and managers at each of the golf courses listed herein.

Many thanks to everyone who played a part in creating the millennium edition of **The Garden State Golf Guide.**

CONTENTS

PREFACE

Golf is a sport that is appealing to both men and women, from the young to the advanced in years. Why is golf such a universal attraction? Most sports require power, speed and stamina. Golf, on the other hand, utilizes more subtle skills such as finesse, judgment and coordination, so that strength and physical endurance are not necessarily the dominant factors. This makes it the perfect sport for everyone and explains its soaring popularity. We wrote those words 5 years ago for the first edition of the **Garden State Golf Guide.** The interest in golf has become more intense and consequently, not only are there many new courses in various stages of planning and construction, but the existing ones are upgrading, refurbishing and expanding. With all these changes and additions, we realized that this millennium edition of the book would be most timely. Now, more than ever, women, youngsters and teenagers have discovered what tried and true golfers have known for years; time spent playing golf can fascinate you, challenge you, introduce you to new friends and places, keep you in touch with nature and help you to stay physically fit.

It's interesting that the small state of New Jersey has some of the world's finest golf facilities. Highly rated **Baltusrol** is just one of the many outstanding courses located in the state. Besides well known private golf clubs such as **Somerset Hills, Plainfield, Ridgewood** and **Forsgate,** there are many less well known but worthy of high regard. **Roxiticus, Metedeconk National, Panther Valley** and the recently completed **Knob Hill** are of comparable status. In addition, New Jersey has some fine publicly owned courses; namely **Howell Park, Hominy Hill** and **Sunset Valley.** Privately owned, but open to the public, are **Seaview** near Atlantic City, **Beaverbrook,** recently opened upscale and outstanding **Roycebrook, Sand Barrens** and **New Jersey National.** Sussex County is becoming a mecca for golf with the well established **Crystal Springs,** the newly operating **Black Bear** and extraordinary **Ballyowen.** Let us not forget the legendary **Pine Valley,** reputed by Golf Digest to be the finest golf course in the world.

With a state the size of New Jersey, it is possible to travel from one end to the other and still enjoy a leisurely round of golf. Why not take the time to learn about the great golfing opportunities within your reach? New Jersey offers play in the mountains, at the seashore, in the Pinelands and on varied terrain in between. The diversity of golf courses can satisfy the budget minded as well as those willing to pay more for beautiful views, excellent facilities and challenging experiences.

In addition to its magnificent array of golf facilities, the bountiful natural beauty of New Jersey makes its residents justifiably proud. With extensive white sand beaches at the Jersey shore, rolling hills of the Watchung and Ramapo Mountains, lush wooded valleys, rich farmlands and well preserved Pinelands, it is fittingly referred to as the "Garden State". Some areas are well known to tourists and draw many visitors from near and far. However, New Jersey offers attractions that are often undiscovered while its more densely populated and developed sectors are familiar and overwhelm the image of the state. There are many New Jersey residents who are not aware of the picturesque horse farms, miles of undeveloped rural areas, many parks, forests and even wildlife sanctuaries. From High Point State Park in the northernmost part of Sussex County to Cape May Migratory Bird Refuge in the southernmost section of Cape May, New Jersey will amaze you with its beauty and natural wonders.

HOW TO USE THIS BOOK

Introduction

We have divided the 21 counties of the State of New Jersey into seven geographical regions. A scrupulous effort has been made to include all the Garden State's golf courses and we have personally visited every one.

Private and Public Golf Courses

Private means the course is open only to members and their guests. Initiation fees and yearly membership dues vary greatly. To obtain specific information, call the individual club. If you belong to a private club, it is possible for your pro to make arrangements with another club for you to play there.

Various private courses are located within adult communities. These are open only to residents of the community and their guests. If you are considering a move to an adult community, it might be a good idea to inquire about playing a round of golf at that facility.

Public is defined as courses that are open to the public and include the following categories:

1. County or municipally owned and operated courses with special rates and reservation policies

2. Daily fee courses open to the public at daily fee rates

3. Semi-private courses with memberships available at widely varying costs offering reduced or prepaid daily fees and tee time priorities - these clubs also encourage daily fee players

4. Resort courses open to the public with reduced rates for hotel guests

Name, Address and Telephone Number

On each page, we have given the full name of the club and its address. In a few cases, we have abbreviated Country Club as CC. For some, a special number for tee time reservations is listed.

Within each region, the courses are arranged alphabetically and therefore listed that way at the beginning of each region. An easy way to find an individual course by name is to refer to the **index** for its page number. The numerical dots on the regional maps give the **approximate** location of the courses with respect to major highways and towns.

Course Information

The first paragraph on each course page includes the number of holes on the course, days and months open, types of memberships and reservation policies. Most New Jersey courses that are open all year or most of the year are dependent on "weather permitting". It is therefore advisable to call in advance for the latest tee time information, as well as for seasonal rate policies. Most private clubs are open six days a week and usually close on Mondays.

Amenities

This box contains a generally self-explanatory check list of the amenities at each course. However, when there are exceptions or clarifications, they are so noted in the text, i.e. Driving Range is checked but practice is limited to irons, or Pull Carts are checked but allowed only during certain hours or days.

Power Carts: Most courses encourage the use of power carts but some do not offer them at all.

Pull Carts: Those courses that permit the use of pull carts may or may not provide them for rent as well.

Food: When this items checked, the facility offers anything from a limited snack bar or vending machines to a full-service restaurant and bar.

Outings: Many clubs make their facilities available to groups of more than 12 golfers for outings usually sponsored by corporations, charities, townships or club members. Most private clubs encourage outings on the days they are closed to their members (usually Mondays).

Caddies: Generally not offered at public courses. Check with individual clubs for their caddie policy.

Soft Spikes: Where required, so noted. Some clubs are now strongly recommending them. Call in advance for policy.

Fees

The fee schedule indicates the prevailing rates, however, it is recommended that you contact the course to make sure it has not been revised. Published rates are subject to change but generally do not vary greatly from one year to the next.

Weekday: Monday to Friday

Weekend: Saturday, Sunday and holidays - some courses include Friday as part of the weekend.

Daily: Greens fee for daily play

Res./ ID: County or township resident with current yearly permit.

Twilight: Twilight starting time differs from club to club in and off-season - check in advance with club.

Cart fees: Generally given for 2 people in a power cart. Sometimes listed (pp).

Course Description

The course description helps you discover what course would be most appropriate and appealing for you. We have discussed degree of difficulty, variety, length and special features. The scorecard shown below each course description gives additional details on course rating, slope and yardages. Whenever possible, information describing what is unique or unusual about these courses has been included; such as historical, anecdotal or interesting features. These descriptions might offer golfers some clue for course strategy.

Many nine hole courses have an additional tee box for the second nine to give the golfer playing 18 holes some added variety. Moreover, courses that have more than two nine hole sets allow combinations of play, i.e. Blue-Red, Blue-White and Red-White.

Course Directions

The first line of directions gives you the course number as indicated on the regional map. Directions progress from major highways to secondary highways to local roads and finally to the club. Care has been taken to alert the driver to landmarks or other helpful navigational features. It is recommended that you bring along a good New Jersey map to track your route in more detail as the maps provided herein show only **approximate** locations.

Professional Staff

Manager: May manage more than just the golf operation.

Supt: Superintendent of greens.

Pro: Head professional is listed; some courses have assistant pros as well. If the pro is PGA affiliated, it is shown following the name.

Architect: The name of the architect(s), year built or redesigned.

Estab: Indicates when the club originated.

Scorecard

Course Rating is an indication of how difficult the course is to a scratch golfer (one who shoots par or better). The higher the rating, the greater the difficulty.

Slope is useful as a comparison of relative difficulty between courses with the higher slope number indicating the more difficult course.

The categories rated on the scorecard on each page of this book are: **Blue/Championship** or **Professional**, **White/Regular** and **Red/Forward** tees. Many courses are offering additional tee boxes which are indicated on the actual scorecard. Some tee positions are designated by other colors or names.

New

Golf courses that were being built at the time of our last **Garden State Golf Guide** edition and have opened recently, or are scheduled to open in 1999, or are in construction as we go to press are designated with a "NEW" on their page.

NORTH EAST REGION

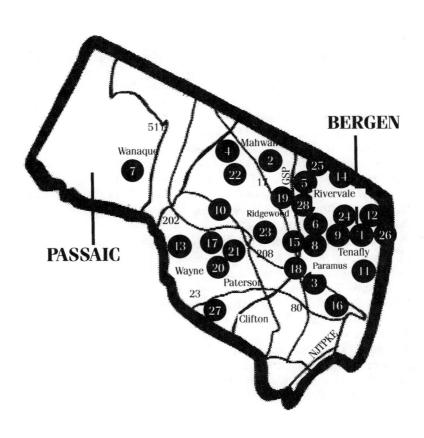

BERGEN

PASSAIC

511
Wanaque
Mahwah
4
7
2
22
GSP
25
14
1?
5
Rivervale
19
28
202
10
Ridgewood
24
12
23
6
9
1
26
13
17
15
8
21
208
18
Tenafly
20
Paramus
11
Wayne
Paterson
3
23
80
16
27
Clifton
NJTPKE

NORTH EAST REGION

Public Courses appear in **_bold italics_**

ALPINE COUNTRY CLUB

80 Anderson Ave., Demarest, NJ 07627   **(201) 768-2121**

Alpine is an 18 hole course that is open 6 days a week from March through December. Guests may play accompanied by a member. Tee time reservations are required on weekends.

- **Driving Range**
- **Practice Green**
- **Power Carts**
- Pull Carts
- **Club Rental**
- **Caddies**
- **Lockers**
- **Showers**
- **Food**
- **Clubhouse**
- **Outings**
- **Soft Spikes**

Course Description: Alpine, one of the most difficult courses in Bergen County, is known for its lush old trees and steep hills. A.W. Tillinghast, the designer of Alpine and Baltusrol as well, followed the contours of the rolling terrain to create a beautiful challenging course. The golfer must be prepared for sidehill, uphill and downhill lies in order to score well here. The greens are fast; many are two tiered. For example, the tenth, a straight uphill par 4, has a blind tee shot and an approach to a small green; a memorable hole! The 18th is a long par 5 that finishes a round of golf that can be frustrating but very enjoyable.

Directions: Bergen County, #1 on Northeast Map
Pal. Interstate Pkwy. to Exit 2, Alpine. At STOP, go left onto Rte. 9W South. Go right at first light onto Closter Dock Rd., then at Anderson Ave., make a left to club on left.

Hole	1	2	3	4	5	6	7	8	9	Out	BLUE	Rating 72.6
BLUE	418	372	331	381	136	436	598	191	510	3373		Slope 134
WHITE	407	350	315	369	127	412	545	166	500	3191		
Par	4	4	4	4	3	4	5	3	5	36	WHITE	Rating 71.7
Handicap	3	9	11	7	17	1	5	15	13			Slope 132
RED	393	272	290	312	110	299	472	153	443	2744		
Par	5	4	4	4	3	4	5	3	5	37	RED	Rating 73.8
Handicap	7	9	11	13	17	3	1	15	5			Slope 130

Hole	10	11	12	13	14	15	16	17	18	In		Totals
BLUE	339	394	316	478	300	404	191	317	570	3309	BLUE	6682
WHITE	317	362	301	452	291	385	184	304	561	3157	WHITE	6348
Par	4	4	4	4	4	4	3	4	5	36	Par	72
Handicap	4	8	16	2	14	6	18	10	12			
RED	216	354	283	443	280	310	164	246	455	2751	RED	5471
Par	4	4	4	5	4	4	3	4	5	36	Par	72
Handicap	14	2	10	6	12	4	18	16	8			

Manager: Robert Mueller   **Pro:** Gary Danback, PGA   **Supt:** Steven Finamore
Architect: A.W. Tillinghast 1928

APPLE RIDGE COUNTRY CLUB

269 East Crescent Ave., Mahwah, NJ 07430   **(201) 327-8000**

Apple Ridge is an 18 hole course that is open 6 days a week, all year. Guests may play accompanied by a member. Tee time reservations are necessary for weekends.

> • **Driving Range**   • **Lockers**
> • **Practice Green**   • **Showers**
> • **Power Carts**   • **Food**
>   Pull Carts   • **Clubhouse**
> • **Club Rental**   • **Outings**
> • **Caddies**   • **Soft Spikes**

Course Description: Apple Ridge is known for the numerous apple, peach and pear trees that line all the fairways. The fruit trees are maintained, providing a welcome snack while playing in season. With undulating fairways, small well-bunkered greens and several challenging water holes, it is considered a sporty course. From the ninth hole, there is a spectacular view of the New York City skyline.

Directions: Bergen County, #2 on Northeast Map
Take Rte. 17 North to Lake St., Ramsey Exit. At first light, make a left onto East Crescent Ave; club is on the right.

Hole	1	2	3	4	5	6	7	8	9	Out	BLUE	Rating 72.2
BLUE	411	381	161	501	415	174	397	363	446	3249		Slope 124
WHITE	386	354	133	476	402	160	382	339	420	3052		
Par	4	4	3	5	4	3	4	4	4	35	WHITE	Rating 70.4
Handicap	5	9	17	13	1	11	7	15	3			Slope 121
RED	362	330	109	453	352	146	367	316	394	2829		
Par	4	4	3	5	4	3	4	4	5	36	RED	Rating 72.0
Handicap	3	7	17	1	11	15	5	13	9			Slope 123

Hole	10	11	12	13	14	15	16	17	18	In		Totals
BLUE	203	368	322	447	563	358	411	188	515	3375	BLUE	6624
WHITE	184	345	307	423	540	341	388	171	493	3192	WHITE	6244
Par	3	4	4	4	5	4	4	3	5	36	Par	71
Handicap	10	8	12	2	4	16	6	18	14			
RED	165	322	290	397	450	324	330	155	472	2905	RED	5734
Par	3	4	4	5	5	4	4	3	5	37	Par	73
Handicap	16	8	10	6	2	12	14	18	4			

Manager: Carol Tonnon   **Pro:** John Curry, PGA   **Supt:** Roy Morris
Architect: Hal Purdy 1966

ARCOLA COUNTRY CLUB

P.O.Box 158., Paramus Rd., Paramus, NJ 07652   **(201) 843-9800**

Arcola is an 18 hole private course that is open all year. Guests play accompanied by a member. Tee time reservations are not necessary.

```
•Driving Range   •Lockers
•Practice Green  •Showers
•Power Carts     •Food
 Pull Carts      •Clubhouse
 Club Rental     •Outings
•Caddies         •Soft Spikes
```

Course Description: Arcola is a gently rolling parkland type course nestled in the hills of Paramus with impressive views, particularly from the first hole. 3 ponds come into play on this tightly bunkered challenging course. With the surrounding commercial development, one is surprised to find such a well-maintained layout in this location. There have been several major renovations in the past few years and one is still going on for 1999 on all the tees and bunkers. Robert Trent Jones and Robert Rulewich are two of several architects who have taken part in the improvements.

Directions: Bergen County, #3 on Northeast Map
From the GWBridge, take Rte. 4 West to the Paramus Road exit. Bear right off exit to course which is immediately on the right.

Hole	1	2	3	4	5	6	7	8	9	Out	BLUE	Rating 72.9
BLUE	436	209	348	380	431	407	204	500	521	3436		Slope 127
WHITE	418	186	317	368	412	383	186	471	494	3235		
Par	4	3	4	4	4	4	3	5	5	36	WHITE	Rating 71.1
Handicap	6	16	18	2	8	4	14	12	10			Slope 125
RED	402	141	283	314	329	352	111	414	413	2759		
Par	5	3	4	4	4	4	3	5	5	37	RED	Rating 72.7
Handicap	13	15	7	1	11	9	17	3	5			Slope 123
Hole	10	11	12	13	14	15	16	17	18	In		Totals
BLUE	432	164	587	341	162	526	348	440	409	3409	BLUE	6845
WHITE	406	154	566	328	150	514	335	419	396	3268	WHITE	6503
Par	4	3	5	4	3	5	4	4	4	36	Par	72
Handicap	5	15	1	13	17	9	11	3	7			
RED	339	96	508	296	132	468	302	395	281	2817	RED	5576
Par	4	3	5	4	3	5	4	5	4	37	Par	74
Handicap	8	16	2	12	18	4	10	6	14			

Manager: Charles Kelly   **Pro:** Bill Burgess, PGA   **Supt:** Mike Mongon
Architect: Herbert Barker 1909, **Renov**: Rees Jones, Roger Rulewich

DARLINGTON GOLF COURSE

PUBLIC

277 Campgaw Rd., Mahwah, NJ 07430   (201) 327-8770

Darlington is an 18 hole Bergen County Course open 7 days a week from mid-March to mid-December. County residents can obtain IDs for $22. There is a computerized reservation system for tee times up to 7 days in advance; call 343-4441.

Amenities	Amenities
• Driving Range	• Lockers
• Practice Green	• Showers
• Power Carts	• Food
• Pull Carts	• Clubhouse
• Club Rental	• Outings
• Soft Spikes	

Fees	Weekday	Weekend
ReswID	$13	$17
Non-res	$24	$31
NonNJ	$45	$45
Sr/Jr	$7	$14.50
Power carts	$20	$20

Course Description: Set in a heavily wooded county park, Darlington, with its rolling hills and lush greens, is an appealing example of a well-maintained public course. Although not extremely long, the par fours are a sure test of the golfer's skill. The pleasant scenery can lull the unwary player into thinking this is just a walk in the woods; however, an errant shot can find the golfer in those woods with an unplayable lie. Some consider the long par 4 ninth the most picturesque hole. This championship style course offers an enjoyable golf experience to players of all levels.

Directions: Bergen County, #4 on Northeast Map
Take Rte. 17 North to Rte.202 South. Pass Ramapo College to Darlington Ave. & turn left. Follow to Campgaw Rd. & turn right. Go 1&1/4 miles & turn left into course before the Police Academy.

Hole	1	2	3	4	5	6	7	8	9	Out	BLUE	Rating 70.6
BLUE	480	175	365	362	189	379	372	390	470	3182		Slope 122
WHITE	452	155	355	352	170	355	357	375	448	3019		
Par	5	3	4	4	3	4	4	4	4	35	WHITE	Rating 68.8
Handicap	9	17	11	13	15	3	7	5	1			Slope 118
RED	380	119	290	313	155	320	320	288	420	2605		
Par	5	3	4	4	3	4	4	4	4	35	RED	Rating 69.9
Handicap	9	17	11	13	15	3	7	5	1			Slope 117
Hole	10	11	12	13	14	15	16	17	18	In		Totals
BLUE	452	500	175	369	489	344	176	382	415	3302	BLUE	6484
WHITE	402	483	150	340	463	325	154	363	350	3030	WHITE	6049
Par	4	5	3	4	5	4	3	4	4	36	Par	71
Handicap	2	8	18	12	10	14	16	4	6			
RED	361	423	131	298	432	295	122	321	312	2695	RED	5300
Par	4	5	3	4	5	4	3	4	4	36	Par	71
Handicap	2	8	18	12	10	14	16	4	6			

Manager/Supt: Peter Evans
Architect: Nicholas Psiahas 1975

EDGEWOOD COUNTRY CLUB

449 River Vale Rd., River Vale, NJ 07675   **(201) 666-1200**

Edgewood is a 27 hole course with 3 separate nines; Red, White & Blue. It is open all year, weather permitting 6 days a week. Guests play accompanied by a member. Tee time reservations are necessary on Saturdays.

- •**Driving Range**
- •**Practice Green**
- •**Power Carts**
- Pull Carts
- •**Club Rental**
- •**Caddies**
- •**Lockers**
- •**Showers**
- •**Food**
- •**Clubhouse**
- •**Outings**
- •**Soft Spikes**

Course Description: Formerly a dairy farm in Bergen County, Edgewood's three nines were built as a public facility then later became a private club. The predominantly flat tree lined terrain has wide fairways and deep bunkers. Many holes present trouble, such as out-of-bounds, ponds and creeks. The Blue offers the most interesting layout with sharp doglegs and water holes. The meandering 5th hole on the Red is known as the "Willow Hole" because of the many willow trees. The course is being renovated. The scorecard below shows the Red Course above & the Blue below. The rating and slope is for the Red-Blue 18.

Directions: Bergen County, #5 on Northeast Map
Pal.Pkwy. North to Exit 6W. At 4th STOP, go left onto Blue Hill Rd.(water on left); for 1.4 miles. Road becomes Orangeburg Rd. in RiverVale. Go left onto RiverVale Rd. Club is on right.

Hole	1	2	3	4	5	6	7	8	9	Out	BLUE	Rating 70.6
BLUE	325	516	365	201	442	510	352	158	449	3318		Slope 122
WHITE	311	474	340	174	413	496	334	144	434	3120		
Par	4	5	4	3	4	5	4	3	4	36	WHITE	Rating 68.6
Handicap	6	5	4	8	1	2	7	9	3			Slope 117
RED	297	461	327	168	337	421	305	135	412	2863		
Par	4	5	4	3	4	5	4	3	5	37	RED	Rating 71.5
Handicap	4	2	6	8	3	1	5	9	7			Slope 119
Hole	10	11	12	13	14	15	16	17	18	In		Totals
BLUE	370	366	380	194	497	519	193	374	191	3084	BLUE	6402
WHITE	349	345	334	180	447	506	148	354	181	2874	WHITE	5994
Par	4	4	4	3	5	5	3	4	3	35	Par	71
Handicap	3	5	1	7	6	2	8	4	9			
RED	320	331	279	152	420	405	106	336	162	2511	RED	5374
Par	4	4	4	3	5	5	3	4	3	35	Par	72
Handicap	3	6	4	7	1	5	9	2	8			

Manager: Danny Palazzola   **Pro:** Keith Larsen, PGA   **Supt:** Paul Dotti
Architect: Orrin Smith 1946

EMERSON GOLF CLUB

99 Palisade Ave., Emerson, NJ 07630   (201) 261-1100

Emerson is an 18 hole course open 7 days a week all year. Weekday memberships are available with unlimited golf and cart fees. Players can purchase guaranteed weekend tee times. Reservations may be made up to 5 days in advance, members up to 8 days.

•Driving Range	•Lockers
•Practice Green	•Showers
•Power Carts	•Food
•Pull Carts	Clubhouse
•Club Rental	•Outings
•Soft Spikes	

Fees	Weekday	Weekend
Daily	$56	$72
Twi (3PM)	$46	$56
Power carts included		

Course Description: The front of the relatively flat Emerson golf course plays longer and straighter than the tighter and shorter back. The signature third hole, a 468 yard par 4, tees off into the wind to a small green. Recently there have been renovations which include the removal of ditches, additional bunkers and landscaping, all of which greatly improve the facility. By stressing ready golf, fast play is encouraged and golfers enjoy the well paced rounds. On a crowded weekend, players can reasonably expect no more than 4 & 1/2 hours to complete a round of 18 holes.

Directions: Bergen County, #6 on Northeast Map
GWBr. to Rte. 4 West to Kinderkamack Rd./RiverEdge exit. Make a left at light onto Kinderkamack Rd. Go 4-5 mi. to town of Emerson, cross RR tracks, make immediate right onto Emerson Plaza E. for 300 yds. Go left onto Palisade Ave. to club on right.

Hole	1	2	3	4	5	6	7	8	9	Out	BLUE	Rating 71.1
BLUE	508	172	468	383	416	448	333	174	556	3458		Slope 115
WHITE	495	162	445	331	404	436	322	162	545	3302		
Par	5	3	4	4	4	4	4	3	5	36	WHITE	Rating 69.8
Handicap	9	17	1	15	5	3	13	11	7			Slope 112
RED	474	157	342	320	349	359	240	134	414	2789		
Par	5	3	4	4	4	4	4	3	5	36	RED	Rating 70.8
Handicap	3	17	9	13	5	1	15	11	7			Slope 117
Hole	10	11	12	13	14	15	16	17	18	In		Totals
BLUE	402	154	513	373	368	385	200	413	437	3245	BLUE	6703
WHITE	390	140	499	358	353	376	176	398	407	3097	WHITE	6399
Par	4	3	5	4	4	4	3	4	4	35	Par	71
Handicap	4	18	10	12	16	6	14	8	2			
RED	374	131	384	349	346	321	145	307	408	2765	RED	5554
Par	4	3	4	4	4	4	3	4	5	35	Par	71
Handicap	4	18	6	14	8	2	10	16	12			

Manager: Steven Murphy   **Pro:** John Trombley   **Supt:** Mike Susshine
Architect: Alec Ternyei 1968

GLENWILD GREENS

102 Glenwild Ave., Bloomingdale, NJ 07403   **(973) 283-0888**

Glenwild Greens is a 9 hole par 3 course. Memberships are available. Tee time reservations are not necessary.

Driving Range	Lockers
Practice Green	Showers
Power Carts	**• Food**
• Pull Carts	Clubhouse
• Club Rental	**• Outings**
• Soft Spikes	

Fees	Weekday	Weekend
Daily	$10	$12
Sr	$8	$8
2nd nine is 1/2 of fee		

Course Description: Carved out of the woods with good grade changes and elevated tees, Glenwild Greens is a very challenging course. Two ponds affect play on two holes. This course is not just a wide open field; there is more interest here. Golfers cannot get hit by another players ball. Glenwild is a great place to practice one's short game.

Directions: Passaic County, #7 on Northeast Map
Rte. 80 to Exit 53, then Rte. 23 North to Rte. 287 North to Exit #53. Go left on Hamburg Tpke. at light. After 1 & 1/2 miles, bear right up hill on Glenwild Ave. Club is 1/2 mile on right.

Hole	1	2	3	4	5	6	7	8	9	Out	BLUE	Rating
BLUE												Slope
WHITE	65	85	75	125	135	100	110	100	170	965		
Par	3	3	3	3	3	3	3	3	3	27	WHITE	Rating
Handicap												Slope
RED												
Par											RED	Rating
Handicap												Slope

Hole	10	11	12	13	14	15	16	17	18	In		Totals
BLUE											BLUE	
WHITE											WHITE	965
Par											Par	27
Handicap												
RED											RED	
Par											Par	
Handicap												

Manager: Clint Campbell   **Supt:** Ron Silvius   **Owner:** Alex J. MacKenn
                                     Built: 1994

HACKENSACK GOLF CLUB

Soldier Hill Rd., Oradell, NJ 07649   **(201) 261-5500**

Hackensack is a private 18 hole course open all year 6 days a week. Tee time reservations are not required. Guests may play accompanied by a member.

- •**Driving Range**   •**Lockers**
- •**Practice Green**   •**Showers**
- •**Power Carts**   •**Food**
- Pull Carts   •**Clubhouse**
- •**Club Rental**   •**Outings**
- •**Caddies**   •**Soft Spikes**

Course Description: Designed in 1928 by architect Charles Banks, Hackensack offers diversity and challenge for any level player. The large bunkers and tree lined fairways make strategic shot placement a must. This is one of the longer courses in Bergen County with 5 difficult par 4s over 400 yards each from the white tees. The club has had a recent renovation under the direction of Rees Jones to reposition the bunkers. The signature 18th is a hole which always seems to stimulate discussion by touring pros who visit here. Hackensack is the home club of Jim McGovern, winner of the 1993 Houston Open.

Directions: Bergen County, #8 on Northeast Map
GSP to Exit #165. Go East on Oradell Ave. to Forest. Turn left, then right on Soldier Hill Rd. Club is on left. From Rte. 4 East or West ; take Kinderkamack Rd. North in River Edge to Oradell. Go left on Soldier Hill to club on right.

Hole	1	2	3	4	5	6	7	8	9	Out	BLUE	Rating 72.3
BLUE	470	429	224	392	377	142	378	524	421	3357		Slope 131
WHITE	440	421	197	383	357	132	355	500	401	3186		
Par	5	4	3	4	4	3	4	5	4	36	WHITE	Rating 70.9
Handicap	15	1	13	5	11	17	9	7	3			Slope 128
RED	416	406	150	373	296	122	267	474	346	2850		
Par	5	5	3	4	4	3	4	5	4	37	RED	Rating 72.4
Handicap	7	5	15	1	9	17	13	3	11			Slope 123

Hole	10	11	12	13	14	15	16	17	18	In		Totals
BLUE	510	425	184	337	336	522	405	160	402	3281	BLUE	6638
WHITE	503	404	177	312	324	502	392	148	387	3149	WHITE	6335
Par	5	4	3	4	4	5	5	3	4	36	Par	72
Handicap	8	2	16	12	14	10	4	18	6			
RED	468	329	139	278	325	439	384	133	325	2820	RED	5670
Par	5	4	3	4	4	5	5	3	4	37	Par	74
Handicap	6	14	18	2	8	4	12	16	10			

Manager: Ed Urben   **Pro:** Michael Dezic, PGA   **Supt:** Richard Lane
Estab: 1899   **Architects:** Charles Banks 1928   Rees Jones 1996

HAWORTH COUNTRY CLUB

5 Lake Shore Dr., Haworth, NJ 07641 **(201) 384-7300**

Haworth is an 18 private course open all year 7 days a week. Tee time reservations should be made in advance. Guests may play accompanied by a member.

•Driving Range	•Lockers
•Practice Green	•Showers
•Power Carts	•Food
•Pull Carts	•Clubhouse
•Club Rental	•Outings
Caddies	•Soft Spikes

Course Description: A complete renovation of the course and clubhouse is planned for 1999. Robert Trent Jones will be doing the redesign. The course will reopen in the year 2000. The scorecard below shows the previous yardages. No more information was available at press time.

Directions: Bergen County, #9 on Northeaest Map
Garden St. Pkwy. North to Oradell Ave. Follow to Grant Ave. (blinking light) & turn left. From Grant Ave., bear left at "Y "to Lake Shore Dr. Proceed along road with reservoir on left approximately 1 mile to entrance road on right and clubhouse on left.

Hole	1	2	3	4	5	6	7	8	9	Out	BLUE	Rating 72.2
BLUE	518	400	211	351	374	560	385	223	418	3440		Slope
WHITE	487	375	183	326	354	539	345	190	403	3202		
Par	5	4	3	4	4	5	4	3	4	36	WHITE	Rating 70.3
Handicap	11	3	13	17	15	1	9	7	5			Slope
RED	464	354	156	308	339	505	319	132	343	2920		
Par	5	4	3	4	4	5	4	3	4	36	RED	Rating 72.2
Handicap	5	3	15	11	9	1	13	17	7			Slope
Hole	10	11	12	13	14	15	16	17	18	In		Totals
BLUE	514	206	384	486	164	387	398	412	433	3384	BLUE	6824
WHITE	486	188	359	455	148	360	372	387	410	3165	WHITE	6327
Par	5	3	4	5	3	4	4	4	4	36	Par	72
Handicap	16	12	4	10	18	14	8	2	6			
RED	463	123	317	424	113	336	331	365	389	2861	RED	5781
Par	5	3	4	5	3	4	4	4	4	36	Par	72
Handicap	14	16	12	10	18	4	8	2	6			

Manager: Akio Nakahara   **Pro:** Charles Podmayersky, PGA
Architects: Albert Zakorus 1966   Robert Trent Jones 1999

HIGH MOUNTAIN GOLF CLUB

PUBLIC

845 Ewing Ave., Franklin Lakes, NJ 07417   **(201) 891-4653**

High Mountain is an 18 hole semi-private course open to the public 7 days a week from mid-March to mid-Dec. Memberships are available. Call for tee times for Mondays and for Wed, Thurs, & Fri. 8-2PM. After 2, and on weekends after 2, 1st come 1st served for foursomes. There is a cash only policy here.

- •Driving Range
- •Practice Green
- •Power Carts
- •Pull Carts
- •Club Rental
- •Soft Spikes

- •Lockers
- •Showers
- •Food
- •Clubhouse
- •Outings

Fees	Weekday	Weekend
Daily	$34	$44
Mbrs	$10	$15
Power carts (req.) $32		

Course Description: The popular semi-private High Mountain is a well maintained playable course. Contoured tree lined fairways, natural ponds and creeks add to its interest. The par 5 16th, 579 yards from the whites, requires an accurate approach shot over water. The most likely birdies encountered are in the form of the feathered neighbors drifting over from the Audobon Society adjacent to the golf course.

Directions: Bergen County, #10 on Northeast Map
Rte. 4 West to Rte. 208 North. Take Ewing Ave. exit and turn left. Club is about 1 mile from exit on left.

Hole	1	2	3	4	5	6	7	8	9	Out	BLUE	Rating 70.0
BLUE	369	385	195	522	150	415	345	365	140	2886		Slope 123
WHITE	350	373	183	511	135	405	331	353	136	2777		
Par	4	4	3	5	3	4	4	4	3	34	WHITE	Rating 68.9
Handicap	10	6	12	4	18	2	14	8	16			Slope 120
RED	305	356	167	443	115	389	314	313	127	2529		
Par	4	4	3	5	3	4	4	4	3	34	RED	Rating 70.7
Handicap	4	4	15	4	13	4	5	5	14			Slope 121
Hole	10	11	12	13	14	15	16	17	18	In		Totals
BLUE	404	480	183	412	403	327	587	200	465	3461	BLUE	6347
WHITE	392	445	162	403	392	307	579	189	455	3324	WHITE	6101
Par	4	5	3	4	4	4	5	3	5	37	Par	71
Handicap	5	13	15	7	3	17	1	9	11			
RED	311	425	132	390	298	276	461	166	438	2897	RED	5426
Par	4	5	3	4	4	4	5	3	5	37	Par	71
Handicap	11	9	15	3	5	17	1	13	7			

Manager: Brian Craig   **Pro:** Joe & Pat Lawlor, PGA   **Supt:** Eliot Lewis
Architect: Alec Ternyei   1967

KNICKERBOCKER COUNTRY CLUB

188 Knickerbocker Rd., Tenafly, NJ 07670   **(201) 568-4034**

Knickerbocker is a private 18 hole course open 6 days a week all year. Guests play accompanied by a member. Tee time reservations are not necessary.

- **Driving Range**
- **Practice Green**
- **Power Carts**
- Pull Carts
- **Club Rental**
- **Caddies**

- **Lockers**
- **Showers**
- **Food**
- **Clubhouse**
- **Outings**
- **Soft Spikes**

Course Description: Nestled in the middle of abundantly treed Tenafly is Knickerbocker Country Club. This very well maintained course has narrow fairways, a flat front nine and a hilly back. It is deceptively challenging. The approach shots are difficult to the true and very fast, undulating greens. The long, demanding par 4 twelfth signature hole has water in play both off the tee and on the second shot. The clubhouse has been recently renovated.

Directions: Bergen County, #11 on Northeast Map
Take Rte. 9W to Clinton Ave., Tenafly. Go left all the way down Clinton Ave. over the RR tracks to Knickerbocker Rd. and make a left. Club is on left; pro shop is on right.

Hole	1	2	3	4	5	6	7	8	9	Out	BLUE	Rating 72.1
BLUE	390	533	422	172	357	182	428	391	349	3224		Slope 123
WHITE	380	518	414	145	343	168	420	383	339	3110		
Par	4	5	4	3	4	3	4	4	4	35	WHITE	Rating 71.1
Handicap	9	5	3	15	11	17	1	7	13			Slope 126
RED	366	469	365	109	306	148	341	370	315	2789		
Par	4	5	4	3	4	3	4	4	4	35	RED	Rating 73.8
Handicap	9	1	5	17	11	15	7	3	13			Slope 129
Hole	10	11	12	13	14	15	16	17	18	In		Totals
BLUE	497	164	430	540	387	357	312	223	494	3404	BLUE	6628
WHITE	486	156	421	525	379	341	302	207	483	3300	WHITE	6410
Par	5	3	4	5	4	4	4	3	5	37	Par	72
Handicap	10	18	2	4	6	8	16	14	12			
RED	458	124	404	445	373	325	294	192	447		RED	5851
Par	5	3	5	5	4	4	4	4	5	39	Par	74
Handicap	4	16	6	2	8	10	14	18	12			

Manager: Don Arrigo   **Pro:** Ed Whitman, PGA   **Supt:** Sam Juliano
Architect: Donald Ross 1914

MONTAMMY GOLF CLUB

Route 9W, Alpine, NJ 07620 **(201) 768-9000**

Montammy is an 18 hole course open 6 days a week, eleven months a year (closed January). Guests play accompanied by a member. Tee times may be reserved 1 week in advance for weekends.

•**Driving Range**	•**Lockers**
•**Practice Green**	•**Showers**
•**Power Carts**	•**Food**
Pull Carts	•**Clubhouse**
•**Club Rental**	•**Outings**
•**Caddies**	•**Soft Spikes**

Course Description: Montammy is a hilly course built on the New Jersey Palisades. It is fairly narrow and tree-lined. The par 3 fourth has a blind uphill tee shot to the undulating green. Landing there does not guarantee a two putt as the breaks are tricky and the surface is fast and interesting. The par 4 seventh, considered the signature hole, is a severe dogleg right with a second shot over a pond. A new pond on the right on the par 5 fifth makes the hole more challenging. This same pond can lure a slice on the 3rd hole which now plays longer as the tee box has been moved back. The course has new mounding on some holes. The clubhouse has been completely renovated and enlarged.   Caddies are required before 2 PM.

Directions: Bergen County, #12 on Northeast Map
G.W.Br. to Pal.Int.Pkwy. to Exit #1. Go right at exit to light. Turn right at light onto 9W and proceed north. After light at Tenafly, watch for club entrance on left.

Hole	1	2	3	4	5	6	7	8	9	Out	BLUE	Rating 72.2
BLUE	397	485	358	186	518	394	352	205	419	3314		Slope 134
WHITE	380	474	347	173	501	374	342	174	379	3144		
Par	4	5	4	3	5	4	4	3	4	36	WHITE	Rating 70.5
Handicap	5	7	13	15	1	3	11	17	9			Slope 130
RED	340	441	330	148	468	349	292	152	305	2825		
Par	4	5	4	3	5	4	4	3	4	36	RED	Rating 73.4
Handicap	5	7	9	15	3	1	11	17	13			Slope 128
Hole	10	11	12	13	14	15	16	17	18	In		Totals
BLUE	389	551	398	526	153	465	352	215	373	3422	BLUE	6736
WHITE	358	517	346	501	134	450	336	184	365	3191	WHITE	6335
Par	4	5	4	5	3	4	4	3	4	36	Par	72
Handicap	8	4	12	10	18	2	16	14	6			
RED	310	423	303	446	98	400	310	171	350	2811	RED	5636
Par	4	5	4	5	3	5	4	3	4	37	Par	73
Handicap	6	4	2	7	9	1	3	8	5			

Director of Golf: James (Spike) Eoff, PGA   **Supt:** Mike Miner
Architect: Frank Duane 1966

NORTH JERSEY COUNTRY CLUB

Hamburg Turnpike, Wayne, NJ 07470   **(201) 595-5150**

North Jersey is a private 18 hole course open 6 days a week 11 months a year. Guests may play accompanied by a member. Tee time reservations are necessary for weekends only.

> • **Driving Range**   • **Lockers**
> • **Practice Green**   • **Showers**
> • **Power Carts**   • **Food**
>   Pull Carts   • **Clubhouse**
> • **Club Rental**   • **Outings**
> • **Caddies**   • **Soft Spikes**

Course Description: The beautiful, hilly and well maintained North Jersey is one of the more difficult courses in this part of the state. With small, undulating greens and tree lined fairways accuracy is at a premium. The golfer is forced to negotiate many uneven lies. The rugged terrain adds even more challenge as well as the many holes that have blind second shots. Several renovations have taken place in the bunkering of the course and in the clubhouse. The club hosted the NJ State Open in 1995.

Directions: Passaic County, #13 on Northeast Map
Rte. 80 West to Rte. 23 North to Alps Rd. and make a right. Follow to 1st traffic light & make left onto Valley Rd. At 1st light, make a right onto Hamburg Tpke. - Club is 3/4 mile on left.

Hole	1	2	3	4	5	6	7	8	9	Out	BLUE	Rating 72.2
BLUE	495	429	335	159	425	439	524	136	397	3339		Slope 134
WHITE	482	414	315	138	413	423	503	131	385	3204		
Par	5	4	4	3	4	4	5	3	4	36	WHITE	Rating 70.5
Handicap	11	1	13	15	3	5	9	17	7			Slope 124
RED	423	368	290	125	343	414	488	127	374	2952		
Par	5	4	4	3	4	5	5	3	4	37	RED	Rating 73.9
Handicap	9	3	13	15	7	11	1	17	5			Slope 136
Hole	10	11	12	13	14	15	16	17	18	In		Totals
BLUE	380	371	372	160	371	164	467	534	398	3217	BLUE	6556
WHITE	353	355	361	153	358	152	400	509	379	3020	WHITE	6224
Par	4	4	4	3	4	3	4	5	4	35	Par	71
Handicap	10	12	4	16	14	18	2	8	6			
RED	312	315	348	118	351	132	350	459	351	2736	RED	5688
Par	4	4	4	3	4	3	4	5	4	35	Par	72
Handicap	14	10	2	16	12	18	4	6	8			

Manager: Ed LaPadula   **Pro:** Chris Dachisen, PGA   **Supt:** Gary Arlio
Architect: Walter Travis 1923 **Estab.** 1894

OLD TAPPAN GOLF COURSE

83 De Wolf Rd., Old Tappan, NJ 07675   **(201) 767-1199**

Old Tappan is a 9 hole municipally owned course with a membership only policy. It is open 6 days a week from 3/15--12/30. All Old Tappan residents are eligible to join. There is a waiting list for non-residents. Tee time reservations are not necessary.

Driving Range	•**Lockers**
•**Practice Green**	•**Showers**
•**Power Carts**	•**Food**
•**Pull Carts**	•**Clubhouse**
•**Club Rental**	•**Outings**
Caddies	•**Soft Spikes**

Course Description: The well maintained Old Tappan has very good drainage and is therefore playable soon after rain. The course features large undulating greens and its many trees help to define the fairways. The par 3 third presents a beautiful view of the lake and requires a well struck tee shot; one must make sure to stay clear of the pond. On the par 3 sixth hole the golfer must hit onto a green elevated 50 feet above the fairway. Old Tappan residents are lucky to have this little gem virtually in their backyards.

Directions: Bergen County, #14 on Northeast Map
Pal.Int.Pkwy. to Exit #6W, Orangeburg. Proceed West on Veterans Memorial Rd. for 1 mile to Blaisdell Rd. which becomes DeWolf. Turn left on DeWolf to course ahead on left. **OR** Piermont Rd. to Broadway in Norwood. Left on Broadway; bear left to Central Ave. At Old Tappan Rd. go right then left onto DeWolf to club.

Hole	1	2	3	4	5	6	7	8	9	Out	BLUE	Rating
BLUE												Slope
WHITE	362	290	202	414	352	112	412	415	517	3076		
Par	4	4	3	4	4	3	4	4	5	35	WHITE	Rating 69.0
Handicap	7	17	11	1	9	15	5	3	13			Slope 115
RED	352	277	186	397	338	95	407	405	504	2961		
Par	4	4	3	5	4	3	4	5	5	37	RED	Rating 71.3
Handicap	2	11	13	9	4	14	1	5	3			Slope 118
Hole	10	11	12	13	14	15	16	17	18	In		Totals
BLUE											BLUE	
WHITE	352	277	186	397	338	95	407	405	504	2961	WHITE	6037
Par	4	4	3	4	4	3	4	4	5	35	Par	70
Handicap	8	18	12	4	10	16	6	2	14			
RED	275	228	150	384	263	81	334	398	434	2547	RED	5508
Par	4	4	3	5	4	3	4	5	5	37	Par	74
Handicap	12	18	16	10	15	17	8	6	7			

Manager/Pro: Doug Meeks, PGA   **Supt:** Paul Pariscondola
Architect: Hal Purdy 1969

ORCHARD HILLS GOLF COURSE

PUBLIC

404 Paramus Rd., Paramus, NJ 07652   **(201) 447-3778**

Orchard Hills is a 9 hole county course open 6 days a week all year. For tee times: residents call 1 week in advance; non residents 1 day. Prices below are for 2 nine hole rounds.

Driving Range	Lockers
Practice Green	Showers
•**Power Carts**	Food
•**Pull Carts**	Clubhouse
Club Rental	Outings

Fees	Weekday	Weekend
ReswID	$13	$17
Non-res	$24	$31
NonNJ	$45	$45
Sr/Jr	$7	$14.50
Power carts	$20	$20

Course Description: Orchard Hills is on the grounds of Bergen Community College and is quite well maintained. Somewhat hilly with plenty of interesting holes, it is a welcome place to play in Bergen County. The par 3 fourth requires an accurate shot over water to a small green. The first hole has a tree in the fairway that makes shots to the green difficult.

Directions: Bergen County, #15 on Northeast Map
Rte. 4 East or West to Paramus Rd. Right on Paramus Rd. for approximately 1 & 1/2 miles. On right is entrance to Bergen Comm. College. Enter & follow signs to course on right.

Hole	1	2	3	4	5	6	7	8	9	Out	BLUE	Rating
BLUE												Slope
WHITE	280	325	465	180	268	325	347	199	387	2776		
Par	4	4	5	3	4	4	4	3	4	35	WHITE	Rating 67.7
Handicap	9	5	7	4	8	1	6	3	2			Slope 109
RED	269	310	461	164	254	313	330	187	376	2664		
Par	4	4	5	3	4	4	4	3	4	35	RED	Rating 70.0
Handicap	9	5	7	4	8	1	6	3	2			Slope 113
Hole	10	11	12	13	14	15	16	17	18	In		Totals
BLUE											BLUE	
WHITE											WHITE	
Par											Par	70
Handicap												
RED											RED	
Par											Par	70
Handicap												

Manager: Bob Pallotta   **Supt:** Vincent Davis
Built: 1920s

East Cedar Lane, Teaneck, NJ 07666   (201) 837-3020

Overpeck is one of four Bergen County public courses. It has 18 holes and is open 7 days a week from mid March to mid Dec. Computerized tee time reservations: call 343-4441 7 days in advance for county residents, 1 day for non residents.

Driving Range	•**Lockers**
•**Practice Green**	•**Showers**
•**Power Carts**	•**Food**
•**Pull Carts**	•**Clubhouse**
•**Club Rental**	Outings

Fees	Weekday	Weekend
ReswID	$13	$17
Non-res	$24	$31
NonNJ	$45	$45
Sr/Jr	$7	$14.50
Power carts	$20	$20

Course Description: Wide open and relatively flat, Overpeck gets quite busy in season. The many water hazards provide interest and a challenge here, and many golfers make their way using pull carts. There are brooks, streams, ditches and lakes to carry over. Overpeck's greens are moderate in size with some break. The back nine is considered more difficult than the front.

Directions: Bergen County, #16 on Northeast Map
Take Rte. 4 to Teaneck Rd. South to Cedar Lane. Go left on Cedar Lane; club is at end of road.

Hole	1	2	3	4	5	6	7	8	9	Out	BLUE	Rating 70.6
BLUE	528	362	141	361	438	441	476	130	342	3219		Slope 115
WHITE	486	349	130	329	425	408	454	120	333	3034		
Par	5	4	3	4	4	4	5	3	4	36	WHITE	Rating 67.9
Handicap	7	13	15	11	3	1	5	17	9			Slope 109
RED	430	335	110	296	415	374	413	93	301	2767		
Par	5	4	3	4	4	4	5	3	4	36	RED	Rating 70.2
Handicap	7	13	15	11	3	1	5	17	9			Slope 113
Hole	10	11	12	13	14	15	16	17	18	In		Totals
BLUE	410	399	484	366	217	431	383	491	159	3340	BLUE	6559
WHITE	368	377	465	340	189	418	370	473	140	3140	WHITE	6174
Par	4	4	5	4	3	4	4	5	3	36	Par	72
Handicap	4	10	8	12	6	2	16	14	18			
RED	318	361	425	298	152	383	312	438	103	2790	RED	5557
Par	4	4	5	4	3	4	4	5	3	36	Par	72
Handicap	4	10	8	12	6	2	16	14	18			

Manager/Supt: Dave Werner
Architect: Michael Burris 1960

PACKANACK GOLF CLUB

7 Osborne Terrace, Wayne, NJ 07470   **(973) 694-9754**

Packanack is a 9 hole private course open 6 days a week and closed between Dec. and Feb. Guests play accompanied by a member. Tee time reservations are necessary on weekends.

> •**Driving Range** •**Lockers**
> •**Practice Green** •**Showers**
> •**Power Carts** •**Food**
> •**Pull Carts** •**Clubhouse**
> •**Club Rental** •**Outings**
> Caddies •**Soft Spikes**

Course Description: Scenic Packanack is flat and tight with water in play on every hole. The medium sized greens are in excellent condition. The signature hole is the par 3 sixth, 180 yards over a lake; more water lurks along the left side. Recent improvements have been made on the drainage ditches. The members here live around Packanack Lake, a community that has tennis courts and beach property for swimming.

Directions: Passaic County, #17 on Northeast Map
Rte. 80 West to Rte. 23 North to Packanack Lake Rd. and go right. Watch for Osborne Terrace and turn right. Clubhouse is on the right.

Hole	1	2	3	4	5	6	7	8	9	Out	BLUE	Rating
BLUE												Slope
WHITE	470	474	211	325	321	180	413	290	327	3011		
Par	5	5	3	4	4	3	4	4	4	36	WHITE	Rating 69.1
Handicap	9	7	3	5	13	15	1	17	11			Slope 119
RED	445	438	158	263	265	136	384	269	237	2595		
Par	5	5	3	4	4	3	5	4	4	37	RED	Rating 70.1
Handicap	7	1	9	6	2	5	8	4	3			Slope 118
Hole	10	11	12	13	14	15	16	17	18	In		Totals
BLUE											BLUE	
WHITE											WHITE	6045
Par											Par	72
Handicap												
RED											RED	5221
Par											Par	73
Handicap												

Manager: Billl Caldwell   **Pro:** Ben Karalis, PGA   **Supt:** Doug Vogel
Architect: Geoffrey Cornish 1965

PARAMUS GOLF & COUNTRY CLUB

PUBLIC

314 Paramus Rd., Paramus, NJ 07652   (201) 447-6067

Paramus is an 18 hole semi-private course open 7 days a week all year. Memberships are available. Reserved tee times are required; must be made in person. For more information, call the pro shop at 447-6079. Fees must be paid in cash only.

Driving Range	• **Lockers**
• **Practice Green**	• **Showers**
• **Power Carts**	• **Food**
• **Pull Carts**	• **Clubhouse**
• **Club Rental**	• **Outings**
• **Soft Spikes**	

Fees	Weekday	Weekend
ParRes./ID	$10	$15
NJRes	$15	$20
Non NJ	$25	$30
Sr Discounts	$1 off	
Power carts	$23	
(1998 rates)		

Course Description: Stephen Kay's five year improvement plan to refurbish Paramus is finally completed. The well maintained course was tightened and is a true gem for players in the area. Mostly flat with small greens, there is a challenge for everyone. The 218 yard par 3 17th has a well bunkered, postage stamp sized elevated green. The signature par 3 12th is made interesting by the stone mausoleum to the right of the green. On the 8th, a dogleg par 4, the golfer encounters water if the tee shot is too long and straight, especially hazardous from the forward tees; the difficult 9th hole, 589 yards from the back, is rarely reached in two. The recently reconstructed 11th, 12th and 13th are longer and trickier than ever before. Scorecard will be revised.

Directions: Bergen County, #18 on Northeast Map
Take Rte. 4 West to Paramus Rd.; follow signs to Bergen Community College. Course is on right just after Century Rd.

Hole	1	2	3	4	5	6	7	8	9	Out	BLUE	Rating
BLUE	343	372	371	314	145	271	371	409	589	3185		Slope
WHITE	322	347	338	295	114	247	351	376	544	2934		
Par	4	4	4	4	3	4	4	4	5	36	WHITE	Rating
Handicap	11	5	7	13	15	17	9	1	3			Slope
RED	259	233	293	285	89	237	239	300	481	2908		
Par	4	4	4	4	3	4	4	4	5	36	RED	Rating
Handicap	11	5	9	13	17	15	7	3	1			Slope
Hole	10	11	12	13	14	15	16	17	18	In		Totals
BLUE	332	508	171	489	332	172	360	218	406	2988	BLUE	6173
WHITE	316	475	158	478	302	156	336	191	378	2790	WHITE	5724
Par	4	5	3	5	4	3	4	3	4	35	Par	71
Handicap	8	14	8	16	10	12	6	2	4			
RED	263	380	123	410	292	108	277	121	344	2318	RED	5226
Par	4	5	3	5	4	3	4	3	4	35	Par	71
Handicap	10	2	18	4	12	16	8	14	6			

Manager/Pro: Madeline Cassano, LPGA   **Supt:** Ken Krausz
Built: 1975   **Architect:** Stephen Kay (redesign 1998)

PASCACK BROOK GOLF & CC

PUBLIC

15 RiverVale Rd., RiverVale, NJ 07675 — (201) 664-5886

Pascack Brook is a public 18 hole course open 7 days a week, all year. Tee time reservations are required.

Driving Range
- **Practice Green**
- **Power Carts**
- **Pull Carts**
- **Club Rental**
- **Soft Spikes**

- **Lockers**
- **Showers**
- **Food**
- **Clubhouse**
- **Outings**

Fees	Weekday	Weekend
Daily	TO BE ANNOUNCED	

Course Description: Pascack Brook, which will be closed in 1999, is located in Bergen County where golfers are always seeking places to play. The newly renovated course will be run by Meadowbrook Management Co. This promises to be an exciting new upscale public golf facility. Pascack Brook runs through the golf course which is adjacent to Lake Tappan, the United Water Company's reservoir. The old scorecard is shown below as a point of reference.

Directions: Bergen County, #19 on Northeast Map
Rte. 4 West to Kinderkamack Rd. Exit. and go left on Kind. Rd.heading north for approx. 5.5 miles to Old Hook Rd. Go right onto Old Hook past Pascack Valley Hospital. After hospital but before next light, go left onto Emerson Rd. Go to end & go right onto RiverVale Rd. Course is 1/2 mile on right.

Hole	1	2	3	4	5	6	7	8	9	Out	BLUE	Rating
BLUE	325	443	175	396	566	364	403	608	172	3452		Slope
WHITE	298	428	164	382	545	352	391	574	156	3290	WHITE	Rating
Par	4	4	3	4	5	4	4	5	3	36		Slope
Handicap	13	1	17	9	3	11	7	5	15			
RED	257	360	121	308	497	262	358	539	124	2826	RED	Rating
Par	4	4	3	4	5	4	4	5	3	36		Slope
Handicap	13	1	17	11	9	7	5	15				

Hole	10	11	12	13	14	15	16	17	18	In		Totals
BLUE	294	293	191	490	300	377	182	352	356	2835	BLUE	6287
WHITE	273	275	176	480	288	367	162	342	338	2701	WHITE	5991
Par	4	4	3	5	4	4	3	4	4	35	Par	71
Handicap	10	12	18	4	14	2	16	8	6			
RED	200	248	143	397	256	305	115	307	270	2241	RED	5067
Par	4	4	3	5	4	4	3	4	4	35	Par	71
Handicap	10	12	18	4	14	2	16	8	6			

Manager/Pro: Don Stenberg, PGA   **Architect:** John Handwerg Jr. 1962

PASSAIC COUNTY GOLF COURSE

207 Totowa Rd., Wayne, NJ 07470   **(973) 881-4921**

Passaic County Golf Course has 36 holes and is the only public course in Passaic County. It is open 7 days a week all year. Private memberships are available; ($40 per year for residents). Tee time reervations are not necessary.

•**Practice Range** •**Lockers**
•**Practice Green** •**Showers**
•**Power Carts** •**Food**
•**Pull Carts** •**Clubhouse**
•**Club Rental** Outings

Fees	Weekday	Weekend
Resident	$9	$10
Non-res	$37	$37
Sr/Jr	$7	$10
Power carts	$17	$17

Course Description: Passaic County Golf Course offers many water hazards, long fairways and large greens creating a challenge for all levels of play. The Red course is flat and wooded, the Blue is hilly, tree lined and open. The first hole on the Red is 453 yards from the back and designed long to avoid congestion at the beginning of the round. It features little undulation and a dogleg surrounded by many beautiful trees. Water makes the hole more interesting. When this course opened in 1931, there was a $1.00 greens fee on weekends! The scorecard below is for the Red course.

Directions: Passaic County, #20 on Northeast Map
Rte. 80 West to Union Blvd., Totowa, Exit #55. Go left on Totowa Rd. and follow curved road for approx. 2 miles. Course is on right.

Hole	1	2	3	4	5	6	7	8	9	Out	BLUE	Rating
BLUE												Slope
WHITE	453	340	436	390	378	176	532	188	360	3253		
Par	4	4	4	4	4	3	5	3	4	35	WHITE	Rating 71.2
Handicap	3	13	5	7	9	15	1	17	11			Slope 122
RED	420	325	426	378	365	140	506	130	340	3030		
Par	5	4	5	4	4	3	5	3	4	37	RED	Rating 74.8
Handicap	3	13	5	7	9	15	1	17	11			Slope 128

Hole	10	11	12	13	14	15	16	17	18	In		Totals
BLUE											BLUE	
WHITE	385	446	370	198	275	438	425	220	408	3165	WHITE	6418
Par	4	4	4	3	4	4	4	3	4	34	Par	69
Handicap	10	2	12	18	14	4	6	16	8			
RED	326	432	352	170	261	399	404	208	394	2946	RED	5976
Par	4	5	4	3	4	5	5	3	5	38	Par	75
Handicap	10	2	12	18	14	4	6	16	8			

Manager/Supt: Nick Roca
Architect: Martin O'Laughlin 1927   **Estab:** 1892

PREAKNESS HILLS COUNTRY CLUB

1050 Ratzer Rd., Wayne, NJ 07470   **(973) 694-2910**

Preakness Hills is an 18 hole course open 6 days a week and closed for the month of January. Guests play accompanied by a member. Tee time reservations are necessary on weekends.

•**Driving Range**	•**Lockers**
•**Practice Green**	•**Showers**
•**Power Carts**	•**Food**
Pull Carts	•**Clubhouse**
Club Rental	•**Outings**
•**Caddies**	•**Soft Spikes**

Course Description: For players and naturalists, Preakness is a challenging course in a majestic setting. There is a large pond adjacent to it stocked with bass and carp. Cranes and other colorful birds are ever-present. Golfers must be accurate to avoid trouble especially with the approach shot over a pond to the 18th green which is just in front of the magnificent clubhouse. The par 4 15th hole, a dogleg right, has a pond to be wary of as well. The 13th green is double-tiered. The sixth hole is densely treed and well-bunkered with a "bowling alley" fairway; careful placement is well rewarded. The 17th hole, 498 yards from the back tees, has 5 bunkers on the left and 2 on the right of the green. Caddies are required until 3 P.M.

Directions: Passaic County, #21 on Northeast Map
Rte. 80 West to Rte. 23 North. Exit on Alps Rd. & take it to Ratzer Rd. Turn right and club is ahead on right.

Hole	1	2	3	4	5	6	7	8	9	Out	BLUE	Rating 72.6
BLUE	480	356	381	441	508	224	428	162	420	3400		Slope 129
WHITE	438	345	377	400	499	210	424	151	411	3255		
Par	5	4	4	4	5	3	4	3	4	36	WHITE	Rating 71.6
Handicap	15	13	3	7	5	11	9	17	1			Slope 126
RED	353	283	334	327	465	188	379	141	398	2868		
Par	4	4	4	4	5	3	4	3	5	36	RED	Rating 73.4
Handicap	5	15	3	13	1	11	7	17	9			Slope 132

Hole	10	11	12	13	14	15	16	17	18	In		Totals
BLUE	497	310	403	359	370	407	187	498	146	3177	BLUE	6577
WHITE	475	300	389	344	365	390	168	489	129	3049	WHITE	6304
Par	5	4	4	4	4	4	3	5	3	36	Par	72
Handicap	10	12	6	2	14	4	16	8	18			
RED	426	219	346	283	336	335	152	408	109	2614	RED	5482
Par	5	4	4	4	4	4	3	5	3	36	Par	72
Handicap	6	12	10	2	14	4	16	8	18			

Manager: Craig Marggraff   **Pro:** Robert Foster, PGA   **Supt:** Jon O'Keefe
Architect: Willie Tucker 1926

RAMSEY GOLF & COUNTRY CLUB

105 Lakeside Dr., Ramsey, NJ 07446   (201) 327-3877

Ramsey is a private 18 hole course open 6 days a week and closed Jan. & Feb. Guests may play accompanied by a member. Tee time reservations are necessary summer weekend mornings.

- **Driving Range**
- **Practice Green**
- **Power Carts**
- **Pull Carts**
- **Club Rental**
- Caddies
- **Lockers**
- **Showers**
- **Food**
- **Clubhouse**
- **Outings**
- **Soft Spikes**

Course Description: Ramsey's golf course circles a peaceful residential development and surrounds 3 spring fed lakes. The course was built after the houses were in place; a difficult task indeed, yet well done. It was originally 220 acres of Ramsey Estates and the pro shop was converted from a stable, then to a bowling alley, later to its present state. The "Abbey Restaurant", of Norman architecture, is constructed of all natural stones. The original 6 hole course was begun in 1940 and Hal Purdy added the 2nd 6 holes about 30 years ago. In 1995, he finished the challenging job of fitting in the final 6 to make this a regulation 18 hole facility. Ramsey is tight, scenic and very well maintained; a lovely amenity for NJ golfers and especially the homeowners who are entitled to automatic membership.

Directions: Bergen County, #22 on Northeast Map
GSP to Rte. 17 North to Allendale exit; at first light, make a right onto Franklin Tpke. (Rte. 507). Pass 1 light, club is ahead on left.

Hole	1	2	3	4	5	6	7	8	9	Out	BLUE	Rating 67.2
BLUE	525	165	290	168	329	372	274	161	423	2707		Slope 117
WHITE	515	160	280	160	316	357	264	156	413	2621		
Par	5	3	4	3	4	4	4	3	4	34	WHITE	Rating 66.3
Handicap	3	15	13	9	17	5	7	11	1			Slope 115
RED	485	135	270	112	310	309	254	131	403	2409		
Par	5	3	4	3	4	4	4	3	5	35	RED	Rating 68.4
Handicap	1	17	9	15	11	7	5	13	3			Slope 115
Hole	10	11	12	13	14	15	16	17	18	In		Totals
BLUE	505	155	376	136	306	383	178	500	294	2833	BLUE	5540
WHITE	475	150	371	124	296	378	163	475	282	2714	WHITE	5335
Par	5	3	4	3	4	4	3	5	4	35	Par	69
Handicap	2	14	4	18	12	8	16	6	10			
RED	441	122	370	114	221	333	151	430	275	2457	RED	4866
Par	5	3	4	3	4	4	3	5	4	35	Par	70
Handicap	2	16	6	18	14	8	12	4	10			

Manager: Norman Forsyth   **Pro:** Mark Mitchell, PGA   **Supt:** Chris Woolbert
Architect: Hal Purdy 1965

40

RIDGEWOOD COUNTRY CLUB

96 West Midland Ave., Paramus, NJ 07450   **(201) 599-3900**

Ridgewood is a 27 hole course open 6 days a week, 11 months a year. Guests play accompanied by a member. Tee time reservations are not necessary.

•**Driving Range**	•**Lockers**
•**Practice Green**	•**Showers**
•**Power Carts**	•**Food**
Pull Carts	•**Clubhouse**
•**Club Rental**	•**Outings**
•**Caddies**	•**Soft Spikes**

Course Description: This tree-lined championship course was designed in 1928 by A.W. Tillinghast. It is rated as one of the top hundred courses in the country in no small part due to the challenge presented by the tee shots. Each hole is surrounded by wonderful elm, maple and oak trees. On the West Course, the par 4 ninth hole is 427 yards, a dogleg right with a cavernous bunker guarding the left front of the green. The sixth on the Center Course is called the "nickel & dime" hole. You either end up with a five or a ten depending on the accuracy of your approach shot. The scorecard below is for the West & East courses.

Directions: Bergen County, #23 on Northeast Map
Take Rte. 4 East or West to Rte. 17 North. Take the 2nd Midland Ave. exit. Travel approximately 1/2 mile to club on left.

Hole	1	2	3	4	5	6	7	8	9	Out	BLUE	Rating 74.2
BLUE	371	384	202	597	413	151	420	569	427	3534		Slope 138
WHITE	358	363	181	531	403	137	380	559	419	3331		
Par	4	5	3	4	5	4	3	4	4	36	WHITE	Rating 72.5
Handicap	7	4	9	6	1	2	8	5	3			Slope 133
RED	340	347	136	456	394	124	305	515	334	2951		
Par	4	4	3	5	5	3	4	5	4	37	RED	Rating 75.1
Handicap	5	3	9	2	6	8	7	1	4			Slope 134
Hole	10	11	12	13	14	15	16	17	18	In		Totals
BLUE	375	177	567	414	407	229	460	403	379	3411	BLUE	6945
WHITE	350	155	544	390	374	205	428	393	369	3208	WHITE	6539
Par	4	3	5	4	4	3	4	4	4	35	Par	71
Handicap	6	9	2	4	3	8	1	7	5			
RED	325	136	507	405	358	187	413	382	328	3041	RED	5992
Par	4	3	5	5	4	3	5	4	4	37	Par	74
Handicap	7	9	1	5	3	8	2	4	6			

Manager: Jonathan Bassi   **Pro:** Bill Adams, PGA   **Supt:** Todd Raisch
Estab: 1890 **Architect:** A.W. Tillinghast 1928

RIVERVALE COUNTRY CLUB
PUBLIC

660 River Vale Rd., River Vale NJ 07675   **(201) 391-2300**

RiverVale is an 18 hole course open all year 7 days a week. Tee time reservations may be made up to 2 weeks in advance; there are no single reserved times. Outings are welcomed here requiring 2 weeks notice for 12 or more players.

- •**Driving Range**
- •**Practice Green**
- •**Power Carts**
-   Pull Carts
- •**Club Rental**
- •**Soft Spikes**

- •**Lockers**
- •**Showers**
- •**Food**
- •**Clubhouse**
- •**Outings**

Fees	Weekday	Weekend
Mon-Thur	$62	$88
Fri	$72	
Twi specials $48		
Power carts included		

Course Description: The immaculately maintained RiverVale is a narrow course with tough, targeted well bunkered greens, many of which are elevated. The fourth hole is a challenging dogleg left; the 18th, the signature hole, features a picturesque pond that fronts the slope to the green. Well played approach shots are required for a chance to score well. With its hilly terrain, the requirement of power carts is appreciated by golfers. The Fuji Restaurant in the clubhouse serves authentic Japanese food.

Directions: Bergen County, #24 on Northeast Map
Pal.Int.Pkwy. to Exit #6W. At 4th light, go left on Blue Hill Rd.(water on left), go 1.4 miles. Blue Hill Rd. becomes Orangeburg Rd. in River Vale. Go left on River Vale Rd. Club is 1/4 mile on left.

Hole	1	2	3	4	5	6	7	8	9	Out	BLUE	Rating 71.3
BLUE	384	325	482	351	233	475	350	133	540	3273		Slope 127
WHITE	365	308	471	321	215	454	334	123	522	3113		
Par	4	4	5	4	3	4	4	3	5	36	WHITE	Rating 69.9
Handicap	3	15	7	11	5	1	13	17	9			Slope 124
RED	326	302	410	267	156	408	309	98	479	2755		
Par	4	4	5	4	3	5	4	3	5	37	RED	Rating 71.3
Handicap	7	11	1	13	15	3	9	17	5			Slope 124

Hole	10	11	12	13	14	15	16	17	18	In		Totals
BLUE	394	345	336	167	508	468	380	164	375	3137	BLUE	6410
WHITE	372	337	325	161	488	450	365	155	364	3017	WHITE	6130
Par	4	4	4	3	5	5	4	3	4	36	Par	72
Handicap	4	14	10	16	6	12	8	18	2			
RED	338	271	268	156	417	442	307	148	302	2649	RED	5404
Par	4	4	4	3	5	5	4	3	5	37	Par	74
Handicap	8	16	12	14	4	2	10	18	6			

Manager: Hitoshi Oshima   **Pro:** John W. Kasper, PGA   **Supt:** Jim Gurzler
Architect: Orrin Smith 1930

ROCKLEIGH GOLF COURSE

PUBLIC

15 Paris Ave., Rockleigh, NJ 07647   **(201) 768-6353**

Rockleigh is a public county course with three nines & is open from mid-March to mid-Dec. 7 days a week. Call 343-4441 for automated tee times up to 7 days in advance (until midnight of the night before.) There is a reservation fee. Scorecard below is Red/White.

Driving Range	•**Lockers**
•**Practice Green**	•**Showers**
•**Power Carts**	•**Food**
•**Pull Carts**	•**Clubhouse**
•**Club Rental**	Outings
•**Soft Spikes**	

Fees	Weekday	Weekend
ReswID	$13	$17
Non-res	$24	$31
NonNJ	$45	$45
Sr/Jr	$7	$14.50
Power carts	$20	$20

Course Description: The traditional design of Rockleigh, the only Bergen County course that has 27 holes, offers something for every level of player. It is wide-open with gently rolling hills and mid-sized greens. The Red course is considered the most challenging, highlighted by the 4th hole which is hilly and has water in play. The White is flatter and the Blue has as the longest hole, the par 5 #8 with a length of 536 yards. Beautiful views of the Palisades can be enjoyed here. The course gets quite busy; as many as 600 people per day play on a weekend. Scorecard below is Red/White; rating & slope are an average of all 3 courses.

Directions: Bergen County, #25 on Northeast Map
Palisades Pkwy. to Exit #5S. Take Rte. 303 South which becomes Livingston Ave. Turn left at the 4th light, Paris Ave., and proceed to course on right. OR Rte. 9W North to Closter Dock Rd. and turn left. Go right on Piermont, then left on Paris to club on left.

Hole	1	2	3	4	5	6	7	8	9	Out	BLUE	Rating
BLUE												Slope
WHITE	349	321	391	155	446	507	437	193	413	3212		
Par	4	4	4	3	5	5	4	3	4	36	WHITE	Rating 68.2
Handicap	6	9	2	8	5	4	1	7	3			Slope 115
RED	327	300	353	92	440	410	422	180	380	2904		
Par	4	4	4	3	5	5	4	3	4	36	RED	Rating 68.2
Handicap	6	9	2	8	5	4	1	7	3			Slope 115

Hole	10	11	12	13	14	15	16	17	18	In		Totals
BLUE											BLUE	
WHITE	304	371	353	185	334	476	171	477	296	2967	WHITE	6179
Par	4	4	4	3	4	5	3	5	4	36	Par	72
Handicap	7	1	4	8	5	2	9	3	6			
RED	269	335	320	154	290	404	163	422	257	2614	RED	5518
Par	4	4	4	3	4	5	3	5	4	36	Par	72
Handicap	7	1	4	8	5	2	9	3	6			

Manager/Supt: Steve Ratto
Architects: Robert Trent Jones 1964 (Blue)   Alfred Tull 1958 (Red & White)

TAMCREST GOLF COURSE

Rte. 9W & Montammy Drive, Alpine, NJ 07620   (201) 767-4610

Tamcrest is a public 9 hole course open 7 days a week and closed in Jan. & Feb. Reserved tee times are necessary. Seasonal memberships for guaranteed weekend tee times are available. Specials available for ladies on Tues. and Srs. on Wed. Electric carts are mandatory; prices below inc. cart. For more info, call 767-1319.

Driving Range	Lockers
•**Practice Green**	Showers
•**Power Carts**	
Pull Carts	•**Food**
•**Club Rental**	Clubhouse
•**Soft Spikes**	•**Outings**

Fees	Weekday	Weekend
9 holes	$32	
18 holes	$44	$62
Twi(after 2)	$40	$42
Sr/Jr(18)	$41	

Course Description: Tamcrest is a tight and hilly course with water on 2 holes; the back tees, not the forward are affected. The greens are undulating, some are two tiered and several are quite difficult to read. Golf at Tamcrest is a fair test with level tree lined fairways, visible hazards and only a few blind shots. One must remain alert during play since some of the fairways are within errant shots of each other. Most golfers who want a full round of 18 holes use alternate tees for the second nine.

Directions: Bergen County, #26 on Northeast Map

Pal. Int.Pkwy. North to Exit #1. Turn right onto Rte. 9 W North. After light for Tenafly, watch for signs to "Montammy CC", turn left, pass Montammy to Tamcrest.

Hole	1	2	3	4	5	6	7	8	9	Out	BLUE	
BLUE												
WHITE	440	337	306	165	471	333	317	150	430	2949		
Par	4	4	4	3	5	4	4	3	4	35	WHITE	Rating 69.8
Handicap	1	11	13	15	3	9	7	17	5			Slope 125
RED	285	200	205	145	400	321	306	145	360	2367		
Par	4	4	4	3	5	4	4	3	4	35	RED	Rating 68.4
Handicap	9	13	11	15	1	5	7	17	3			Slope 115
Hole	10	11	12	13	14	15	16	17	18	In		Totals
BLUE											BLUE	
WHITE											WHITE	2949
Par											Par	35
Handicap												
RED											RED	2367
Par											Par	35
Handicap												

Pro: Jeff Bohr, PGA   **Supt:** Ken Duggan
Architect: Tamburelli 1971

UPPER MONTCLAIR COUNTRY CLUB

177 Hepburn Rd., Clifton, NJ 07012   (973) 779-7505

Upper Montclair is a private 27 hole course open 6 days a week all year. Guests play accompanied by a member. Tee time reservations are not necessary. The scorecard below is for the East & South courses.

•**Driving Range**	•**Lockers**
•**Practice Green**	•**Showers**
•**Power Carts**	•**Food**
•**Pull Carts**	•**Clubhouse**
•**Club Rental**	•**Outings**
•**Caddies**	•**Soft Spikes**

Course Description: This championship course is the site of the Cadillac NFL Golf Classic. Originally A.W. Tillinghast designed 36 holes for Upper Montclair but the GSP took 9 away and Robert Trent Jones redesigned the course for 27 holes. The fairways are tree lined and well maintained. Many of the immaculately groomed greens are elevated and all are fast with subtle breaks. Water on the par 4 third hole requires a well placed tee shot followed by a demanding second shot. Characteristic of Robert Trent Jones are the long tee boxes and narrow fairways.

Directions: Passaic County, #27 on Northeast Map
Garden State Pkwy. to Exit # 153. Then take Rte. 3 East. Almost immediately, make a right to the club entrance on Rte. 3.

Hole	1	2	3	4	5	6	7	8	9	Out	BLUE	Rating 72.9
BLUE	440	182	550	300	185	520	400	370	430	3467		Slope 131
WHITE	427	170	535	370	165	500	365	350	401	3283		
Par	4	3	5	4	3	5	4	4	4	36	WHITE	Rating 71.3
Handicap	1	8	3	6	9	4	5	7	2			Slope 127
RED	410	165	415	335	140	410	350	330	355	2910		
Par	5	3	5	4	3	5	4	4	4	37	RED	Rating 73.5
Handicap	2	8	3	6	9	1	7	5	4			Slope 124
Hole	10	11	12	13	14	15	16	17	18	In		Totals
BLUE	420	495	425	355	375	180	390	215	590	3445	BLUE	6912
WHITE	410	478	408	340	357	168	360	195	550	3266	WHITE	6549
Par	4	5	4	4	4	3	4	3	5	36	Par	72
Handicap	4	3	1	7	6	9	5	8	2			
RED	356	385	355	320	325	135	350	170	469	2865	RED	5775
Par	4	5	5	4	4	3	4	3	5	37	Par	74
Handicap	4	2	3	7	6	9	5	8	1			

Manager: Ed Jaworski   **Pro:** John Heuser, PGA   **Supt:** Bob Dickison
Architect: A.W. Tillinghast 1901   **Redesign:** Robert Trent Jones 1929

WHITE BEECHES GOLF & CC

70 Haworth Dr., Haworth, NJ 07641   **(201) 385-8531**

White Beeches is a private 18 hole course open 6 days a week and closed for the month of Feb. Guests play accompanied by a member. Reserved tee times are suggested for weekends.

•**Driving Range**	•**Lockers**
•**Practice Green**	•**Showers**
•**Power Carts**	•**Food**
Pull Carts	•**Clubhouse**
•**Club Rental**	•**Outings**
•**Caddies**	•**Soft Spikes**

Course Description: White Beeches is a relatively flat, parkland style course with an abundance of trees and many doglegs. The greens are postage stamp in size and extremely hard to hold. Excellent chipping and putting skills are necessary to get up and down. The player faces a difficult decision on the par 5 eleventh hole where a brook crosses the fairway; to lay up on the second shot or to try to carry the green. The 18th is a daunting finishing hole, a par 3 over water. White Beeches is presently being enhanced with many new bunkers and tees.

Directions: Bergen County, #28 on Northeast Map
From Rte. 4East take Kinderkamack Rd. North to Oradell. Go right on Oradell Ave. to blinking light and make a left on Grant Ave. and right on Sunset. Left on Haworth Dr. to club on left.

Hole	1	2	3	4	5	6	7	8	9	Out	BLUE	Rating 71.7
BLUE	392	326	527	349	374	148	299	570	368	3353		Slope 134
WHITE	371	289	514	331	365	134	285	557	354	3200		
Par	4	4	5	4	4	3	4	5	4	37	WHITE	Rating 70.9
Handicap	3	13	5	11	7	17	15	1	9			Slope 131
RED	351	255	405	322	353	420	262	500	340	2949		
Par	4	4	5	4	4	4	3	5	4	37	RED	Rating 73.0
Handicap	3	15	7	11	9	17	13	1	5			Slope 129
Hole	10	11	12	13	14	15	16	17	18	In		Totals
BLUE	396	509	366	185	429	366	336	428	215	3230	BLUE	6583
WHITE	376	481	346	174	413	347	315	411	202	3065	WHITE	6265
Par	4	5	4	3	4	4	4	4	3	35	Par	72
Handicap	6	8	10	18	2	14	12	4	16			
RED	355	421	310	162	401	329	284	400	145	2807	RED	5756
Par	4	5	4	3	5	4	4	5	3	37	Par	74
Handicap	8	2	12	16	4	14	10	6	18			

Manager: Cindy Williams   **Pro:** Paul Meseck, PGA   **Supt:** Armand LaSage
Architects: Val Flood 1902   Walter Travis 1919   Alfred Tull 1950

NORTHWEST REGION

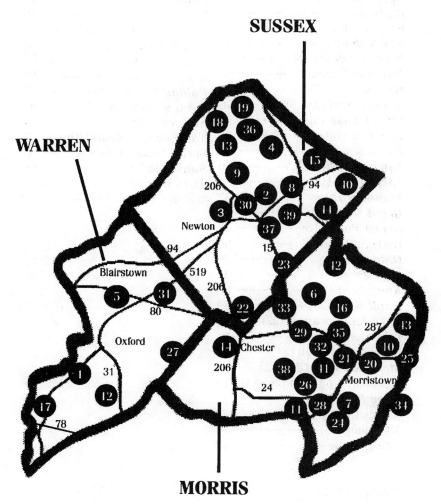

SUSSEX

WARREN

MORRIS

NORTHWEST REGION

Public Courses appear in **bold italics**

* Military Course

APPLE MOUNTAIN GOLF & CC

PUBLIC

624 Hazen Oxford Rd., Belvidere, NJ 07823   **(908) 453-3023**

Apple Mountain is an 18 hole semi-private course open to the public 7 days a week all year. Memberships are available. Tee times may be reserved up to 2 weeks in advance. Power carts are required until 2PM on weekends. Soft spikes are optional. Call 800 PLAYGOLF as alternate for tee times.

Driving Range	• Lockers
• Practice Green	• Showers
• Power Carts	• Food
• Pull Carts	• Clubhouse
• Club Rental	• Outings

Fees	Weekday	Weekend
Daily	$24	$52/cart
After 12	$19	$42/cart
9 hole	$15/cart	$5
Power carts	$12pp	

Course Description: Apple Mountain is a hilly well-maintained golf course. Although there are many beautiful mature trees lining the fairways, additional ones are planted periodically and tees are upgraded on a regular basis. Water comes into play on eleven holes. The severe dogleg left and water to carry on the par 5 third signature hole makes it a golfer's nightmare. The unique par 6 17th is a 650 yard downhill dogleg. The greens have variety; some are elevated, some are two-tiered. The 13th and 15th holes are at high elevation and the Delaware Water Gap can be seen in the distance.

Directions: Warren County, #1 on Northwest Map
Rte.80 to Exit #12. Go south on Rte.519 crossing over Rte.46. Go left onto Rte.623 and then a quick left onto Rte.624. Club is 2mi on right. From Rte. 78 take Exit #17 to Rte.31N; and left on Rte. 624 in Oxford. Club 2mi ahead on the left.

Hole	1	2	3	4	5	6	7	8	9	Out	BLUE	Rating 71.8
BLUE	284	381	560	170	394	379	401	397	229	3195		Slope 122
WHITE	262	365	501	120	364	362	372	379	135	2860		
Par	4	4	5	3	4	4	4	4	3	35	WHITE	Rating 68.8
Handicap	16	4	2	18	6	14	12	8	10			Slope 118
RED	232	321	453	109	262	273	265	371	122	2408		
Par	4	4	5	3	4	4	4	4	3	35	RED	Rating 69.8
Handicap	16	4	2	18	6	14	12	8	10			Slope 123
Hole	10	11	12	13	14	15	16	17	18	In		Totals
BLUE	201	376	373	568	339	261	419	656	280	3473	BLUE	6668
WHITE	130	356	351	541	327	182	372	632	260	3151	WHITE	6011
Par	3	4	4	5	4	3	4	5	3	35	Par	70
Handicap	15	17	7	5	9	13	3	1	11			
RED	111	332	312	457	294	159	331	559	250	2805	RED	5213
Par	3	4	4	5	4	3	4	6	4	37	Par	72
Handicap	15	17	7	5	9	13	3	1	11			

Manager: Drew J. Kiszonak   **Supt:** Andrew Kiszonak
Built: 1973

BALLYOWEN

Wheatsworth Rd., Hamburg, NJ 07419

(973) 827-5996

Ballyowen is an 18 hole semi-private course open 7 days a week March through Dec. weather permitting. Quad memberships are available that include playing privileges at Black Bear, Crystal Springs and The Spa. Tee time reservations up to 10 days in advance. Caddies must be reserved 48 hours ahead.

- •Driving Range
- •Practice Green
- •Power Carts
- Pull Carts
- •Club Rental
- •Soft Spikes

- •Lockers
- •Showers
- •Food
- •Clubhouse
- •Outings
- •Caddies

NEW

Fees	Weekday	Weekend
Daily	$90	$115
After 3PM	$60	$75
Power carts included		

Course Description: With panoramic views of the Great Gorge area and mountains in the distance, Ballyowen takes advantage of the unique natural landscape. The property was reclaimed from a former sand and gravel mine and is virtually treeless. Multiple tee locations give golfers of all skill levels a chance to enjoy this links style lay-out. The architect specializes in environmentally sensitive design. The broad verdant rolling contoured fairways, the bent grass greens, the wind shifts and the wheat-like native grasses in the rough, make this an unusual and challenging course with a true Scottish flavor.

Directions: Sussex County, #2 on Northwest Map
Rte. 80 West or East to Exit 53. Take Rte.23 North approximately 35 miles to Hamburg. Go left on Rte.94S for 2 miles to Wheatsworth Rd. Turn left & go 1 m. to course on right.

Hole	1	2	3	4	5	6	7	8	9	Out	BLUE	Rating 70.5
BLUE	351	312	546	180	530	174	384	395	393	3265		Slope 126
WHITE	328	282	505	159	509	159	347	374	364	3027		
Par	4	4	5	3	5	3	4	4	4	36	WHITE	Rating 68.6
Handicap	15	17	5	11	7	3	1	13	9			Slope 115
RED	286	212	423	95	422	107	285	283	282	2395		
Par	4	4	5	3	5	3	4	4	4	36	RED	Rating 66.4
Handicap	15	17	5	11	7	3	1	13	9			Slope 103
Hole	10	11	12	13	14	15	16	17	18	In		Totals
BLUE	482	161	328	360	448	167	420	490	387	3243	BLUE	6508
WHITE	460	140	315	338	409	143	394	475	365	3039	WHITE	6066
Par	5	3	4	4	4	3	4	5	4	36	Par	72
Handicap	18	8	16	14	4	6	2	12	10			
RED	396	87	247	303	354	99	355	357	310	2508	RED	4903
Par	5	3	4	4	4	3	4	5	4	36	Par	72
Handicap	18	8	16	14	4	6	2	12	10			

Manager: Art Walton, PGA   **Pro:** Dave Glenz, PGA   **Supt:** Rich La Bar
Architect: Roger Rulewich 1998

BEAR BROOK GOLF CLUB

527 Route 94, Fredon Township, NJ 07860   **(973) 300-5775**

Bear Brook will open in the summer of 1999. It will be a private 18 hole course open 6 days a week from Apr. 1 to Nov. 28th. Guests will play accompanied by a member. Caddies may be available as needed. Clubhouse will be ready by the end of 1999.

- •Driving Range
- •Practice Green
- •Power Carts
- Pull Carts
- •Club Rental
- Caddies
- •Lockers
- •Showers
- •Food
- •Clubhouse
- •Outings
- •Soft Spikes

Course Description: This course is being built within a gated community of 44 estate homes and 42 golf villas. From the championship tees, the course will play about 6800 yards, and 6300 from the Blues, 5800 from the Whites and 4800 from the forward tees to a par of 71. Bear Brook Golf Club features a links style layout of varying topography. The 4th hole offers two separate and distinct greens. The picturesque par 3 9th requires a shot over a wildlife zone to a green surrounded by pot bunkers. On the 14th hole, the long hitters will face a challenge; it is a 708 yard par 6 and very narrow. A brook crosses the 18th both on the fairway and the approach shot. Water is in play on 6 holes.

Directions: Sussex County, #3 on Northwest Map
Rte.80W to Exit 34B. Take Rte.15N and continue on Rte.206N. Then take Rte.618 to Rte. 94 to course.

Supt: Jeff Lansdowne
Architect: Ron Pritchard 1999

BLACK BEAR GOLF & CC

138 Route 23 North, Franklin, NJ 07416   **(973) 209-2226**

Black Bear is a semi-private 18 hole course open to the public 7 days a week from Mar. 1 to Dec.31, weather permitting. Motorized pull carts may be rented. Quad memberships are available featuring reciprocity with Crystal Springs, The Spa, & Ballyowen. Members may make tee times up to 15 days in advance; non-mbrs up to 10 days.

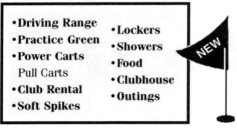

- •Driving Range
- •Practice Green
- •Power Carts
- Pull Carts
- •Club Rental
- •Soft Spikes
- •Lockers
- •Showers
- •Food
- •Clubhouse
- •Outings

NEW

Fees	Weekday	Weekend
Daily	$55	$70
After 3 PM	$35	$45
Power carts	included	

Course Description: The 6,673 yard layout of Black Bear combines the specatacular beauty of the Great Gorge area with an array of amenities that rivals any golf facility in the Metropolitan area. There is a diversity of topography, an abundance of wildlife and remarkable scenery. This course is the headquarters for the well known David Glenz Golf Academy. There are two distinct nines on 280 acres of a former farm; the front weaves in and out of forests and sloping terrain, while the back offers interesting mounding. The 2nd and 7th cross over a large pond stocked with a variety of fish.

Directions: Sussex County, #4 on Northwest Map
Rte. 80 West or East to Exit 53. Take Rte. 23 North for approximately 32 miles. Course is on the right 1/4 mile after the intersection of Rte. 631 in Franklin.

Hole	1	2	3	4	5	6	7	8	9	Out	BLUE	Rating 72.2
BLUE	384	506	445	406	195	566	204	343	420	3490		Slope 130
WHITE	349	451	394	386	158	500	142	295	400	3075		
Par	4	5	4	4	3	5	3	4	4	36	WHITE	Rating 66.4
Handicap	9	11	1	5	17	13	7	15	3			Slope 121
RED	240	382	329	310	120	437	122	251	305	2496		
Par	4	5	4	4	3	5	3	4	4	36	RED	Rating 67.7
Handicap	11	5	1	7	17	9	13	15	3			Slope 115
Hole	10	11	12	13	14	15	16	17	18	In		Totals
BLUE	382	148	385	555	164	275	496	389	389	3183	BLUE	6673
WHITE	335	123	350	496	137	230	455	340	342	2808	WHITE	5873
Par	4	3	4	5	3	4	5	4	4	36	Par	72
Handicap	8	18	4	2	16	14	12	6	10			
RED	266	103	335	366	111	164	380	267	297	2260	RED	4756
Par	4	3	4	5	3	4	5	4	4	36	Par	72
Handicap	12	18	4	2	16	14	6	10	8			

Manager: Karl Fitz, PGA   **Pro:** Dave Glenz, PGA   **Supt:** Eric Tomzic
Architects: Jack Kurlander, David Glenz 1996

BLAIR ACADEMY GOLF COURSE   **PUBLIC**

Blair Academy, Blairstown, NJ 07825   **(908) 362-6218**

Blair Academy is a 9 hole course open 7 days a week from mid March to the end of Nov., weather permitting. Students at Blair have priority here. Memberships are available. Reservations for tee times available for members only until 12PM weekends and holidays.

Driving Range	Lockers
•**Practice Green**	Showers
Power Carts	Food
•**Pull Carts**	Clubhouse
Club Rental	Outings
•**Soft Spikes**	

Fees	Weekday	Weekend
Daily	$13	$18
Twi	$10	$13
Discounts for Srs. & Jrs.		

Course Description: The layout at Blair academy is beautifully maintained and very hilly. As power carts are not allowed at all, some say you've got to be a billy goat to play here. The course is generally uncrowded except when the school golf team practices. Different tees may be used for the second nine. The par 3 2nd has both the tee and the green elevated. On a number of holes the green can't be seen from the tee. The 9th hole has been redone recently.

Directions: Warren County, #5 on Northwest Map
Rte. 80 West to Exit #12. Go right toward Blairstown onto Rte. 521 for 5 miles. At end, make left and after Coastal Sta., make right onto Park St. Pass 2 STOP signs to Blair Academy gate. Follow signs to golf course.

Hole	1	2	3	4	5	6	7	8	9	Out	BLUE	Rating
BLUE												Slope
WHITE	372	188	375	267	503	186	491	138	350	2870		
Par	4	3	4	4	5	3	5	3	4	35	WHITE	Rating
Handicap	5	13	7	1	9	15	11	17	3			Slope
RED	360	132	241	257	405	149	423	118	300	2385		
Par	4	3	4	4	5	3	5	3	4	35	RED	Rating
Handicap	4	8	3	2	6	7	5	9	1			Slope

Hole	10	11	12	13	14	15	16	17	18	In		Totals
BLUE											BLUE	
BLUE	372	182	375	267	503	207	491	157	356	2910	WHITE	5780
Par	4	3	4	4	5	3	5	3	4	35	Par	70
Handicap	6	14	8	2	10	16	12	8	4			
GOLD	362	180	358	257	462	172	463	124	327	2705	RED	5090
Par	4	3	4	4	5	3	5	3	4	35	Par	70
Handicap	3	7	1	4	5	8	6	9	2			

Manager/Pro: Hal Eaton   **Supt:** Joe Antonioli

BOWLING GREEN GOLF CLUB

53 Schoolhouse Rd., Milton, NJ 07438   (973) 697-8688

Bowling Green is a semi-private 18 hole course open to the public 7 days a week from mid March until mid Dec. Memberships are available. Call 5 days in advance for tee times, members 10 days. Foursomes only on weekends and holidays.

•Driving Range	•Lockers
•Practice Green	•Showers
•Power Carts	•Food
•Pull Carts	•Clubhouse
Club Rental	•Outings
•Soft Spikes	

Fees	M-Thurs	Weekend
Daily	$32	$50
After 4PM	$20	$25
9holes	$20	
Power carts	$18pp	9hole/$9

Course Description: With Bowling Green Mountain as a backdrop, this picturesque course is appealing to nature lovers and all levels of golfers. The tee shot over water on the #1 handicap fourth hole requires accuracy and water is still in play on the approach to the green. The 601 yard long 18th is made more difficult by the uphill terrain leading to the putting surface. The drives out of a chute of pines on the 5th and 10th holes make them both challenging and memorable. Attentive rangers assist the players in maintaining the pace of play. Carts are not mandatory.

Directions: Morris County, #6 on Northwest Map
Rte.80 West to Exit 34B. Take Rte.15N. At 3rd light, turn right at Berkshire Valley Rd. Go north for 8.5 miles to traffic light and turn left onto Ridge Rd. Go 1 mi. to blinker and turn left onto Schoolhouse Rd. Course is 1 mile on right.

Hole	1	2	3	4	5	6	7	8	9	Out	BLUE	Rating 72.4
BLUE	358	375	220	482	351	417	431	210	492	3336		Slope 131
WHITE	330	359	198	456	331	397	405	184	474	3134		
Par	4	4	3	5	4	4	4	3	5	36	WHITE	Rating 70.3
Handicap	13	7	15	1	11	3	5	17	9			Slope 126
RED	298	285	178	420	262	266	314	110	382	2515		
Par	4	4	3	5	4	4	4	3	5	36	RED	Rating 69.4
Handicap	13	7	15	1	11	3	5	17	9			Slope 122
Hole	10	11	12	13	14	15	16	17	18	In		Totals
BLUE	389	167	403	351	493	350	199	400	601	3353	BLUE	6689
WHITE	363	144	381	291	474	313	176	376	572	3090	WHITE	6224
Par	4	3	4	4	5	4	3	4	5	36	Par	72
Handicap	10	16	4	12	8	14	18	6	2			
RED	265	120	282	265	357	239	145	312	466	2451	RED	4966
Par	4	3	4	4	5	4	3	4	5	36	Par	72
Handicap	10	16	4	12	8	14	18	6	2			

Manager: Bruce Salmon   **Pro:** Tom Staples, PGA   **Supt:** Dave Mayer
Architect: Geoffrey Cornish 1965

BROOKLAKE COUNTRY CLUB

139 Brooklake Rd., Florham Park, NJ 07932   **(973) 377-6751**

Brooklake is an 18 hole course open 6 days a week from Apr.1 to Dec 10th. Guests play accompanied by a member. Tee time reservations are not necessary.

•**Driving Range**	•**Lockers**
•**Practice Green**	•**Showers**
•**Power Carts**	•**Food**
Pull Carts	•**Clubhouse**
•**Club Rental**	•**Outings**
•**Caddies**	•**Soft Spikes**

Course Description: Brooklake is relatively flat and well treed with tricky, carefully manicured greens and water in play on seven holes. Additional fairway bunkers have recently been installed. The layout begins with a long par 3. The fifth is a lengthy par 4 that has a stream running through the fairway. The tenth hole has an island green, one of many obstacles to posting a low score. The tee shot over water on the par 3 17th is to a narrow target surrounded by bunkers. The signature par 5 18th hole is 600 yards with a creek and sparkling pond confronting the golfer.

Directions: Morris County, #7 on Northwest Map
Rte. 80W or E to Rte. 287S. Exit at Rte. 24E. Take the Florham Park exit to Columbia Tpke. (Rte. 510). Make right onto Ridgedale Ave. Turn left onto Brooklake Rd. to club on right.

Hole	1	2	3	4	5	6	7	8	9	Out	BLUE	Rating 73.0
BLUE	190	514	380	185	466	366	642	414	574	3433		Slope 127
WHITE	183	500	372	175	436	329	330	411	566	3302		
Par	3	5	4	3	4	4	4	4	5	36	WHITE	Rating 72.0
Handicap	13	11	7	17	1	15	9	3	5			Slope 125
RED	164	480	320	126	385	278	315	400	465	2933		
Par	3	5	4	3	5	4	4	5	5	38	RED	Rating 73.8
Handicap	11	1	3	17	7	15	9	13	5			Slope 125
Hole	10	11	12	13	14	15	16	17	18	In		Totals
BLUE	402	414	390	420	512	426	166	162	600	3502	BLUE	6935
WHITE	371	387	382	387	502	405	157	157	589	3337	WHITE	6639
Par	4	4	4	4	5	4	3	3	5	36	Par	72
Handicap	4	12	6	8	16	10	18	14	2			
RED	300	325	345	325	480	305	133	100	500	2813	RED	5746
Par	4	4	4	4	5	4	3	3	5	36	Par	74
Handicap	6	10	8	12	4	14	16	18	2			

Manager: Don Neeb   **Pro:** Basil Amorosano, PGA   **Supt:** Scott Carpenter
Architect: Herb Strong 1921

CRYSTAL SPRINGS GOLF CLUB PUBLIC

123 Crystal Springs Rd., Hamburg, NJ 07419   (973) 827-1444

Crystal Springs is an 18 hole semi-private course within an upscale housing development and is open to the public Mar. to Dec. 7 days a week. Memberships are available. Tee times for members; up to 15 days in advance, non-members 10 days. One new course is in construction as we go to press and another is being planned here.

- **Driving Range**
- **Practice Green**
- **Power Carts**
- Pull Carts
- **Club Rental**
- **Soft Spikes**

Lockers
Showers
- **Food**
- **Clubhouse**
- **Outings**

Fees	Weekday	Weekend
Daily	$62	$82
Off-peak	$52	$72
Twi 3PM	$39	$49
Power carts included		

Course Description: Crystal Springs is a course of breathtaking views and dramatic golf holes, a truly unique experience. A links layout, it has moguls and hills on every hole and large contoured greens, some multi-tiered. Water is in play on 5 holes. The signature par 3 10th tees off from an 80 foot elevation to a large butterfly shaped green. The sparkling crystal spring on the left is the depository of many balls. The par 3 8th requires an accurate carry over water to a green surrounded by bunkers. The par 4 9th tees off over water to a severe dogleg left and an uphill shot to a two-tiered green with a beautiful view.

Directions: Sussex County, #8 on Northwest Map
Rte. 80 West to Exit 53. Take Rte. 23North through Franklin and just before Hamburg, make a right onto Rte. 517 North. Course is 2 miles ahead on the left.

Hole	1	2	3	4	5	6	7	8	9	Out	BLUE	Rating 74.1
BLUE	420	433	485	153	406	419	553	153	413	3435		Slope 137
WHITE	356	383	403	113	343	366	493	130	347	2934		
Par	4	4	5	3	4	4	5	3	4	36	WHITE	Rating 69.7
Handicap	5	1	11	17	9	13	7	15	3			Slope 125
RED	313	323	375	100	303	382	443	106	297	2592		
Par	4	4	5	3	4	4	5	3	4	36	RED	Rating 70.5
Handicap	5	1	11	17	9	13	7	15	3			Slope 123
Hole	10	11	12	13	14	15	16	17	18	In		Totals
BLUE	186	541	165	564	140	416	410	396	563	3381	BLUE	6816
WHITE	160	475	125	524	105	356	350	330	503	2954	WHITE	5888
Par	3	5	3	5	3	4	4	4	5	36	Par	72
Handicap	14	6	16	2	18	4	8	12	10			
RED	105	425	100	465	85	306	300	250	453	2499	RED	5091
Par	3	5	3	5	3	4	4	4	5	36	Par	72
Handicap	14	6	16	2	18	4	8	12	10			

Manager: Joe Fotino   **Pro:** Dave Glenz, PGA   **Supt:** Craig Worts
Architect: Robert Von Hagge 1990

CULVER LAKE GOLF CLUB

PUBLIC

Box G, Branchville, NJ 07826   (973) 948-5610

Culver Lake is a 9 hole course open 7 days a week between March and December. Tee time reservations are not necessary. Memberships are available. Tuesday is Ladies Day and discounts prevail. Alternate phone: (973) 948-6959.

Driving Range
- **Practice Green**
- **Power Carts**
- **Pull Carts**
- **Club Rental**

Soft Spikes

- **Lockers**
- **Showers**
- **Food**
- **Clubhouse**
- **Outings**

Fees	Weekday	Weekend
9 holes	$10	$15
18 holes	$16	$20
Power carts	$20/18	$12/9

Course Description: Culver Lake was closed for a time in 1935 to become a game preserve. In 1962, it reopened as a golf course; much of the wildlife remained. This accounts for sightings of deer, wild turkeys and other animals roaming here. It is by no means an executive course. Tight, well wooded with small well-maintained greens, it can be an enjoyable golf experience. There is a second set of White tees.

Directions: Sussex County, #9 on Northwest Map
Rte. 80 West to Exit 34B. Take Rte. 15N and continue when it becomes Rte. 206North for about 4 & 1/2 miles. At Dale's Market, make right onto East Shore of Culver Lake. Club is about 1 mile ahead on the right.

Hole	1	2	3	4	5	6	7	8	9	Out	BLUE	Rating
BLUE												Slope
WHITE	129	339	142	302	408	391	163	336	297	2507		
Par	3	4	3	4	4	4	3	4	4	33	WHITE	Rating
Handicap	18	7	17	11	2	3	15	5	9			Slope
RED	124	300	140	270	402	360	135	220	224	2175		
Par	3	4	3	4	5	4	3	4	4	34	RED	Rating
Handicap												Slope
Hole	10	11	12	13	14	15	16	17	18	In		Totals
BLUE											BLUE	
WHITE	171	361	168	331	504	397	174	349	324	2779	WHITE	5286
Par	3	4	3	4	5	4	3	4	4	34	Par	67
Handicap	13	4	16	12	1	6	14	10	8			
RED											RED	4350
Par											Par	68
Handicap												

Manager: Robert Lupine   **Supt:** Ed Riley
Built: 1962

DEER RUN GOLF & TENNIS CLUB

1 Gettysburg Way, Lincoln Park, NJ 07035   **(973) 694-0758**

Deer Run is a 9 hole course found within a private condo development. It is open all year 7 days a week. Guests may play accompanied by a member. This course was formerly called Meadows One. Tee time reservations are not necessary.

- **Driving Range**   Lockers
- **Practice Green** Showers
- **Power Carts**   Food
- **Pull Carts**   • **Clubhouse**
- **Club Rental**   • **Outings**
- Caddies   • **Soft Spikes**

Course Description: Deer Run is a very walkable golf course surrounded by lovely town homes. It is wide open with some ponds to traverse. Water is in play on four holes and there are no fairway bunkers. The greens are large and well maintained. It is a links type course, contoured but generally flat. New tee boxes have been built on 5 holes. An improved irrigation system is being installed. For variety, a second set of tees may be used for the back nine.

Directions: Morris County, #10 on Northwest Map
Take Rte.80 to Exit 52. At exit make right & then turn left onto Two Bridges Rd. Go over a bridge and turn left at STOP sign (still Two Bridges). Continue to another STOP and turn left. Go up hill & make left onto Pinebrook Rd. Go 1 mi. & turn left into Deer Run development and to golf course.

Hole	1	2	3	4	5	6	7	8	9	Out	BLUE	Rating 71.2
BLUE	436	485	344	401	222	427	390	380	150	3235		Slope 120
WHITE	408	475	329	359	165	414	338	372	142	3002		
Par	4	5	4	4	3	4	4	4	3	35	WHITE	Rating 70.1
Handicap	2	10	16	8	15	5	13	12	18			Slope 119
RED	397	393	225	291	125	313	321	327	134	2526		
Par	5	5	4	4	3	4	4	4	3	36	RED	Rating 69.2
Handicap	1	5	15	7	13	3	11	9	17			Slope 121
Hole	10	11	12	13	14	15	16	17	18	In		Totals
BLUE											BLUE	6470
WHITE											WHITE	6004
Par											Par	70
Handicap												
RED											RED	5052
Par											Par	72
Handicap												

Pro: Vinnie Traina, PGA   **Supt:** John Fitzgerald
Built: 1980s

FAIRMOUNT COUNTRY CLUB

400 Southern Blvd., Chatham, NJ 07928   (973) 377-8901

Fairmount is an 18 hole golf club open 6 days a week and closed in February. Guests may play accompanied by a member. Tee time reservations are necessary for weekends.

> • **Driving Range**   • **Lockers**
> • **Practice Green**   • **Showers**
> • **Power Carts**   • **Food**
> • **Pull Carts**   • **Clubhouse**
> • **Club Rental**   • **Outings**
> • **Caddies**   • **Soft Spikes**

Course Description: Fairmount is a typical Hal Purdy design, long with difficult, crown style greens that fall off on all sides. It is a relatively tight and flat course. The creeks and ponds affect play on 8 holes. It borders the Great Swamp, a National Refuge, so the course stays soft all year. The signature par 4 14th, is one of several great doglegs; its green has a severe break. The LPGA Chrysler-Plymouth tournament was held here.

Directions: Morris County, #11 on Northwest Map
GSP or NJ Tpke to Rte. 78West. Exit at Rte. 24West and take the Summit-River Rd. Exit. Go straight to 4th light and make a left on Noe Ave. Proceed to the end and turn right onto Southern Blvd. and to the club on the right.

Hole	1	2	3	4	5	6	7	8	9	Out	BLUE	Rating 73.1
BLUE	553	400	415	156	338	429	172	527	346	3336		Slope 134
WHITE	536	387	410	150	332	419	152	514	342	3242		
Par	5	4	4	3	4	4	3	5	4	36	WHITE	Rating 72.2
Handicap	3	9	1	15	11	5	17	7	13			Slope 132
RED	502	357	395	132	252	401	131	429	429	2930		
Par	5	4	5	3	4	5	3	5	4	38	RED	Rating 75.6
Handicap	3	9	1	15	11	7	17	5	13			Slope 136
Hole	10	11	12	13	14	15	16	17	18	In		Totals
BLUE	553	478	359	217	408	524	405	198	430	3396	BLUE	6732
WHITE	367	470	350	203	399	512	396	193	421	3311	WHITE	6553
Par	4	5	4	3	4	5	4	3	4	36	Par	72
Handicap	12	4	14	15	10	2	8	18	6			
RED	351	433	335	177	377	449	337	173	403	3035	RED	5965
Par	4	5	4	3	4	5	4	3	5	36	Par	75
Handicap	12	4	14	16	2	6	8	18	10			

Manager: Scott Wright   **Pro:** Mark Giuliano, PGA   **Supt:** Vince Bracken
Architect: Hal Purdy 1958

FAIRWAY VALLEY GOLF CLUB

76 Mine Hill Rd., Washington, NJ 07882　　　**(908) 689-1530**

Fairway Valley is a 9 hole course open to the public 7 days a week all year weather permitting. Memberships are available. Tee times may be made up to one month in advance.

Driving Range	Lockers	Fees	Weekday	Weekend
• **Practice Green**	Showers	9 holes	$14	$17
• **Power Carts**	• **Food**	18 holes	$19	$25
• **Pull Carts**	• **Clubhouse**	Srs	$12/9	$17/18
• **Club Rental**	• **Outings**	Power carts	$10/9	$12/18
Soft Spikes				

Course Description: Fairway Valley is a flat, wide open, scenic and easy to walk facility. Originally built as a 6 hole layout, played 3 times for 18, it was converted later into the present 9. It provides wonderful practice for beginners. Ponds are encountered on the fourth, seventh and eighth holes. The par 4 5th could be considered the signature hole, the #1 handicap from the back tees requiring a shot to a narrow fairway and an approach to a target green. On weekends and holidays this course becomes quite busy.

Directions: Warren County, #12 on Northwest Map
Rte.80 West to Exit 26(Budd Lake). Take Rte.46W to Hackettstown. Take Rte.57W for approx. 10 miles, crossing over Rte.31. Road is now Main St., Washington. At 1st light, make right onto Belvedere Ave. Go straight, at 4 way STOP road becomes Mine Hill. Course is 1 mile up on right.

Hole	1	2	3	4	5	6	7	8	9	Out	BLUE	Rating 67.4
BLUE	490	312	300	140	410	138	480	185	480	2935		Slope 107
WHITE	475	297	280	130	346	135	386	149	471	2669		
Par	5	4	4	3	4	3	4	3	5	35	WHITE	Rating 65.4
Handicap	4	2	9	8	1	7	3	5	6			Slope 103
RED	450	282	220	118	326	130	336	129	414	2405		
Par	5	4	4	3	4	3	5	3	5	36	RED	Rating 68.3
Handicap	2	6	7	9	4	8	3	5	1			Slope 108
Hole	10	11	12	13	14	15	16	17	18	In		Totals
BLUE											BLUE	5870
WHITE											WHITE	5338
Par											Par	70
Handicap												
RED											RED	4810
Par											Par	72
Handicap												

Manager/Supt: Jim Stern　　　**Pro:** Craig Utt, PGA　　　**Built:** 1960s

FARMSTEAD GOLF & CC

88 Lawrence Rd., Lafayette, NJ 07848   (973) 383-1666

Farmstead is a 27 hole course open 7 days a week from Mar. to Dec. Tee times may be made up to one week in advance. Limited memberships are available. On weekends and holidays, carts are required before 3 PM.

Driving Range	•Lockers
•Practice Green	•Showers
•Power Carts	•Food
•Pull Carts	•Clubhouse
•Club Rental	•Outings
•Soft Spikes	

Fees	Weekday	Weekend
Daily	$27	$42
After 3	$20	$26
After 5	$13	$16
Power carts	$26	$26

Course Description: Farmstead is more challenging than the golfer realizes at first glance. The Valley nine, although short, is very tight with 6 holes having OB on the right. A good short game is essential to conquer the undulating greens throughout the course. On the longer "Lake" & "Club" nines, the trees and doglegs can block shots that miss the fairway. All the layouts are well contoured and heavily treed. The signature par 3 9th on Lake is an all water carry to what is virtually an island green. At this busy course, rangers assist in moving the pace of play. The scorecard below is for Lakeview and Clubview.

Directions: Sussex County, #13 on Northwest Map
Rte. 80 West to Exit 34B. Go north on Rte. 15 for 15 miles. At intersection for Rte.94, turn left onto Rte.623S. Go 3 & 3/10 miles to course on left.

Hole	1	2	3	4	5	6	7	8	9	Out	BLUE	Rating 71.3
BLUE	357	433	219	550	561	238	384	367	201	3310		Slope 118
WHITE	285	380	182	508	503	219	369	304	124	2874		
Par	4	4	3	5	5	3	4	4	3	35	WHITE	Rating 68.4
Handicap	8	1	6	3	4	2	5	7	9			Slope 112
RED	226	370	126	397	444	166	306	234	93	2362		
Par	4	4	3	4	5	3	4	4	3	34	RED	Rating 67.0
Handicap	6	4	8	2	1	7	3	5	9			Slope 112

Hole	10	11	12	13	14	15	16	17	18	In		Totals
BLUE	368	410	189	586	497	353	350	437	180	3370	BLUE	6680
WHITE	356	384	188	497	458	329	343	432	172	3159	WHITE	6033
Par	4	4	3	5	5	4	4	4	3	36	Par	71
Handicap	4	2	6	3	7	8	9	1	5			
RED	329	282	154	432	343	225	270	408	105	2548	RED	4910
Par	4	4	3	5	4	4	4	5	3	34	Par	68
Handicap	4	5	7	1	3	8	6	2	9			

Manager: Sandy Howarth   **Pros:** Scott Pruden, PGA Leslie Van Syckle, LPGA
Supt: Mike Pruzer   **Built:** Byron Phoebus 1960s

FLANDERS VALLEY GOLF COURSE

PUBLIC

81 Pleasant Hill Rd., Flanders, NJ 07836   (973) 584-5382

Flanders Valley has two 18 hole layouts, Blue-White and Red-Gold. Run by the Morris County Park Commission, it is open 7 days a week from Apr. 1 to Nov. 30. Resident ID$30, non-res $20. With ID, automated phone system reservations 7 days in advance for res. 5 days for non-res. Reservation fees $2.50pp res., $5pp for non-res.

Driving Range	
•**Practice Green**	•**Lockers**
•**Power Carts**	•**Showers**
•**Pull Carts**	•**Food**
•**Club Rental**	•**Clubhouse**
•**Soft Spikes**	Outings

Fees	Weekday	Weekend
Res/ID	$15	$20.50
Sr.	$10	
Non-res	$30	$41
Non-NJ	$40	$60
Power carts	$25	

Course Description: Rated by Golf Digest as one of the top 100 public courses, in the US, Flanders Valley has a well deserved reputation. Extremely busy with about 85,000 rounds played yearly, the course has very large undulating greens, some terraced. Trees come into play on many fairways. The 7th, on the Red course is a long par 4; with a creek running across it. The scorecard below is for the Red-Gold layout. Most tournaments are played on White - Blue. Although somewhat difficult to get a choice tee time in advance, single walk-ons often get to play. **Cash** only for greens fees.

Directions: Morris County, #14 on Northwest Map
Take Rte. 80 to Exit 27A. Take Rte. 206S approximately 3 mi to 2nd light and make left onto Main St., Flanders. Follow road to course on left.

Hole	1	2	3	4	5	6	7	8	9	Out	BLUE	Rating 71.6
BLUE	380	510	413	371	149	541	478	166	396	3404		Slope 126
WHITE	361	487	398	351	135	526	455	151	379	3243		
Par	4	5	4	4	3	5	4	3	4	36	WHITE	Rating 70.5
Handicap	4	5	2	6	9	3	15	8	7			Slope 123
RED	304	409	355	286	111	466	412	120	346	2809		
Par	4	5	4	4	3	5	5	3	4	37	RED	Rating 71.8
Handicap	5	4	2	7	9	1	5	8	6			Slope 123

Hole	10	11	12	13	14	15	16	17	18	In		Totals
BLUE	476	192	403	550	362	213	426	394	350	3366	BLUE	6770
WHITE	476	162	380	528	332	189	410	369	340	3186	WHITE	6429
Par	5	3	4	5	4	3	4	4	4	36	Par	72
Handicap	2	8	3	1	6	7	4	5	9			
RED	422	141	338	451	298	150	332	314	285	2731	RED	5540
Par	5	3	4	5	4	3	4	4	4	36	Par	73
Handicap	1	7	2	3	4	8	5	6	9			

Manager: Tim Reid   **Pro:** Renee Klose, LPGA   **Supt:** Mark Johnson
Architects: Hal Purdy 1963   Rees Jones second nine 1982

GREAT GORGE COUNTRY CLUB

PUBLIC

P.O. Box 1140 Route 517., McAfee, NJ 07428   (973) 827-5757

Great Gorge CC is adjacent to the grounds of the Legends Resort. It is a privately owned 27 hole course open 7 days a week from mid March to the end of Nov. Reservations may be made up to 30 days in advance for tee times.

- **Driving Range**
- **Practice Green**
- **Power Carts**
- Pull Carts
- **Club Rental**
- Soft Spikes
- **Lockers**
- **Showers**
- **Food**
- **Clubhouse**
- **Outings**

Fees	Weekday	Weekend
Daily(M-Thurs)	$50	$79
Fri	$60	
After 3 PM	$35	$45
Sussex res	$40	

Course Description: A tight, picturesque shot maker's course, Great Gorge has three holes rated among the best public golf holes in the Garden State. The layout is hilly and quarry rocks line the fairways. The signature first on Lake features an elevated tee and a very small green with water on the right. The five sets of tees give golfers of all levels an interesting challenge. Pace of play is carefully monitored. The scorecard below is for the Quarry and Rail nines.

Directions: Sussex County, #15 on Northwest Map
Rte. 80 West to Exit 53. Take Rte. 23N to Hamburg. Go right to Rte. 94N. At light, go straight up hill (road becomes Rte. 517N.) Go approx. 1//10th mi to Hotel and golf course. Driveway is 1/4 mi. on the right.

Hole	1	2	3	4	5	6	7	8	9	Out	BLUE	Rating 72.8
BLUE	175	592	230	364	443	180	449	502	427	3362		Slope 128
WHITE	167	538	191	352	434	170	403	490	422	3167		
Par	3	5	3	4	4	3	4	5	4	35	WHITE	Rating 70.9
Handicap	8	3	6	7	2	9	1	5	4			Slope 125
RED	134	488	152	318	395	114	367	436	283	2687		
Par	3	5	3	4	4	3	4	5	4	35	RED	Rating 71.7
Handicap	8	3	6	7	2	9	1	5	4			Slope 122
Hole	10	11	12	13	14	15	16	17	18	In		Totals
BLUE	456	429	182	341	156	586	519	412	383	3464	BLUE	6826
WHITE	440	360	166	328	151	566	498	370	373	3252	WHITE	6419
Par	4	4	3	4	3	5	5	4	4	36	Par	71
Handicap	3	1	8	7	9	2	5	6	4			
RED	321	335	136	293	128	518	455	319	347	2852	RED	5539
Par	4	4	3	4	3	5	5	4	4	36	Par	71
Handicap	3	1	8	7	9	2	5	6	4			

Manager: Sutomo Yauchi   **Pro:** Terry Manziano, PGA   **Supt:** David Brubaker
Architect: George Fazio 1970

GREEN POND GOLF CLUB

765 Green Pond Rd., Marcella, NJ 07866   **(973) 983-9494**

Green Pond is a privately owned 9 hole course open to the public 7 days a week from
April through November. Reserved tee times are not necessary.

<table>
<tr><td>Driving Range
Practice Green
•**Power Carts**
Pull Carts
•**Club Rental**
Soft Spikes</td><td>Lockers
Showers
•**Food**
•**Clubhouse**
Outings</td></tr>
</table>

Fees	Weekday	Weekend
Daily	$17	$23
Power carts	$14/9	$26/18

Course Description: Short, hilly and narrow, Green Pond gives the golfer a chance to
develop skill with irons. The par 3 finishing hole requires an accurate tee shot to carry
over a pond that makes this ninth and eighteenth, if you play the layout twice,a
demanding and interesting experience.

Directions: Morris County, #16 on Northwest Map
Rte. 80 West to Exit 37. Take Green Pond Road north for 6 miles. Course is on the left.

Hole	1	2	3	4	5	6	7	8	9	Out	BLUE	Rating
BLUE												Slope
WHITE	485	320	332	129	474	178	355	314	128	2715		
Par	5	4	4	3	5	3	4	4	3	35	WHITE	Rating
Handicap	3	9	7	17	1	13	5	11	15			Slope
RED	470	250	300	120	434	132	260	228	112	2306		
Par	5	4	4	3	5	3	4	4	3	35	RED	Rating
Handicap	3	9	7	17	1	13	5	11	15			Slope
Hole	10	11	12	13	14	15	16	17	18	In		Totals
BLUE											BLUE	
WHITE											WHITE	2715
Par											Par	35
Handicap												
RED											RED	2306
Par											Par	35
Handicap												

Manager: Karen McCoy

HARKERS HOLLOW GOLF & CC

950 Uniontown Rd., Phillipsburg, NJ 08865   **(908) 859-0448**

Harkers Hollow is a private 18 hole course located in Harmony Township. It is open all year 7 days a week, weather permitting. Pro shop is closed Dec. 24-Mar.14. Guests play accompanied by a member. Members call in advance for tee times.

- **Driving Range**
- **Practice Green**
- **Power Carts**
- **Pull Carts**
- **Club Rental**
- Caddies
- **Lockers**
- **Showers**
- **Food**
- **Clubhouse**
- **Outings**
- **Soft Spikes**

Course Description: Harkers Hollow is a windy course with numerous uneven lies that are more up and downhill on the front nine and sidehill on the back. The small greens are fast with considerable break; a creek runs through eight of the fairways. The signature is the par 5 4th hole. Its green slopes back to front and is difficult to hold. The greens are hand mown to improve consistency. A set of gold tees has been added recently.

Directions: Warren County, #17 on Northwest Map
Take Rte. 80W to Exit 12, Blairstown-Hope. Take Rte. 521S for 1 mile. At blinker, road becomes Rte. 519S. Continue about 21 mi. to course on left. OR take Rte.78W to the exit for Phillipsburg. Go to the 2nd traffic light and right onto Rte. 519N. Proceed about 4 miles to club on right.

Hole	1	2	3	4	5	6	7	8	9	Out	BLUE	Rating 71.7
BLUE	420	375	376	524	157	422	423	429	154	3280		Slope 126
WHITE	408	365	365	510	148	413	411	419	148	3187		
Par	4	4	4	5	3	4	4	4	3	35	WHITE	Rating 70.8
Handicap	3	11	15	1	17	9	5	7	13			Slope 124
RED	359	362	356	439	107	402	358	408	99	2890		
Par	4	4	4	5	3	5	4	5	3	37	RED	Rating 72.7
Handicap	11	9	13	1	15	5	7	3	17			Slope 128
Hole	10	11	12	13	14	15	16	17	18	In		Totals
BLUE	501	189	391	392	390	371	202	403	432	3271	BLUE	6551
WHITE	492	179	379	378	378	362	194	395	417	3174	WHITE	6361
Par	5	3	4	4	4	4	3	4	4	35	Par	70
Handicap	2	18	8	6	10	12	16	14	4			
RED	442	169	367	309	299	285	178	387	355	2791	RED	5681
Par	5	3	4	4	4	4	3	4	4	35	Par	72
Handicap	2	18	4	10	12	14	16	6	8			

Manager: Quentin Huber   **Pro:** Peter Dachisen, PGA   **Supt:** Donald Zeffer
Architect: Robert White 1929

HIDDEN ACRES GOLF COURSE

Ayers Rd., Hainesville, NJ 07851   **(973) 948-9804**

HIdden Acres is a 9 hole privately owned course open to the public 7 days a week from April through November. Tee time reservations are not necessary.

Driving Range	Lockers
•**Practice Green**	Showers
•**Power Carts**	Food
•**Pull Carts**	Clubhouse
•**Club Rental**	Outings
Soft Spikes	

Fees	Weekday	Weekend
Daily	$11	$11
Power carts	$12/9	$24/18

Course Description: At Hidden Acres, the first 3 holes are wide open; the last six are more tree lined. The greens are small and of average speed. The par 3 ninth requires a tee shot over a pond. The course is a very friendly family operation that is constantly being upgraded.

Directions: Sussex County, #18 on Northwest Map
Rte. 80 West to Exit 34B. Take Rte. 15N and continue as it becomes Rte. 206N. In Hainesville, at De Angeli's Restaurant, turn left. At "T", turn right and then first left onto Rte. 646. Proceed for 1mile and turn right onto Ayers Rd and golf course.

Hole	1	2	3	4	5	6	7	8	9	Out	BLUE	Rating
BLUE												Slope
WHITE	290	410	500	140	340	280	175	425	165	2725		
Par	4	4	5	3	4	4	3	5	3	35	WHITE	Rating
Handicap	9	1	2	6	5	8	4	7	3			Slope
RED	250	340	380	140	290	270	125	410	145	2350		
Par											RED	Rating
Handicap												Slope
Hole	10	11	12	13	14	15	16	17	18	In		Totals
BLUE											BLUE	
WHITE											WHITE	5450
Par											Par	70
Handicap												
RED											RED	4700
Par											Par	70
Handicap												

Manager: Pam Green   **Pro:** Floyd Romynes   **Supt:** Harry Green
Architect: Harold Green 1977

HIGHPOINT COUNTRY CLUB

PUBLIC

Clove Rd., Montague, NJ 07827   **(973) 293-3282**

Highpoint ia an 18 hole course open 7 days a week and closed in Jan. & Feb. Various memberships are available. Tee times: 2 weeks in advance for members, 1 week for all others. Tues: Senior Day, Thurs: Ladies. **Cash** only for greens fees.

• **Driving Range**
• **Practice Green**
• **Power Carts**
Pull Carts
• **Club Rental**
• **Soft Spikes**

- **Lockers**
- **Showers**
- **Food**
- **Clubhouse**
- **Outings**

Fees	Weekday	Weekend
Daily	$34	$59
After 3PM	$27	
After 2PM		$37
Fees include cart		

Course Description: Highpoint is a traditional links course, narrow with no parallel fairways. Overlooking beautiful Holiday Lake and with several creeks in evidence throughout the course, water comes into play on 14 holes. The first hole is a daunting par 5 dogleg requiring substantial carry over water on the approach shot. The greens are fast some sharply two tiered. Try not to land above the hole. People travel to Highpoint from PA, NY and other parts of NJ. Weekday specials are an attraction. The air is crystal clear this far north in New Jersey, giving your lungs a break.

Directions: Sussex County, #19 on Northwest Map
Rte. 80 West to Exit 34B. Take Rte. 15N which becomes Rte. 206. Continue approx. 15 mi. to Clove Rd. (Rte. 653) and turn right. Club is 3 miles up on the right.

Hole	1	2	3	4	5	6	7	8	9	Out	BLUE	Rating 73.3
BLUE	500	330	428	532	213	448	215	442	411	3519		Slope 128
WHITE	481	312	392	513	197	416	196	420	394	3321		
Par	5	4	4	5	3	5	3	4	4	37	WHITE	Rating 71.6
Handicap	9	17	3	11	7	13	15	1	5			Slope 126
RED	465	265	367	408	208	351	155	415	315	2949		
Par	5	4	4	5	4	5	3	4	4	38	RED	Rating 70.0
Handicap	1	13	5	11	17	7	15	3	9			Slope 120
Hole	10	11	12	13	14	15	16	17	18	In		Totals
BLUE	522	408	378	348	190	551	302	433	132	3264	BLUE	6783
WHITE	518	377	362	305	140	506	278	404	115	3005	WHITE	6326
Par	5	4	4	4	3	5	4	4	3	36	Par	73
Handicap	6	8	12	14	16	4	10	2	18			
RED	429	349	298	285	68	425	137	295	120	2406	RED	5355
Par	5	4	4	4	3	5	3	4	3	35	Par	73
Handicap	4	4	15	4	13	4	5	5	14			

    Manager/Pro: John Carrasco   **Supt:** Bret Roby
                Built: Gerald Roby 1960s

KNOLL EAST GOLF CLUB

Knoll & Greenbank Rd., Parsippany, NJ 07054   (973) 263-7115

Knoll East is owned by the township of Parsippany and is open to the public from March to December, 7 days a week. Tee time reservations are not necessary during the week. On weekends: must book in person for that day or can call after 6AM for tee times 11AM or later that same day.

Driving Range	Lockers
•Practice Green	Showers
•Power Carts	•Food
•Pull Carts	•Clubhouse
•Club Rental	•Outings
•Soft Spikes	

Fees	Weekday	Weekend
Res/ID	$10	$14
Non-res	$20	$28
Mbrs 6-8AM		$8.50
Carts	$28.50	$17/9

Course Description: Knoll East is a wide open golf course with scenic views especially spectacular during the fall foliage season. The greens are small and well-conditioned, the 9th and 18th severly sloped. The signature par 5 5th challenges the golfer to hit the tee shot along the right, avoiding the dry creek on that side, to be in position to go for the green. A creek runs across the 7th fairway. The long par 3 3rd requires accuracy; an errant shot does not yield an easy recovery.

Directions: Morris County, #20 on Northwest Map
Rte. 80 West to Exit 47, Parsippany. Take Rte. 46W to 2nd light and make a right onto Beverwick Rd. Go about 2 mi and turn left at end of road. At 2nd driveway, turn right and follow signs to club entrance. From Rte. 287, see directions for Knoll West.

Hole	1	2	3	4	5	6	7	8	9	Out	BLUE	Rating
BLUE												Slope
WHITE	390	431	230	348	476	307	313	182	337	3014		
Par	4	4	3	4	5	4	4	3	4	35	WHITE	Rating 67.9
Handicap	5	1	9	11	3	17	13	15	17			Slope 112
RED	365	415	197	315	443	247	260	152	313	2707		
Par	4	5	3	4	5	4	4	3	4	36	RED	Rating 67.9
Handicap	5	3	7	11	1	17	13	15	9			Slope 112

Hole	10	11	12	13	14	15	16	17	18	In		Totals
BLUE											BLUE	
WHITE	503	325	154	376	127	347	543	165	330	2870	WHITE	5884
Par	5	4	3	4	3	4	5	3	4	35	Par	70
Handicap	6	10	16	4	18	12	2	14	8			
RED	472	300	135	348	117	315	525	135	255	2602	RED	5309
Par	5	4	3	4	3	4	5	3	4	35	Par	71
Handicap	4	12	14	6	18	10	2	16	8			

Manager/Pro: Ken Congleton   **Supt:** John Grady
Architect: Hal Purdy 1960s

KNOLL WEST COUNTRY CLUB

PUBLIC

Knoll & Greenbank Rd., Parsippany, NJ 07054   (973) 263-7110

Knoll West is an 18 hole course owned by the township of Parsippany open 7 days a week from Mar. to Dec. There is a waiting list for memberships. Tee times; members may reserve up to 1 week in advance. Daily fee golfers: when time is available.

Driving Range	• Lockers
• Practice Green	• Showers
• Power Carts	• Food
• Pull Carts	• Clubhouse
• Club Rental	• Outings
• Soft Spikes	

Fees	Weekday	Weekend
Res/mbr	$11	$15.50
Mbrs	$22	$28
Non/mbr	$35	$47.50
Power Carts	$29.50	

Course Description: The original clubhouse, destroyed by fire, was rebuilt on a high knoll that overlooks the property and offering wonderful views; thus the name Knoll. The course was the brainchild of a few extremely wealthy men who wanted a superb private layout for their golfing pleasure. The 339 acre design is one of the finest for a semi-private club in New Jersey. It is long with many bunkers along the fairways and protecting the difficult greens, characteristic of the course architect. The par 4 18th is a favorite due to its length and well-bunkered green. Power carts are required until 3:30PM.

Directions: Morris County, #21 on Northwest Map
Rte. 80 to Rte. 287N. Exit at Wootton St. At 2nd STOP, make right onto Vreeland Ave. Go 1/2 mile down hill and follow signs on right to Knoll East & West. For access via Rte.80 and Rte. 46, see directions to Knoll East.

Hole	1	2	3	4	5	6	7	8	9	Out	BLUE	Rating 72.4
BLUE	416	445	194	394	550	154	367	416	388	3324		Slope 127
WHITE	409	426	188	383	525	142	355	406	380	3214		
Par	4	4	3	4	5	3	4	4	4	35	WHITE	Rating 71.3
Handicap	5	1	15	9	3	17	13	7	11			Slope 125
RED	374	361	148	303	430	130	330	384	355	2815		
Par	5	4	3	4	5	3	4	4	4	36	RED	Rating 74.1
Handicap	3	7	15	13	1	17	11	5	9			Slope 127
Hole	10	11	12	13	14	15	16	17	18	In		Totals
BLUE	391	418	383	248	430	530	383	170	439	3392	BLUE	6716
WHITE	385	407	370	217	410	520	371	158	427	3265	WHITE	6479
Par	4	4	4	3	4	5	3	4	4	35	Par	70
Handicap	10	6	14	12	2	8	16	18	4			
RED	359	386	356	189	365	493	345	145	400	3038	RED	5853
Par	4	5	4	4	4	5	4	3	5	38	Par	74
Handicap	10	6	12	16	8	2	14	18	4			

Manager: Pat De Falco   **Pro:** Steele King, PGA   **Supt:** John Grady
Architect: Charles Banks 1929

LAKE LACKAWANNA GOLF COURSE

155 Lake Drive, Stanhope, NJ 07874   (973) 347-9701

Lake Lackawanna is a 9 hole course open to the public 7 days a week from March until the first snowfall. Tee time reservations are not necessary.

Driving Range	Lockers
•**Practice Green**	Showers
Power Carts	•**Food**
•**Pull Carts**	Clubhouse
•**Club Rental**	Outings
Soft Spikes	

Fees	Weekday	Weekend
Daily/9	$15	$18
18 holes	$20	$24
Sr	$14/9,	
"	$19/18	

Course Description: Lake Lackawanna is a pleasant, flat nine hole course, good for practicing your game. The only hill on this layout is on the 8th, resulting in an elevated green. Two holes have water in play. The course is wide open and easy to walk.

Directions: Sussex County, #22 on Northwest Map
Take Rte.80West to Exit 25. Take Rte.206North for 3 traffic lights. Go right at Barones Restaurant for 1 and 1/4 mile. At the sign for Lake Lackawanna Golf Course, make a right. Go 2 blocks and then left to the course.

Hole	1	2	3	4	5	6	7	8	9	Out	BLUE	Rating
BLUE												Slope
WHITE	315	165	150	215	135	400	440	200	220	2240		
Par	4	3	3	3	3	4	5	4	3	32	WHITE	Rating
Handicap	3	7	6	4	8	1	2	9	5			Slope
RED												
Par											RED	Rating
Handicap												Slope

Hole	10	11	12	13	14	15	16	17	18	In		Totals
BLUE											BLUE	
WHITE											WHITE	4480
Par											Par	64
Handicap												
RED											RED	
Par											Par	
Handicap												

Manager: Grex Corporation

LAKE MOHAWK GOLF CLUB

471 West Shore Trail, Sparta, NJ 07871　　　(973) 729-9200

Lake Mohawk is an 18 hole private course open 6 days a week from March through November. Guests play accompanied by a member. Tee time reservations are necessary for weekends.

- •Driving Range　•Lockers
- •Practice Green　•Showers
- •Power Carts　•Food
- •Pull Carts　•Clubhouse
- •Club Rental　•Outings
- •Caddies　•Soft Spikes

Course Description: This challenging hilly golf course situated above Lake Mohawk is surrounded by many lovely homes. It is short with elevated greens and tees. A stream meanders through the narrow layout making it interesting and picturesque. The first hole, a 452 yard par 4, is made more difficult by dense woods on the left, out of bounds on the right and an uphill second shot to a well bunkered green. Pull carts are permitted only during the week here.

Directions: Sussex County, #23 on Northwest Map
Rte.80 to Exit 34B. Take Rte.15N to sign "Lake Mohawk Business District". Exit right and go back over Rte.15, which is Rte.181, until 2nd light and sign for Lake Mohawk Country Club (not the golf club). Go left and cross over the Plaza. Make left onto West Shore Trail. Follow winding road, keeping lake on left, to club on right.

Hole	1	2	3	4	5	6	7	8	9	Out	BLUE	Rating 71.1
BLUE	452	368	471	193	334	312	444	408	174	3156		Slope 126
WHITE	442	363	451	170	330	302	404	380	160	3002		
Par	4	4	5	3	4	4	4	4	3	35	WHITE	Rating 69.9
Handicap	1	5	7	15	9	17	3	11	13			Slope 124
RED	432	326	405	151	328	250	394	309	135	2730		
Par	5	4	5	3	4	4	5	4	3	37	RED	Rating 72.9
Handicap	1	9	7	15	3	17	5	11	13			Slope 127

Hole	10	11	12	13	14	15	16	17	18	In		Totals
BLUE	495	528	194	428	148	314	383	439	195	3124	BLUE	6280
WHITE	490	518	187	415	133	305	370	425	175	3018	WHITE	6020
Par	5	5	3	4	3	4	4	4	3	35	Par	70
Handicap	12	4	14	6	18	16	8	2	10			
RED	406	457	169	408	120	300	334	411	132	2737	RED	5467
Par	5	5	3	5	3	4	4	5	3	37	Par	74
Handicap	6	2	16	12	18	10	8	4	14			

Manager: Cheryl Schiess　　**Pro:** Davis De Rosa, PGA　**Supt:** Eric Carlson
Architect: David Sewell 1927

MADISON GOLF CLUB

Green Avenue, Madison, NJ 07940   **(973) 377-5264**

Madison is a 9 hole private golf course open 6 days a week, from April 1 through November 30. Guests play accompanied by a member. Tee time reservations are required on weekends.

Driving Range	•**Lockers**
•**Practice Green**	•**Showers**
•**Power Carts**	Food
Pull Carts	•**Clubhouse**
Club Rental	•**Outings**
•**Caddies**	•**Soft Spikes**

Course Description: Madison is an extremely well-maintained course. It is characterized by small greens and narrow fairways. Target golf is imperative to score well here. On two of the holes it is necessary to hit over a much-traveled road. The par 4 5th has a gully to traverse. On the signature 9th, also a par 4, a tree is in the middle of the fairway affecting the second shot. This interesting course attracts a waiting list even though Madison is only 9 holes. The NJ Assistant Pro Match Play Tournament is held here annually.

Directions: Morris County, #24 on Northwest Map
Rte. 80 to Rte. 287S. Exit at Madison Ave(old Rte. 24). Go left and follow to downtown Madison. Turn left on Waverly which becomes Green Ave; club is on the right. From GSP, exit at #142. Take Rte. 24West to Madison and follow as above.

Hole	1	2	3	4	5	6	7	8	9		BLUE	Rating
BLUE												Slope
WHITE	154	254	202	217	391	334	138	155	374	2219		
Par	3	4	3	3	4	4	3	3	4	31	WHITE	Rating 61.8
Handicap	15	11	9	7	1	5	13	17	3			Slope 109
RED	150	250	200	210	328	281	132	150	370	2071		
Par	3	4	3	4	4	5	3	3	5	34	RED	Rating 64.5
Handicap	15	7	9	11	1	5	13	17	3			Slope 111
Hole	10	11	12	13	14	15	16	17	18	In		Totals
BLUE											BLUE	
WHITE	158	263	210	226	400	341	158	160	381	2289	WHITE	4508
Par	3	4	3	3	4	4	3	3	4	31	Par	62
Handicap	16	12	10	8	2	6	14	18	4			
RED	154	254	202	217	328	281	140	155	374	2105	RED	4176
Par	3	4	3	4	4	5	3	3	5	34	Par	68
Handicap	16	8	10	12	2	6	14	18	4			

Manager/Pro: Dan Pasternak, PGA   **Supt:** Keith Rose
Built: 1896

MEADOWS GOLF CLUB

79 Two Bridges Rd., Lincoln Park, NJ 07035   **(973) 696-7212**

Meadows is an 18 hole course open 7 days a week all year. Tee times are first come first served weekdays and 7 days in advance on weekends. Carts are mandatory before 1PM weekends and holidays.

Driving Range	Lockers
• **Practice Green**	• **Lockers**
• **Power Carts**	• **Showers**
• **Pull Carts**	• **Food**
• **Club Rental**	• **Clubhouse**
• **Soft Spikes**	• **Outings**

Fees	Weekday	Weekend
Daily	$27	
Pre 1PM		$47
After1PM		$38
After 5PM	$18	$24
Carts	$30	

Course Description: The Meadows is in the process of a major renovation. The course will measure more than 6200 yards and 2 new par 4s will be created which will eliminate back to back par 3s. The owner is also adding new bunkers as well as cart paths throughout the property. The layout is predominantly flat and open with water in play on 15 of the holes. The par 3 9th has a substantial carry over water and is 226 yards from the whites. A computerized sprinkler system is being installed. The new scorecard will reflect the changes and the course will be rerated.

Directions: Morris County, #25 on Northwest Map
Rte. 80 to Exit 52. Make a left onto Two Bridges Rd. Go to the end and turn left. Course is on the right about 1/2 mile ahead.

Hole	1	2	3	4	5	6	7	8	9	Out	BLUE	Rating
BLUE												Slope
WHITE	394	375	495	187	172	379	423	365	226	3016		
Par	4	4	5	3	3	4	4	4	3	34	WHITE	Rating 68.5
Handicap	15	7	9	17	11	5	3	13	1			Slope 116
RED	315	190	345	165	135	185	315	335	160	2145		
Par	4	4	5	3	3	4	4	4	3	34	RED	Rating 66.2
Handicap	15	7	9	17	11	5	3	13	1			Slope 105
Hole	10	11	12	13	14	15	16	17	18	In		Totals
BLUE											BLUE	
WHITE	400	523	436	198	354	152	184	391	362	3000	WHITE	6016
Par	4	5	4	3	4	3	3	4	4	34	Par	68
Handicap	2	10	8	6	16	18	14	4	12			
RED	325	400	340	140	290	125	170	335	325	2540	RED	4595
Par	4	5	4	3	4	3	3	4	4	34	Par	68
Handicap	2	10	8	6	16	18	14	4	12			

Manager: Dennis Rogers   **Pro:** Pete Cherone, PGA   **Supt:** Andy Shuckers
Architect: Frank Duane 1963

MENDHAM GOLF CLUB

Golf Lane, Mendham, NJ 07945   **(973) 543-7297**

Mendham Golf Club, known as Mendham Golf & Tennis Club, is an 18 hole private course open 6 days a week from April through November. Guests play accompanied by a member. Tee time reservations are not necessary.

•**Driving Range**	•**Lockers**
•**Practice Green**	•**Showers**
•**Power Carts**	•**Food**
•**Pull Carts**	•**Clubhouse**
•**Club Rental**	Outings
Caddies	•**Soft Spikes**

Course Description: Mendham is a relatively short and narrow layout with rolling hills demanding all varieties of shots. The back is longer and more wide open than the short tight front nine. The signature par 4 6th, with a large oak tree in the middle of the fairway, has one of the six ponds that come into play and exemplifies the difficulties of the layout. The 18th, considered one of the premiere holes in Morris County, has a narrow driving area, out of bounds on the left, woods on the right and a brook in front of the two-tiered small green.

Directions: Morris County, #26 on Northwest Map
Rte.80 to Rte.287S towards Morristown. Take exit #33(Harter Rd.) and turn left. Make left onto Rte. 202S and go 2 miles to Tempe Wicke Rd. At light (Jockey Hollow Park), go right. Go 3.4 mi and turn right at Kenneday Rd. Club is 1/2 mile ahead on the right.

Hole	1	2	3	4	5	6	7	8	9	Out	BLUE	Rating 70.5
BLUE	347	386	492	391	155	371	203	520	366	3231		Slope 125
WHITE	340	360	465	340	140	352	135	480	330	2942		
Par	4	4	5	4	3	4	3	5	4	36	WHITE	Rating 76.1
Handicap	14	8	12	2	18	6	16	4	10			Slope 134
RED	321	268	463	308	127	298	121	425	262	2593		
Par	4	4	5	4	3	4	3	5	4	36	RED	Rating 72.2
Handicap	12	10	4	2	18	14	16	6	8			Slope 127
Hole	10	11	12	13	14	15	16	17	18	In		Totals
BLUE	564	432	183	352	221	423	343	555	376	3449	BLUE	6680
WHITE	540	366	170	330	150	360	330	525	360	3131	WHITE	6073
Par	5	4	3	4	3	4	4	5	4	36	Par	72
Handicap	1	9	17	13	11	5	15	3	7			
RED	443	366	98	325	147	55	300	479	355	2868	RED	5461
Par	4	4	5	4	3	5	4	3	4	36	Par	72
Handicap	5	9	17	11	15	7	13	1	3			

Pro: Al Sutton, PGA   **Supt:** Chris Boyle
Architect: Alfred Tull 1961

MINE BROOK GOLF CLUB

PUBLIC

500 Schooleys Mtn. Rd., Hackettstown, NJ 07840   (908) 979-0366

Mine Brook is a privately owned 18 hole course open 7 days a week all year. Tee time reservations may be made up to 1 week in advance, two weeks for season pass holders. Carts are required before 2PM on weekends.

Driving Range
- **Practice Green**
- **Power Carts**
- **Pull Carts**
- **Club Rental**
- **Soft Spikes**
- **Lockers**
- **Showers**
- **Food**
- **Clubhouse**
- **Outings**

Fees	M-Thurs	Weekend
Daily	$40	$55
Fri	$45	

Fees include cart
Twilight discounts available

Course Description: Golfers from NJ, PA & NY flock to play this par 70, traditional links style course, formerly called Hidden Hills. This challenging sporty and scenic layout has something for every level of player. There are 6 holes with ponds and lakes affecting play and the fairways are lined with mature trees. The signature par 5 15th is difficult due to its length and dogleg left. The 18th, a 589 par 5, is one of the longest in New Jersey and is bordered by the Musconetcong River. The course is now owned by Arnold Palmer Golf Management.

Directions: Morris County, #27 on Northwest Map
Rte.80 West to Exit 26. Take Rte.46W to Hackettstown and go left onto Rte.57W. At light go straight onto Rte.24/517 (over a bridge). Mine Brook is immediately on the left.

Hole	1	2	3	4	5	6	7	8	9	Out	BLUE	Rating 70.9
BLUE	470	178	385	397	340	387	140	387	445	3129		Slope 128
WHITE	455	167	340	380	315	382	125	369	427	2960		
Par	5	3	4	4	4	4	3	4	4	35	WHITE	Rating 69.6
Handicap	14	16	10	6	12	8	18	4	2			Slope 126
RED	440	140	320	350	300	330	100	330	421	2731		
Par	5	3	4	4	4	4	3	4	5	36	RED	Rating 73.0
Handicap	14	16	10	6	12	8	18	4	2			Slope 122
Hole	10	11	12	13	14	15	16	17	18	In		Totals
BLUE	395	449	139	385	214	487	350	212	589	3220	BLUE	6349
WHITE	383	385	129	361	183	462	336	212	576	3027	WHITE	5987
Par	4	4	3	4	3	5	4	3	5	35	Par	70
Handicap	9	1	17	11	5	7	13	15	3			
RED	361	365	110	315	135	445	333	160	550	2774	RED	5505
Par	4	4	3	4	3	5	4	3	6	36	Par	72
Handicap	9	1	17	11	5	7	13	15	3			

Manager/Pro: Don Miller, PGA   **Supt:** Mark Wallace
Built: 1919, 2nd nine James M. Rocco 1965

MORRIS COUNTY GOLF CLUB

Punch Bowl Rd., Convent Station, NJ 07961   **(973) 539-1188**

Morris County is an 18 hole private course open all year, 6 days a week. Guests play accompanied by a member. Tee time reservations may be made on weekends.

•**Driving Range**	•**Lockers**
•**Practice Green**	•**Showers**
•**Power Carts**	•**Food**
Pull Carts	•**Clubhouse**
•**Club Rental**	•**Outings**
•**Caddies**	•**Soft Spikes**

Course Description: Nestled in the contours of the rolling terrain, Morris County is a beautiful old hilly course. The greens are small and undulating; the fairways tree-lined. The signature par 3 13th, "Redan", has an elevated green with a difficult slope. Many holes have been named for world famous ones. The 18th, "Home", features a double dogleg and is one of the highlights of the course.

Directions: Morris County, #28 on Northwest Map
From Rte. 80, take Rte. 287S toward Morristown. Proceed to 2nd Morristown exit (Rte. 24, Madison Ave). Go left at top of ramp and continue 1.3 miles to Punch Bowl Rd. (after 3 traffic lights). Turn left and go 1 mile past RR tracks. Club is on the left.

Hole	1	2	3	4	5	6	7	8	9	Out	BLUE	Rating
BLUE												Slope
WHITE	300	491	108	355	303	300	452	422	408	3139		
Par	4	5	3	4	4	4	4	4	4	36	WHITE	Rating 69.8
Handicap	15	11	18	7	13	9	1	3	5			Slope 124
RED	280	480	100	315	300	290	452	310	405	2932		
Par	4	5	3	4	4	4	5	4	5	38	RED	Rating 73.0
Handicap	15	1	18	5	13	7	3	9	11			Slope 123
Hole	10	11	12	13	14	15	16	17	18	In		Totals
BLUE											BLUE	
WHITE	440	515	315	178	404	222	398	182	395	3049	WHITE	6188
Par	4	5	4	3	4	3	4	3	4	34	Par	70
Handicap	2	10	16	12	4	14	6	17	8			
RED	433	378	315	175	388	165	356	164	321	2695	RED	5627
Par	5	4	4	3	5	3	4	3	4	35	Par	73
Handicap	6	2	12	10	14	16	4	17	8			

Manager: David Harnois   **Pro:** Ted O'Rourke, PGA   **Supt:** Mark Antonaccio
Architect: Seth Raynor 1894

MT. TABOR COUNTRY CLUB

Country Club Road, Mt. Tabor, NJ 07878 **(973) 627-5995**

Mt. Tabor is a private 9 hole course open 6 days a week from April 1 to November 1. Guests play accompanied by a member. Tee time reservations are advised on weekends. Soft spikes are suggested but not required.

> • **Driving Range**   • **Lockers**
> • **Practice Green**   • **Showers**
> • **Power Carts**   • **Food**
> • **Pull Carts**   • **Clubhouse**
> • **Club Rental**   • **Outings**
>   Caddies   Soft Spikes

Course Description: A challenging, tight course, Mt. Tabor has small undulating greens and many uneven lies. Accuracy is the key to scoring well on this nine hole layout. Throughout the scenic hilly terrain, there are creeks across and along the fairways. The signature par 4 4th has an old tree in the middle of the fairway that affects both the tee and second shots; the green slopes away front to back. The club changes the tee position for the second nine with differing yardages as shown on the scorecard below.

Directions: Morris County, #29 on Northwest Map
Rte. 80 To Exit #39. Take Rte. 53South. Make a left on Country Club Road to club.

Hole	1	2	3	4	5	6	7	8	9	Out	BLUE	Rating
BLUE												Slope
WHITE	255	283	430	400	140	171	311	465	344	2799		
Par	4	4	4	4	3	3	4	5	4	35	WHITE	Rating 67.6
Handicap	13	15	5	1	17	11	7	3	9			Slope 115
RED	250	265	430	392	138	147	303	417	328	2670		
Par	4	4	5	5	3	3	4	5	4	37	RED	Rating 71.4
Handicap	13	15	5	1	17	11	7	3	9			Slope 120
Hole	**10**	**11**	**12**	**13**	**14**	**15**	**16**	**17**	**18**	**In**		Totals
BLUE											BLUE	
WHITE	240	274	365	462	198	151	307	433	355	2785	WHITE	5584
Par	4	4	4	5	3	3	4	4	4	35	Par	70
Handicap	14	12	6	2	18	16	10	4	8			
RED	236	258	360	457	185	136	296	417	338	2683	RED	5353
Par	4	4	4	5	4	3	4	5	4	37	Par	74
Handicap	14	12	6	2	18	16	10	4	8			

Pro: Mark McCormick, PGA   **Supt:** Chris Holenstein
Built: 1900

77

NEWTON COUNTRY CLUB

25 Club Rd., Newton, NJ 07860   **(973) 383-9394**

Newton is a private 18 hole course open 6 days a week from April through December. Guests play accompanied by a member. Tee time reservations are not necessary.

> • **Driving Range**   • **Lockers**
> • **Practice Green** • **Showers**
> • **Power Carts**   • **Food**
> • **Pull Carts**   • **Clubhouse**
>   Club Rental   • **Outings**
>   Caddies   • **Soft Spikes**

Course Description: Newton is a difficult, hilly course with uneven lies and small greens. The atmosphere is quiet and peaceful. Water can be found mainly on the par 4 18th, a beautiful signature hole. The golfer tees off from a hill to a dogleg left. The second shot is over a pond to an elevated green guarded by a stone wall. From the blues and whites, the 8th is the #1 handicap hole, a long par 4. Originally, this course was the nine hole Sussex Country Club.

Directions: Sussex County, #30 on Northwest Map
Rte.80 to Exit 34B. Take Rte.15North. Take the Newton exit to Rte.517. Stay on the Newton-Sparta Road to club on the right.

Hole	1	2	3	4	5	6	7	8	9	Out	BLUE	Rating 70.2
BLUE	350	385	360	162	368	181	355	429	525	3115		Slope 122
WHITE	340	375	353	147	353	174	350	417	502	3011		
Par	4	4	4	3	4	3	4	4	5	35	WHITE	Rating 69.0
Handicap	9	11	7	17	13	15	5	1	3			Slope 120
RED	305	365	274	137	343	123	345	409	453	2754		
Par	4	4	4	3	4	3	4	5	5	36	RED	Rating 70.8
Handicap	11	7	13	15	9	17	5	3	1			Slope 123
Hole	10	11	12	13	14	15	16	17	18	In		Totals
BLUE	369	532	393	178	356	419	355	174	404	3180	BLUE	6295
WHITE	354	518	378	164	336	404	342	147	389	3032	WHITE	6043
Par	4	5	4	3	4	4	4	3	4	35	Par	70
Handicap	12	2	6	16	14	4	10	18	8			
RED	266	436	305	107	268	350	285	107	303	2427	RED	5181
Par	4	5	4	3	4	4	4	3	4	35	Par	71
Handicap	12	2	6	16	14	4	10	18	8			

Manager: Steve Kerrins   **Pro:** Robin Kohberger, PGA   **Supt:** Les Carpenter
Architects: Front nine: Gordon & Gordon 1904   Back: 1969

PANTHER VALLEY GOLF & CC

Route 517, Hackettstown, NJ 07840

(908) 852-6120

Panther Valley is a private 18 hole course open 6 days a week. It closes the beginning of Dec. and reopens Apr. 1. Guests play accompanied by a member. Reserved tee times are suggested for weekends.

- •Driving Range
- •Practice Green
- •Power Carts
- Pull Carts
- •Club Rental
- •Caddies
- •Lockers
- •Showers
- •Food
- •Clubhouse
- •Outings
- •Soft Spikes

Course Description: Located on a former estate in the woods of western New Jersey, Panther Valley is a beautiful and hilly course. The rural setting is abundant with wildlife; deer, muskrat, beaver and even an occasional black bear have been spotted. The golfers do not have to return to the clubhouse after nine, but can stop at a halfway house for food, etc. The course has Penn Cross bent grass fairways and greens. The latter are fast and undulating, a true test of skill. From the signature 9th hole, players can see water on one side and mountains in the distance. The handsome clubhouse and separate golf shop were rebuilt after a fire in 1989. Panther Valley has one of the most picturesque driving ranges in the Northeast.

Directions: Warren County, #31 on Northwest Map
Rte.80W to Exit 19, Hackettstown-Andover. At exit, turn left onto Rte. 517. The club is one mile ahead on the right.

Hole	1	2	3	4	5	6	7	8	9	Out	BLUE	Rating 71.5
BLUE	510	169	388	360	431	162	523	411	418	3372		Slope 133
WHITE	488	153	378	345	398	151	502	391	389	3195		
Par	5	3	4	4	4	3	5	4	4	36	WHITE	Rating 69.9
Handicap	9	15	7	13	3	17	11	1	5			Slope 129
RED	452	121	349	303	381	127	471	365	370	2939		
Par	5	3	4	4	5	3	5	4	4	37	RED	Rating 72.4
Handicap	9	17	7	11	13	15	5	1	3			Slope 127
Hole	10	11	12	13	14	15	16	17	18	In		Totals
BLUE	174	501	337	184	348	361	353	355	380	2993	BLUE	6365
WHITE	161	482	314	160	330	344	337	341	360	2829	WHITE	6024
Par	3	5	4	3	4	4	4	4	4	35	Par	71
Handicap	14	2	10	18	6	8	16	12	4			
RED	118	450	283	133	283	327	310	297	329	2530	RED	5469
Par	3	5	4	3	4	4	4	4	4	35	Par	72
Handicap	18	2	4	16	6	8	14	12	10			

Manager: Jacques Labbye   **Pro:** Richard Hughes, PGA   **Supt:** Pat Campbell
Architect: Robert Trent Jones, Sr. 1969

PEACE PIPE COUNTRY CLUB

2 Lee Rd., Denville, NJ 07834   **(973) 625-5041**

Peace Pipe is a 9 hole private golf course open all year 7 days a week. Reservations for tee times are not necessary.

```
    Driving Range        Lockers
   •Practice Green       Showers
   •Power Carts          •Food
   •Pull Carts           •Clubhouse
   •Club Rental          •Outings
    Caddies              •Soft Spikes
```

Course Description: Peace Pipe started as a 6 hole facility and later graduated to the present layout. This 9 hole course is tight, short and moderately contoured with small greens. A pond and a river come in to play. The signature par 3 8th has a rocky background which adds to the scenery. The 9th is a par 4 with an island green. It is advisable to check playability after a heavy rain.

Directions: Morris County, #32 on Northwest Map
Rte. 80 To Exit 39. Take Rte. 46E. Go to 2nd light and turn left. Take immediate right and at 1st light, turn left onto Diamond Springs Rd. Go 2 miles and turn right onto River Rd. Make a left onto Lee Rd. to club.

Hole	1	2	3	4	5	6	7	8	9	Out	BLUE	Rating 66.0
BLUE	286	270	398	445	201	285	263	155	323	2626		Slope 106
WHITE	271	255	372	405	184	270	248	133	313	2451		
Par	4	4	4	5	3	4	4	3	4	35	WHITE	Rating 66.2
Handicap	9	15	1	2	11	13	7	17	5			Slope 111
RED	252	225	340	345	167	245	175	120	270	2139		
Par	4	4	4	5	3	4	4	3	4	35	RED	Rating 67.9
Handicap	9	15	1	2	11	13	7	17	5			Slope 115
Hole	10	11	12	13	14	15	16	17	18	In		Totals
BLUE											BLUE	5252
WHITE											WHITE	4902
Par											Par	70
Handicap												
RED											RED	4278
Par											Par	70
Handicap												

Manager/Supt: David Lee   **Pro:** Pat Hill, PGA
Built: Sid Lee 1960

PICATINNY GOLF CLUB

Building 121A, Picatinny, NJ 07806   (973) 989-2466

Picatinny is an 18 hole private course open 6 days a week between Apr.1 & Nov. 30. It is available to military civilian employees of the Arsenal and retired and active duty military personnel. Tee time reservations are required. Only active members may reserve.

Driving Range	•Lockers
•Practice Green	•Showers
•Power Carts	•Food
•Pull Carts	•Clubhouse
•Club Rental	•Outings
Caddies	•Soft Spikes

Course Description: Picatinny is relatively flat with small greens and heavily tree-lined fairways. On the tight front nine, there are approximately 50 bunkers. Water is in play on seven of the 18 holes. On the 17th, a short par 4, the golfer must hit over a road on the approach shot. Golfers often find this course more difficult than it appears.

Directions: Morris County, #33 on Northwest Map
Rte. 80 To Exit 34B. Take Rte. 15N. After 1/4 mile, take entrance to Picatinny Arsenal. At first light, bear right. At 1st left, turn left to Clubhouse.

Hole	1	2	3	4	5	6	7	8	9	Out	BLUE	Rating 72.8
BLUE	438	160	502	390	400	213	391	417	533	3444		Slope 125
WHITE	425	145	485	380	385	200	385	400	525	3330		
Par	4	3	5	4	4	3	4	4	5	36	WHITE	Rating 71.8
Handicap	11	17	13	9	7	15	5	3	1			Slope 123
RED	365	110	420	300	310	155	300	325	415	2700		
Par	4	3	5	4	4	3	4	4	5	36	RED	Rating 71.4
Handicap	5	15	7	9	11	3	17	1	13			Slope 122
Hole	10	11	12	13	14	15	16	17	18	In		Totals
BLUE	170	350	524	422	446	545	230	312	373	3372	BLUE	6816
WHITE	160	330	512	410	430	538	225	300	365	3270	WHITE	6600
Par	3	4	5	4	4	5	3	4	4	36	Par	72
Handicap	18	4	8	10	14	2	16	6	12			
RED	140	300	450	315	310	430	160	300	325	2730	RED	5430
Par	3	4	5	4	4	5	3	4	4	36	Par	72
Handicap	14	2	6	8	16	10	12	18	4			

Manager: Doug Moran   **Pro:** Clay Murray, PGA   **Supt:** Chris Kunkel
Built: 1st nine 1928   2nd nine 1940

PINCH BROOK GOLF COURSE

PUBLIC

234 Ridgedale Ave., Florham Park, NJ 07932   **(973) 377-2039**

Pinch Brook is a short 18 hole Morris County course open 7 days a week from Apr. 1 to Nov.30. Residents with ID may make tee times 1 week in advance, $2.50 pp fee. Non-residents; $5pp fee, 5 days in advance under automated program.

Driving Range	
•**Practice Green**	•**Lockers**
•**Power Carts**	•**Showers**
•**Pull Carts**	•**Food**
•**Club Rental**	•**Clubhouse**
•**Soft Spikes**	Outings

Fees	Weekday	Weekend
Res/ID	$15	$20.50
Res/Sr	$10	
Non-res	$30	$41
Power cart	$25/18	$15/9

Course Description: Pinch Brook is a flat, short and easy course to walk. The greens are large and fast. Woods may be found on either side of many holes; ponds affect play on four of them. A creek runs all the way along the left side on the ninth. A big ravine confronts the golfer on the tee on the 18th tee. Pinch Brook was originally called Canary Cottage and then Florham Park CC. Later, Morris County bought the course to be used primarily by residents.

Directions: Morris County, #34 on Northwest Map
Rte.80West to Rte.287S towards Morristown. Exit at Rte.10East (not Pleasant Ave.) Turn right onto Ridgedale Ave. Course is 3 miles ahead on the left.

Hole	1	2	3	4	5	6	7	8	9	Out	BLUE	Rating 63.7
BLUE	177	178	466	369	351	364	158	153	187	2403		Slope 98
WHITE	159	163	445	349	340	341	144	127	163	2231		
Par	3	3	5	4	4	4	3	3	3	32	WHITE	Rating 62.1
Handicap	15	13	1	9	7	5	3	17	11			Slope 95
RED	136	143	407	333	325	325	103	109	131	2012		
Par	3	3	5	4	4	4	3	3	3	32	RED	Rating 63.1
Handicap	15	13	1	7	5	3	11	17	9			Slope 96
Hole	10	11	12	13	14	15	16	17	18	In		Totals
BLUE	174	476	385	337	343	190	177	358	164	2604	BLUE	5007
WHITE	157	453	368	327	336	169	144	337	142	2433	WHITE	4664
Par	3	5	4	4	4	3	3	4	3	33	Par	65
Handicap	18	6	8	14	2	4	16	10	12			
RED	139	408	286	301	316	124	117	314	100	2105	RED	4117
Par	3	5	4	4	4	3	3	4	3	33	Par	65
Handicap	18	4	6	14	2	10	16	8	12			

Manager: Tony Palmieri   **Pro:** Renee Klose, LPGA   **Supt:** Bill Engler
Architect: Rees Jones 1983

ROCKAWAY RIVER COUNTRY CLUB

39 Pocono Rd., Denville, NJ 07834   **(973) 681-4461**

Rockaway River is a private 18 hole course open 6 days a week between March 15 & December 31. Guests play accompanied by a member. Tee time reservations are not necessary.

- **Driving Range**
- **Practice Green**
- **Power Carts**
- Pull Carts
- **Club Rental**
- **Caddies**

- **Lockers**
- **Showers**
- **Food**
- **Clubhouse**
- **Outings**
- **Soft Spikes**

Course Description: Rockaway River is a short, gently rolling and fairly tight course with small well-bunkered greens, some elevated. It is noted for its long par 5s. The tenth, a par 4 dogleg left can prove to be very difficult especially on the approach shot to the severely elevated landing area. On the signature par 5 18th, the Rockaway River is in play on both the tee and second shot. Recent changes in the hole yardages are reflected in the totals on the scorecard below.

Directions: Morris County, #35 on Northwest Map
Rte.80W to Exit 42B. Bear right and then make left at 2nd light onto Rte.46W. Turn right at 2nd light onto the Boulevard. At 1st light, go left onto Pocono Rd. Club is 1 mile ahead on the right.

Hole	1	2	3	4	5	6	7	8	9	Out	BLUE	Rating 71.8
BLUE	578	404	426	552	307	198	416	354	144	3379		Slope 127
WHITE	565	394	404	546	296	175	402	344	135	3261		
Par	5	4	4	5	4	3	4	4	3	36	WHITE	Rating 70.5
Handicap	3	9	7	1	11	15	5	13	17			Slope 125
RED	437	307	360	414	285	152	341	300	95	2691		
Par	5	4	4	5	4	3	4	4	3	36	RED	Rating 72.4
Handicap	7	11	1	5	9	15	3	13	17			Slope 126

Hole	10	11	12	13	14	15	16	17	18	In		Totals
BLUE	415	217	259	325	173	572	350	333	538	3182	BLUE	6561
WHITE	413	212	254	312	167	530	343	327	528	3086	WHITE	5762
Par	4	3	4	4	3	5	4	4	5	36	Par	72
Handicap	2	8	16	12	18	6	10	14	4			
RED	375	176	249	293	146	448	326	278	475	2766	RED	5457
Par	5	3	4	4	3	5	4	4	5	36	Par	72
Handicap	8	16	12	10	18	6	2	14	4			

Manager: Noel Coad   **Pro:** Gregory J. Baker, PGA
Architect: Devereaux Emmet 1915

ROCK VIEW GOLF CLUB

60 River Rd., Montague, NJ 07826   **(973) 293-9891**

Rock View is a 9 hole course open to the public 7 days a week from April 1 to Oct. 31. Memberships are available. Tee time reservations are not necessary.

Driving Range	
•Practice Green	Lockers
•Power Carts	Showers
•Pull Carts	•Food
•Club Rental	•Clubhouse
•Soft Spikes	Outings

Fees	Weekday	Weekend
9 holes	$9	$10
18 holes	$14	$15
Power carts $6pp per 9 holes		

Course Description: Although located in a valley and predominantly flat, Rock View has hilly 8th and 9th holes and an elevated 8th green. From the 1st hole, New York and Pennsylvania may be seen in the distance. The scenery is picturesque and the air is cool and clear. People come to play here from NY and PA as well as from New Jersey.

Directions: Sussex County, #36 on Northwest Map
Rte.80 to Exit 34B. Go north on Rte.15 to Rte.206. Continue north up to Monatague and bear left onto River Rd. (Rte.521). Club is on the right.

Hole	1	2	3	4	5	6	7	8	9	Out	BLUE	Rating
BLUE												Slope
WHITE	283	273	331	144	251	283	382	152	410	2464		
Par	4	4	4	3	4	4	4	3	5	35	WHITE	Rating
Handicap	7	5	3	9	6	4	2	8	1			Slope
RED												
Par											RED	Rating
Handicap												Slope
Hole	10	11	12	13	14	15	16	17	18	In		Totals
BLUE											BLUE	
WHITE											WHITE	4928
Par											Par	70
Handicap												
RED											RED	
Par											Par	
Handicap												

Manager/Supt: James Seeger
Built: 1935

ROLLING GREENS GOLF CLUB

PUBLIC

214 Newton Sparta Rd., Newton, NJ 07860   **(973) 383-3082**

Rolling Greens is an 18 hole semi-private course open to the public 7 days a week all year. Annual memberships are available. Tee time reservations may be made up to 7 days in advance. **Specials:** Ladies/Wed $12, Seniors/M & Thurs. $12.

Driving Range
- **Practice Green**
- **Power Carts**
- **Pull Carts**
- **Club Rental**
- Soft Spikes

Lockers
Showers
- **Food**
Clubhouse
- **Outings**

Fees	Weekday	Weekend
Daily	$18	$25
After 3	$12	$17
Power carts	$12pp	

Course Description: Although Rolling Greens golf club is a relatively short course, it is rather tricky with small well bunkered greens. It is flat and easy to walk; ponds can be found on the par 3 9th and 18th holes. A creek runs across or alongside five other holes as well. The fairways and greens are well conditioned.

Directions: Sussex County, #37 on Northwest Map
Rte.80 West to Exit 34B. Take Rte.15 North. Go 11 miles then take the 2nd Sparta exit labeled Rte.517S. Turn left at light at end of exit and then go straight for 4 lights. Club is 1/4 mile past 4th light on the left.

Hole	1	2	3	4	5	6	7	8	9	Out	BLUE	Rating 64.5
BLUE	355	310	350	237	269	510	347	210	185	2773		Slope 116
WHITE	333	270	307	210	260	483	315	187	167	2532		
Par	4	4	4	3	4	5	4	3	3	34	WHITE	Rating 62.4
Handicap	4	9	6	11	13	2	8	16	14			Slope 103
RED	300	247	289	150	215	463	297	120	100	2181		
Par	4	4	4	3	4	5	4	3	3	34	RED	Rating 62.2
Handicap	4	9	6	11	13	2	8	16	14			Slope 104
Hole	10	11	12	13	14	15	16	17	18	In		Totals
BLUE	367	200	197	460	235	383	157	197	220	2416	BLUE	5189
WHITE	333	167	167	450	235	327	133	152	183	2147	WHITE	4679
Par	4	3	3	5	3	4	3	3	3	31	Par	65
Handicap	5	18	15	1	12	3	17	7	10			
RED	313	146	150	394	207	297	100	100	100	1807	RED	3988
Par	4	3	3	5	4	5	3	3	3	33	Par	67
Handicap	5	18	15	1	12	3	17	7	10			

Manager/Supt: Ian Kunesch   **Pro:** Glenn Holterman
Architect: Nicholas Psiahas 1954

ROXITICUS GOLF CLUB

Bliss Rd., Mendham, NJ 07945　　　　　　　　**(973) 543-4017**

Roxiticus is a private member owned 18 hole course open 6 days a week and closed from Christmas until Apr. 1. Guests may play accompanied by a member. Tee time reservations are required on Sundays.

•**Driving Range**	•**Lockers**
•**Practice Green**	•**Showers**
•**Power Carts**	•**Food**
Pull Carts	•**Clubhouse**
•**Club Rental**	•**Outings**
Caddies	•**Soft Spikes**

Course Description: One of the finest of the Morris County courses, Roxiticus Golf Club is extremely picturesque and hilly. This layout features narrow fairways, many uneven lies and truly magnificent scenery. The thick natural woods block one's views of adjoining holes. The par 3 signature 12th has an elevated tee, woods on the left, a brook and woods on the right and a pond in front. The pro shop, located in a former carriage house, is well stocked and beautifully designed.

Directions: Morris County, #38 on Northwest Map
Rte.80 to Rte. 287S to the Bernardsville exit. Take Rte. 202S to center of Bernardsville and bear right onto Anderson Rd. Go about 3 miles to Bliss Rd. and turn left. Proceed 1 mile to club on the right.

Hole	1	2	3	4	5	6	7	8	9	Out	BLUE	Rating 71.3
BLUE	368	526	233	442	560	201	344	317	139	3130		Slope 124
WHITE	357	508	218	410	541	186	325	305	130	2980		
Par	4	5	3	4	5	3	4	4	3	35	WHITE	Rating 69.6
Handicap	13	5	9	1	3	11	7	15	17			Slope 121
RED	341	469	169	334	488	160	301	284	117	2663		
Par	4	5	3	4	5	3	4	4	3	35	RED	Rating 72.6
Handicap	11	3	13	5	1	9	7	15	17			Slope 130
Hole	10	11	12	13	14	15	16	17	18	In		Totals
BLUE	425	375	194	389	529	423	135	410	428	3308	BLUE	6438
WHITE	405	357	178	369	495	395	115	392	396	3102	WHITE	6082
Par	4	4	3	4	5	4	3	4	4	35	Par	70
Handicap	8	14	16	6	2	12	18	10	4			
RED	342	280	152	348	453	358	114	321	363	2731	RED	5394
Par	4	4	3	4	5	4	3	4	4	35	Par	70
Handicap	10	18	14	4	2	12	16	8	6			

Manager: Lisa Lonergan　　**Pro:** Rick Taylor, PGA　　**Supt:** Leslie Carpenter
Architect: Hal Purdy 1967

SKY VIEW GOLF & COUNTRY CLUB

226 Lafayette Rd., Sparta, NJ 07871   (973) 729-7313

Sky View will be an 18 hole par 71 semi-private course opening in the Spring of 2000. Memberships will be available. Reservations for tee times will be 7-10 days in advance As indicated below, the exact amenities available and fees are still to be determined.

•**Driving Range**	Lockers?	
•**Practice Green**	Showers?	
•**Power Carts**	•**Food**	
Pull Carts?	•**Clubhouse**	
Club Rental?	•**Outings**	
•**Soft Spikes**		

Fees	Weekday	Weekend
Daily	$65	$85
fees are approx.		

Course Description: On the former Smith Farm, 80 new one family homes are being built in conjunction with this course that overlooks Fox Hollow Lake in Sparta. Variety can be found here in elevation changes, grand sheer rock cliffs and outcroppings of stone. Four or five holes could be classified as signature because of the spectacular views and the environmental sensitivity displayed as these holes weave through striking natural terrain. The 18th has a lake on one side and a pond on the other. The course will measure 6525 from the championship tees. Handicaps, ratings and slopes are not yet available.

Directions: Sussex County, #39 on Northwest Map
Rte.80 to Exit 34B. Take Rte.15N for 12 miles to "End of Freeway" sign. At jughandle, make left onto Rte. 181(Lafayette Road). Course is 1/4 mile on the right.

Hole	1	2	3	4	5	6	7	8	9	Out	BLUE	Rating
BLUE	310	515	180	550	390	170	330	420	415	3280		Slope
WHITE	290	480	150	500	365	140	295	400	380	3000		
Par	4	5	3	5	4	3	4	4	4	36	WHITE	Rating
Handicap												Slope
RED	265	425	115	440	285	120	270	350	355	2625		
Par	4	5	3	5	4	3	4	4	4	36	RED	Rating
Handicap												Slope

Hole	10	11	12	13	14	15	16	17	18	In		Totals
BLUE	365	155	355	405	175	485	335	200	490	2965	BLUE	6245
WHITE	335	140	345	385	145	470	305	175	480	2780	WHITE	5780
Par	4	3	4	4	3	5	4	3	5	35	Par	71
Handicap												
RED	305	105	315	295	130	425	275	125	410	2385	RED	5010
Par	4	3	4	4	3	5	4	3	5	35	Par	71
Handicap												

Manager: Arnold Palmer Golf Management
Architect: Robert McNeil 2000

THE SPA GOLF CLUB

Route 94, McAfee, NJ 07428   (973) 827-3710

The Spa is a 9 hole course open 7 days a week and closed between November and March. Quad memberships are available with Crystal Springs, Ballyowen and Black Bear. Members may reserve tee time 2 weeks in advance, the public, 10 days.

Driving Range	Lockers
•**Practice Green**	Showers
•**Power Carts**	•**Food**
•**Pull Carts**	•**Clubhouse**
•**Club Rental**	•**Outings**
•**Soft Spikes**	

Fees	Weekday	Weekend
Daily	$20	$45
9 holes	$17	$29
Power carts included		

Course Description: The Spa is a picturesque executive type course; it offers five par 3s and four par 4s. The signature par 3 4th requires a shot of 180 yards over a pond in front of a rock wall. This hilly and challenging layout does not get very crowded. It is near Mountain Creek and adjacent to a development of condo units.

Directions: Sussex County, #40 on Northwest Map
Rte.80West to Exit 53. Take Rte.23N to Rte.515N. Take 515 into the town of Vernon. Make a left onto Rte. 94S. Go 2.5 mi and turn left into The Great Gorge Resort.

Hole	1	2	3	4	5	6	7	8	9	Out	BLUE	Rating
BLUE	346	178	363	181	323	231	407	176	100	2305		Slope
WHITE	316	136	337	150	292	186	374	163	100	2044		
Par	4	3	4	3	4	3	4	3	3	31	WHITE	Rating
Handicap	9	11	7	3	13	5	1	17	15			Slope
RED	281	103	294	88	265	152	312	131	100	1726		
Par											RED	Rating
Handicap												Slope

Hole	10	11	12	13	14	15	16	17	18	In		Totals
BLUE											BLUE	
WHITE											WHITE	
Par											Par	
Handicap												
RED											RED	
Par											Par	
Handicap												

Manager: Tom Tawpash   **Pro:** John Buck
Architect: Robert Trent Jones 1988

SPRING BROOK COUNTRY CLUB

9 Spring Brook Rd., Morristown, NJ 07960   (973) 538-7959

Spring Brook is an 18 hole course open 6 days a week and closed in February. Guests play accompanied by a member. Tee time reservations are necessary on weekends after 12PM.

•Driving Range	•Lockers
•Practice Green	•Showers
•Power Carts	•Food
Pull Carts	•Clubhouse
•Club Rental	•Outings
•Caddies	•Soft Spikes

Course Description: A par 70 from the back tees, Spring Brook is a very picturesque, fair and enjoyable course. On 14 of the holes, the golfer encounters out of bounds and on five, water from natural springs. Part of the land was once a private estate. The 10th hole tee is a peninsula that extends into one of the ponds. Spring Brook may be the only club in the country where there are 3 par 3s in a row, an unusual feature. A renovation and redesign is in process as this book goes to press.

Directions: Morris County, #41 on Northwest Map
Rte. 80W to Rte. 287S. Exit at Harter Rd., #33. Go left off ramp for 3/4 mile and then a sharp right onto **Old** Harter Rd. Go 50 yards and make a sharp right onto Alvord Rd. to club. Entrance is straight ahead.

Hole	1	2	3	4	5	6	7	8	9	Out	BLUE	Rating 72.6
BLUE	417	223	532	386	374	495	395	428	192	3442		Slope 130
WHITE	402	195	502	362	360	487	376	413	173	3270		
Par	4	3	5	4	4	5	4	4	3	36	WHITE	Rating 71.4
Handicap	3	17	5	9	13	11	7	1	15			Slope 128
RED	323	155	395	309	347	402	361	400	122	2814		
Par	4	3	5	4	4	5	4	5	3	37	RED	Rating 72.5
Handicap	7	17	5	15	11	9	1	3	13			Slope 126
Hole	10	11	12	13	14	15	16	17	18	In		Totals
BLUE	164	210	349	448	204	427	446	417	397	3062	BLUE	6504
WHITE	162	197	335	430	193	414	441	417	393	2982	WHITE	6252
Par	3	3	4	4	3	4	5	4	4	34	Par	70
Handicap	14	16	10	2	18	6	12	4	8			
RED	95	175	322	375	168	319	404	404	322	2718	RED	5398
Par	3	3	4	4	3	4	5	5	4	35	Par	72
Handicap	18	14	8	2	16	12	4	6	10			

Manager: Tom Hurly   **Pro:** Don Vallario, PGA   **Supt:** James Wortman
Architect: Robert Hucknell 1922

SUNSET VALLEY GOLF COURSE **PUBLIC**

West Sunset Rd., Pompton Plains, NJ 07444   **(973) 835-1515**

Sunset Valley is part of the Morris County Park System. It is an 18 hole course open 7 days a week from Apr.1st to Dec. 7th. ID obtained is valid at Flanders Valley & Pinch Brook as well. Automated tee times: 7 days for res., 5 days for registered non-res.

Driving Range
- **Practice Green**
- **Power Carts**
- **Pull Carts**
- **Club Rental**
- **Soft Spikes**
- **Lockers**
- **Showers**
- **Food**
- **Clubhouse**

Outings

Fees	Weekday	Weekend
Res./ID	$15	$20.50
Senior	$10	
Non.resNJ	$30	$41
Power Cart	$25/dbl	$15pp

Course Description: Sunset Valley is a demanding and hilly course with contoured and sloping greens. The difficult par 5 7th requires the golfer to decide whether to go for the green in two or play conservatively. The tight fairways lead up to 3 of the toughest finishing holes in the state of NJ. From the tee on the 555 yard par 5 16th the shot should be right to left to keep the drive in the narrow fairway; the hole ends with a severe uphill slope leading to the green. Sunset Valley is well managed and worthwhile visiting to see the spectacular views of the mountains in the distance.

Directions: Morris County, #42 on Northwest Map
Rte.80 West to Exit 53. Take Rte. 23N to Newark-Pompton Tpke. Take the jughandle and cross over Rte. 23 to Jacksonville Rd. and turn left. Look for Sunset Rd. on right. Make the right and follow Sunset to club on the right.

Hole	1	2	3	4	5	6	7	8	9	Out	BLUE	Rating 71.7
BLUE	360	409	224	406	396	173	508	375	378	3229		Slope 129
WHITE	335	375	183	383	360	147	495	332	356	2966		
Par	4	4	3	4	4	3	5	4	4	35	WHITE	Rating 69.7
Handicap	13	7	15	3	5	17	1	11	9			Slope 124
RED	285	302	163	323	338	111	437	293	317	2569		
Par	4	4	3	4	4	3	5	4	4	35	RED	Rating 70.8
Handicap	13	7	15	3	5	17	1	11	9			Slope 123
Hole	10	11	12	13	14	15	16	17	18	In		Totals
BLUE	421	329	203	353	398	147	555	430	418	3254	BLUE	6483
WHITE	406	299	194	330	367	134	523	418	402	3073	WHITE	6039
Par	4	4	3	4	4	3	5	4	4	35	Par	70
Handicap	10	14	16	12	8	18	2	4	6			
RED	367	267	170	207	336	119	448	405	386	2705	RED	5274
Par	4	4	3	4	4	3	5	4	4	35	Par	70
Handicap	10	14	16	12	8	18	2	4	6			

Manager/Pro: Renee Klose, LPGA   **Supt:** Joanne Eberle
Architect: Hal Purdy 1974

TWIN WILLOWS GOLF COURSE

PUBLIC

167 Ryerson Rd., Lincoln Park, NJ 07035   **(973) 694-9726**

Twin Willows is 9 hole par 3 course located at the Lincoln Park Swim Club. It is open to the public 7 days a week from April through November. Reserved tee times are not necessary.

Driving Range	Lockers
•**Practice Green**	
Power Carts	Showers
•**Pull Carts**	•**Food**
•**Club Rental**	Clubhouse
•**Soft Spikes**	Outings

Fees	Weekday	Weekend
Daily	$8	$10
Sr/Jr 8AM-1PM $5		
Fees are for 9 holes		

Course Description: This course consists entirely of par 3s between 80 and 150 yards in length. It affords the player an opportunity to practice the short game. The local rule states that there is a 5 stroke limit on any hole.

Directions: Morris County, #43 on Northwest Map
Rte.80West to Exit 53. Take Rte. 23North to 1st exit (Lincoln Park-Rte.202). Take Rte.202 to Ryerson Rd and turn right. Club is 1 mile ahead on right.

Hole	1	2	3	4	5	6	7	8	9	Out	BLUE	Rating
BLUE												Slope
WHITE	80	100	105	110	105	125	140	140	150	1055		
Par	3	3	3	3	3	3	3	3	3	27	WHITE	Rating
Handicap												Slope
RED												
Par											RED	Rating
Handicap												Slope
Hole	10	11	12	13	14	15	16	17	18	In		Totals
BLUE											BLUE	
WHITE											WHITE	
Par											Par	
Handicap												
RED											RED	
Par											Par	
Handicap												

Manager: Richard Ward

WALKILL COUNTRY CLUB

Maple Rd., Franklin, NJ 07416   **(973) 827-9620**

Walkill is a 9 hole course open 7 days a week. The club closes between December and mid April. Guests play accompanied by a member. Reserved tee times are not required. Soft spikes are requested.

Driving Range	•Lockers
•Practice Green	•Showers
•Power Carts	•Food
•Pull Carts	•Clubhouse
•Club Rental	•Outings
Caddies	Soft Spikes

Course Description: Deceptively difficult, Walkill is a short course with small greens; the Walkill River meanders through this very hilly property. On the 4th hole, the golfer encounters both the river and a creek. The 7th is called the "teacup hole" due to the high rim around the 2 tiered green. Walkill was originally designed with 6 holes for the NJ Zinc Co. officials and their guests. It was later incorporated as Walkill Golf Club in 1915. Sometime in the 1920s, it was expanded to the present 9 holes. The members are proud to show off their little "gem" in Franklin, NJ.

Directions: Sussex County, #44 on Northwest Map
Rte.80 to Exit 52. Take Rte.23North. When entering Franklin, make a left on Franklin Ave (Rte.631) past a pond and waterfall and onto Cork Hill Rd. Immediately after the municipal building, go right onto Maple Rd. Club is ahead on right.

Hole	1	2	3	4	5	6	7	8	9	Out	BLUE	Rating
BLUE												Slope
WHITE	315	169	485	225	285	398	147	512	333	2869		
Par	4	3	5	3	4	4	3	5	4	35	WHITE	Rating 67.3
Handicap	14	17	4	11	10	1	16	5	8	·		Slope 114
RED	268	137	350	163	234	235	116	374	246	2123		
Par	4	3	5	3	4	4	3	5	4	35	RED	Rating 66.3
Handicap	13	17	3	11	9	1	15	5	7			Slope 111
Hole	10	11	12	13	14	15	16	17	18	In		Totals
BLUE											BLUE	
WHITE	326	152	520	205	310	380	158	480	350	2881	WHITE	5750
Par	4	3	5	3	4	4	3	5	4	35	Par	70
Handicap	13	18	3	12	9	2	15	6	7			
RED											RED	4246
Par											Par	70
Handicap												

Manager/Pro: Frank Vnuk   **Supt:** Richard Fodor
Built: 1910

EAST CENTRAL REGION

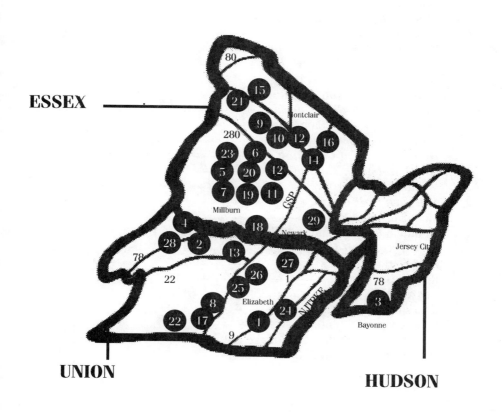

ESSEX

80

15

21

Montclair

9

280

10 12

16

23 6

14

5 20 12

7 19 11

GSP

Millburn

18

29

Newark

4

28 2

13

Jersey City

78

27

22

26

1

25

78

8

Elizabeth

24

3

22 17

1

Bayonne

9

UNION

HUDSON

EAST CENTRAL

Public Courses appear in **bold italics**

ASH BROOK GOLF COURSE

1210 Raritan Rd., Scotch Plains, NJ 07076   **(908) 756-0414**

Ash Brook, part of the Union County Parks System, is an 18 hole course open 7 days a week all year. Residents purchase ID and may reserve up to 1 week in advance, non res. with ID up to 3 days. Reciprocity: Bergen & Middlesex for Srs/ID on weekdays.

Driving Range	
•**Practice Green**	•**Lockers**
•**Power Carts**	•**Showers**
•**Pull Carts**	•**Food**
•**Club Rental**	•**Clubhouse**
•**Soft Spikes**	Outings

Fees	Weekday	Weekend
Res/ID	$12	$14
Srs.	$8	$13.50
Non.res	$24	$28
Power Carts $22		$14/9

Course Description: The rolling terrain at Ash Brook is relatively wooded. The front nine has recently been renovated and the back is being worked on; all overseen by architect, Stephen Kay. The greens have been replaced and bunkers have been added. A new scorecard will reflect these changes. The par 5 16th is a difficult uphill dogleg right with a lake at the corner. Considered a good test of golf, this course is very busy. This facility has a 9 hole pitch and putt course on the premises.

Directions: Union County, #1 on East Central Map
GSP to Exit 135 (Central Ave). Make the 1st left at light onto Raritan Rd. At 4th light, turn right onto Lake Ave. Go 3 lights and turn left onto Old Raritan Rd. Watch for signs for golf course.

Hole	1	2	3	4	5	6	7	8	9	Out	BLUE	Rating 72.2
BLUE	417	380	420	185	511	155	435	548	426	3477		Slope 117
WHITE	377	351	389	176	471	135	400	484	392	3175		
Par	4	4	4	3	5	3	4	5	4	36	WHITE	Rating 69.5
Handicap	12	14	6	16	8	18	2	10	4			Slope 111
RED	324	332	351	136	410	115	341	426	356	2791		
Par	4	4	4	3	5	3	4	5	4	36	RED	Rating 71.8
Handicap	12	14	10	16	8	18	6	2	4			Slope 119

Hole	10	11	12	13	14	15	16	17	18	In		Totals
BLUE	428	353	539	222	466	303	525	423	180	3439	BLUE	6962
WHITE	401	342	517	193	432	287	483	386	157	3198	WHITE	6410
Par	4	4	5	3	4	4	5	4	3	36	Par	72
Handicap	11	9	5	15	1	13	3	7	17			
RED	378	303	490	170	402	278	430	338	125	2914	RED	5661
Par	4	4	5	3	5	4	5	4	3	37	Par	73
Handicap	9	11	3	15	5	13	1	7	17			

Manager: Harry Goett III   **Pro:** Ron Regner, PGA   **Supt:** Peter McCoy
Built: 1953

BALTUSROL GOLF CLUB

Shunpike Rd., Springfield, NJ 07081   **(973) 376-5160**

Baltusrol has two 18 hole courses, the Upper and the Lower, open all year 7 days a week. Guests play accompanied by a member. Reservations for tee times are not necessary. The scorecard below is for the Lower course.

- **Driving Range**
- **Practice Green**
- **Power Carts**
- Pull Carts
- **Club Rental**
- **Caddies**

- **Lockers**
- **Showers**
- **Food**
- **Clubhouse**
- **Outings**
- **Soft Spikes**

Course Description: This traditional setting is suffused with pure golf atmosphere. Jack Nicklaus won two US Opens here; numerous other championships took place at this world famous club. The finely maintained courses feature rolling fairways, a multitude of bunkers and subtle greens. The Lower is dauntingly long, particularly from the Blues. The par 5 17th is 630 yards!! John Daly was the first to reach the green in two shots. The signature and memorable par 3 fourth requires an accurate shot over a formidable pond to a well bunkered green. The courses have been redesigned by Robert Trent Jones and Rees Jones.

Directions: Union County, #2 on East Central Map

GSP or NJTpke to Rte. 78West. Take Rte. 24West to sign marked 'Springfield, Summit, Millburn. Follow sign to Summit. You are now on Broad St. Turn left onto Orchard St. which changes to Shunpike at Morris Ave. Turn right at caution blinker into club.

Hole	1	2	3	4	5	6	7	8	9	Out	BLUE	Rating 75.4
BLUE	478	381	443	194	393	470	505	374	205	3443		Slope 139
WHITE	470	362	405	143	375	411	494	360	189	3209		
Par	5	4	4	3	4	4	5	4	3	36	WHITE	Rating 72.5
Handicap	11	7	1	17	3	5	13	9	15			Slope 133
RED	453	300	402	101	342	406	461	342	171	2978		
Par	5	4	5	3	4	5	5	4	3	38	RED	Rating 75.8
Handicap	4	14	6	18	8	12	2	10	16			Slope 134
Hole	10	11	12	13	14	15	16	17	18	In		Totals
BLUE	454	428	193	393	409	430	216	630	542	3695	BLUE	7195
WHITE	444	388	188	374	379	383	180	543	511	3390	WHITE	6637
Par	4	4	3	4	4	4	3	5	5	36	Par	72
Handicap	2	8	16	12	14	4	18	6	10			
RED	416	377	151	359	329	368	114	448	423	2985	RED	5963
Par	5	4	3	4	4	4	3	5	5	37	Par	75
Handicap	11	3	15	9	13	5	17	1	7			

Manager: Mark DeNoble   **Pro:** Doug Steffan, PGA   **Supt:** Joe Flaherty
Architect: A. W. Tillinghast 1922

HYATT HILLS GOLF COURSE

PUBLIC

Raritan Rd., Clark, NJ 07066 **Phone unavailable**

Hyatt Hills will be a 3,000 yard 9 hole course open to the public 7 days a week. Residents of Clark and Cranford who are members will have reduced fees and preferred tee times. It will be run by a Clark/Cranford Golf Authority. Completion is projected for 2001.

- •Driving Range
- •Practice Green
- •Power Carts
- •Pull Carts
- •Club Rental
- •Soft Spikes
- •Lockers
- •Showers
- •Food
- •Clubhouse
- •Outings

Fees	Weekday	Weekend
Not available at press time.		

Course Description: The property was formerly a GM Roller Bearing factory that is now being prepared for construction. Rail cars of soil are being brought in and as a result, there will be elevation changes that will give some undulation to this course. On this 88 acre terrain, there will be 2 par 5s, 3 par 4s and 4 par 3s. Four different tee boxes are planned so that a 2nd nine may be played from a different perspective. Three holes will be over water with the 7th green surrounded by a pond. The driving range is expected to open in the year 2,000, the course a year later. The architect is Brian Ault.

Directions: Union County, #17 on East Central Map
GSP to Exit 135. Go right onto Central Ave. At 1st light make right onto Raritan Rd. Property is on the left immediately over the RR tracks.

BAYONNE GOLF COURSE

Hudson County will have the first golf course within its borders when this 403 acre property at Constable Hook is finished being prepared and then developed. The land is on NY Bay adjacent to the Military Ocean Terminal and within sight of the World Trade Center and the Statue of Liberty. The Orion of Elizabeth New Jersey (OENJ Corp) is preparing this abandoned municipal landfill and will dredge material from the harbor. The expectation is that the layout will be links style and the waterside winds will affect play. The as yet unnamed 18 hole course will be open to the public in 2001. The actual architect has not been selected. It is possible that in a second phase a private golf course will be built as well. No further information is available at press time.

Hudson County, #3 on East Central Map

CANOE BROOK COUNTRY CLUB PRIVATE

1108 Morris Turnpike, Summit, NJ 07901   **(908) 277-2683**

Canoe Brook is a private club with 36 holes and open 6 days a week, all year, weather permitting. Guests play accompanied by a member. Tee time reservations are not necessary.

> - **Driving Range**   - **Lockers**
> - **Practice Green**   - **Showers**
> - **Power Carts**   - **Food**
>   Pull Carts   - **Clubhouse**
> - **Club Rental**   - **Outings**
> - **Caddies**   - **Soft Spikes**

Course Description: An original C.H. Allison design, Canoe Brook's North course is considered one of the most difficult in NJ due to its length, small greens, penalizing rough and its tree-lined fairways. The club hosts qualifying rounds for the US Open and hosted the The Women's National Amateur of 1938, '83 and '90. Both layouts have had extensive redesign by Robert Trent Jones and Rees Jones. The South course features gently rolling fairways and ponds that may create havoc for the average golfer. Canoe Brook has won several awards for its beautifully stocked and meticulously kept pro shop. The scorecard below is for the North course.

Directions: Union County, #4 on East Central Map
GSP or NJTpke to Rte. 78W to Exit 48. Take Rte.24West to Summit Ave exit. Go through light on north service road. Club is ahead on the right.

Hole	1	2	3	4	5	6	7	8	9	Out	BLUE	Rating 71.5
BLUE	399	572	390	362	173	442	212	528	417	3495		Slope 126
WHITE	380	534	358	346	148	402	184	501	401	3254		
Par	4	5	4	4	3	4	3	5	4	36	WHITE	Rating 69.9
Handicap	7	1	13	11	17	5	15	9	3			Slope 124
RED	358	460	323	282	110	352	153	435	355	2828		
Par	4	5	3	4	5	4	3	4	4	36	RED	Rating 72.7
Handicap	7	1	9	6	2	5	8	4	3			Slope 126
Hole	10	11	12	13	14	15	16	17	18	In		Totals
BLUE	374	173	538	391	226	382	431	455	601	3571	BLUE	7066
WHITE	360	148	512	370	201	360	395	424	567	3337	WHITE	6591
Par	4	3	5	4	3	4	4	4	5	36	Par	72
Handicap	12	18	4	14	10	16	8	6	2			
RED	333	125	434	326	166	331	334	330	496	2875	RED	5703
Par	4	3	5	4	3	4	4	4	5	36	Par	72
Handicap	12	18	2	8	14	16	6	10	4			

Manager: Rudolf Fisher   **Pro:** Greg Lecker, PGA
Architects: North: Charles Allison 1902   **South:** Alfred Tull, Walter Travis 1924

CEDAR HILL COUNTRY CLUB

100 Walnut St., Livingston, NJ 07039   (973) 992-6455

Cedar Hill is a private 18 hole course open 6 days a week from Mar. 1 to Nov. 30. Guests play accompanied by a member. Tee times may be made 2 or 3 days in advance for weekends.

•**Driving Range**	•**Lockers**
•**Practice Green**	•**Showers**
•**Power Carts**	•**Food**
Pull Carts	•**Clubhouse**
•**Club Rental**	•**Outings**
•**Caddies**	•**Soft Spikes**

Course Description: Cedar Hill is known for its fast, undulating, small greens. Some consider the par four 4th hole the most difficult due to the out of bounds along the right side of the fairway. Its severely sloped green is well protected by bunkers. The back nine includes a memorable par 3. The par 5 18th is a good uphill finishing hole. Accuracy is a necessity in order to score well at Cedar Hill. The course has been upgraded in the last few years to make it more interesting and challenging.

Directions: Essex County, #5 on East Central Map
GSP or NJTpke to Rte.280West. Exit at 4A (Eisenhower Parkway). Follow parkway for 6 traffic lights (approx. 3 miles) to Walnut Street and turn right. Club is ahead on left.

Hole	1	2	3	4	5	6	7	8	9	Out	BLUE	Rating 71.5
BLUE	458	375	385	465	178	503	317	348	428	3436		Slope 126
WHITE	447	362	374	450	161	472	309	333	418	3303		
Par	4	4	4	4	3	5	4	4	4	36	WHITE	Rating 69.9
Handicap	1	11	9	5	17	7	15	13	3			Slope 124
RED	393	348	362	383	157	400	263	290	364	2955		
Par	5	4	4	5	3	5	4	4	4	38	RED	Rating 72.7
Handicap	3	11	5	7	17	9	15	13	1			Slope 126
Hole	**10**	**11**	**12**	**13**	**14**	**15**	**16**	**17**	**18**	**In**		Totals
BLUE	157	379	394	192	542	373	133	369	475	3007	BLUE	6443
WHITE	145	323	375	176	530	359	120	358	462	2789	WHITE	6092
Par	3	4	4	3	5	4	3	4	5	35	Par	71
Handicap	18	12	4	14	2	8	16	10	6			
RED	137	303	356	159	430	345	109	332	384	2531	RED	5486
Par	3	4	4	3	5	4	3	4	5	35	Par	73
Handicap	2	16	14	18	6	4	10	8	12			

Manager: Ron Winarich   **Pro**: Ron Korn, PGA   **Supt**: Dennis Wrede
Architect: Nicholas Psiahas 1921

CRESTMONT COUNTRY CLUB

750 Eagle Rock Ave , West Orange, NJ 07052 **(973) 731-0833**

Crestmont is an 18 hole course that is open from February through December, 6 days a week. Guests play accompanied by a member. Tee times are by assignment on weekends.

•**Driving Range**	•**Lockers**
•**Practice Green**	•**Showers**
•**Power Carts**	•**Food**
Pull Carts	•**Clubhouse**
Club Rental	•**Outings**
•**Caddies**	•**Soft Spikes**

Course Description: Crestmont opened in 1912 with 12 holes as the Newark Athletic Club. This Donald Ross course is known for its small, undulating greens, some two tiered and extremely difficult to putt when fast. Uneven lies are characteristic of hilly Crestmont. The tee shot on the par 5 1st hole is from an elevation. The approach shot is uphill. The green on the signature par 3 11th is elevated with a back to front slope; landing above the hole would be a big mistake. A carry over water is necessary to reach the 12th hole. The par 3 8th is also over water. The 1997 NJ State Open was held here.

Directions: Essex County, #6 on East Central Map
From GSP or NJTpke take Rte. 280West to Exit 6A, Laurel Ave. Club is about 1/2 mile up on the right just before intersection of Eagle Rock Ave.

Hole	1	2	3	4	5	6	7	8	9	Out	BLUE	Rating 72.7
BLUE	489	448	412	162	402	404	307	216	510	3350		Slope 130
WHITE	478	432	398	148	382	392	295	205	502	3232		
Par	5	4	4	3	4	4	4	3	5	36	WHITE	Rating 71.7
Handicap	11	1	5	17	9	7	15	13	3			Slope 128
RED	467	416	293	132	282	320	292	179	448	2829		
Par	5	5	4	3	4	4	4	3	5	37	RED	Rating 73.8
Handicap	3	5	9	17	11	7	13	15	1			Slope 126
Hole	10	11	12	13	14	15	16	17	18	In		Totals
BLUE	422	163	414	356	521	362	406	230	508	3382	BLUE	6732
WHITE	415	157	402	346	493	353	393	222	494	3275	WHITE	6507
Par	4	3	4	4	5	4	4	3	5	36	Par	72
Handicap	6	18	2	10	14	12	4	16	8			
RED	407	147	327	314	442	308	375	182	384	2886	RED	5715
Par	5	3	4	4	5	4	4	3	5	37	Par	74
Handicap	12	18	2	14	8	6	4	16	10			

Manager: Mark Shan   **Pro:** Peter Famiano, PGA   **Supt:** Peter Pedrazzi, Jr.
Architect: Donald Ross 1912

EAST ORANGE GOLF COURSE

PUBLIC

440 Parsonage Hill Rd., Short Hills, NJ 07078   (973) 379-7190

East Orange is a municipal 18 hole course, considered to be semi-private, owned by the City of East Orange and open to the public 7 days a week all year. Memberships are available with the privilege of reserving tee times. Irons only for driving range.

•**Driving Range**	•**Lockers**
•**Practice Green**	•**Showers**
•**Power Carts**	•**Food**
•**Pull Carts**	•**Clubhouse**
Club Rental	Outings
•**Soft Spikes**	

Fees	Weekday	Weekend
Mbrs	$7	$10
Non-mbrs	$30	$35
Power carts	$20	

Course Description: This golf course is on the property of the East Orange water Reserve which supplies water to the area. Adjacent to a wildlife preserve, it sometimes has drainage problems in wet weather. The layout is open and relatively flat. Recently, considerable improvements have been made to the clubhouse and a beautiful patio has been added. New cart paths have been installed; the tees and greens have been renovated.

Directions: Essex County, #7 on East Central Map
GSP or NJ Tpke to Rte.78W. Take Rte.24West to Exit 7C (JFK Pkwy) toward Livingston. Go past Short Hills Mall. Make left onto Parsonage Hill Rd. Club is 1/4 mi on left.

Hole	1	2	3	4	5	6	7	8	9	Out	BLUE	Rating
BLUE												Slope
WHITE	342	396	178	343	500	305	488	204	375	3131		
Par	4	4	3	4	5	4	5	3	4	36	WHITE	Rating 67.6
Handicap	5	1	9	11	15	17	13	3	7			Slope 117
RED	280	355	175	330	419	295	448	199	261	2762		
Par	4	4	3	4	5	4	5	3	4	36	RED	Rating 69.8
Handicap	13	5	17	7	3	9	1	11	15			Slope 122
Hole	10	11	12	13	14	15	16	17	18	In		Totals
BLUE											BLUE	
WHITE	497	344	330	150	419	344	272	149	484	2989	WHITE	6120
Par	5	4	4	3	4	4	4	3	5	36	Par	72
Handicap	8	6	12	16	2	4	18	14	10			
RED	490	334	326	145	409	336	248	144	446	2878	RED	5640
Par	5	4	4	3	5	4	4	3	5	37	Par	73
Handicap	2	8	14	18	6	10	12	16	4			

Manager: Grassella Oliphant   **Supt:** Joe Ciccone
Built: Tom Bendelow 1926

ECHO LAKE COUNTRY CLUB

Springfield Ave., Westfield, NJ 07091   **(908) 232-4288**

Echo Lake is an 18 hole course open all year 6 days a week. Guests play accompanied by a member. Tee time reservations are not necessary.

- **Driving Range**   • **Lockers**
- **Practice Green** • **Showers**
- **Power Carts**   • **Food**
- Pull Carts   • **Clubhouse**
- **Club Rental**   • **Outings**
- **Caddies**   • **Soft Spikes**

Course Description: Echo Lake CC is an interesting Donald Ross layout with some hills causing uneven lies. Many of the greens are small and there are numerous bunkers. The signature par 3 7th requires a shot over a pond. The 6th and 14th holes have water in play. From the first tee, the scenic view to the east includes the World Trade Center and the Empire State Building. The club hosted the 1994 US Junior Amateur Championship.

Directions: Union County, #8 on East Central Map
GSP to Exit 140A. Take Rte. 22West to Exit "Westfield-Cranford-Echo Lake Park". Follow Springfield Ave (Rte. 577) south. Club is ahead on right.

Hole	1	2	3	4	5	6	7	8	9	Out	BLUE	Rating 72.2
BLUE	401	247	363	493	365	383	147	418	393	3210		Slope 128
WHITE	391	241	357	489	353	378	138	367	384	3098		
Par	4	4	4	5	4	4	3	4	4	36	WHITE	Rating 71.4
Handicap	10	18	14	2	4	8	16	6	12			Slope 127
RED	365	176	310	483	262	330	126	326	382	2760		
Par	4	4	4	5	4	4	3	4	5	37	RED	Rating 72.8
Handicap	15	5	13	1	7	3	17	11	9			Slope 129
Hole	10	11	12	13	14	15	16	17	18	In		Totals
BLUE	410	546	526	437	214	448	406	170	417	3596	BLUE	6806
WHITE	386	536	521	417	209	433	380	156	398	3436	WHITE	6534
Par	4	5	5	4	3	4	4	3	4	36	Par	72
Handicap	7	1	3	11	15	5	9	17	13			
RED	369	421	422	258	145	428	327	142	279	2791	RED	5551
Par	4	5	5	4	3	5	4	3	4	37	Par	74
Handicap	8	6	2	14	16	4	10	18	12			

Manager: Manny Gugliuzza   **Pro:** Mike Preston, PGA   **Supt:** Chris Carson
Architect: Donald Ross 1913

ESSEX COUNTY COUNTRY CLUB

350 Mt. Pleasant Ave., West Orange, NJ 07052   **(973) 731-9764**

Essex County is an 18 hole course open six days a week all year. Guests play accompanied by a member. Tee times can be reserved up to one week in advance for weekends and holidays.

> - **Driving Range**
> - **Practice Green**
> - **Power Carts**
> - Pull Carts
> - **Club Rental**
> - **Caddies**
> - **Lockers**
> - **Showers**
> - **Food**
> - **Clubhouse**
> - **Outings**
> - **Soft Spikes**

Course Description: Essex County was established in 1887 and occupied a location which has now become a residential community. Taking over from a course that Tillinghast and Seth Raynor had worked on, Charles Banks imposed his inimitable style with many deep bunkers and large rolling slick greens. The club, which is on the first mountain of West Orange, is characterized by quite hilly terrain and sprawling fairways. From an elevated tee on the par 3 11th, the golfer needs an accurate shot over a ravine towards the hole. The beautiful 12th is back over the ravine. The 18th is a very long uphill par 4. The NJPGA holds match play championships here yearly in honor of Jack Mitchell, the club pro for thirty years. NJ State Open was held here in 1987.

Directions: Essex County, #9 on East Central Map
GSP or NJ Tpke to Rte. 280West to Exit 8A (Prospect Ave.) At 3rd light, go right onto Mt. Pleasant Ave. Entrance is 300 yards ahead on the left.

Hole	1	2	3	4	5	6	7	8	9	Out	BLUE	Rating 72.9
BLUE	383	298	375	420	460	176	614	524	165	3415		Slope 128
WHITE	377	292	365	414	450	170	560	475	146	3249		
Par	4	4	4	4	4	3	5	5	3	36	WHITE	Rating 71.5
Handicap	11	17	7	5	1	13	3	9	15			Slope 126
RED	320	246	326	360	410	141	452	421	92	2770		
Par	4	4	4	4	5	3	5	5	3	37	RED	Rating 73.4
Handicap	12	14	10	4	8	16	2	6	18			Slope 128
Hole	10	11	12	13	14	15	16	17	18	In		Totals
BLUE	445	192	440	548	336	220	439	390	455	3465	BLUE	6901
WHITE	440	180	405	508	310	203	424	380	440	3290	WHITE	6554
Par	4	3	4	5	4	3	4	4	4	35	Par	71
Handicap	8	12	2	14	18	16	4	10	6			
RED	425	173	379	478	284	166	349	314	367	2935	RED	5705
Par	5	3	4	5	4	3	4	4	4	36	Par	73
Handicap	7	9	1	3	15	17	11	13	5			

Manager: Robert Osborne   **Pro:** Bill Nash, PGA   **Supt:** Sean Klotzbach
Architects: A.W. Tillinghast, Seth Raynor, Charles Banks 1918

ESSEX FELLS COUNTRY CLUB

219 Devon Rd., Essex Fells, NJ 07021   **(973) 226-5800**

Essex Fells is an 18 hole course open 6 days a week all year.   Guests play accompanied by a member. Tee time reservations are not necessary.

- •**Driving Range**   •**Lockers**
- •**Practice Green**   •**Showers**
- •**Power Carts**   •**Food**
-   Pull Carts   •**Clubhouse**
- •**Club Rental**   •**Outings**
- •**Caddies**   •**Soft Spikes**

Course Description: Essex Fells is a magnificent, long, and hilly course with spectacular panoramic views and flowers in abundance. The small, fast greens are mostly elevated with bunkers guarding the front and back of the target areas. Correct club selection is a must for the approach shot. Water is in play on seven holes. The signature #10 is a challenging par 3. The brook on the par 4 15th adds to the course's difficulty. The NJ State Open was held here in 1996.

Directions: Essex County, #10 on East Central Map
From GSP or NJTpke take Rte. 280West to Laurel Ave Exit 6A. Proceed north on Laurel Ave.and left onto Eagle Rock Ave. Bear right onto Old Eagle Rock. Turn right into Devon Rd. Club is ahead on right.

Hole	1	2	3	4	5	6	7	8	9	Out	BLUE	Rating 71.9
BLUE	452	320	178	396	544	183	357	463	356	3249		Slope 128
WHITE	446	311	149	388	531	168	340	450	308	3091		
Par	4	4	3	4	5	3	4	4	4	35	WHITE	Rating 70.6
Handicap	3	13	17	5	7	15	9	1	11			Slope 126
RED	431	264	119	334	488	149	294	440	269	2788		
Par	5	4	3	4	5	3	4	5	4	37	RED	Rating 74.9
Handicap	7	1	9	6	2	5	8	4	3			Slope 135
Hole	10	11	12	13	14	15	16	17	18	In		Totals
BLUE	208	502	185	385	411	453	439	366	346	3295	BLUE	6544
WHITE	203	491	167	377	404	448	435	340	294	3159	WHITE	6250
Par	3	5	3	4	4	4	4	4	4	35	Par	70
Handicap	12	10	18	8	6	4	2	14	16			
RED	194	476	150	368	401	438	429	302	281	3039	RED	5827
Par	3	5	3	4	5	5	5	4	4	38	Par	75
Handicap	16	2	18	10	8	6	4	12	14			

Manager: Michael Brasher   **Pro:** Russell Helwig, PGA   **Supt:** Richard La Flamme
Estab: 1896 **Architect:** Donald Ross 1918

FOREST HILL FIELD CLUB

9 Belleville Ave., Bloomfield, NJ 07003   **(973) 743-9611**

Forest Hill is an 18 hole course open 6 days a week and closed for one month in winter. Guests play accompanied by a member. Tee time reservations are not necesary.

- •**Driving Range**
- •**Practice Green**
- •**Power Carts**
- Pull Carts
- •**Club Rental**
- •**Caddies**

- •**Lockers**
- •**Showers**
- •**Food**
- •**Clubhouse**
- •**Outings**
- •**Soft Spikes**

Course Description: Mostly narrow fairways, uneven lies and elevated small greens characterize this densely treed challenging course. The par 4 signature #7 is very long and uphill. The shot on the downhill par 3 8th is to a small well bunkered green, difficult to read, typical at Forest Hill. On the par 4 11th the fairway is three tiered and all uphill. It has an extremely fast bunkered green that requires a delicate touch. The uphill par 3 18th needs an accurate shot to carry over the bunker in front and to avoid another on the side. Recently, all the bunkers have been made deeper.

Directions: Essex County, #11 on East Central Map
GSP to Exit 149. At exit, turn right to traffic light. Then right onto Belleville Ave. Watch carefully for entrance road to club on left at light.

Hole	1	2	3	4	5	6	7	8	9	Out	BLUE	Rating 71.4
BLUE	363	364	542	502	163	381	416	216	390	3337		Slope 126
WHITE	358	346	523	334	489	147	373	400	377	3222		
Par	4	4	5	5	3	4	4	3	4	36	WHITE	Rating 70.4
Handicap	13	11	3	5	17	9	1	15	7			Slope 124
RED	322	304	388	439	136	360	375	194	353	2871		
Par	4	4	5	5	3	4	4	3	4	36	RED	Rating 73.5
Handicap	11	13	5	3	17	9	1	15	7			Slope 127
Hole	10	11	12	13	14	15	16	17	18	In		Totals
BLUE	366	396	303	446	475	356	171	444	209	3166	BLUE	6503
WHITE	361	389	297	439	459	343	158	425	173	3044	WHITE	6266
Par	4	4	4	4	5	4	3	4	3	35	Par	71
Handicap	10	4	16	2	8	12	18	6	14			
RED	320	380	276	408	430	334	143	383	153	2827	RED	5698
Par	4	5	4	4	5	4	3	5	3	37	Par	73
Handicap	12	6	14	4	2	10	18	8	16			

Manager: David Schutzenhoser   **Pro:** Charlie Cowell, PGA   **Supt:** Jeff Drake
Estab: 1896 **Architect:** A.W. Tillinghast 1926

FRANCIS BYRNE GOLF COURSE | PUBLIC

1100 Pleasant Valley Way, West Orange, NJ 07052   (973) 736-2306

Francis A. Byrne is an 18 hole course, part of the Essex County Dept. of Parks. It is open 7 days a week and closes Jan. & Feb. County residents may purchase an ID. Non ID holders may get tee times after noon on weekends.

Driving Range
- •Practice Green
- •Power Carts
- •Pull Carts
- Club Rental
- •Soft Spikes

Lockers
- •Showers
- •Food
- •Clubhouse
- •Outings

Fees	Weekday	Weekend
Res/ID	$11	$13
Sr/Jr	$6	$11
NJnon-res.	$22	$26
Power Carts	$12pp	

Course Description: Francis Byrne golf course has an interesting history. It was originally the West layout and second 18 of Essex County CC. Purchased by the county for its citizens and the general public, it is lengthy with gently rolling terrain. The par 4 15th signature hole is a long sharp dogleg left measuring 442 from the Blues & Whites as well. The 16th, 17th and 18th have water in play in the form of a stream. This golf facility gets very crowded; it handled about 56,000 rounds in 1997.

Directions: Essex County, #12 on East Central Map

GSP or NJTpke to Rte. 280West. Exit at #7(Pleasant Valley Way). Go south for 1/4 mile. Course is on the left.

Hole	1	2	3	4	5	6	7	8	9	Out	BLUE	Rating 70.2
BLUE	465	230	400	405	140	417	395	385	435	3262		Slope 128
WHITE	456	211	390	365	129	407	360	352	435	3105		
Par	5	3	4	4	3	4	4	4	4	35	WHITE	Rating 70.2
Handicap	16	4	8	6	18	10	12	14	2			Slope 125
RED	427	184	340	210	118	347	246	340	420	2632		
Par	5	3	4	4	3	4	4	4	5	36	RED	Rating 70.8
Handicap	2	6	4	14	16	8	18	12	10			Slope 120
Hole	10	11	12	13	14	15	16	17	18	In		Totals
BLUE	381	405	430	395	160	442	428	360	390	3391	BLUE	6653
WHITE	363	388	430	365	130	442	418	330	367	3233	WHITE	6338
Par	4	4	4	4	3	4	4	4	4	35	Par	70
Handicap	7	9	1	13	17	3	5	15	11			
RED	310	347	350	345	110	346	377	220	347	2752	RED	5384
Par	4	4	4	4	3	4	5	4	4	36	Par	72
Handicap	7	9	1	11	17	3	5	15	13			

Manager/Pro: Bob Schubert, PGA   **Supt:** John Di Palo
Architect: Charles Banks 1920

GALLOPING HILL GOLF COURSE **PUBLIC**

Galloping Hill Rd., Union, NJ 07083   **(908) 686-1556**

Galloping Hill is a 27 hole Union County facility open 7 days a week all year. As we go to press, 9 of the holes are under construction. Residents purchase IDs and may reserve tee times. Non res. may walk on. A pitch & putt course is on the premises.

Driving Range	
•**Practice Green**	•**Lockers**
•**Power Carts**	•**Showers**
•**Pull Carts**	•**Food**
Club Rental	•**Clubhouse**
•**Soft Spikes**	Outings

Fees	Weekday	Weekend
Res/ID	$12	$14
Sr/Jr	$8	$10
Non-res	$24	$28
Power carts	$22/18,	$14/9

Course Description: This very busy, wide open county course is hilly with virtually no flat lies, hence the name. The golfer encounters a variety of uphill and downhill terrain. The well kept undulating greens can be tricky and very hard to read with more difficult pin placements. A major refurbishment has been in progress for several years including improved drainage, cart paths, tees and greens. The yardages and ratings will change when the project is finished so that the hole distances for the scorecard below are temporary. An area is available for practice using your own golf balls.

Directions: Union County, #13 on East Central Map
GSP to Exit #138. At light, take jughandle for the U-turn; course is immediately on the right.

Hole	1	2	3	4	5	6	7	8	9	Out	BLUE	Rating 68.5
BLUE	347	333	439	368	135	553	354	279	555	3363		Slope 115
WHITE	335	323	421	345	135	463	354	279	545	3200		
Par	4	4	4	4	3	5	4	4	5	37	WHITE	Rating 65.9
Handicap	16	14	2	8	17	4	12	18	6			Slope 110
RED	335	300	380	330	111	411	327	259	391	2844		
Par	4	4	5	4	3	5	4	4	5	38	RED	Rating 69.4
Handicap	13	11	3	7	17	5	9	15	1			Slope 116
Hole	10	11	12	13	14	15	16	17	18	In		Totals
BLUE	398	195	505	427	376	184	364	383	495	3327	BLUE	6160
WHITE	398	176	505	414	365	170	364	332	449	3173	WHITE	5639
Par	4	3	5	4	4	3	4	4	5	36	Par	73
Handicap	7	9	13	1	5	15	10	11	3			
RED	274	162	433	414	365	143	342	229	317	2670	RED	4975
Par	4	3	5	5	5	3	4	4	5	38	Par	76
Handicap	14	16	4	2	10	18	8	12	6			

Manager: Ron Goodwin   **Pro:** Ron Regner, PGA   **Supt:** Joe Adassa
Architect: Willard Wilkinson 1927

GLEN RIDGE COUNTRY CLUB

555 Ridgewood Ave., Glen Ridge, NJ 07028   **(973) 744-7803**

Glen Ridge is an 18 hole course open 6 days a week all year. Guests play accompanied by a member. Tee time reservations are not required.

Driving Range	• **Lockers**
• **Practice Green**	• **Showers**
• **Power Carts**	• **Food**
Pull Carts	• **Clubhouse**
Club Rental	• **Outings**
• **Caddies**	• **Soft Spikes**

Course Description: Glen Ridge was established in 1894 making it one of the oldest clubs in New Jersey. It was redesigned by A. W. Tillinghast and Robert Trent Jones and it is said to be the "longest 6000 yards you'll ever play." The small, contoured greens have sizeable bunkers guarding them, notably the one on the par 4, 329 yard first hole. A stone-walled brook must be crossed on four different approach shots; ponds come into play on several other locations. The uphill, long par 4 18th challenges the golfer with a blind second shot.

Directions: Essex County, #14 on East Central Map
GSP to Exit 151 (Watchung Ave.) Go west on Watchung past Broad St. to Ridgewood Ave. and turn left; club is on the left.

Hole	1	2	3	4	5	6	7	8	9	Out	BLUE	Rating 69.8
BLUE	342	138	519	140	384	474	374	172	364	2907		Slope 125
WHITE	329	132	512	129	377	462	372	152	355	2820		
Par	4	3	5	3	4	5	4	3	4	35	WHITE	Rating 69.0
Handicap	11	17	1	15	3	9	7	13	5			Slope 123
RED	317	128	496	120	359	455	371	134	340	2720		
Par	4	3	5	3	4	5	4	3	4	35	RED	Rating 73.6
Handicap	11	17	1	15	3	7	5	13	9			Slope 132
Hole	10	11	12	13	14	15	16	17	18	In		Totals
BLUE	394	192	488	334	342	330	484	154	405	3123	BLUE	6030
WHITE	384	187	479	321	333	317	477	136	402	3036	WHITE	5856
Par	4	3	5	4	4	4	5	3	4	36	Par	71
Handicap	8	14	2	12	10	16	6	18	4			
RED	379	185	476	320	328	305	474	113	400	2980	RED	5700
Par	4	3	5	4	4	4	5	3	5	37	Par	72
Handicap	10	12	2	16	8	14	6	18	4			

Manager: Cyrus Reitmeyer   **Pro:** Greg Mulhern, PGA   **Supt:** Mike Vacchiano
Architect: Willie Park, Jr. 1894

GREEN BROOK COUNTRY CLUB

100 W. Green Brook Rd., North Caldwell, NJ 07006   **(973) 226-2406**

Green Brook is an 18 hole course open 6 days a week and closed in February . Guests play accompanied by a member. Tee time reservations are necessary for Fridays and weekends. Power caddies are available for walkers.

•**Driving Range**	•**Lockers**
•**Practice Green**	•**Showers**
•**Power Carts**	•**Food**
Pull Carts	•**Clubhouse**
•**Club Rental**	•**Outings**
•**Caddies**	•**Soft Spikes**

Course Description: Green Brook is a beautifully maintained course; hilly on the front nine and flatter on the back. The difficult greens add to its character. The par 5 3rd has a spectacular view of western New Jersey from the fairway. The elevated tee of the par 3 5th is the highest point in Essex County. Improvements have been made here recently; new tees and greens and new cartpaths were installed throughout. The bunkers were redone as well.

Directions: Essex County, #15 on East Central Map
Rte. 80W to Exit 53. Take Rte. 46W to Passaic Ave. South. Proceed 1 & 1/2 miles to 6th light, Green Brook Rd. Turn left and club is 1/4mile ahead on the right.

Hole	1	2	3	4	5	6	7	8	9	Out	BLUE	Rating 72.3
BLUE	408	434	513	270	179	380	367	211	390	3152		Slope 130
WHITE	390	423	508	261	170	368	355	204	385	3064		
Par	4	4	5	4	3	4	4	3	4	35	WHITE	Rating 71.1
Handicap	7	3	1	15	17	2	13	11	5			Slope 128
RED	401	379	451	256	152	315	348	175	345	2822		
Par	5	4	5	4	3	4	4	3	4	36	RED	Rating 74.0
Handicap	15	5	1	9	17	11	7	13	3			Slope 130
Hole	10	11	12	13	14	15	16	17	18	In		Totals
BLUE	420	412	441	454	178	528	395	167	401	3396	BLUE	6548
WHITE	399	378	421	440	162	516	385	160	381	3242	WHITE	6306
Par	4	4	4	5	3	5	4	3	4	36	Par	71
Handicap	4	10	2	12	16	6	8	18	14			
RED	401	348	418	420	144	467	324	137	311	2970	RED	5792
Par	5	4	5	5	3	5	4	3	4	38	Par	74
Handicap	14	8	10	4	12	2	6	18	16			

Manager: Michael McCarthy   **Pro:** George Sauer, PGA   **Supt:** Joe Kennedy
Architect: Robert White 1923

HENDRICKS FIELD GOLF CLUB   **PUBLIC**

Franklin Ave., Belleville, NJ 07109   **(973) 751-0178**

Hendricks Field is an 18 hole Essex County course. It is open 7 days a week all year. County residents purchase an ID and may make tee time reservations through an automated system $1.50pp. Non residents $3pp to reserve.

Driving Range	• **Lockers**
Practice Green	• **Showers**
• **Power Carts**	• **Food**
• **Pull Carts**	• **Clubhouse**
• **Club Rental**	• **Outings**
• **Soft Spikes**	

Fees	**Weekday**	**Weekend**
Res/ID	$11	$13
Sr	$7	
Non-res	$22	$26
Power carts $12pp		

Course Description: Hendricks Field is wide open with tree lined fairways. It is generally flat and thus conducive to walking. No water is in play. Golfers can score well here making it a very popular and busy course in the heart of Essex County. The 400 yard par 4 5th is a difficult dogleg left. The ninth, also a long par 4, is downhill; both give the golfer a formidable challenge. The tee boxes are being redone.

Directions: Essex County, #16 on East Central Map
GSP to Exit #150 (Hoover Ave.) Turn right at Jeroloman. Make a right into Franklin Ave; course is ahead on the left.

Hole	1	2	3	4	5	6	7	8	9	Out	BLUE	Rating 69.4
BLUE	386	382	406	372	400	152	437	472	445	3452		Slope 116
WHITE	378	370	402	359	393	140	432	450	406	3330		
Par	4	4	4	4	4	3	4	5	4	36	WHITE	Rating 68.4
Handicap	11	9	3	15	7	13	1	17	5			Slope 114
RED	338	254	398	292	290	132	353	410	366	2833		
Par	4	4	4	4	4	3	4	5	4	36	RED	Rating 68.4
Handicap	11	9	1	15	13	17	5	7	3			Slope 114
Hole	10	11	12	13	14	15	16	17	18	In		Totals
BLUE	475	120	367	295	170	358	377	240	369	2771	BLUE	6223
WHITE	469	112	361	285	161	348	370	222	360	2688	WHITE	6018
Par	5	3	4	3	3	4	4	4	4	34	Par	70
Handicap	10	16	6	12	8	14	4	18	2			
RED	393	103	355	120	153	277	363	213	350	2327	RED	5160
Par	4	3	4	3	3	4	4	4	4	33	Par	69
Handicap	2	18	8	16	14	10	4	12	6			

Manager/Pro: Jimmy Feaster, PGA   **Supt:** Joe Ciccone
Architect: Charles Banks 1929

MAPLEWOOD COUNTRY CLUB   PRIVATE

28 Baker St., Maplewood, NJ 07040   **(973) 762-0215**

Maplewood is an 18 hole course open 6 days a week and closed in February. Guests play accompanied by a member. Tee time reservations are required for weekends.

•Driving Range	•Lockers
•Practice Green	•Showers
•Power Carts	•Food
Pull Carts	•Clubhouse
•Club Rental	•Outings
•Caddies	•Soft Spikes

Course Description: Maplewood is a relatively short, very tree-lined course. The small greens are difficult; the golfer must hit straight for a good score. Water is in play on holes 4, 9, 11, 12 and 18 in the form of a creek meandering through them. The recent renovation has included work on the bunkers, tee boxes and fairway mounding. Maplewood is considered the birthplace of the golf tee. In the 1920s, Dr. William Lowell, a dentist, was dissatisfied with the tradition of forming a tee from dirt. He carved out a peg with a rounded cup on top for use on the tee. Some time later, he had the idea patented as the "Reddy Tee".

Directions: Essex County, #18 on East Central Map
GSP or NJTPke to Rte. 78W. Exit at Springfield Ave (Rte. 124). Bear left onto Valley Ave. Course can be seen on left. Turn left onto Baker St. to club entrance.

Hole	1	2	3	4	5	6	7	8	9	Out	BLUE	Rating 70.3
BLUE	502	369	324	312	333	393	325	185	406	3149		Slope 131
WHITE	489	361	317	289	320	375	291	168	392	3004		
Par	5	4	4	4	4	4	4	3	4	36	WHITE	Rating 69.3
Handicap	5	9	11	17	15	3	7	13	1			Slope 128
RED	475	333	287	216	292	339	275	148	363	2728		
Par	5	4	4	4	4	4	4	3	5	37	RED	Rating 72.3
Handicap	1	5	9	11	15	3	7	17	13			Slope 127

Hole	10	11	12	13	14	15	16	17	18	In		Totals
BLUE	153	379	334	394	394	509	383	418	149	3113	BLUE	6262
WHITE	140	371	322	383	386	496	376	405	140	3019	WHITE	6023
Par	3	4	4	4	4	5	4	4	3	35	Par	71
Handicap	16	10	14	6	4	8	12	2	18			
RED	127	353	239	330	324	413	338	372	95	2591	RED	5319
Par	3	4	4	4	4	5	4	5	3	36	Par	73
Handicap	16	4	14	6	8	2	12	10	18			

Manager: Michael Lusk   **Pro:** Mickie Gallagher, 3rd, PGA   **Supt:** Greg Nicoll
Built: 1911

MILLBURN GOLF COURSE

White Oak Ridge Rd., Short Hills, NJ 07078   **(973) 379-4156**

Millburn is a 9 hole municipal par 3 course run by the Dept. of Recreation and open 7 days a week from Apr. 1 to Nov. 1. Memberships are available for residents of Millburn and its surrounding communities. Reserved tee times are not necessary.

Driving Range
• **Practice Green**
Power Carts
• **Pull Carts**
• **Club Rental**
• **Soft Spikes**

Lockers
Showers
Food
Clubhouse
• **Outings**

Fees	Weekday	Weekend
Daily	$2.50	$3.75
Guests	$5	$7.50
Indiv. mbrship	$55	

Course Description: Considered to be one of the best par 3 layouts, Millburn gives its residents a good place to practice and play on an interesting Hal Purdy designed short course. There are wooded areas here with an abundance of ditches along the sides and across the fairways to add to the variety and difficulty.

Directions: Essex County, #19 on East Central Map
GSP or NJ Tpke to Rte. 78West. Take Rte.24West and exit at Hobart Gap Rd. Bear left onto White Oak Ridge. Entrance to golf is through Gero Park Recreational Center for Millburn Township.

Hole	1	2	3	4	5	6	7	8	9	Out	BLUE	Rating
BLUE												Slope
WHITE	90	125	125	110	150	175	175	125	110	1185		
Par	3	3	3	3	3	3	3	3	3	27	WHITE	Rating
Handicap												Slope
RED												
Par											RED	Rating
Handicap												Slope

Hole	10	11	12	13	14	15	16	17	18	In		Totals
BLUE											BLUE	
WHITE											WHITE	1185
Par											Par	27
Handicap												
RED											RED	
Par											Par	
Handicap												

Director of Recreation: Tom Sharpe
Architect: Hal Purdy 1970s

MONTCLAIR GOLF CLUB

25 Prospect Ave., West Orange, NJ 07052   **(973) 239-0160**

Montclair is a golf club with 4 separate nines that can be played in various combinations. It is open 6 days a week all year. Guests play accompanied by a member. Reserved tee times are not necessary. The scorecard below is for the first and second nines.

> • **Driving Range**   • **Lockers**
> • **Practice Green**   • **Showers**
> • **Power Carts**   • **Food**
>   Pull Carts   • **Clubhouse**
> • **Club Rental**   • **Outings**
> • **Caddies**   • **Soft Spikes**

Course Description: Montclair celebrated its 100th anniversary in 1993. These courses, built by Donald Ross and Charles Banks, have elevation changes up to 500 feet. Each nine starts on a hill and plays into a valley where creeks meander. Grassy hollows with lush greens can be found here. The demanding 454 yard 2nd hole on the 4th nine requires a long approach shot to an elevated green and provides the ultimate in shot-making opportunities. Montclair can boast of beautiful, well-manicured greens and great views.

Directions: Essex County, #20 on East Central Map
GSP or NJTpke to Rte. 280West. Take Exit 8B(Cedar Grove-Prospect Ave.) Follow Prospect for 1 mile; club is on the left.

Hole	1	2	3	4	5	6	7	8	9	Out	BLUE	Rating 70.9
BLUE	387	386	410	420	181	557	326	160	416	3243		Slope 126
WHITE	361	365	397	411	174	529	315	130	396	3078		
Par	4	4	4	4	3	5	4	3	4	35	WHITE	Rating 70.2
Handicap	9	6	4	1	5	2	7	8	3			Slope 124
RED	340	352	357	402	167	444	304	123	371	2860		
Par	4	4	4	5	3	5	4	3	5	37	RED	Rating
Handicap	8	6	4	1	7	2	5	8	3			Slope
Hole	10	11	12	13	14	15	16	17	18	In		Totals
BLUE	570	163	460	360	207	443	353	324	396	3276	BLUE	6519
WHITE	567	154	440	354	200	387	346	315	383	3146	WHITE	6224
Par	5	3	4	4	3	4	4	4	4	35	Par	70
Handicap	2	9	1	6	8	4	5	7	3			
RED	511	143	405	347	155	367	283	306	368	2885	RED	5745
Par	5	3	5	4	3	4	4	4	5	37	Par	74
Handicap	1	8	2	4	9	6	7	5	3			

Manager: Alan Gamble   **Pro:** Mike Stubblefield, PGA   **Supt:** Gregg Vadala
Architects: Donald Ross, Charles Banks 1893

MOUNTAIN RIDGE COUNTRY CLUB

713 Passaic Ave., West Caldwell, NJ 07006   (973) 575-0734

Mountain Ridge is an 18 hole course open 6 days a week from March through December. Guests play accompanied by a member. Tee time reservations are necessary for weekends.

•**Driving Range**	•**Lockers**
•**Practice Green**	•**Showers**
•**Power Carts**	•**Food**
Pull Carts	•**Clubhouse**
•**Club Rental**	•**Outings**
•**Caddies**	•**Soft Spikes**

Course Description: Mountain Ridge is a traditional meticulously maintained Donald Ross layout with wide fairways, old trees and difficult undulating greens. The course is well watered and plays long. It is nearly 6000 yards from the forward tees with seven par 5s!! The par 3 16th requires accuracy on the carry over water to avoid the many bunkers around the green. The long beautiful 8th always has the wind in your face. The uphill 18th needs careful placement; the golfer should bear left, but not so much as to go OB. Landing to the right will cause the approach shot to be blocked by a tree. The back to front severely sloped green makes the smart golfer go for a spot below the hole.

Directions: Essex County, #21 on East Central Map
Rte. 80 to Exit 52. Make a right turn onto Passaic Ave.South and go through 3 traffic lights (about 3 miles). Club is ahead on the right.

Hole	1	2	3	4	5	6	7	8	9	Out	BLUE	Rating 73.0
BLUE	414	435	338	213	410	498	161	476	491	3436		Slope 129
WHITE	408	425	324	205	395	480	150	463	473	3323		
Par	4	4	4	3	4	5	3	4	5	36	WHITE	Rating 71.9
Handicap	9	3	15	11	5	13	18	1	7			Slope 127
RED	402	416	271	187	326	437	131	442	457	3069		
Par	4	5	4	3	4	5	3	5	5	38	RED	Rating 75.2
Handicap	7	9	15	13	11	3	17	5	1			Slope 131
Hole	10	11	12	13	14	15	16	17	18	In		Totals
BLUE	412	413	370	454	169	392	157	548	452	3367	BLUE	6803
WHITE	401	401	355	441	160	383	130	535	442	3248	WHITE	6571
Par	4	4	4	4	3	4	3	5	4	35	Par	71
Handicap	12	6	14	2	16	10	18	8	4			
RED	390	343	287	399	152	353	107	455	431	2917	RED	5986
Par	4	4	4	5	3	4	3	5	5	37	Par	75
Handicap	8	12	14	4	16	10	18	2	6			

Manager: Stephen Wolsky   **Pro:** Mike Burke, Jr. PGA   **Supt:** Steve Kopach
Architect: Donald Ross 1929

OAK RIDGE GOLF COURSE

PUBLIC

136 Oak Ridge Rd., Clark, NJ 07066   **(732) 574-0139**

Oak Ridge is an 18 hole Union County Park System course open 7 days a week all year. Tee times are made through an automated system. County residents purchase an ID. Union Cty has reciprocity with Middlesex & Bergen Seniors w/ID on weekdays.

Driving Range	Lockers
• **Practice Green**	Showers
• **Power Carts**	• **Food**
• **Pull Carts**	• **Clubhouse**
• **Club Rental**	Outings
• **Soft Spikes**	

Fees	Weekday	Weekend
Res/ID	$12	$14
Sr/ID	$8	$13.50
Non-res	$24	$28
Power carts	$22/18	$14/9

Course Description: Oak Ridge is a relatively short course with small, fairly fast undulating greens. Recent upgrades have made the fairways more narrow and the rough more challenging. Out of bounds on the right, where an errant shot may land on the railroad tracks, can cause some difficulty. The course is well-bunkered and carefully maintained.

Directions: Union County, #22 on East Central Map
GSP to Exit 135. Go right to Central Ave. At first light, make a left onto Raritan Rd. Go 2 miles on Raritan which becomes Oak Ridge to club on right.

Hole	1	2	3	4	5	6	7	8	9	Out	BLUE	Rating 70.0
BLUE	391	480	129	405	410	217	432	400	334	3198		Slope 110
WHITE	378	454	111	382	380	182	422	363	317	2989		
Par	4	5	3	4	4	3	4	4	4	35	WHITE	Rating 68.0
Handicap	10	8	18	4	6	16	1	12	14			Slope 107
RED	330	400	93	317	352	151	383	333	227	2586		
Par	4	5	3	4	4	3	5	4	4	36	RED	Rating 69.7
Handicap	4	4	15	4	13	4	5	5	14			Slope 106
Hole	10	11	12	13	14	15	16	17	18	In		Totals
BLUE	422	340	400	155	432	457	348	213	423	3190	BLUE	6388
WHITE	416	320	394	127	378	450	339	192	396	3012	WHITE	6001
Par	4	4	4	3	4	5	4	3	4	35	Par	70
Handicap	5	13	9	17	7	3	11	15	2			
RED	333	285	362	110	343	407	297	168	370	2675	RED	5261
Par	4	4	4	3	4	5	4	3	5	36	Par	72
Handicap	5	11	9	17	7	1	13	15	3			

Manager: Nick Renna   **Pro:** Bill McCluney, PGA   **Supt:** Cormac Hamilton
Architect: Willard Wilkinson 1928

ROCK SPRING CLUB

Rock Spring Rd., West Orange, NJ 07052   **(973) 731-6466**

Rock Spring is an 18 hole course open all year 6 days a week.   Guests play accompanied by a member. Reservations may be necessary on weekends.

•**Driving Range**	•**Lockers**
•**Practice Green**	•**Showers**
•**Power Carts**	•**Food**
Pull Carts	•**Clubhouse**
•**Club Rental**	•**Outings**
•**Caddies**	•**Soft Spikes**

Course Description: The builder of this course, Charles "Steamshovel" Banks, is responsible for the deep bunkers, characteristic of this architect's style. With narrow fairways and tricky approach shots, the golfer must deal with formidable challenges. Upon reaching the green of the long par 3 third hole, a magnificent view of the New York City skyline can be seen. Cable Lake comes into play on the first and second holes and adds to the picturesque quality of this interesting layout.

Directions: Essex County, #23 on East Central Map
GSP to Exit 145. Take Rte. 280West to Exit 10 (Northfield Ave.) Turn left and go through 3 lights on Northfield. At top of mountain, turn left onto Rock Spring Rd., just before the 4th light and proceed to club.

Hole	1	2	3	4	5	6	7	8	9	Out	BLUE	Rating
BLUE												Slope
WHITE	346	384	194	443	396	526	374	318	411	3392		
Par	4	4	3	4	4	5	4	4	4	36	WHITE	Rating 71.2
Handicap	15	3	9	1	7	13	11	17	5			Slope 124
RED	327	374	177	435	389	520	345	246	397	3232		
Par	4	4	3	5	4	5	4	4	5	38	RED	Rating 75.3
Handicap	7	1	9	6	2	5	8	4	3			Slope 132

Hole	10	11	12	13	14	15	16	17	18	In		Totals
BLUE											BLUE	
WHITE	140	377	419	467	311	416	178	410	335	3053	WHITE	6445
Par	3	4	4	5	4	4	3	4	4	35	Par	71
Handicap	18	8	2	14	16	6	10	4	12			
RED	139	368	402	449	304	405	150	364	322	2894	RED	6126
Par	3	4	5	5	4	5	3	4	4	37	Par	75
Handicap	18	6	8	2	12	10	16	4	14			

Pro: Baker Maddera, PGA   **Supt:** Wayne Remo
Architect: Charles Banks 1925

ROSELLE GOLF CLUB

417 Raritan Rd., Roselle, NJ 07203   **(908) 245-9671**

Roselle is a 9 hole course open 6 days a week and closed for the month of February. Guests play accompanied by a member. Tee time reservations are necessary for weekends.

•**Driving Range**	•**Lockers**
•**Practice Green**	•**Showers**
•**Power Carts**	•**Food**
•**Pull Carts**	•**Clubhouse**
•**Club Rental**	•**Outings**
Caddies	•**Soft Spikes**

Course Description: Roselle is a fairly flat course in excellent condition. The greens are fast and substantially sloped. A pond and two streams affect play on 3 of the holes. There is a separate set of tees for the second nine. Although a short course, it is interesting enough to demand the golfer's concentration. A new clubhouse has recently been completed.

Directions: Union County, #24 on East Central Map
GSPNorth to Exit 136. Make a right at exit and left onto Raritan Rd. Club is ahead on right. OR GSPSouth to Exit 136. Turn right and go to jughandle for Raritan Rd and turn left. Club is ahead on the right.

Hole	1	2	3	4	5	6	7	8	9	Out	BLUE	Rating
BLUE												Slope
WHITE	358	549	453	426	342	212	291	138	335	3104		
Par	4	5	5	4	4	3	4	3	4	36	WHITE	Rating 70.4
Handicap	9	3	11	1	7	5	17	15	13			Slope 121
RED	320	436	381	395	330	209	217	120	298	2706		
Par	4	5	5	5	4	4	4	3	4	38	RED	Rating 66.9
Handicap	9	3	1	5	7	15	13	17	11			Slope 113
Hole	10	11	12	13	14	15	16	17	18	In		Totals
BLUE											BLUE	
WHITE	371	530	458	404	355	326	150	124	329	3047	WHITE	6151
Par	4	5	5	4	4	4	3	3	4	36	Par	72
Handicap	6	4	10	2	8	12	16	18	14			
RED	328	435	381	395	259	305	144	111	306	2664	RED	5390
Par	4	5	5	5	4	4	3	3	4	37	Par	75
Handicap	10	4	2	6	14	8	16	18	12			

Pro: Vincent Harmon, PGA   **Supt:** Gregg M. Sullivan
Architect: Seth Raynor 1917

SCOTCH HILLS COUNTRY CLUB

PUBLIC

820 Jerusalem Rd., Scotch Plains, NJ 07076   **(908) 232-9748**

Scotch Hills is a municipally owned, 9 hole course open to the public 7 days a week from Mar. 15 to Dec. 15. Memberships are available. Tee time reservations are not necessary. Greens fee is good all day.

Driving Range	Lockers
• **Practice Green**	Showers
• **Power Carts**	Food
• **Pull Carts**	Clubhouse
• **Club Rental**	Outings
• **Soft Spikes**	

Fees	Weekday	Weekend
Mbrs	$8	$10
Sr.	$6	$10
Non-mbrs	$15	$20
Power carts	$10/9	

Course Description: Scotch Hills, a short, hilly and tight course, is well groomed and known for its small well conditioned, fast greens. At one time, it was called Shady Rest CC and was the first black CC in the country. John Shippen, the pro at Scotch Hills in the late 19th century, was part black and part Shinnecock Indian. He was the first American born US Pro and played, after some controversy, in the 1896 US Open at Shinnecock. Cab Calloway, Louis Armstrong and Count Basie golfed here. It is now a popular golf course for all players in the area.

Directions: Union County, #25 on East Central Map
Take GSP to Exit 140A to Rte. 22West. Exit at Mountain Ave. in Scotch Plains (not Mtn. Ave. in Westfield). Take Mountain Ave 3 blocks to Jerusalem Rd. and turn left. Go to the last driveway on the right to club.

Hole	1	2	3	4	5	6	7	8	9	Out	BLUE	Rating
BLUE												Slope
WHITE	298	324	164	309	230	210	166	358	188	2247		
Par	4	4	3	4	4	4	3	4	3	33	WHITE	Rating 61.2
Handicap	7	3	13	5	9	11	15	1	17			Slope 106
RED	287	278	141	280	212	169	148	239	168	2022		
Par	4	5	3	4	4	4	3	5	3	35	RED	Rating 64.6
Handicap	5	3	13	1	9	11	17	7	15			Slope 110
Hole	10	11	12	13	14	15	16	17	18	In		Totals
BLUE											BLUE	
WHITE											WHITE	4494
Par											Par	66
Handicap												
RED											RED	4044
Par											Par	70
Handicap												

Manager/Pro: John Turnbull, PGA   **Supt:** Chuck De Francesco
Built: 1889

SHACKAMAXON GOLF & CC

Shackamaxon Drive, Scotch Plains, NJ 07076   **(908) 233-3989**

Shackamaxon is an 18 hole course open 6 days a week all year. Guests play accompanied by a member. Tee time reservations are necessary on weekends.

- **Driving Range**
- **Practice Green**
- **Power Carts**
- Pull Carts
- **Club Rental**
- **Caddies**

- **Lockers**
- **Showers**
- **Food**
- **Clubhouse**
- **Outings**
- **Soft Spikes**

Course Description: Shackamaxon golf course is an example of the classic Tillinghast design characterized by gently rolling fairways and small fast greens. The signature par 4 ninth hole is one of the most intimidating in the metropolitan area due in part to its island green and the lake to carry on the tee shot. Five other holes have water in play. In the 1950s, Shackamaxon hosted a PGA tour event known as the "Cavalcade of Golf."

Directions: Union County, #26 on East Central Map
GSPSouth to Exit 135 (Central Ave). Go past light & make left onto Terminal Ave. Turn right onto Westfield Ave (Rahway Ave on one side) over RR crossing. Take first left onto Lambert Mill Rd. Proceed 2 miles and turn left onto Shackamaxon Dr. Go 1 block to clubhouse.

Hole	1	2	3	4	5	6	7	8	9	Out	BLUE	Rating 71.3
BLUE	281	401	330	402	205	364	480	449	393	3305		Slope 126
WHITE	274	389	321	387	191	356	469	437	376	3200		
Par	4	4	4	4	3	4	5	4	4	36	WHITE	Rating 70.0
Handicap	17	7	13	1	15	11	9	3	5			Slope 123
RED	234	372	312	368	169	344	391	401	299	2890		
Par	4	4	4	4	3	4	5	5	4	37	RED	Rating 71.6
Handicap	17	5	15	1	13	9	3	7	11			Slope 126
Hole	10	11	12	13	14	15	16	17	18	In		Totals
BLUE	552	152	422	533	219	403	457	200	349	3287	BLUE	6592
WHITE	540	140	405	520	204	394	454	189	340	3186	WHITE	6386
Par	5	3	4	5	3	4	5	3	4	36	Par	72
Handicap	2	18	6	4	14	8	10	16	12			
RED	440	126	388	445	190	384	386	179	307	2845	RED	5735
Par	5	3	4	5	3	4	5	3	4	36	Par	73
Handicap	2	18	6	4	14	8	10	12	16			

Manager: George Pluhar   **Pro:** Peter Busch, PGA   **Supt:** Jack Martin
Architect: A. W. Tillinghast 1916

SUBURBAN GOLF CLUB

1730 Morris Ave., Union, NJ 07083   **(908) 686-0444**

Suburban is an 18 hole course open 6 days a week all year. Guests play accompanied by a member. Tee time reservations are not necessary.

•**Driving Range**	•**Lockers**
•**Practice Green**	•**Showers**
•**Power Carts**	•**Food**
Pull Carts	•**Clubhouse**
•**Club Rental**	•**Outings**
•**Caddies**	•**Soft Spikes**

Course Description: Suburban is relatively short with narrow rolling fairways and small, undulating greens. Uneven lies abound. The course is well tree-lined; not much water is in play. The bunkering is typical of the traditional Tillinghast architectual style. Originally designed with six holes, it was later expanded to the full 18. A challenging layout, it is particularly picturesque during the fall foliage season. 1996 was Suburban's Centennial year.

Directions: Union County, #27 on East Central Map
GSPSouth to Exit 140A. Take Rte.82East (Morris Ave.) towards Elizabeth and Goethals Bridge by bearing right off exit ramp and turning right. Club is ahead on the right.

Hole	1	2	3	4	5	6	7	8	9	Out	BLUE	Rating 71.7
BLUE	361	385	210	430	472	372	339	341	366	3276		Slope 133
WHITE	348	365	196	416	464	355	312	328	354	3138		
Par	4	4	3	4	5	4	4	4	4	36	WHITE	Rating 70.4
Handicap	13	11	15	1	7	3	17	5	9			Slope 130
RED	330	339	180	324	447	337	291	322	345	2915		
Par	4	4	3	4	5	4	4	4	4	36	RED	Rating 72.4
Handicap	11	13	16	9	1	3	15	5	7			Slope 123
Hole	10	11	12	13	14	15	16	17	18	In		Totals
BLUE	314	167	540	403	393	382	160	388	400	3147	BLUE	6423
WHITE	294	157	515	390	377	365	141	369	377	2985	WHITE	6123
Par	4	3	5	4	4	4	3	4	4	35	Par	71
Handicap	16	14	6	4	2	10	18	12	8			
RED	258	130	488	373	361	348	119	349	360	2786	RED	5701
Par	4	3	5	4	5	4	3	4	4	36	Par	72
Handicap	14	17	2	6	4	10	18	12	8			

Manager: Dan McHugh   **Pro:** Kevin Syring, PGA   **Supt:** Ken Givens
Architect: A. W. Tillinghast 1896

SUMMIT MUNICIPAL GOLF COURSE

River Rd. & Route 24, Summit, NJ 07901   (908) 277-6828

Summit Municipal is a par 3 course open 7 days a week from the 3rd week in March to early Dec. Memberships are available only to residents of Summit. Guests play accompanied by a member.

Driving Range	Lockers
• **Practice Green**	Showers
Power Carts	Food
• **Pull Carts**	Clubhouse
• **Club Rental**	Outings
Caddies	• **Soft Spikes**

Course Description: This par 3 nine hole course is appreciated by the residents of Summit for its proximity and availability. It affords its townspeople a good place to learn and play inexpensively. Children and seniors can get to play often and practice the basics. The short layout means that woods are generally not used here. There is even a lake in the middle of the course, on the 4th hole, to give players the opportunity to hitover water.

Directions: Union County, #28 on East Central Map
GSP or NJTpke to Rte. 78West. At exit #48, take Rte. 24West to River Rd. Look for Short Hills Mall; go around circle and course is on right on River Rd.

Hole	1	2	3	4	5	6	7	8	9	Out	BLUE	Rating
BLUE												Slope
WHITE	82	106	65	122	100	73	159	142	140	989		
Par	3	3	3	3	3	3	3	3	3	27	WHITE	Rating
Handicap												Slope
RED												
Par											RED	Rating
Handicap												Slope
Hole	10	11	12	13	14	15	16	17	18	In		Totals
BLUE											BLUE	
WHITE											WHITE	
Par											Par	
Handicap												
RED											RED	
Par											Par	
Handicap												

Director of Recreation: Bruce Kaufman
Built: 1960s

WEEQUAHIC PARK GOLF COURSE

PUBLIC

Elizabeth Åve., Newark, NJ 07114   **(201) 923-1838**

Weequahic Park is an 18 hole Essex County course open 7 days a week all year. Through an automated system, ID holders may make tee times up to 7 days in advance.

Driving Range	
• **Practice Green**	Lockers
• **Power Carts**	Showers
Pull Carts	• **Food**
Club Rental	• **Clubhouse**
• **Soft Spikes**	• **Outings**

Fees	Weekday	Weekend
Res/ID	$11	$22
Non-res	$22	$26
Power Carts	$12pp	

Course Description: Weequahic Park is located in a county park along a lake fed by artesian wells that keep it clean. The fairways are narrow with elevated greens. Few level lies can be found on this hilly layout. The golfer finds little relief when reaching the greens that rarely yield straight putts. The 3rd would be considered the signature hole, a long par 5. Water is in play on a few holes. New tee boxes have been installed recently and the clubhouse is being renovated.

Directions: Essex County, #29 on East Central Map
NJTpke to Exit 14. Take Rte.78West to Rte.22West in Newark. Exit at Frelinghuysen Ave. South. After Meeker Ave, bear right onto Dayton St. and continue into Weequahic Park. Follow signs to golf course.

Hole	1	2	3	4	5	6	7	8	9	Out	BLUE	Rating
BLUE												Slope
WHITE	323	141	490	383	101	477	300	142	326	2683		
Par	4	3	5	4	3	5	4	3	4	35	WHITE	Rating 66.0
Handicap	10	16	1	6	18	2	12	15	9			Slope 106
RED	303	135	410	377	101	462	294	142	321	2542		
Par	4	3	5	4	3	5	4	3	4	35	RED	Rating
Handicap	7	16	2	3	18	1	9	15	6			Slope

Hole	10	11	12	13	14	15	16	17	18	In		Totals
BLUE											BLUE	
WHITE	466	173	372	408	334	285	397	127	364	2926	WHITE	5609
Par	5	3	4	4	4	4	4	3	4	35	Par	70
Handicap	3	13	7	4	11	14	5	17	8			
RED	368	168	302	338	284	255	263	125	274	2377	RED	4922
Par	5	3	4	4	4	4	4	3	4	35	Par	70
Handicap	4	14	8	5	10	13	12	17	11			

Manager/Pro: Jim Feaster, PGA   **Supt:** Joe Ciccone
Built: 1915 1st nine   1959 2nd nine

WEST CENTRAL REGION

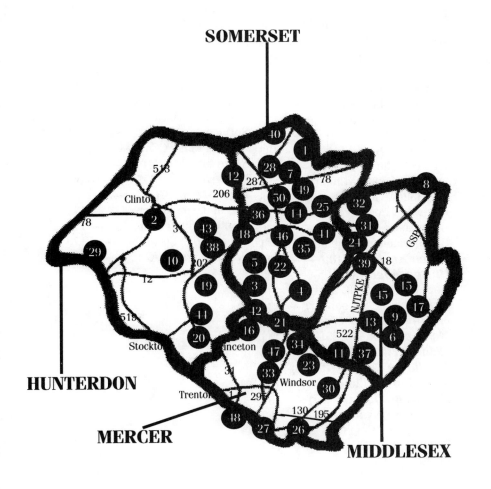

SOMERSET

HUNTERDON

MERCER

MIDDLESEX

WEST CENTRAL REGION

Public Courses appear in
bold italics

BASKING RIDGE COUNTRY CLUB

185 Madisonville Rd., Basking Ridge, NJ 07920   (908) 766-8200

Basking Ridge is an 18 hole course that is open from mid-March through Dec. 15, 6 days a week. Guests may play accompanied by a member. Tee time reservations are necessary; call between 8-10 AM, Tues.-Sun.

•Driving Range	•Lockers
•Practice Green	•Showers
•Power Carts	•Food
•Pull Carts	•Clubhouse
•Club Rental	•Outings
Caddies	•Soft Spikes

Course Description: Designed in 1926 by Alexander Findlay, (the architect of over 500 golf courses in various parts of the US), Basking Ridge is relatively long and flat with tight tree-lined fairways and small fast greens. Originally a public course called Pembroke Golf Club, Basking Ridge is set amidst the serene beauty of the neighboring national wildlife refuge. Three holes have elevation changes and water is in play on several holes. The par 3 signature 18th has one of the largest greens in New Jersey; it is three tiered and penalizes the errant shot with a possible 3 putt or chip and two putts. The clubhouse was recently renovated.

Directions: Somerset County, #1 on West Central Map
Take Rte. 80 West to Rte. 287 South to Exit #30A (North Maple Ave.). Go 1/2 mile to light and turn left onto Madisonville Rd. Club is second driveway on right.

Hole	1	2	3	4	5	6	7	8	9	Out	BLUE	Rating 72.7
BLUE	379	525	127	454	188	533	453	333	377	3369		Slope 125
WHITE	344	496	115	411	170	497	434	309	361	3137		
Par	4	5	3	4	3	5	4	4	4	36	WHITE	Rating 71.4
Handicap	13	1	17	9	15	3	7	11	5			Slope 123
RED	293	392	89	391	116	404	391	280	335	2691		
Par	4	5	3	4	3	5	5	4	4	37	RED	Rating 72.2
Handicap	13	1	17	5	15	7	9	11	3			Slope 117
Hole	10	11	12	13	14	15	16	17	18	In		Totals
BLUE	425	330	367	410	461	449	153	389	190	3174	BLUE	6543
WHITE	402	316	337	400	447	424	137	379	180	3022	WHITE	6159
Par	4	4	4	4	5	4	3	4	3	35	Par	71
Handicap	4	10	12	8	18	2	16	6	14			
RED	325	284	276	396	382	364	114	323	168	2632	RED	5323
Par	4	4	4	5	5	4	3	4	3	36	Par	73
Handicap	8	12	16	2	10	4	18	6	14			

Manager: David Karner   **Pro:** Bill Spicer, PGA   **Supt:** Les Stout
Architect: Alexander Findlay 1926

BEAVER BROOK COUNTRY CLUB

PUBLIC

PO Box 5171 Rte.#31, Clinton, NJ 08809   **(908) 735-4022**

Beaver Brook is an 18 hole semi-private course open to the public 7 days a week in season and 6 days off season. Memberships are available. Call up to 7 days in advance for tee times; members 14 day advance. Info: 1-800 433-8567.

• **Driving Range**	• **Lockers**
• **Practice Green**	• **Showers**
• **Power Carts**	• **Food**
• **Pull Carts**	• **Clubhouse**
• **Club Rental**	• **Outings**
• **Soft Spikes**	

Fees	Weekday	Weekend
Mon-Thur	$54	$72
Fri.		$72
Twi (Mon-Th) $35		$45
Power carts included		

Course Description: Formerly a private club, Beaver Brook presents a challenging and interesting layout. It is located in a country setting, with stately oaks, maples and other beautiful trees. Its hilly rolling terrain is a strong test of golf. The large, well contoured greens are difficult to read with some deceptive breaks. The signature par 4 # 11 has a big tree in the center of the fairway. Water comes into play on the 6th, 7th and 15th holes. The pro shop is attractive and well stocked.

Directions: Hunterdon County, #2 on West Central Map
Take Rte. 78 West to Exit #17. Follow signs to Rte. 31 South. Watch for club on right shortly after entering Rte. 31 S.

Hole	1	2	3	4	5	6	7	8	9	Out	BLUE	Rating 71.7
BLUE	462	501	400	164	400	399	174	395	290	3185		Slope 125
WHITE	437	478	390	134	371	384	159	380	254	2987		
Par	5	5	4	3	4	4	3	4	4	36	WHITE	Rating 70.4
Handicap	3	11	7	17	9	5	15	1	13			Slope 122
RED	407	434	275	101	316	369	144	325	194	2565		
Par	5	5	4	3	4	4	3	4	4	36	RED	Rating 71.7
Handicap	9	7	13	17	5	1	11	3	15			Slope 122
Hole	10	11	12	13	14	15	16	17	18	In		Totals
BLUE	354	384	136	380	155	446	467	510	506	3338	BLUE	6523
WHITE	349	361	112	367	143	436	414	482	471	3135	WHITE	6122
Par	4	4	3	4	3	4	4	5	5	36	Par	72
Handicap	10	6	18	4	14	2	8	16	12			
RED	277	290	100	341	115	384	349	402	460	2718	RED	5283
Par	4	4	3	4	3	4	4	5	5	36	Par	72
Handicap	10	6	18	4	12	2	14	16	8			

Manager: Matt Kerins   **Pro:** Rod Granger, PGA   **Supt:** Chuck Lane
Architect: Alex Ternyei 1965

THE BEDENS BROOK CLUB

Rolling Hill Rd., Skillman, NJ 08558   **(609) 466-3063**

Bedens Brook is a private 18 hole golf course open 6 days a week between April 15 and Dec. 15. Guests may play accompanied by a member. Reservations for tee times are not necessary.

•**Driving Range**	•**Lockers**
•**Practice Green**	•**Showers**
•**Power Carts**	•**Food**
•**Pull Carts**	•**Clubhouse**
•**Club Rental**	•**Outings**
•**Caddies**	•**Soft Spikes**

Course Description: Excellently maintained and constantly being upgraded under the supervision of its architect, Dick Wilson, Bedens Brook is a fine example of New Jersey golf. Hilly with well bunkered greens, accuracy is at a premium here. The 17th, "The Dick Wilson" hole, is 581 yards from the back tees and is a long dogleg left. The Bedens Brook crosses the signature hole twice. This facility is well managed and challenging.

Directions: Somerset County, #3 on West Central Map
NJTpke. to Exit #9. Take Rte. 1 South for 6 miles to Finnegan's Lane & turn right. At first light (Rte.27), go left. Proceed for about 3 miles to Rte. 518 (forks to right). Go 3 traffic lights & after 3rd, look for & take 1st left onto Rolling Hill Rd. to club.

Hole	1	2	3	4	5	6	7	8	9	Out	BLUE	Rating 73.2
BLUE	382	149	578	397	331	188	515	388	379	3307		Slope 134
WHITE	367	134	527	382	320	173	507	377	367	3154		
Par	4	3	5	4	4	3	5	4	4	36	WHITE	Rating 71.9
Handicap	7	17	1	3	13	15	11	9	5			Slope 131
RED	337	119	429	322	279	156	440	292	318	2692		
Par	4	3	5	4	4	3	5	4	4	36	RED	Rating 72.6
Handicap	9	17	3	5	11	15	1	13	7			Slope 128
Hole	10	11	12	13	14	15	16	17	18	In		Totals
BLUE	414	395	496	175	317	433	225	581	437	3473	BLUE	6780
WHITE	403	383	466	158	307	417	202	567	427	3330	WHITE	6484
Par	4	4	5	3	4	4	3	5	4	36	Par	72
Handicap	8	6	14	18	16	4	12	10	2			
RED	316	299	400	144	291	352	174	485	418	2879	RED	5571
Par	4	4	5	3	4	4	3	5	5	37	Par	73
Handicap	12	10	8	18	14	6	16	2	4			

Manager: Michael Rudon   **Pro:** Doug Schamback, PGA   **Supt:** Benny Peta
Architect: Dick Wilson 1965

BUNKER HILL GOLF COURSE

Bunker Hill Rd. RD #1, Princeton, NJ 08540   **(908) 359-6335**

Bunker Hill is a privately owned 18 hole course open to the public 7 days a week all year. Tee times can be reserved for weekends 7 days in advance.

Driving Range	•**Lockers**
•**Practice Green**	•**Showers**
•**Power Carts**	•**Food**
•**Pull Carts**	•**Clubhouse**
•**Club Rental**	•**Outings**
•**Soft Spikes**	

Fees	**Weekday**	**Weekend**
Daily	$31.50	$45
Sr.	$28.50	
Power carts included in price		

Course Description: Bunker Hill is an open course that can be quite challenging. The signature third is a par 4 with an elevated tee box. Its tee shot is over a creek and the approach shot is tight. This creek comes into play on five holes. The par 3 sixth hole is from an elevated tee to a green surrounded by trees. Numbers 9 and 18 have uphill approach shots to the green. Bunker Hill can get quite busy in season.

Directions: Somerset County, #4 on West Central Map
From North: NJTPK to Exit #9. Follow signs to Rte. 1 South and take it to New Rd. Go right and cross Rte. 27 to Bunker Hill Rd. Course is ahead on right.

Hole	1	2	3	4	5	6	7	8	9	Out	BLUE	Rating
BLUE												Slope
WHITE	361	302	376	160	325	183	502	335	486	3030		
Par	4	4	4	3	4	3	5	4	5	36	WHITE	Rating 67.9
Handicap	5	11	1	17	9	13	7	15	3			Slope 111
RED	350	292	360	150	313	170	488	323	478	2924		
Par	4	4	5	3	4	3	5	4	5	37	RED	Rating 72.6
Handicap	6	9	2	8	5	4	1	7	3			Slope 113
Hole	10	11	12	13	14	15	16	17	18	In		Totals
BLUE											BLUE	
WHITE	330	286	492	186	365	145	347	301	483	2935	WHITE	5965
Par	4	4	5	3	4	3	4	4	5	36	Par	72
Handicap	4	14	8	16	6	18	10	12	2			
RED	312	275	480	173	355	140	340	290	477	2842	RED	5766
Par	5	4	5	3	4	3	4	4	5	37	Par	74
Handicap	6	12	4	16	8	18	10	14	2			

Manager: Dave Wasnick   **Pro:** Tedd Torkildsen   **Supt:** Joe Gunson
Architect: Holliss Yarbough 1972

CHERRY VALLEY COUNTRY CLUB

133 Country Club Dr., Skillman, NJ 08558   **(609) 466-4464**

Cherry Valley is an 18 hole golf course that is open 6 days a week from Feb. through December. Guests play accompanied by a member; no member needed from Tues.-Thurs. Tee times may be made up to 4 days in advance.

- •**Driving Range**
- •**Practice Green**
- •**Power Carts**
- Pull Carts
- •**Club Rental**
- •**Caddies**
- •**Lockers**
- •**Showers**
- •**Food**
- •**Clubhouse**
- •**Outings**
- •**Soft Spikes**

Course Description: Under the creative brilliance of Rees Jones, Cherry Valley was conceived and beautifully designed; the front in 1991 & the wooded back in 1992. This challenging course is built in a links style on a former farm. Cherry Valley has bent grass fairways and greens; some creeks and mounds are encountered on the front nine. The large undulating greens are well bunkered and have a lot of break. The par 4 eleventh signature hole has a huge cherry tree left of the tee. There are large new homes surrounding the property. The new pro shop and clubhouse are outstanding.

Directions: Somerset County #5 on West Central Map
NJTPKE South to Exit #9; follow signs to Rte. 18 to Rte.1 South. Take Rte. 1 to the Raymond Rd. exit (approx. 13 miles). Then take Rte.27 thru Princeton to Rte.206South. Almost immediately, turn right onto Elm Rd. which becomes The Great Road for approx. 4 miles; look for Country Club Dr. on left. Go left to club.

Hole	1	2	3	4	5	6	7	8	9	Out	BLUE	Rating 72.3
BLUE	363	212	513	430	360	441	408	165	555	3447		Slope 126
WHITE	332	187	477	399	330	396	360	137	531	3149		
Par	4	3	5	4	4	4	4	3	5	36	WHITE	Rating 70.5
Handicap	7	15	5	1	13	11	9	17	3			Slope 128
RED	310	100	435	376	310	370	338	115	410	2764		
Par	4	3	5	4	4	4	4	3	5	36	RED	Rating 71.6
Handicap	13	17	3	5	11	7	9	15	1			Slope 124
Hole	10	11	12	13	14	15	16	17	18	In		Totals
BLUE	526	179	393	358	174	466	496	440	451	3483	BLUE	6930
WHITE	490	162	360	335	143	417	452	413	395	3167	WHITE	6316
Par	5	3	4	4	3	4	5	4	4	36	Par	72
Handicap	2	16	6	12	18	14	4	10	8			
RED	420	123	326	283	130	387	412	327	287	2695	RED	5399
Par	5	3	4	4	3	4	5	4	4	36	Par	72
Handicap	2	16	6	12	18	4	8	10	14			

Manager: Dave Whalen   **Pro:** Allan Bowman, PGA   **Supt:** Dennis Shea
Architect: Rees Jones 1991

CLEARBROOK GOLF CLUB

Applegarth Rd., Cranbury, NJ 08512   **(609) 655-3443**

Clearbrook is an adult community with a 9 hole golf course open 7 days a week 10 months a year. Guests play accompanied by a member. Tee times may be made in advance between 7AM-11AM in season. Memberships are available.

•**Driving Range**	Lockers
•**Practice Green**	Showers
•**Power Carts**	Food
•**Pull Carts**	•**Clubhouse**
Club Rental	•**Outings**
Caddies	•**Soft Spikes**

Course Description: Easily walkable and convenient to its community members, Clearbrook is playable almost all year round. With its rolling terrain and water in play on 5 holes, it presents an interesting round of golf without a great degree of difficulty. People who might be contemplating buying a house here should try the golf course. One can vary the feel of the course by changing tee placements on the second nine.

Directions: Middlesex County, #6 on West Central Map
NJTPKE South to Exit #8A. Then go East on Rte. 32 (Forsgate) to first light. Turn right on Applegarth Rd. Clearbrook is about 2 miles on the left.

Hole	1	2	3	4	5	6	7	8	9	Out	BLUE	Rating
BLUE												Slope
WHITE	474	147	501	360	173	363	405	371	154	2948		
Par	5	3	5	4	3	4	4/5	4	3	35/36	WHITE	Rating 67.7
Handicap	3	17	1	11	13	9	5	7	15			Slope 107
RED	457	125	442	330	153	326	353	325	125	2636		
Par	5	3	5	4	3	4	4/5	4	3	35/36	RED	Rating 68.9
Handicap	3	17	1	11	13	9	5	7	15			Slope 109
Hole	10	11	12	13	14	15	16	17	18	In		Totals
BLUE											BLUE	
WHITE											WHITE	5902
Par											Par	70/72
Handicap												
RED											RED	5225
Par											Par	70/72
Handicap												

Manager: Tony Wilcenski   **Pro:** Vic Calvaresi, PGA   **Supt:** Dave Lerner
Architect: Hal Purdy 1973

COAKLEY-RUSSO GOLF COURSE PRIVATE

151 Knollcroft Rd., Lyons, NJ 07939   **(908) 604-2582**

Coakley-Russo is a 9 hole private course for the use of out and in-patients, employees and volunteers of Lyons V.A. Hospital. It is open 7 days a week from April to Nov. Tee times may be made up to 1 week in advance.

Driving Range	Lockers
•**Practice Green**	Showers
Power Carts	Food
•**Pull Carts**	Clubhouse
Club Rental	Outings
Caddies	•**Soft Spikes**

Course Description: Relatively flat, open, and easy to walk, Coakley-Russo is a course that is run by the Basking Ridge Recreation Department and is part of the Lyons V.A. Hospital. There are no bunkers but there are 2 brooks affecting play on three holes; one brook runs across the entire course. The facility was built for the use of the patients for therapeutic purposes. Many volunteers play with the patients during the week and in tournaments. Golf gear will be gladly accepted as a donation.

Directions: Somerset County, #7 on West Central Map
Rte. 80 West to Rte.287 South to Exit #24. Go South on Maple Ave. to Basking Ridge. Make a left onto Finley Ave. (Rte. 527 spur). Road becomes Stonehouse Rd. Turn right onto Valley Rd. Hospital is on right; enter grounds and course is on the left.

Hole	1	2	3	4	5	6	7	8	9	Out	BLUE	Rating
BLUE												Slope
WHITE	495	215	375	127	430	336	370	455	317	3120		
Par	5	3	4	3	4	4	4	4	4	35	WHITE	Rating 70.4
Handicap	7	5	11	17	3	13	9	1	15			Slope 115
RED	436	165	300	127	350	310	320	380	270	2658		
Par	5	3	4	3	4	4	4	4	4	35	RED	Rating 70.8
Handicap	7	5	11	17	3	13	9	1	15			Slope 115
Hole	10	11	12	13	14	15	16	17	18	In		Totals
BLUE											BLUE	
WHITE											WHITE	6406
Par											Par	70
Handicap												
RED											RED	5316
Par											Par	70
Handicap												

Manager: Matt LaCourte, Jr.   **Supt:** Peter Wright
Architect: Robert Trent Jones, 1946

COLONIA COUNTRY CLUB

Colonia Blvd., Colonia, NJ 07067 **(732) 381-9500**

Colonia is an 18 hole private course open all year 6 days a week. Guests may play accompanied by a member. Reserved tee times are suggested.

•**Driving Range**	•**Lockers**
•**Practice Green**	•**Showers**
•**Power Carts**	•**Food**
Pull Carts	•**Clubhouse**
•**Club Rental**	•**Outings**
Caddies	•**Soft Spikes**

Course Description: Built in the late 1890s, Colonia is a relatively short and sporty traditional course (just celebrating its 100 year anniversary). Offering tight, tree lined fairways, its small undulating greens are usually fast and well bunkered. Water comes into play on several holes. The par five 4th could be considered the signature hole; it is a dogleg left with a pond in front of the green.

Directions: Middlesex County, #8 on West Central Map
GSP to Exit #131. Turn left onto Rte. 27 North. Go approx. 2 miles to traffic light and make a sharp left onto Colonia Blvd. Club is 1 mile on left.

Hole	1	2	3	4	5	6	7	8	9	Out	BLUE	Rating 70.4
BLUE	317	205	304	523	394	171	396	541	347	3198		Slope 120
WHITE	307	200	301	510	381	155	385	528	341	3108		
Par	4	3	4	5	4	3	4	5	4	36	WHITE	Rating 69.6
Handicap	15	11	13	1	5	17	7	3	9			Slope 118
RED	290	122	250	380	370	133	352	426	322	2645		
Par	4	3	4	5	5	3	4	5	4	37	RED	Rating 71.4
Handicap	11	17	13	1	5	15	7	3	9			Slope 121
Hole	10	11	12	13	14	15	16	17	18	In		Totals
BLUE	358	330	313	180	475	576	197	365	360	3154	BLUE	6352
WHITE	339	306	305	162	464	563	184	351	350	3024	WHITE	6132
Par	4	4	4	3	5	5	3	4	4	36	Par	72
Handicap	6	18	16	14	4	2	12	8	10			
RED	333	291	273	143	461	437	153	261	333	2685	RED	5330
Par	4	4	4	3	5	5	3	4	4	36	Par	73
Handicap	6	14	12	18	2	4	16	10	8			

Manager: Sal Vigilante   **Pro:** Len Siter, PGA   **Supt:** Lance Rogers
Architects: Tom Bendelow, Robert White, Hal Purdy, Frank Duane   **Built:** 1898

CONCORDIA GOLF COURSE

3 Clubhouse Dr., Cranbury, NJ 08512 **(609) 655-5631**

Concordia is a private 18 hole course on the grounds of an adult community. Some non-residents are members. It is open 7 days a week 10 months a year. Tee times may be reserved up to 3 days in advance.

- •**Driving Range**
- •**Practice Green**
- •**Power Carts**
- •**Pull Carts**
- •**Club Rental**
- Caddies
- •**Lockers**
- •**Showers**
- •**Food**
- •**Clubhouse**
- •**Outings**
- •**Soft Spikes**

Course Description: Narrow fairways, out of bounds on every hole and tricky pin placement contribute to Concordia's challenge. Its signature par 4 fourteenth hole has water off the tee and then again further up the hill. The boomerang shaped green provides various degrees of difficulty depending on the location of the pin. Water affects play on 11 holes; wayward shots do not often get caught in heavy rough. This section of New Jersey is one of the largest retirement areas in the United States. When available, a new scorecard will reflect new yardages and ratings.

Directions: Middlesex County, #9 on West Central Map
NJTPKE to Exit #8A. Go East on Forsgate Drive to Applegarth and turn right. Proceed to Prospect Plains Rd. Club is 1 & 1/2 miles on right.

Hole	1	2	3	4	5	6	7	8	9	Out	BLUE	Rating 69.0
BLUE	317	455	315	180	303	386	186	318	350	2810		Slope 117
WHITE	300	438	255	150	275	343	162	298	327	2548		
Par	4	5	4	3	4	4	3	4	4	35	WHITE	Rating 66.3
Handicap	16	10	12	6	8	2	14	18	4			Slope 112
RED	283	421	234	111	249	296	144	268	301	2307		
Par	4	5	4	3	4	4	3	4	4	35	RED	Rating 68.3
Handicap	7	1	9	6	2	5	8	4	3			Slope 113
Hole	10	11	12	13	14	15	16	17	18	In		Totals
BLUE	283	167	511	404	389	166	404	503	386	3213	BLUE	6039
WHITE	270	151	485	393	365	130	375	460	350	2979	WHITE	5527
Par	4	3	5	4	4	3	4	5	4	36	Par	71
Handicap	17	13	11	3	1	15	7	9	5			
RED	257	136	432	371	322	108	349	420	319	2714	RED	5021
Par	4	3	5	4	4	3	4	4	4	36	Par	71
Handicap	13	15	7	3	1	17	9	5	11			

Manager/Owner: Castle Golf Mgmt.   **Pro:** Kevin Kriews, PGA   **Supt:** Rolf Strobel
Architect: Edmund Ault 1983

COPPER HILL COUNTRY CLUB

Copper Hill Rd., Flemington, NJ 08822   (908) 782-4279

Copper Hill is an 18 hole private golf course that is open 6 days a week, 11 months a year (closed Jan.) Guests may play accompanied by a member. Reserved tee times are not necessary.

•**Driving Range**	•**Lockers**
•**Practice Green**	•**Showers**
•**Power Carts**	•**Food**
•**Pull Carts**	•**Clubhouse**
•**Club Rental**	•**Outings**
Caddies	•**Soft Spikes**

Course Description: The meandering stream that runs through Copper Hill affects play on seven holes. Four sets of tees, sloping terrain, exceedingly small greens and tight fairways add to the challenge here. The signature par 4 18th is the most outstanding hole; it is long with a three tiered elevated green, unusually large for this course. The hole has a downhill lie for the approach shot. In addition, overshooting the green can result in trouble. On thirteen holes, out of bounds on the left awaits an errant shot.

Directions: Hunterdon County, #10 on West Central Map
GSP to Exit 142 OR NJTPK to Exit 14 to I-78 West. Proceed to I-287S to Rte. 202S. Follow signs to Flemington(at Flemington Circle, Rte 202 is joined by Rte. 31S). Go approx. 3 miles South (pass Stewart's Root Beer Stand on right) & turn right at Country Club Rd. to club entrance.

Hole	1	2	3	4	5	6	7	8	9	Out	BLUE	Rating 71.5
BLUE	391	235	488	156	366	351	341	416	484	3228		Slope 128
WHITE	372	218	472	132	348	338	307	393	471	3051		
Par	4	3	5	3	4	4	4	4	5	36	WHITE	Rating 70.1
Handicap	3	9	11	17	5	15	13	1	7			Slope 125
RED	337	143	416	100	287	267	250	301	415	2516		
Par	4	3	5	3	4	4	4	4	5	36	RED	Rating 70.1
Handicap	3	17	5	15	7	13	9	11	1			Slope 119
Hole	10	11	12	13	14	15	16	17	18	In		Totals
BLUE	372	165	370	504	165	556	345	384	428	3289	BLUE	6517
WHITE	353	156	352	482	159	532	334	375	410	3153	WHITE	6204
Par	4	3	4	5	3	5	4	4	4	36	Par	72
Handicap	6	18	10	14	16	4	12	8	2			
RED	332	118	289	420	112	416	293	299	401	2680	RED	5196
Par	4	3	4	5	3	5	4	4	5	37	Par	73
Handicap	10	18	6	8	16	2	12	14	4			

Manager: Rob Weisberg   **Pro:** Robert Nicolson, PGA **Supt:** Robert Mlynarski
Estab: 1928   **Architect:** Michael Hurdzan 1991(Redesign)

CRANBURY GOLF CLUB

49 Southfield Rd., Cranbury, NJ 08512   (609) 799-0341

Cranbury Golf Club is a privately owned 18 hole course open to the public 7 days a week all year. Memberships are available to West Windsor, Cranbury and Plainsboro residents. Tee times: up to 1 week in advance; 2 weeks for members. Members only may play until 10:30 on weekend mornings. Weekend prices are for Fri. Sat. Sun.

• Driving Range	• Lockers
• Practice Green	• Showers
• Power Carts	• Food
• Pull Carts	• Clubhouse
• Club Rental	• Outings
• Soft Spikes	

Fees	Weekday	Weekend
Daily	$27	$37
Twi(1PM)	$22	$27
Twi(4PM)	$16	$22
Power carts $14pp		

Course Description: The wide open front nine at Cranbury Golf Course was once farmland and is designed around a working farm. Relatively flat with some undulation, the wooded well bunkered back nine is tight. The signature par 3 fifth hole is 211 yards over a pond. There is water in play on three other holes, including the 3rd, known as "Bog Hole" because one must hit over a bog. This busy course draws players from all over, including Staten Island. The restaurant "The Bog" is a major attraction.

Directions: Mercer County, #11 on West Central Map
NJTPKE to Exit #8. Then take Rte. 33 West and at the end of the road, make a left at the firehouse. At first light, go right onto Rte. 571(Stockton St.) Go 3 miles and make a left onto Southfield Rd. Club is 1 mile on right.

Hole	1	2	3	4	5	6	7	8	9	Out	BLUE	Rating 69.5
BLUE	519	333	155	460	211	495	163	419	398	3153		Slope 122
WHITE	506	333	145	420	187	485	142	401	383	3002		
Par	5	4	3	4	3	5	3	4	4	35	WHITE	Rating 68.3
Handicap	11	13	15	3	5	7	17	1	9			Slope 120
RED	470	310	110	310	115	475	115	395	360	2660		
Par	5	4	3	4	3	5	3	5	4	36	RED	Rating 69.1
Handicap	11	13	15	3	5	7	17	1	9			Slope 123

Hole	10	11	12	13	14	15	16	17	18	In		Totals
BLUE	376	175	393	225	347	498	189	371	538	3112	BLUE	6265
WHITE	360	175	378	197	347	490	170	356	529	3002	WHITE	6004
Par	4	3	4	3	4	5	3	4	5	35	Par	70
Handicap	12	14	6	8	18	2	16	10	4			
RED	335	160	335	175	300	460	150	330	490	2735	RED	5395
Par	4	3	4	3	4	5	3	4	5	35	Par	71
Handicap	12	14	6	8	18	2	16	10	4			

Manager: Mike Attara, PGA   **Pro:** Alex Bushman, PGA   **Supt:** John Alexander
Built: 1963

FIDDLER'S ELBOW COUNTRY CLUB

Rattlesnake Bridge Rd., Bedminster, NJ 07921   (908) 439-2513

Fiddler's Elbow is made up of three separate courses, Meadow, Forest and River. It is open 7 days a week, March through Dec. Membership is reserved exclusively for private corporations. Tee times should be reserved in advance.

- •Driving Range
- •Practice Green
- •Power Carts
- Pull Carts
- •Club Rental
- Caddies

- •Lockers
- •Showers
- •Food
- •Clubhouse
- •Outings
- •Soft Spikes

Course Description: Designed and built on former farmland with picturesque views, Fiddler's Elbow was originally named because the clubhouse resembled a fiddler with a crooked arm. The Meadows has a links type design on the back nine; the front is tree lined with water in play on several holes. The 16th hole on the River Course is rated one of the most difficult in New Jersey; its green is on a peninsula. The Rees Jones designed Forest Course has a man made lake and is just as exciting as the other 2 courses. The 1994 NJ Pro & Asst. Pro Tournaments were held here. The opportunity to play here is a great bonus for those who work for member corporations. The scorecard below is for the River Course.

Directions: Somerset County, #12 on West Central Map
NJTPKE or GSP to Rte. 78 West to Exit #26 (Lamington/North Branch). Go left at STOP, cross over Rte. 78 on Rattlesnake Bridge Rd. Club is on right.

Hole	1	2	3	4	5	6	7	8	9	Out	BLUE	Rating 70.8
BLUE	382	514	155	549	158	418	386	148	451	3161		Slope 122
WHITE	336	494	150	506	152	408	375	140	443	3004		
Par	4	5	3	5	3	4	4	3	5	36	WHITE	Rating 69.7
Handicap	8	10	16	4	14	2	6	18	12			Slope 120
RED	305	452	137	460	131	362	307	132	349	2635		
Par	4	5	3	5	3	4	4	3	5	36	RED	Rating 70.7
Handicap	8	10	16	4	14	2	6	18	12			Slope 119
Hole	10	11	12	13	14	15	16	17	18	In		Totals
BLUE	324	168	360	386	200	510	518	184	576	3226	BLUE	6387
WHITE	314	159	352	375	192	499	510	174	569	3144	WHITE	6148
Par	4	3	4	4	3	5	5	3	5	36	Par	72
Handicap	13	17	15	5	11	3	7	9	1			
RED	305	117	346	300	189	378	424	164	498	2721	RED	5356
Par	4	3	4	4	3	5	5	3	5	36	Par	72
Handicap	13	17	15	5	11	3	7	9	1			

Manager: David McGhee   **Pro:** Michael Sparks, PGA   **Supt:** Thomas Breiner
Architects: River & Meadow; Hal Purdy, Brian Silver   Forest; Rees Jones 1994

FORSGATE COUNTRY CLUB

Forsgate Drive, Jamesburg, NJ 08831   **(732) 521-0070**

Forsgate is a private club that has two 18 hole courses open to members and guests all year 7 days a week. Tee time reservations should be made in advance

•**Driving Range**	•**Lockers**
•**Practice Green**	•**Showers**
•**Power Carts**	•**Food**
Pull Carts	•**Clubhouse**
•**Club Rental**	•**Outings**
Caddies	•**Soft Spikes**

Course Description: The "Banks" was originally to be a private personal golf course with the holes replicating the famous golf links of Europe. John Forster, who owned the farmland, commissioned the renowned Charles "Steam Shovel" Banks to design the course on his property which became known as Forsgate. Banks provided his trademark gargantuan deep bunkers and large undulating greens to confront the unwary golfer. The West Course, a more contemporary style, is designed by the Arnold Palmer Group and has smaller bunkers and greens with a multitude of water hazards. The 2nd hole is a long par 5, 623 from the blues. Both courses are beautifully maintained and enjoyable to play. The scorecard below is for the Banks Course.

Directions: Middlesex County, #13 on West Central Map
NJTPKE to Exit #8A. Take Forsgate Drive East to club on left.

Hole	1	2	3	4	5	6	7	8	9	Out	BLUE	Rating 71.4
BLUE	375	403	194	347	417	344	187	570	501	3338		Slope 126
WHITE	367	398	182	332	403	334	179	551	484	3230		
Par	4	4	3	4	4	4	3	5	5	36	WHITE	Rating 70.4
Handicap	9	7	15	13	3	11	17	1	5			Slope 123
RED	350	386	169	317	348	317	165	468	405	2925		
Par	4	4	3	4	4	4	3	5	5	36	RED	Rating 72.9
Handicap	9	5	15	13	3	11	17	1	7			Slope 124
Hole	10	11	12	13	14	15	16	17	18	In		Totals
BLUE	416	357	140	529	411	328	402	235	421	3239	BLUE	6577
WHITE	408	349	140	519	396	318	388	201	398	3117	WHITE	6347
Par	4	4	3	5	4	4	4	3	4	35	Par	71
Handicap	4	12	18	2	10	14	8	16	6			
RED	394	267	133	462	325	313	340	150	369	2753	RED	5678
Par	4	4	3	5	4	4	4	3	4	35	Par	71
Handicap	2	14	18	4	10	12	8	16	6			

Manager: Tom Grant **Pro:** Doug Pearce, PGA **Supt:** Robert Ribbans
Architects: Charles Banks 1931 (West Course) Hal Purdy, Arnold Palmer 1962

FOX HOLLOW GOLF CLUB

59 Fox Chase Run, Somerville, NJ 08876   **(908) 526-0010**

Fox Hollow is a private 18 hole course open 7 days a week from April through Oct. and 6 days a week the rest of the year. Guests play accompanied by a member. Tee times should be reserved in advance.

```
• Driving Range    • Lockers
• Practice Green   • Showers
• Power Carts      • Food
• Pull Carts       • Clubhouse
• Club Rental      • Outings
  Caddies          • Soft Spikes
```

Course Description: Partially renovated in 1994, Fox Hollow is a wooded course set in the scenic hills of Somerset County. Golfers here encounter varied tree lined terrain with many elevation changes. Water comes into play on about half of the holes and rather extensively on the signature 18th hole. The 15th is difficult because it is all downhill.

Directions: Somerset County, # on West Central Map
NJTPKE or GSP to Rte. 78 West. Take Rte. 287 South to Rtes. 202/206 South. Proceed to Rte. 28 in Somerville and go right on Rte.28 to Lamington Rd. Make a right and then the 2nd left at Fox Chase Run to club.

Hole	1	2	3	4	5	6	7	8	9	Out	BLUE	Rating 70.5
BLUE	350	162	535	179	432	547	395	351	181	3132		Slope 120
WHITE	343	151	525	165	421	540	379	341	155	3020		
Par	4	3	5	3	4	5	4	4	3	35	WHITE	Rating 69.5
Handicap	9	17	3	13	1	5	7	11	15			Slope 118
RED	301	115	495	105	320	490	359	309	108	2602		
Par	4	3	5	3	4	5	4	4	3	35	RED	Rating 71.2
Handicap	9	17	1	15	5	3	7	11	13			Slope 122
Hole	10	11	12	13	14	15	16	17	18	In		Totals
BLUE	584	348	189	434	171	565	352	366	185	3194	BLUE	6326
WHITE	565	341	178	421	151	555	344	358	176	3089	WHITE	6109
Par	5	4	3	4	3	5	4	4	3	35	Par	70
Handicap	2	8	10	4	18	6	14	12	16			
RED	480	299	145	415	140	472	326	342	108	2727	RED	5329
Par	5	4	3	5	3	5	4	4	3	36	Par	71
Handicap	4	14	10	6	18	2	12	8	16			

Manager: Mark McAvoy **Pro:** Vaughan Abel, PGA **Supt:** Tim McAvoy
Architect: Hal Purdy 1962

GLENWOOD COUNTRY CLUB

1655 Rte. 9 & Fairway Lane, Old Bridge, NJ 08857   **(732) 607-2582**

Glenwood is an 18 hole course open 6 days a week all year. Guests play accompanied by a member. Reserved tee times are required on weekends only.

•Driving Range	•Lockers
•Practice Green	•Showers
•Power Carts	•Food
•Pull Carts	•Clubhouse
•Club Rental	•Outings
Caddies	•Soft Spikes

Course Description: Glenwood provides a good test of golf; the course offers right and left doglegs, tight fairways, elevated greens and tees and water in play on many holes. Wind can be a factor here as well. The signature hole, the par 4 sixth, is a dogleg left with water coming into play. A NJ State Open qualifying round is held here almost every year. PGA Junior tournaments take place at Glenwood as well.

Directions: Middlesex County, #15 on West Central Map
GSP to Exit #123. Then take Rte. 9 South to Fairway Lane & turn right to club. From South: GSP to Exit #105 to Rte. 18 North to Rte. 9 North to Fairway Lane.

Hole	1	2	3	4	5	6	7	8	9	Out	BLUE	Rating 73.7
BLUE	539	445	158	406	378	187	396	359	582	3450		Slope 132
WHITE	496	425	138	386	353	167	374	329	552	3220		
Par	5	4	3	4	4	3	4	4	5	36	WHITE	Rating 71.5
Handicap	9	1	17	7	11	15	3	13	5			Slope 126
RED	457	371	117	334	290	115	321	278	489	2767		
Par	5	5	3	4	4	3	4	4	5	37	RED	Rating 71.2
Handicap	2	4	15	7	14	16	8	13	1			Slope 122
Hole	10	11	12	13	14	15	16	17	18	In		Totals
BLUE	410	185	515	414	537	381	395	204	437	3478	BLUE	6928
WHITE	385	162	493	392	470	355	375	179	417	3228	WHITE	6448
Par	4	3	5	4	5	4	4	3	4	36	Par	72
Handicap	14	18	6	2	12	8	10	16	4			
RED	276	115	450	326	369	247	272	124	344	2523	RED	5290
Par	4	3	5	4	5	4	4	3	5	37	Par	74
Handicap	10	17	3	11	5	9	12	18	6			

Manager/Pro: Brian Bauer, PGA   **Architect:** Hal Purdy 1967

GREENACRES COUNTRY CLUB `PRIVATE`

2170 Lawrenceville Rd., Lawrenceville, NJ 08648   **(609) 896-0276**

Greenacres is an 18 hole private club that is open 7 days a week from March through December. Reserved tee times are required on weekends. Guests play accompanied by a member.

```
• Driving Range      • Lockers
• Practice Green     • Showers
• Power Carts        • Food
  Pull Carts         • Clubhouse
• Club Rental        • Outings
• Caddies            • Soft Spikes
```

Course Description: With its difficult, demanding layout, Greenacres requires accuracy. There are many tee shots out of chutes on this narrrow tree lined layout. The greens are well bunkered and undulating. Because they are small, fast and in some cases elevated, it is tough to get up and down if they are missed on the approach shot. The signature hole is the par 3 fourth with water right of the green. In recent years, the architect, Stephen Kay has made some changes at this course.

Directions: Mercer County, #16 on West Central Map
NJTPKE to Exit #9 and follow signs to Rte.1South to Lawrenceville. Pass Quaker Bridge Mall on left & take Rte. 295 and 95 (next right turn) sign says "To Pennsylvania." Exit at 69B "Rte. 206 South-Trenton" Greenacres is 1st driveway on left on 206.

Hole	1	2	3	4	5	6	7	8	9	Out	BLUE	Rating 71.7
BLUE	415	368	397	204	510	360	134	334	377	3099		Slope 126
WHITE	395	328	364	173	500	344	120	323	338	2885		
Par	4	5	5	3	5	4	3	4	4	35	WHITE	Rating 70.1
Handicap	1	9	3	15	7	13	17	11	5			Slope 122
RED	375	268	327	130	466	300	110	311	320	2607		
Par	5	4	4	3	5	4	3	4	4	36	RED	Rating 71.6
Handicap	3	11	5	15	1	9	17	13	7			Slope 122
Hole	10	11	12	13	14	15	16	17	18	In		Totals
BLUE	503	377	182	446	181	490	389	413	365	3346	BLUE	6445
WHITE	477	363	160	376	171	475	365	398	333	3118	WHITE	6003
Par	5	4	3	4	3	5	4	4	4	36	Par	71
Handicap	2	6	16	10	18	14	8	4	12			
RED	420	311	129	309	142	423	376	366	291	2767	RED	5374
Par	5	4	3	4	3	5	5	5	4	38	Par	74
Handicap	2	12	18	14	16	4	6	8	10			

Manager: Larry Bienapfle **Pro:** Ron Chmura, PGA   **Supt:** Jeff Wetterling
Architects: Devereux Emmet, Alfred Tull, George Fazio   **Built:**1932

GREENBRIAR AT WHITTINGHAM

101 Whittingham Drive, Jamesburg, NJ 08831   (609) 860-6621

Greenbriar at Whittingham is a 9 hole course that is part of an adult community. Only residents may join here. It is open 7 days a week and closed in Jan. & Feb. Guests may play accompanied by a member. Reservations for tee times are necessary.

Driving Range
- **Practice Green**
- **Power Carts**
- **Pull Carts**
- **Club Rental**
Caddies
- **Lockers**
- **Showers**
- **Food**
- **Clubhouse**
Outings
- **Soft Spikes**

Course Description: There are three sets of tees at Greenbriar giving variety to a second nine. Water comes into play on several holes and the mounding adds to the character of the layout. The 485 yard par 5 eighth hole is carved out of the woods. Greenbriar offers another option for golfers looking to reside in one of New Jersey's many adult communities. Scorecard below shows totals for a second nine.

Directions: Middlesex County, #17 on West Central Map
NJTPKE to Exit 8A, Go east on Forsgate Drive to 2nd traffic light. Make a right; club is on left about 1 mile.

Hole	1	2	3	4	5	6	7	8	9	Out	BLUE	Rating 68.2
BLUE	350	390	325	135	525	380	200	485	345	3135		Slope 118
WHITE	305	360	315	120	475	355	180	475	300	2885		
Par	4	4	4	3	5	4	3	5	4	36	WHITE	Rating 64.8
Handicap	13	1	11	17	5	3	9	7	15			Slope 108
RED	225	340	265	105	420	325	170	430	275	2555		
Par	4	4	4	3	5	4	3	5	4	36	RED	Rating 66.8
Handicap	13	5	15	17	3	7	9	1	11			Slope 110
Hole	10	11	12	13	14	15	16	17	18	In		Totals
BLUE											BLUE	6270
WHITE											WHITE	5770
Par											Par	72
Handicap												
RED											RED	5710
Par											Par	72
Handicap												

Pro: Peter Wyndorf, PGA   **Supt:** Harry Harsin
Architect: Brian Ault 1996

GREEN KNOLL GOLF COURSE

PUBLIC

587 Garretson Rd., Bridgewater, NJ 08807   (908) 722-1301

Green Knoll is an 18 hole public course operated by Somerset County. It is open all year, 7 days a week. A 9 hole pitch & putt is on the premises. Tee times may be made 7 days in advance for residents with ID. For $60/year non-res. have privilege to reserve tee times 5 days in advance. Reservation # is 231-1122.

Driving Range	Lockers
•**Practice Green**	Showers
•**Power Carts**	•**Food**
•**Pull Carts**	•**Clubhouse**
•**Club Rental**	•**Outings**
•**Soft Spikes**	

Fees	**Weekday**	**Weekend**
Res/ID	$12	$14
Sr/Jr	$7.50	$14
Non-res	$24	$28
Power carts $24		

Course Description: Moderately hilly and well maintained, Green Knoll is relatively long, 6443 from the blues. It is known for its tight fairways and rolling contours. The signature hole is the par 4 17th where water is encountered three times as a brook meanders through it. As in the case of all the Somerset County courses, Green Knoll is well worth the greens fee, and offers a challenge for the average golfer. The course has cross-country skiing in the winter when snow covered.

Directions: Somerset County, #18 on West Central Map
Rte. 287 South to Rte. 202/206 South. Exit right to Commons Way. At light at top of ramp, go right. At next light turn onto Garretson Rd. Course is on right opposite the high school.

Hole	1	2	3	4	5	6	7	8	9	Out	BLUE	Rating 70.5
BLUE	531	332	194	397	552	356	178	387	405	3332		Slope 120
WHITE	512	322	174	374	543	332	159	374	387	3177		
Par	5	4	3	4	5	4	3	4	4	36	WHITE	Rating 69.0
Handicap	13	15	7	3	9	11	17	1	5			Slope 117
RED	445	301	150	347	497	306	131	290	286	2753		
Par	5	4	3	4	5	4	3	4	4	36	RED	Rating 71.1
Handicap	3	13	15	7	1	11	17	9	5			Slope 124

Hole	10	11	12	13	14	15	16	17	18	In		Totals
BLUE	404	360	165	346	183	356	427	387	483	3111	BLUE	6443
WHITE	377	347	145	329	160	337	410	370	452	2927	WHITE	6104
Par	4	4	3	4	3	4	4	4	5	35	Par	71
Handicap	6	10	18	4	16	2	8	14	12			
RED	352	333	130	303	131	270	361	345	371	2596	RED	5349
Par	4	4	3	4	3	4	5	4	5	36	Par	72
Handicap	4	8	18	12	16	10	6	14	2			

Dir. of Golf: Bill Anderson   **Manager:** Joe Bozzomo   **Supt:** John Zujowski
Architect: William F. Gordon 1960

HILLSBOROUGH COUNTRY CLUB

PUBLIC

146 Wertsville Rd., Flemington, NJ 08822   **(908) 369-3322**

Hillsborough is an 18 hole semi-private course open all year, 7 days a week. Memberships are available for 5 day advance tee time reservations. Non-member threesomes or more may reserve on Mondays for weekends. Cash or check for fees.

•**Driving Range**	Lockers
•**Practice Green**	Showers
•**Power Carts**	•**Food**
•**Pull Carts**	•**Clubhouse**
•**Club Rental**	•**Outings**
•**Soft Spikes**	

Fees	Weekday	Weekend
Daily	$39	$50
Twi (2PM)	$34	$42
Power carts included		

Course Description: Adjacent to a barn and a polo field (which doubles as a driving range), Hillsborough's 450 acres is set on the side of the Sourland Mountains. Spectacular views abound and a constant breeze prevails here. The back nine is tighter and more severely sloped than the front with many sharp doglegs. Many holes have right to left sloping fairways that don't hold drives unless aimed strategically. The uneven lies and out of bounds contribute to the course's difficulty. The signature par 3 eleventh hole overlooks the entire Amwell Valley.

Directions: Hunterdon County, #19 on West Central Map
Rte. 80 or Rte. 78 West to Rte. 287 South to Exit #13 (either left or right from 287)for Rtes. 202/206 South out of the Somerville Circle. Turn right onto Amwell Rd. after McDonald's. Go straight thru 3-way STOP to top of hill. Make a left onto Wertsville Rd. for 3 miles to club on right.

Hole	1	2	3	4	5	6	7	8	9	Out	BLUE	Rating
BLUE												Slope
WHITE	475	195	360	550	145	305	305	190	510	3035		
Par	5	3	4	5	3	4	4	3	5	36	WHITE	Rating 68.2
Handicap	13	3	15	5	17	11	9	1	7			Slope 114
RED	460	185	345	495	140	300	295	180	475	2875		
Par	5	4	4	5	3	4	4	4	5	38	RED	Rating 74.1
Handicap	3	15	11	5	17	7	9	13	1			Slope 119

Hole	10	11	12	13	14	15	16	17	18	In		Totals
BLUE											BLUE	
WHITE	375	155	295	180	350	530	375	390	155	2805	WHITE	5840
Par	4	3	4	3	4	5	4	4	3	34	Par	70
Handicap	12	16	14	10	4	2	8	6	18			
RED	365	145	285	170	320	440	315	380	150	2570	RED	5445
Par	4	3	4	4	4	5	4	4	3	35	Par	73
Handicap	12	16	6	14	8	2	10	4	18			

Manager: Drew Munro   **Pro:** Cindy Cooper, PGA   **Supt:** Jared Smith
Architect: George Fazio

HOPEWELL VALLEY GOLF CLUB PRIVATE

114 Pennington-Hopewell Rd., Hopewell, NJ 08525   (609) 466-9070

Hopewell Valley is an 18 hole course open 6 days a week and closed for the month of January. Guests play accompanied by a member. Tee time reservations are required for weekends.

```
•Driving Range    •Lockers
•Practice Green   •Showers
•Power Carts      •Food
•Pull Carts       •Clubhouse
•Club Rental      •Outings
 Caddies          •Soft Spikes
```

Course Description: Built in 1927, Hopewell Valley is short, tight and about 6500 yards from the blues. The land was formerly a trotter horse farm and is quite picturesque. The Stony Brook meanders through this wooded course and affects play on holes 1,7,8,10 and 16. Adding to the challenge are the small fast bent grass greens. The par 3 #13 signature hole is downhill over a lake. A qualifying round for the NJ State Amateur (Southern Region) was played here.

Directions: Mercer County, #20 on West Central Map
(From North)NJTPKE to Exit #9. Take Rte. 1 South and after the Quaker Bridge Mall, take Rte.295/95 on right to Exit #4. Then take Rte. 31North for 5 miles to Rte. 654 and make a right. Club is ahead on right. (Rte. 95 can be reached from the South off of Rte. 295).

Hole	1	2	3	4	5	6	7	8	9	Out	BLUE	Rating 71.0
BLUE	374	381	166	476	432	396	495	400	132	3252		Slope 127
WHITE	357	348	154	457	404	389	469	373	126	3077		
Par	4	4	3	5	4	4	5	4	3	36	WHITE	Rating 69.9
Handicap	9	5	15	13	1	7	11	3	17			Slope 124
RED	316	295	125	414	341	385	426	284	113	2699		
Par	4	4	3	5	4	4	5	4	3	36	RED	Rating 71.3
Handicap	5	11	15	3	7	1	9	13	17			Slope 122
Hole	10	11	12	13	14	15	16	17	18	In		Totals
BLUE	389	404	356	148	352	414	456	209	570	3298	BLUE	6550
WHITE	374	395	344	146	343	383	474	195	550	3204	WHITE	6281
Par	4	4	4	3	4	4	5	3	5	36	Par	72
Handicap												
RED	329	347	331	119	317	298	413	127	455	2736	RED	5435
Par	4	4	4	3	4	4	5	3	5	36	Par	72
Handicap	8	6	12	16	10	14	4	18	2			

Manager: Paul Walstad   **Pro:** Joe Conboy, PGA   **Supt:** Steve Bradley
Architect: Thomas Winton 1927

LAWRENCEVILLE SCHOOL COURSE

Rte. 206, Lawrenceville, NJ 08648   (609) 896-1481

The Lawrenceville School has a private 9 hole facility open 7 days a week to parents of students and alumni, and a limited number of Lawrence Township residents. Guests may play accompanied by a member. Tee time reservations are not necessary. Current students at the school have playing priority.

•**Driving Range**	Lockers
•**Practice Green**	Showers
Power Carts	Food
•**Pull Carts**	Clubhouse
Club Rental	•**Outings**
Caddies	•**Soft Spikes**

Course Description: Several creeks run through this relatively flat par 70 course. There are double tees usable for the second nine. The eighth and (seventeenth) holes have a pond in play off the tee. Lawrenceville provides an excellent opportunity for short game practice. The facility is open when students are not using it; mornings in Spring and Fall and all day from mid June until Labor Day. An individual or family membership is required for non-current student use. The scorecard below shows the tees moved back for the second nine.

Directions: Mercer County, #21 on West Central Map
Rte. 1 South thru Princeton to Franklin Corner Rd. Make a right and at 2nd light turn right onto Rte. 206 North. Go past the main entrance of the Lawrenceville School and turn right into the school; pass the tennis courts. Parking lot & golf shack is on left.

Hole	1	2	3	4	5	6	7	8	9	Out	BLUE	Rating
BLUE												Slope
WHITE	309	331	188	358	368	155	336	337	470	2875		
Par	4	4	3	4	4	3	4	4	5	35	WHITE	Rating
Handicap	15	7	13	1	3	17	9	11	5			Slope
RED												
Par											RED	Rating
Handicap												Slope

Hole	10	11	12	13	14	15	16	17	18	In		Totals
BLUE											BLUE	
WHITE	322	306	205	332	425	145	359	312	365	2748	WHITE	5623
Par	4	4	3	4	5	3	4	4	4	35	Par	70
Handicap	8	14	4	10	12	18	2	16	6			
RED											RED	
Par											Par	
Handicap												

Manager/Pro: Ron Kane
Built: 1897

THE MATTAWANG GOLF CLUB

PUBLIC

295 Township Line Rd., Belle Mead, NJ 08502   (908) 281-0778

Mattawang is an 18 hole semi-private course open to the public 7 days a week all year. Annual memberships available. Members may make tee times 12 days in advance and the public 5 days. A small reservation fee is charged. Mandatory carts weekends.

Driving Range
- Practice Green
- Power Carts
- Pull Carts
- Club Rental
- Soft Spikes

- Lockers
- Showers
- Food
- Clubhouse

Outings

Fees	Weekday	Weekend
Daily	$43	$54
Twi	$30	$38
Power carts included		
Weekend is Fri-Sun		

Course Description: Hilly, well bunkered and not as easy as it appears at first, Mattawang is very well laid out. There are small greens and not much water in play, however those holes that do have water are quite intriguing. The owners are doing their utmost to upgrade the quality of the course. The bunkers have been improved and a new irrigation system installed. The new clubhouse is convenient and attractive. Jack Nicklaus played here some years ago and shot a 66.

Directions: Somerset County, #22 on West Central Map
Rte. 80 West to Rte. 287 South to Rtes. 202/206 South to the Somerville Circle. Follow 206 South for 9 miles into Belle Mead. Bear left at fork; go over bridge and pass RR sign that says "Mattawang." Make a left onto Township Line Rd. Club is 1 & 1/2 miles on right.

Hole	1	2	3	4	5	6	7	8	9	Out	BLUE	Rating 71.0
BLUE	333	323	182	328	528	198	492	400	390	3174		Slope 120
WHITE	292	318	170	320	498	150	440	381	320	2889		
Par	4	4	3	4	5	3	5	4	4	36	WHITE	Rating 69.3
Handicap	11	15	17	13	3	9	5	1	7			Slope 116
RED	283	315	114	323	446	139	395	342	311	2668		
Par	4	4	3	4	5	3	5	5	4	37	RED	Rating 71.6
Handicap	11	13	15	9	1	17	3	7	5			Slope 120

Hole	10	11	12	13	14	15	16	17	18	In		Totals
BLUE	388	142	540	221	407	486	437	287	426	3334	BLUE	6508
WHITE	313	135	490	157	377	464	375	285	394	2990	WHITE	5879
Par	4	3	5	3	4	5	4	4	4	36	Par	72
Handicap	14	18	8	12	2	10	6	16	4			
RED	306	122	484	153	313	410	372	273	366	2301	RED	5469
Par	4	3	5	3	4	5	5	4	5	38	Par	75
Handicap	6	18	2	16	4	8	12	14	10			

Manager/Pro: Mahlon Dow, PGA   **Supt:** Chip Kern
Architect: Mike Myles 1960

Village Rd. West, West Windsor, NJ 08561　(609) 936-9603

Mercer Oaks is an 18 hole county course open between April 1 & Thanksgiving, 7 days a week. ID cards are available for $20 (Jr/Sr $14). Tee time policy: Res. with ID; Call 936-TIME Mon. for Sat., Tues. for Sun., Wed. for following week. Non-res call Thurs. for weekends.

- **Driving Range** Lockers
- **Practice Green** Showers
- **Power Carts** • **Food**
- **Pull Carts** • **Clubhouse**
- **Club Rental** • **Outings**
- **Soft Spikes**

Fees	Weekday	Weekend
ReswID	$15	$17
No ID	$ 30	$34
Sr/Jr wID	$9	
Power carts	$23	
Twi discounts available		

Course Description: Many old trees have been preserved on the relatively new Mercer Oaks golf course. The greens are large and have sizeable moguls protecting them along with well placed bunkers that affect play. Somewhat flat and tree lined, Mercer Oaks gets quite busy in season. The par 4 signature 17th, 405 yards from the back tees, has a lake alongside of it and water influences the approach shot.

Directions: Mercer County, #23 on West Central Map
NJTPKE to Exit #9. Follow signs to Rte. 18 West and then almost immediately, take Rte. 1 South. Go left over Quaker Bridge Rd., then left onto Village Rd. West; club is 1 mile on right.

Hole	1	2	3	4	5	6	7	8	9	Out	BLUE	Rating 73.5
BLUE	395	365	445	535	213	454	600	165	380	3552		Slope 126
WHITE	360	335	375	505	160	400	535	155	350	3175		
Par	4	4	4	5	3	4	5	3	4	36	WHITE	Rating 70.3
Handicap	15	13	5	7	9	1	3	17	11			Slope 120
RED	320	310	340	445	110	360	460	110	275	2730		
Par	4	4	4	5	3	4	5	3	4	36	RED	Rating 70.2
Handicap	15	13	5	7	9	1	3	17	11			Slope 120
Hole	10	11	12	13	14	15	16	17	18	In		Totals
BLUE	390	450	425	160	355	505	240	405	535	3465	BLUE	7017
WHITE	360	410	380	130	325	465	185	365	510	3130	WHITE	6305
Par	4	4	4	3	4	5	3	4	5	36	Par	72
Handicap	14	2	6	18	12	10	4	8	16			
RED	325	340	340	115	300	415	155	300	335	2625	RED	5355
Par	4	4	4	3	4	5	3	4	5	36	Par	72
Handicap	14	2	6	18	16	12	10	4	8			

Director of Golf: John Kostin　**Pro**: Steve Bowers, PGA　**Supt**: Bob Bishop
Architect: Brian Ault 1990

METUCHEN GOLF & COUNTRY CLUB

Plainfield Rd., Edison, NJ 08818   **(732) 548-3003**

Metuchen is an 18 hole golf course open all year, 6 days a week. Guests may play accompanied by a member. Tee time reservations are required for weekends.

Driving Range   •**Lockers**
•**Practice Green** •**Showers**
•**Power Carts**   •**Food**
•**Pull Carts**   •**Clubhouse**
•**Club Rental**   •**Outings**
•**Caddies**   •**Soft Spikes**

Course Description: With its rolling land, amply bunkered greens and heavily treed terrain, Metuchen presents a challenge to all golfers. A feature of this well conditioned relatively flat course is the variety of its greens; each has a different shape and contour. The seventh and twelfth holes have double greens. Water is not a major factor at this busy facility; 23,000 rounds were played here in 1997.

Directions: Middlesex County, #24 on West Central Map
GSP to Exit #131. Go right to Rte. 27 South. At 6th traffic light, make a right onto Central Ave. which becomes Plainfield Rd. Club is about 1 & 1/2 miles on right.

Hole	1	2	3	4	5	6	7	8	9	Out	BLUE	Rating 71.8
BLUE	398	199	387	376	353	522	457	446	376	3514		Slope 127
WHITE	387	178	365	350	331	478	441	402	364	3296		
Par	4	3	4	4	4	5	4	4	4	36	WHITE	Rating 70.3
Handicap	5	11	17	9	15	7	1	3	13			Slope 124
RED	375	156	352	329	319	412	378	391	345	3057		
Par	4	3	4	4	4	5	4	5	4	37	RED	Rating 73.4
Handicap	3	17	15	9	11	1	5	7	13			Slope 124
Hole	10	11	12	13	14	15	16	17	18	In		Totals
BLUE	281	555	292	542	408	314	156	394	167	3109	BLUE	6623
WHITE	262	521	284	534	400	287	144	381	147	2960	WHITE	6256
Par	4	5	4	5	4	4	3	4	3	36	Par	72
Handicap	14	4	12	6	2	10	18	8	16			
RED	257	454	276	459	376	270	126	317	133	2668	RED	5725
Par	4	5	4	5	5	4	3	4	3	37	Par	74
Handicap	14	6	10	2	4	12	18	8	16			

Manager: John Schoellner   **Pro:** Jim Miller, PGA   **Supt:** Brett Price
Architects: Marty O'Loughlin, Charles Laing   **Built:** 1915

MIDDLESEX COUNTY GOLF COURSE

PUBLIC

Sidney Road, Piscataway, NJ 08854

(201) 768-6353

Middlesex County Golf Course is an 18 hole executive par 58 course open 7 days a week, all year. A telephone reservation system will be installed; call 1-800-676-7888.

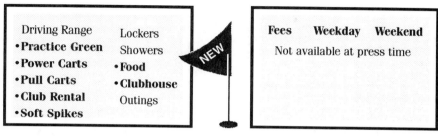

Driving Range	Lockers
•Practice Green	Showers
•Power Carts	•Food
•Pull Carts	•Clubhouse
•Club Rental	Outings
•Soft Spikes	

NEW

| Fees | Weekday | Weekend |
| Not available at press time | | |

Course Description: Scheduled to open for full play in the late summer of 1999, Middlesex County GC at Piscataway (name may change) will be an 18 hole executive style 3400 yard par 58 public course. There will be 14 par 3s & 4 par 4s. The 103 acres of county owned land is adjacent to Ambrose-Doty Brook off Sydney Rd. Environmentally friendly in design, the builders have preserved trees, natural rolling terrain and vegetation. It will be a course for beginners, families and golfers with limited time to play.

Directions: Middlesex County, #25 on West Central Map
NJTPKE North to Exit #9, bear right to Rte. 18N. Proceed on Rte. 18 thru N.Bruns, over Lynch Bridge & go left at River Rd. to 2nd light; on top of hill go right onto Old Hoes Lane to end of road & at light go left onto Hoes Lane. Make a right at Sidney Rd. to course on right.

Hole	1	2	3	4	5	6	7	8	9	Out	BLUE	Rating
BLUE												Slope
WHITE	105	100	115	135	165	320	325	140	170	1575		
Par	3	3	3	3	3	4	4	3	3	29	WHITE	Rating
Handicap												Slope
RED												
Par											RED	Rating
Handicap												Slope

Hole	10	11	12	13	14	15	16	17	18	In		Totals
BLUE											BLUE	
WHITE	135	125	245	140	165	130	335	150	160	1585	WHITE	3160
Par	3	3	4	3	3	3	4	3	3	29	Par	58
Handicap												
RED											RED	
Par											Par	
Handicap												

Manager: Castle Golf Mgmt.   **Architect:** Stephen Kay 1999

MIRY RUN COUNTRY CLUB

106 B Sharon Rd., Robbinsville, NJ 08691   **(609) 259-1010**

Miry Run is an 18 hole semi-private course open all year, 7 days a week. Memberships are available as well as daily fee rates. Members may reserve tee times up to 7 days in advance and non-members up to 4 days.

- **Driving Range**
- **Practice Green**
- **Power Carts**
- **Pull Carts**
- **Club Rental**
  Soft Spikes

- **Lockers**
- **Showers**
- **Food**
- **Clubhouse**
- **Outings**

Fees	Weekday	Weekend
Daily	$20	$25
Twi(3PM)	$17	$17
Power carts	$24	

Course Description: Originally known as Skyview CC, Miry Run was later named for the Miry Run Creek that runs through the course. It is well maintained and relatively flat with fast greens that vary in size. The front is somewhat open; the back more so. The signature third hole has a lake and creek in front of the green. The 18th, a dogleg left, features a horseshoe shaped bunker that protects the rear and both sides of the green. The clubhouse was recently renovated.

Directions: Mercer County, #26 on West Central Map
From North: NJTPKE to Exit 7A. Take Rte. I-95 West; exit at Rte. 130 North. Go to 4th light and make a right onto Sharon Rd. Club is ahead on right. From South: NJTPKE to Exit 7 to Rte. 206 North which goes into Rte. 130 N. Go 3 lights past I-95 interchange to Sharon Rd.

Hole	1	2	3	4	5	6	7	8	9	Out	BLUE	Rating 71.9
BLUE	543	166	386	382	520	385	394	197	405	3378		Slope 116
WHITE	528	151	371	367	505	370	379	182	389	3242		
Par	5	3	4	4	5	4	4	3	4	36	WHITE	Rating 70.7
Handicap	15	13	1	9	17	7	5	11	3			Slope 114
RED	463	122	330	300	460	305	341	167	354	2842		
Par	5	3	4	4	5	4	4	3	4	36	RED	Rating 70.7
Handicap	6	12	2	14	8	16	10	18	4			Slope 114
Hole	10	11	12	13	14	15	16	17	18	In		Totals
BLUE	221	405	403	345	377	552	434	231	503	3471	BLUE	6849
WHITE	206	390	388	330	362	537	419	216	488	3336	WHITE	6578
Par	3	4	4	4	4	5	4	3	5	36	Par	72
Handicap	10	4	6	18	12	8	2	14	16			
RED	141	355	375	315	347	422	400	170	435	2960	RED	5802
Par	3	4	4	4	4	5	5	3	5	37	Par	73
Handicap	17	5	1	15	9	11	3	13	7			

Pro: Jeff Bonicky, PGA   **Supt:** Dick Potts
Architect: Fred Lambert 1966

MOUNTAIN VIEW GOLF COURSE

PUBLIC

Bear Tavern Rd., West Trenton, NJ 08628   (609) 882-4093

Mountain View is a Mercer County public course that is open 7 days a week, all year. Tee time reservations are not necessary. Mercer County ID is $20, Jr/Sr $14.

•Driving Range	•Lockers
•Practice Green	•Showers
•Power Carts	•Food
•Pull Carts	•Clubhouse
•Club Rental	•Outings
•Soft Spikes	

Fees	Weekday	Weekend
Daily/ID	$11	$13
Non-res	$22	$26
Jr/Sr	$7	$13
Power carts	$23	

Course Description: Well maintained with beautiful mountain views, Mountain View is a relatively flat public course. The back nine is more hilly than the front. The layout has wide fairways with two holes affected by water. The par 4 twelfth, uphill over water, is the most difficult. There are golf leagues that play here making the course very busy in summer.

Directions: Mercer County, #27 on West Central Map

NJTPKE to Exit #9, then take Rte. 1 South. At Lawrenceville, watch for exit to Rtes. I-95 & 295. Exit at Bear Tavern Rd. (Rte. 579). Go right on Nursery which becomes Mountain View Rd.; course is ahead on right.

Hole	1	2	3	4	5	6	7	8	9	Out	BLUE	Rating 72.0
BLUE	390	375	350	235	545	410	145	420	425	3295		Slope 124
WHITE	365	350	335	190	450	380	135	395	405	3005		
Par	4	4	4	3	5	4	3	4	4	35	WHITE	Rating 69.5
Handicap	13	15	16	11	5	8	18	1	3			Slope 119
RED	330	300	290	165	410	340	125	300	330	2590		
Par	4	4	4	3	5	4	3	4	4	35	RED	Rating 71.4
Handicap	13	15	16	11	5	8	18	1	3			Slope 116
Hole	10	11	12	13	14	15	16	17	18	In		Totals
BLUE	530	470	440	165	375	345	430	210	515	3480	BLUE	6775
WHITE	490	440	405	140	340	330	390	190	490	3215	WHITE	6220
Par	5	5	4	3	4	4	4	3	5	37	Par	72
Handicap	9	7	2	17	10	12	4	6	14			
RED	460	375	350	110	320	310	380	155	450	2910	RED	5500
Par	5	5	4	3	4	4	5	3	5	38	Par	73
Handicap	9	7	2	17	10	12	4	6	14			

Manager: Butch Minelli   **Pro:** Steve Bowers, PGA   **Supt:** Steve Nictakis
Built: 1958

NEW JERSEY NATIONAL GOLF CLUB

579 Allen Rd., Basking Ridge, NJ 07920   (908) 781-2575

NJ National is an 18 hole semi-private course open 7 days a week all year. Temporary greens are utilized in winter. Memberships are available with tee time reservations up to 14 days in advance. Non-members can reserve 6 days in advance.

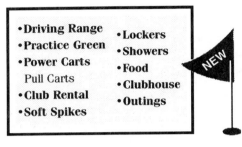

- **Driving Range**
- **Practice Green**
- **Power Carts**
- Pull Carts
- **Club Rental**
- **Soft Spikes**

- **Lockers**
- **Showers**
- **Food**
- **Clubhouse**
- **Outings**

Fees	M-Thurs	Fri-Sun
Daily	$70	$90
Members	$30	$40
Twi	$45	$60
Power Carts included		

Course Description: New Jersey National is carved out of heavily treed terrain and natural wetlands. It is an impressive and beautiful course having virtually no parallel fairways. The holes are each memorable; differing lengths, unique topography and level changes add interest. The large bent grass greens are fast and well bunkered. The signature par 4 #17 requires a long carry over a catch basin from the back tees. The 8th is a double dogleg with a lengthy carry over a ditch. The 5 sets of tees make the course playable for golfers of every skill level.

Directions: Somerset County, #28 on West Central Map
Rte.287South to Exit 22. Bear right at exit and then make an immediate U turn onto Rtes.202/206South. Get in left lane, go under Rte.287 and turn left onto Schley Mt. Rd. Proceed through Hills development. Course is about 2 miles ahead on left.

Hole	1	2	3	4	5	6	7	8	9	Out	BLUE	Rating 72.2
BLUE	400	495	388	165	395	387	140	539	369	3278		Slope 134
WHITE	365	471	367	145	380	371	131	515	361	3106	WHITE	Rating 70.6
Par	4	5	4	3	4	4	3	5	4	36		Slope 131
Handicap	8	4	10	16	14	6	18	2	12			
RED	298	412	281	118	257	288	107	405	235	2401	RED	Rating 68.8
Par	4	5	4	3	4	4	3	5	4	36		Slope 121
Handicap	10	2	8	16	12	6	18	4	14			

Hole	10	11	12	13	14	15	16	17	18	In		Totals
BLUE	450	202	367	546	431	182	341	375	553	3447	BLUE	6725
WHITE	423	184	355	521	409	170	335	335	535	3267	WHITE	6373
Par	4	3	4	5	4	3	4	4	5	36	Par	72
Handicap	1	13	9	7	5	15	17	11	3			
RED	325	130	310	468	345	122	270	219	429	2618	RED	5019
Par	4	3	4	5	4	3	4	4	5	36	Par	72
Handicap	7	17	9	3	5	15	13	11	1			

Manager/Pro: Charles Kilkenny, PGA   **Supt:** Steve Fritsch
Architect: Roy Case 1997

OAK HILL GOLF CLUB

15 Fernwood Rd., Milford, NJ 08848   **(908) 995-2285**

Oak Hill is an 18 hole private club open 7 days a week, all year. Guests may play accompanied by a member. Tee time reservations are not necessary. Caddies are available on request.

•**Driving Range**	•**Lockers**
•**Practice Green**	•**Showers**
•**Power Carts**	•**Food**
•**Pull Carts**	•**Clubhouse**
•**Club Rental**	•**Outings**
•**Caddies**	•**Soft Spikes**

Course Description: A hilly course, Oak Hill is a challenge for all: its severely sloped greens make three putting commonplace. The picturesque layout offers panoramic views, including the entire Delaware Valley. The course is very well maintained and has excellent drainage. Its signature 15th hole, which is considered a very difficult par 3, is tight and features a dramatically contoured green. In the past, Oak Hill has hosted several MGA and NJSGA tournaments.

Directions: Hunterdon County, #29 on West Central Map
NJTPKE or GSP to Rte. 78 West to Exit 11. Follow signs to Pattenburg and take bridge over Rte. 78 & bear right onto Rte. 614. Stay on 614 for about 6 miles following signs carefully for Rte. 614 West. Go right onto Rte. 519 for 1 mile; at Fernwood, go right to club.

Hole	1	2	3	4	5	6	7	8	9	Out	BLUE	Rating 71.2
BLUE	388	373	182	418	167	535	400	515	396	3374		Slope 122
WHITE	377	362	171	385	154	520	387	510	360	3226		
Par	4	4	3	4	3	5	4	5	4	36	WHITE	Rating 70.0
Handicap	9	11	17	7	15	3	13	1	5			Slope 120
RED	365	351	160	368	119	446	360	420	321	2910		
Par	4	4	3	4	3	5	4	5	4	36	RED	Rating 72.8
Handicap	11	7	15	13	17	1	9	3	5			Slope 126
Hole	10	11	12	13	14	15	16	17	18	In		Totals
BLUE	541	146	418	387	369	228	355	356	528	3328	BLUE	6702
WHITE	530	119	407	371	358	215	325	345	513	3183	WHITE	6409
Par	5	3	4	4	4	3	4	4	5	36	Par	72
Handicap	4	18	2	12	8	6	10	16	14			
RED	475	102	320	360	347	153	291	334	443	2825	RED	5735
Par	5	3	4	4	4	3	4	4	5	36	Par	72
Handicap	2	18	8	16	6	10	14	12	4			

Pro: Michael P. Knight, PGA   **Supt:** Jim Martin
Architect: William Gordon 1963

PEDDIE SCHOOL GOLF COURSE  PRIVATE

S.Main St. (PO Box A), Hightstown, NJ 08520   **(609) 490-7542**

Peddie School Golf Course is an 18 hole private club open 7 days a week, all year. Guests may play accompanied by a member. There is a waiting list to get into this club.

•Driving Range	•Lockers
•Practice Green	•Showers
•Power Carts	•Food
•Pull Carts	•Clubhouse
•Club Rental	•Outings
Caddies	•Soft Spikes

Course Description: The European style golf course at the Peddie School is tight with many old trees lining the fairways. There are small greens that play hard and fast; well placed approach shots are necessary to score well. Some consider the par 4 fourth the signature hole because of its picturesque tree lined fairway and water to carry in front of the green. Various state-wide tournaments are held here. Students at the school have privileges at the course.

Directions: Mercer County, #30 on West Central Map
NJTPKE to Exit #8. Take Rte. 33 West to first light, then go left. Turn at 2nd light onto Ward St. Make the next left at STOP sign onto S. Main St. Course is 1 mile on left.

Hole	1	2	3	4	5	6	7	8	9	Out	BLUE	Rating
BLUE												Slope
WHITE	523	352	115	380	121	381	492	350	413	3127		
Par	5	4	3	4	3	4	5	4	4	36	WHITE	Rating 68.8
Handicap	7	13	17	3	15	5	9	11	1			Slope 116
RED	485	306	115	334	109	333	441	350	413	2886		
Par	5	4	3	4	3	4	5	4	5	37	RED	Rating 71.8
Handicap	5	11	15	1	17	9	3	7	13			Slope 125
Hole	10	11	12	13	14	15	16	17	18	In		Totals
BLUE											BLUE	
WHITE	385	307	560	135	485	360	157	177	550	3151	WHITE	6278
Par	4	4	5	3	5	4	3	3	5	36	Par	72
Handicap	2	18	6	12	14	8	16	10	4			
RED	320	307	471	105	412	301	157	130	470	2673	RED	5559
Par	4	4	5	3	5	4	3	3	5	36	Par	73
Handicap	10	12	2	18	6	8	14	16	4			

Manager/Pro: John Bolla, PGA   **Supt:** George Thompson
Built: 1st nine 1920s, 2nd nine 1950s

PLAINFIELD COUNTRY CLUB

Box 311 Woodland Ave., Plainfield, NJ 07061   **(908) 769-3666**

Plainfield CC is an 18 hole private course open all year, 6 days a week. Guests may play accompanied by a member. Tee time reservations are advisable. Outings are held on Mondays and Thursdays.

•**Driving Range**	•**Lockers**
•**Practice Green**	•**Showers**
•**Power Carts**	•**Food**
Pull Carts	•**Clubhouse**
•**Club Rental**	•**Outings**
•**Caddies**	•**Soft Spikes**

Course Description: A true Donald Ross gem, Plainfield ranks as one of the finest and most difficult courses in the US and has an illustrious history. Over 100 years old, it has hosted the 1978 US Amateur Tournament won by John Cook and the 1987 Ladies US Open won by Laura Davies. The course is hilly, scenic and very well maintained. Even the driving range has a spectacular view of the Watchung Mountains. The dogleg par 4 seventeenth is considered the signature hole. The par 3 third hole requires a 160 yard carry over water from the blue tees. A ravine comes into play on the 2nd shot of the par 5 twelfth hole.

Directions: Middlesex County, #31 on West Central Map
GSP South to Exit #131, Iselin-Metuchen. Keep right to 1st light. Turn right onto Wood Ave. At 1st light go left onto Oak Tree Rd. for 3 & 1/2 mi. to Woodland Ave. Turn right and club is 1 mile on right.

Hole	1	2	3	4	5	6	7	8	9	Out	BLUE	Rating 73.6
BLUE	431	450	179	331	525	141	458	510	367	3392		Slope 136
WHITE	421	445	160	312	509	130	400	482	356	3215		
Par	4	4	3	4	5	3	4	5	4	36	WHITE	Rating 72.0
Handicap	5	1	13	15	11	17	3	9	7			Slope 132
RED	404	423	151	265	486	102	327	450	310	2918		
Par	5	5	3	4	5	3	4	5	4	38	RED	Rating 74.8
Handicap	13	5	15	7	1	17	11	3	9			Slope 139
Hole	10	11	12	13	14	15	16	17	18	In		Totals
BLUE	360	147	585	447	224	371	554	423	384	3495	BLUE	6887
WHITE	349	139	555	394	188	357	537	404	366	3289	WHITE	6504
Par	4	3	5	4	3	4	5	4	4	36	Par	72
Handicap	16	18	6	4	12	10	8	2	14			
RED	274	132	512	313	136	320	490	313	321	2811	RED	5729
Par	4	3	5	4	3	4	5	4	4	36	Par	74
Handicap	14	18	2	12	16	6	4	8	10			

Manager: Roger Regimbol   **Pro:** Scott Paris, PGA   **Supt:** Greg James
Architect: Donald Ross 1890

PLAINFIELD CC - WEST NINE

Corner Woodland & Maple Ave., Edison, NJ 08818   **(908) 769-3672**

Plainfield West Country Club is a 9 hole golf course open to the public 7 days a week all year. Memberships are available with discounts for seniors and juniors. Tee time reservations are not necessary.

Driving Range	Lockers
•**Practice Green**	Showers
•**Power Carts**	•**Food**
•**Pull Carts**	Clubhouse
•**Club Rental**	Outings
•**Soft Spikes**	

Fees	Weekday	Weekend
Member	$12	$14
Non-Mbr	$23	$28
Sr	$9	$12
Power carts	$20/18	$10/9

Course Description: This well maintained nine hole course is ideal for seniors and beginners. Plainfield West has wide open undulating fairways, rolling terrain and small greens, some of which are a punch-bowl type. The first and second holes are long and challenging with difficult rough. The property is owned by Plainfield Country Club which can be seen across the field. Green fees are for all day play. A second round may be played changing the tee position.

Directions: Middlesex County, #32 on West Central Map
GSP to Exit #13. Keep right to 1st traffic light and turn right onto Wood Ave. At 1st light, make a left onto Oak Tree Ave. Go approx. 3 & 1/2 miles to Woodland Ave. and turn right. Club is 1 mile on right.

Hole	1	2	3	4	5	6	7	8	9	Out	BLUE	Rating
BLUE												Slope
WHITE	409	413	151	241	179	339	189	274	308	2503		
Par	4	4	3	4	3	4	3	4	4	33	WHITE	Rating 63.0
Handicap	1	3	9	15	7	5	13	17	11			Slope 97
RED												
Par	5	5	3	4	3	4	3	4	4	35	RED	Rating 67.0
Handicap												Slope 102

Hole	10	11	12	13	14	15	16	17	18	In		Totals
BLUE											BLUE	
WHITE											WHITE	5006
Par											Par	66
Handicap												
RED											RED	4986
Par											Par	70
Handicap												

Manager: Kumi Fujii   **Pro:** Ed Famula, PGA   **Supt:** Greg James
Architect: Tom Bendelow 1932   **Estab:** 1898

PRINCETON COUNTRY CLUB

PUBLIC

1 Wheeler Way, Princeton, NJ 08540 · (609) 452-9382

Princeton Country Club is an 18 hole public golf course operated by the Mercer County Park Commission. It is open 7 days a week, all year. Tee time reservations are not necessary.

Driving Range	• Lockers
• Practice Green	Showers
• Power Carts	• Food
• Pull Carts	• Clubhouse
• Club Rental	• Outings
• Soft Spikes	

Fees	Weekday	Weekend
Res w/ID	$11	$13
Non-res	$22	$26
Sr/Jr	$7	$13
Power carts	$23	

Course Description: This popular county course is short, well bunkered and tightly wooded. Seniors like Princeton Country Club because it is flat and easy to walk. Several of the greens are elevated and water comes into play on the 13th hole. The most challenging hole is the par 5 second, a dogleg right with water in play on the second and third shots. It gets quite busy in summer.

Directions: Mercer County, #33 on West Central Map
From North: NJTPKE to Exit #9 to Rte. 1 South. In Princeton, from Rte. 1 go right on Emmons Drive, then left on Wheeler Way to club on right.
From South: Take Rte. 1 North, make a left from the Meadow Rd. jughandle back onto Rte.1 South, then right onto Emmons Drive as above.

Hole	1	2	3	4	5	6	7	8	9	Out	BLUE	Rating 68.6
BLUE	345	515	420	150	370	360	180	355	325	3020		Slope 113
WHITE	335	500	410	140	355	345	170	340	310	2905		
Par	4	5	4	3	4	4	3	4	4	35	WHITE	Rating 67.7
Handicap	11	1	3	17	5	9	13	7	15			Slope 113
RED	300	470	380	110	325	320	145	315	290	2655		
Par	4	5	5	3	4	4	3	4	4	36	RED	Rating 69.9
Handicap	11	1	3	17	5	9	13	7	15			Slope 113
Hole	10	11	12	13	14	15	16	17	18	In		Totals
BLUE	370	335	355	175	395	300	170	510	430	3040	BLUE	6060
WHITE	360	325	345	165	385	290	160	490	420	2940	WHITE	5845
Par	4	4	4	3	4	4	3	5	4	35	Par	70
Handicap	10	14	12	8	4	18	16	2	6			
RED	335	300	320	110	360	280	135	465	400	2705	RED	5360
Par	4	4	4	3	4	4	3	5	5	36	Par	72
Handicap	10	14	12	8	4	18	16	2	6			

Pro: Steve Bowers, PGA   **Supt:** Steve Nictakis
Architects: William & David Gordon 1964

PRINCETON MEADOWS GOLF CLUB

PUBLIC

70 Hunters Glen Dr., Plainsboro, NJ 08536   **(609) 799-4000**

Princeton Meadows is an 18 hole semi-private course open to the public 7 days a week all year. It will become a Middlesex County course. The details of the arrangement were unavailable at press time. Call the course for fees and policies. The information offered below is as of 1998.

Driving Range	• **Lockers**
• **Practice Green**	• **Showers**
• **Power Carts**	• **Food**
• **Pull Carts**	• **Clubhouse**
• **Club Rental**	Outings
• **Soft Spikes**	

Fees	Weekday	Weekend
Daily	$30	$50
Fri	$40	
Twi(3PM)	$10 reduction	
Power carts $15pp		

Course Description: Built in conjunction with housing units, Princeton Meadows is a flat, open, easy to walk course with greens that are small with some break. The back nine is much more difficult than the front. There is an abundance of water available to help keep the course green even during hot dry summers. The par 3 17th signature hole requires a shot over a pond and is considered most picturesque. This interesting course is worth travelling to; one can visit the nearby Princeton community as well. Power carts are mandatory until 2PM on weekends. Check current status.

Directions: Middlesex County, #34 on West Central Map
NJTPKE to Exit #8. Make a right and bear left to 2nd light to Rte. 130 South(Georges Rd.) Turn left to 2nd light & turn right onto Dey Rd. At 2nd light turn left onto Scudder;s Mill Rd. After 2 lights & 300 yards turn left onto Hunters Glen Rd. (part of a condo dev.) Proceed 3/8 mile to course on left.

Hole	1	2	3	4	5	6	7	8	9	Out	BLUE	Rating 70.3
BLUE	525	155	350	390	410	160	515	160	325	2990		Slope
WHITE	495	131	323	369	398	150	502	147	300	2817		
Par	5	3	4	4	4	3	5	3	4	35	WHITE	Rating 68.7
Handicap	4	12	14	8	2	18	10	16	6			Slope
RED	475	120	290	360	388	139	472	135	290	2669		
Par	5	3	4	4	4	3	5	3	4	35	RED	Rating 71.5
Handicap	4	12	14	8	2	18	10	16	6			Slope
Hole	10	11	12	13	14	15	16	17	18	In		Totals
BLUE	195	430	510	452	400	220	435	148	510	3300	BLUE	6290
WHITE	185	326	498	442	392	208	426	137	500	3114	WHITE	5931
Par	3	4	5	4	4	3	4	3	5	35	Par	70
Handicap	15	9	11	1	13	5	3	17	7			
RED	150	270	450	395	385	165	390	130	465	2800	RED	5469
Par	3	4	5	4	4	3	4	3	5	35	Par	70
Handicap	15	9	11	1	13	5	3	17	7			

Manager: Tara Sola   **Supt:** Dennis Kaminski
Architect: Joe Finger 1978

QUAIL BROOK GOLF COURSE

625 New Brunswick Rd., Somerset, NJ 08873   **(732) 560-9199**

Quail Brook is one of four courses operated by Somerset County and open to the public all year, 7 days a week. Automated tee time subscribers call 7 days in advance; 1 day for non-subscribers at (732) 231-1122.

•**Driving Range**	Lockers
•**Practice Green**	Showers
•**Power Carts**	•**Food**
•**Pull Carts**	•**Clubhouse**
•**Club Rental**	•**Outings**
•**Soft Spikes**	

Fees	Weekday	Weekend
Resw/ID	$12	$14
Non-res	$24	$28
Sr/Jr	$7.50	$14
Power carts	$24	

Course Description: Quail Brook can be proud of two of the best holes on a public course in New Jersey; numbers 17 & 18. The lengthy hole #17 has a tree blocking the tee shot, and needs super accuracy to a green surrounded by traps. The eighteenth is equally difficult. Water comes into play only on holes one and two with an errant shot likely to land in Quail Brook Lake. This course is very busy on weekends and draws players from Staten Island and Middlesex County, as well as Somerset.

Directions: Somerset County, #35 on West Central Map
Rte. 287 to Exit #6. Exit off ramp and take a right at 2nd light onto Cedar Grove Lane. Go to New Brunswick Rd. and turn left. Course is on right.

Hole	1	2	3	4	5	6	7	8	9	Out	BLUE	Rating 71.4
BLUE	519	359	352	191	398	538	404	166	346	3273		Slope 123
WHITE	456	315	324	163	355	500	357	145	313	2928		
Par	5	4	4	3	4	5	4	3	4	36	WHITE	Rating 68.9
Handicap	5	11	9	15	3	1	7	17	13			Slope 118
RED	436	298	296	135	337	413	312	124	287	2638		
Par	5	4	4	3	4	5	4	3	4	36	RED	Rating 70.9
Handicap	1	9	11	15	5	3	7	17	13			Slope 119
Hole	10	11	12	13	14	15	16	17	18	In		Totals
BLUE	353	151	407	384	525	151	336	470	424	3201	BLUE	6474
WHITE	308	133	356	344	486	128	323	435	394	2907	WHITE	5835
Par	4	3	4	4	5	3	4	4	4	35	Par	71
Handicap	12	16	8	10	6	18	14	2	4			
RED	292	123	301	327	462	105	298	401	327	2636	RED	5385
Par	4	3	4	4	5	3	4	5	4	36	Par	72
Handicap	14	16	10	8	2	18	12	4	6			

Manager: Fred Bobrowski   **Supt:** Thomas Grigal
Architect: Edmund Ault 1982

RARITAN VALLEY COUNTRY CLUB

PO Box 1075, Somerville, NJ 08876   **(908) 722-2002**

Raritan Valley is an 18 hole course open 6 days a week and closed for the month of February. Guests play accompanied by a member. Tee time reservations are required after 11:30 AM on weekends.

•**Driving Range**	•**Lockers**
•**Practice Green**	•**Showers**
•**Power Carts**	•**Food**
Pull Carts	•**Clubhouse**
Club Rental	•**Outings**
•**Caddies**	•**Soft Spikes**

Course Description: The beautifully maintained Raritan Valley seems cool on hot days due to the winds from the west. With its gently rolling and well bunkered fairways, it is a deceivingly difficult layout. Well placed shots are rewarded on this fairly narrow course. The par 3 seventh signature hole requires a shot over a pond with a stone wall between the tee and the green. Water also affects play on the 4th, 15th and 16th holes.

Directions: Somerset County, #36 on West Central Map
NJTPKE to Exit #10. Then take Rte. 287 North to Somerville. Exit at Rte. 22. Go west and take Rtes. 202/206 South towards Princeton. At 1st traffic circle take 1st right to Rte. 28. Raritan Valley is immediately after circle on right.

Hole	1	2	3	4	5	6	7	8	9	Out	BLUE	Rating 72.5
BLUE	570	414	424	337	343	205	173	432	493	3390		Slope 127
WHITE	563	401	418	332	334	198	135	424	480	3285		
Par	5	4	4	4	4	3	3	4	5	36	WHITE	Rating 71.4
Handicap	3	5	7	11	13	15	17	1	9			Slope 125
RED	444	301	310	252	295	167	79	328	440	2616		
Par	5	4	4	4	4	3	3	4	5	36	RED	Rating 71.3
Handicap	3	11	9	13	7	15	17	5	1			Slope 124
Hole	10	11	12	13	14	15	16	17	18	In		Totals
BLUE	151	530	528	390	381	205	427	405	400	3417	BLUE	6808
WHITE	147	524	511	353	361	190	417	390	388	3281	WHITE	6566
Par	3	5	5	4	4	3	4	4	4	36	Par	72
Handicap	18	6	4	14	12	16	2	8	10			
RED	127	462	417	307	287	138	366	310	315	2729	RED	5345
Par	3	5	5	4	4	3	4	4	4	36	Par	72
Handicap	18	4	2	12	14	16	6	10	8			

Manager: Bill Hofferer   **Pro:** John Fagan, PGA   **Supt:** Al Rathjens
Architect: Herbert Barker 1911

ROSSMOOR GOLF COURSE

10 Clubhouse Drive, Jamesburg, NJ 08831   **(609) 655-3182**

Rossmoor is an 18 hole course open 7 days a week all year. Memberships are available to the public. Guests may play accompanied by a member. Tee time reservations are necessary on weekends.

•**Driving Range**	•**Lockers**
•**Practice Green**	•**Showers**
•**Power Carts**	Food
•**Pull Carts**	•**Clubhouse**
•**Club Rental**	•**Outings**
Caddies	•**Soft Spikes**

Course Description: Located within an adult community, Rossmoor is characterized by tree lined fairways and large elevated bent grass greens that are well protected by bunkers making the layout a challenge to golfers at all levels. The course record here is a 67. Water comes into play on 7 holes in the form of three large ponds. The signature par 3 4th has a substantial carry over water. The New Jersey State Pro Am is played here every year.

Directions: Middlesex County, #37 on West Central Map
NJTPKE to Exit #8A. Proceed to Forsgate Drive towards Jamesburg. Club is ahead on right before Applegarth Road.

Hole	1	2	3	4	5	6	7	8	9	Out	BLUE	Rating 70.2
BLUE	410	425	360	125	340	160	310	435	510	3075		Slope 117
WHITE	395	420	340	115	305	150	280	410	425	2840		
Par	4	5	4	3	4	3	4	4	5	36	WHITE	Rating 67.7
Handicap	1	3	5	17	13	7	15	11	9			Slope 114
RED	375	335	320	105	290	140	270	330	405	2570		
Par	4	5	4	3	4	3	4	4	5	36	RED	Rating 70.5
Handicap	5	1	7	17	11	15	13	9	3			Slope 116
Hole	10	11	12	13	14	15	16	17	18	In		Totals
BLUE	410	285	185	520	385	150	525	350	420	3230	BLUE	6305
WHITE	375	275	145	475	375	120	500	340	355	2960	WHITE	5800
Par	4	4	3	5	4	3	5	4	4	36	Par	72
Handicap	2	16	14	8	4	18	12	6	10			
RED	355	265	135	460	365	105	435	330	275	2725	RED	5295
Par	4	4	3	5	4	3	5	4	4	36	Par	72
Handicap	8	16	12	2	6	18	4	10	14			

Pro: Tony Wilcenski, PGA   **Supt:** Dave Lerner
Architect: Desmond Muirhead 1967

ROYCE BROOK GOLF CLUB

201 Hamilton Rd., Somerville, NJ 08876   (888) 434-3673

Royce Brook is semi-private with 2 18 hole courses, East & West, open to the public 7 days a week and closed Jan. & Feb. Corporate memberships are available. Tee times may be made up to 7 days in advance. Walking, at reduced fees, on East after 1PM.

•Driving Range	•Lockers
•Practice Green	•Showers
•Power Carts	•Food
•Pull Carts(elec)	•Clubhouse
•Club Rental	•Outings
•Soft Spikes	•Caddies

Fees	M-Thurs	Fri-Sun
East	$55	$70
West	$65	$90
Power carts included		

Course Description: The West is links style featuring numerous and severe bunkers along the fairways and around the greens as well as fescue grass in the rough. Strategically placed bunkers and a more traditional, somewhat wooded terrain characterize the East Course. Both have bent grass tees, greens and fairways. The architect, Steve Smyers, is known for enhancing the natural landscape by following the gently rolling topography and leaving the land relatively undisturbed except to incorporate interesting challenges. The setting is made more beautiful by the absence of residential or commercial development within view. Scorecard is for West Course.

Directions: Somerset County, #38 on West Central Map
Rte. 287 South to Exit #17. Follow signs carefully for Rte. 206S. At the Somerville Circle, continue on 206S. Approx. 5 mi. from circle, look for Hamilton Rd. & take jughandle left onto Hamilton Rd. Club is 1.5 mi. on left.

Hole	1	2	3	4	5	6	7	8	9	Out	BLUE	Rating 72.5
BLUE	388	405	520	411	208	445	533	151	438	3499		Slope 129
WHITE	351	376	491	378	190	420	495	135	391	3227		
Par	4	4	5	4	3	4	5	3	4	36	WHITE	Rating 69.9
Handicap	17	5	7	15	11	3	13	9	1			Slope 124
RED	304	335	433	308	95	337	461	113	354	2740		
Par	4	4	5	4	3	4	5	3	4	36	RED	Rating 70.6
Handicap	17	5	7	15	11	3	13	9	1			Slope 119

Hole	10	11	12	13	14	15	16	17	18	In		Totals
BLUE	405	505	191	409	426	415	303	162	531	3347	BLUE	6846
WHITE	375	475	170	362	386	366	278	141	489	3042	WHITE	6269
Par	4	5	3	4	4	4	4	3	5	36	Par	72
Handicap	8	6	12	14	2	10	16	18	4			
RED	308	438	108	329	345	352	204	120	422	2626	RED	5366
Par	4	5	3	4	4	4	4	3	5	36	Par	72
Handicap	8	6	12	14	2	10	16	18	4			

Manager: Bill Troyanoski   **Pro:** Jeffrey Pope, PGA   **Supt:** Trent Inman
Architect: Steve Smyers 1998

RUTGERS GOLF COURSE

777 Hoes Lane, Piscataway, NJ 08854   **(732) 445-2631**

Rutgers is an 18 hole course located on the Rutgers University campus, open 7 days a week from March through December. Call on Thurs. noon for tee times the following Mon. thru Friday. Weekends: 1 week in advance in person.

Driving Range	Lockers
•**Practice Green**	Showers
•**Power Carts**	•**Food**
•**Pull Carts**	Clubhouse
Club Rental	Outings
•**Soft Spikes**	

Fees	Weekday	Weekend
Daily	$21	$30
Twi	$15	$15
Sr (registered at Rutgers)	$17	
Power carts	$28	

Course Description: Noted for its impressive evergreen trees and its fair test of skill, Rutgers is an interesting layout. Each hole is named for a tree that can be found on the course. The many fairway bunkers are an obstacle for golfers of all levels. Water is not a major factor although there is some in play on several holes. The par 3 eleventh is both picturesque and challenging with an elevated tee that requires a shot over a stream and a ravine to an uphill well bunkered green.

Directions: Middlesex County, #39 on West Central Map
NJTPKE to Exit #9. Take Rte. 18 North to River Rd. and make a left. At 2nd light, make a right onto Hoes Lane to course up ahead.

Hole	1	2	3	4	5	6	7	8	9	Out	BLUE	Rating 69.9
BLUE	353	381	178	483	349	369	531	201	448	3293		Slope 115
WHITE	335	365	155	469	323	350	522	184	434	3137		
Par	4	4	3	5	4	4	5	3	4	36	WHITE	Rating 68.3
Handicap	13	9	17	5	11	7	3	15	1			Slope 112
RED	318	307	127	453	284	322	488	172	413	2884		
Par	4	4	3	5	4	4	5	3	5	37	RED	Rating 71.3
Handicap	11	13	17	5	15	3	1	7	9			Slope 116
Hole	10	11	12	13	14	15	16	17	18	In		Totals
BLUE	381	158	539	382	170	363	345	197	512	3047	BLUE	6340
WHITE	361	140	520	367	147	348	330	184	496	2893	WHITE	6334
Par	4	3	5	4	3	4	4	3	5	35	Par	71
Handicap	6	18	2	10	16	8	12	14	4			
RED	327	128	397	355	149	334	330	172	428	2620	RED	5461
Par	4	3	5	4	3	4	4	3	5	35	Par	72
Handicap	2	18	12	4	16	8	6	14	10			

Manager/Pro: Art DeBlasio, PGA   **Supt:** Terry Sedon
Architect: Hal Purdy 1963

SOMERSET HILLS COUNTRY CLUB `PRIVATE`

Mine Mount Rd., Bernardsville, NJ 07924 **(908) 766-0044**

Somerset Hills is an 18 hole course that is open all year, 6 days a week.   Guests may play accompanied by a member. Tee time reservations are not necessary.

```
• Driving Range    • Lockers
• Practice Green   • Showers
• Power Carts      • Food
• Pull Carts       • Clubhouse
• Club Rental      • Outings
• Caddies          • Soft Spikes
```

Course Description: The back nine of Somerset Hills is tight and cut out of the woods, while the front is built in an open links design. Golf is taken very seriously at this truly spectacular Tillinghast style course. Each hole is named after a well known Scottish hole. There are 109 bunkers around the undulating greens. The signature par 3 2nd hole, "Redan" (meaning a fortress guarded by bunkers), has beautiful views and is well protected. Some say the "Duke of Windsor' or "Happy Valley"hole is the most appealing requiring a carry over a creek and a waterfall. The "Racetreck" used to be an actual racetrack and its grooves and paddock can still be seen. The 12th, "Despair" is all water and an island green. Many New Yorkers are members; a waiting list exists.

Directions: Somerset County, #40 on West Central Map
Rte. 80 West towards Morristown to Rte. 287S; exit at Mt. Airy-Bernardsville #26B. Go 2.1 mi. on Rte. 202S to Claremont Rd. & turn right for 0.3 mi. to Mine Mt. Rd. At church turn left. Club is 1/4 mile on left.

Hole	1	2	3	4	5	6	7	8	9	Out	BLUE	Rating 71.8
BLUE	448	175	358	427	343	476	445	230	514	3416		Slope 129
WHITE	408	175	358	418	329	465	402	194	514	3263		
Par	4	3	4	4	4	5	4	3	5	36	WHITE	Rating 70.4
Handicap	5	15	11	3	17	9	1	13	7			Slope 126
RED	440	148	324	353	285	448	360	186	465	3009		
Par	5	3	4	4	4	5	4	3	5	37	RED	Rating 73.5
Handicap	7	17	5	11	15	3	9	13	1			Slope 126
Hole	10	11	12	13	14	15	16	17	18	In		Totals
BLUE	496	411	144	409	396	394	167	387	319	3123	BLUE	6539
WHITE	480	388	130	391	372	375	162	362	295	2955	WHITE	6218
Par	5	4	3	4	4	4	3	4	4	35	Par	71
Handicap	10	4	18	2	12	6	16	8	14			
RED	417	370	107	360	352	301	132	324	271	2634	RED	5643
Par	5	4	3	4	4	4	3	4	4	35	Par	72
Handicap	8	2	18	4	10	12	16	6	14			

Manager: Elizabeth Grant   **Pro:** Dan Colvin, PGA **Supt:** Bob Dwyer
Architect: A.W. Tillinghast 1917

SPOOKY BROOK GOLF COURSE | PUBLIC

Elizabeth Ave., Franklin Township, NJ 08734   (732) 873-2242

Spooky Brook is an 18 hole course operated by Somerset County open all year, 7 days a week. Tee times may be made 7 days in advance for residents with ID. For $60/year non-residents have privilege to reserve tee times 5 days in advance. Call 231-1122.

- **Driving Range**
- **Practice Green**
- **Power Carts**
- **Pull Carts**
- **Club Rental**
- **Soft Spikes**

Lockers
Showers
- **Food**
- **Clubhouse**
- **Outings**

Fees	Weekday	Weekend
Res/ID	$12	$14
Sr/Jr	$7.50	$14
Non-res	$24	$28
Power carts $24		

Course Description: Spooky Brook is a relatively flat course with spacious greens, tees and wide open fairways. The signature par 4 17th has an approach shot over water. The first, second and fourteenth are the most difficult holes. It gets quite busy on weekends. This course is one of four Somerset County courses; Green Knoll, Warrenbrook and Quail Brook are the others.

Directions: Somerset County, #41 on West Central Map
NJTPKE to Exit #10. Take Rte. 287 South to Exit #7. At Weston Canal Rd. make a right. Proceed about 100 yds. & go right onto Edgewood Terrace. At light, turn right onto Elizabeth Ave. Course is on right just past Colonial Park entrance.

Hole	1	2	3	4	5	6	7	8	9	Out	BLUE	Rating 71.0
BLUE	458	424	148	438	536	404	358	196	375	3337		Slope 121
WHITE	422	405	134	418	531	384	339	178	358	3169		
Par	4	4	3	4	5	4	4	3	4	35	WHITE	Rating 69.5
Handicap	1	3	17	7	5	11	13	15	9			Slope 118
RED	349	284	118	319	526	361	321	158	258	2694		
Par	4	4	3	4	5	5	4	3	4	36	RED	Rating 70.8
Handicap	5	11	17	9	1	3	7	15	13			Slope 122
Hole	10	11	12	13	14	15	16	17	18	In		Totals
BLUE	363	188	373	525	409	364	167	379	507	3275	BLUE	6612
WHITE	347	169	356	503	383	340	155	366	492	3111	WHITE	6280
Par	4	3	4	5	4	4	3	4	5	36	Par	71
Handicap	12	16	14	8	2	10	18	4	6			
RED	336	159	339	483	288	257	142	281	402	2687	RED	5381
Par	4	3	4	5	4	4	3	4	5	36	Par	72
Handicap	10	18	6	2	12	14	16	8	4			

Manager: Michael Zoda   **Supt:** Billy Martin
Architect: Edmund B. Ault 1970

SPRINGDALE GOLF CLUB

26 College Road West, Princeton, NJ 08540 **(609) 924-3198**

Springdale is an 18 hole private course open 6 days a week and closed for January. Guests may play accompanied by a member. Tee time reservations are necessary on weekends.

```
• Driving Range    • Lockers
• Practice Green   • Showers
• Power Carts      • Food
• Pull Carts       • Clubhouse
• Club Rental      • Outings
  Caddies          • Soft Spikes
```

Course Description: Situated on the grounds of Princeton University, Springdale Golf Club was expanded to its present 18 holes in the early part of the century. It is a mature course with narrow fairways. The small bent grass greens have subtle breaks and are tightly bunkered. The seventeenth, a difficult par 4 starts from an elevated tee, curves and slopes to the right to the fairway bordered by a brook. The par 3s are very challenging as well.

Directions: Mercer County, #42 on West Central Map
From North: NJTPKE to Exit #9, then Rte. 1 South to Princeton. Make a right onto Alexander Rd. East in Princeton. Go 3 lights; at College Rd. turn left. Club is on left.
From South: Rte. 1 North and go left at Alexander Rd; follow as above.

Hole	1	2	3	4	5	6	7	8	9	Out	BLUE	Rating 70.8
BLUE	296	180	424	405	364	343	442	526	193	3173		Slope 128
WHITE	275	168	369	388	359	331	430	502	186	3008		
Par	4	3	4	4	4	4	4	5	3	35	WHITE	Rating 69.2
Handicap	15	17	3	7	9	11	1	5	13			Slope 125
RED	271	130	360	372	324	325	423	445	147	2798		
Par	4	3	4	4	4	4	5	5	3	36	RED	Rating 73.1
Handicap	15	17	9	3	7	5	11	1	13			Slope 126
Hole	10	11	12	13	14	15	16	17	18	In		Totals
BLUE	572	318	413	185	470	126	336	404	383	3207	BLUE	6380
WHITE	525	300	397	156	453	122	322	374	360	3009	WHITE	6400
Par	5	4	4	3	5	3	4	4	4	36	Par	71
Handicap	2	16	4	12	10	18	14	6	8			
RED	497	293	386	148	432	116	306	351	328	2857	RED	5655
Par	5	4	4	3	5	3	4	4	4	36	Par	72
Handicap	2	14	4	12	8	18	16	6	10			

Manager: Donna DiLorenzo   **Pro:** Peter Consoli, PGA   **Supt:** Charles Dey
Built: 1895   **Architects:** William Dunn, Howard Toomey & William Flynn

STANTON RIDGE GOLF & CC   PRIVATE

Clubhouse Drive, Stanton, NJ 08885 **(908) 534-1234**

Stanton Ridge is an 18 hole course that is open 6 days a week and closed in Jan. & Feb. Guests may play accompanied by a member. Tee time reservations are not necessary.

- •**Driving Range**   •**Lockers**
- •**Practice Green**   •**Showers**
- •**Power Carts**   •**Food**
- Pull Carts   •**Clubhouse**
- •**Club Rental**   •**Outings**
- •**Caddies**   •**Soft Spikes**

Course Description: Built on spectacular terrain, Stanton Ridge is a Scottish style layout located in the Cushetunk Mountains. As its architect Stephen Kay said, "it is old style elegance that is at one with the land; a modern course that looks seventy years old." The 555 acre property is surrounded by about 150 residences. The lush fairways are cut through virgin woods, the latter a haven for deer and pheasant. The elevated tees, strategically placed bunkers and fine bent grass greens add beauty and interest. An easy trip from NY, Phila. and Princeton, the course is attracting new members at a fast pace. It is one of the newer courses in NJ.

Directions: Hunterdon County, #43 on West Central Map
GSP to Exit #142 or NJTPKE to Exit #14 to I-78 West. Proceed to Exit 24 (Rte. 523 South). Proceed on Rte. 523S approx. 6.4 miles to club on right.

Hole	1	2	3	4	5	6	7	8	9	Out	BLUE	Rating 73.1
BLUE	365	407	371	310	119	527	207	504	378	3188		Slope 132
WHITE	345	373	352	297	111	491	195	481	365	3010		
Par	4	4	4	4	3	5	3	5	4	36	WHITE	Rating 71.4
Handicap	15	11	7	13	17	1	5	3	9			Slope 128
RED	287	335	251	245	95	425	110	423	335	2506		
Par	4	4	4	4	3	5	3	5	4	36	RED	Rating 69.7
Handicap	15	11	7	13	17	1	5	3	9			Slope 126
Hole	10	11	12	13	14	15	16	17	18	In		Totals
BLUE	445	407	192	322	542	450	351	196	412	3317	BLUE	6505
WHITE	410	380	170	310	525	412	315	185	385	3092	WHITE	6102
Par	4	4	3	4	5	4	4	3	4	35	Par	71
Handicap	4	8	18	16	6	2	14	12	10			
RED	351	333	75	269	485	328	282	135	320	2578	RED	5084
Par	4	4	3	4	5	4	4	3	4	35	Par	71
Handicap	4	8	18	16	6	2	14	12	10			

Manager: Lynn Moskalski   **Pro:** Jeffrey Rickenbach, PGA   **Supt:** Doug Baier
Architect: Stephen Kay 1993

STONYBROOK GOLF CLUB

PUBLIC

Stonybrook Rd., Hopewell, NJ 08525

(609) 466-2215

Stonybrook is a par 62 course that is open 7 days a week all year. Memberships are available. Tee time reservations are not necessary; walk ons only.

Driving Range
- **Practice Green**
- **Power Carts**
- **Pull Carts**
- **Club Rental**
Soft Spikes

Lockers
Showers
Food
Clubhouse
- **Outings**

Fees	Weekday	Weekend
Daily	$15	$21
Sr(60+)	$13	$15
Twi(4PM)	$12	
Power carts	$20	

Course Description: Stonybrook is a short tree lined, well bunkered course with four par 4's and two par 5's; the rest par 3's. A stream runs throughout. The signature par 3 first hole, is 223 yards from the back tees and is quite difficult. Rounds can be played in less than three hours making the course perfect for seniors, women, beginners and those whose golfing time is limited.

Directions: Mercer County, #44 on West Central Map
Rte. 295 to Exit #14, then take Rte. 31 North toward Pennington. Make a right onto Rte. 654. Follow road and make a left onto Stonybrook.

Hole	1	2	3	4	5	6	7	8	9	Out	BLUE	Rating
BLUE												Slope
WHITE	223	240	81	310	182	505	82	125	101	1849		
Par	3	4	3	4	3	5	3	3	3	31	WHITE	Rating 57.3
Handicap	3	7	17	5	9	1	13	11	16			Slope 91
RED	212	233	76	300	172	490	77	115	91	1766		
Par	4	4	3	4	3	5	3	3	3	32	RED	Rating 59.2
Handicap	11	5	9	3	7	1	15	13	16			Slope 93
Hole	10	11	12	13	14	15	16	17	18	In		Totals
BLUE											BLUE	
WHITE	273	72	142	235	201	468	160	135	68	1754	WHITE	3603
Par	4	3	3	4	3	5	3	3	3	31	Par	62
Handicap	6	18	12	8	4	2	10	14	15			
RED	263	65	132	225	188	458	150	125	63	1669	RED	3435
Par	4	3	3	4	4	5	3	3	3	32	Par	64
Handicap	4	18	12	6	10	2	8	14	17			

Manager: Leo Hughs   **Architect:** Robert Kraeger 1964

TAMARACK GOLF COURSE

PUBLIC

97 Hardenburg Lane, East Brunswick, NJ 08816   (732) 821-8881

Tamarack is a 36 hole Middlesex County course open 7 days a week, all year. Residents can obtain an ID for $25/year. Tee times may be made by calling 1-800-676-7888. A reservation fee will be charged.

• **Driving Range**	• **Lockers**
• **Practice Green**	• **Showers**
• **Power Carts**	• **Food**
• **Pull Carts**	• **Clubhouse**
• **Club Rental**	• **Outings**
• **Soft Spikes**	

Fees	Weekday	Weekend
Res w/ID	$13	$15
Non-res w/ID	$34	$38
Sr/Jr	$8	
NonNJ	$42	$47
Power carts	$26	

Course Description: With four different nines to choose from at Tamarack, there is a good variety of play. The dogleg right par 5 third on the Red course is long and uphill. The 7th on this same nine is 589 yards from the championship tees; even a low handicapper must put together two long shots to land within a reasonable distance for the approach shot. Tamarack gets very busy and has earned its popularity. Scorecard below is for Red/White.

Directions: Middlesex County, #45 on West Central Map
NJTPKE to Exit #9, then take Rte. 18 North to Rte. 1 South to 2nd Milltown exit. Continue on Main St. in Milltown. At Riva Ave. make a right; then a left at 2nd blinking light to Hardenburg Lane to course.

Hole	1	2	3	4	5	6	7	8	9	Out	BLUE	Rating 73.4
BLUE	375	385	531	376	168	452	589	397	192	3465		Slope
WHITE	350	362	496	335	134	420	546	364	159	3166		
Par	4	4	5	4	3	4	5	4	3	36	WHITE	Rating 69.8
Handicap	7	4	3	5	9	2	1	6	8			Slope
RED	336	340	476	310	111	400	517	340	139	2969		
Par	4	4	5	4	3	4	5	4	3	36	RED	Rating 72.5
Handicap	7	4	3	5	9	2	1	6	8	3		Slope

Hole	10	11	12	13	14	15	16	17	18	In		Totals
BLUE	403	225	515	442	205	423	367	510	470	3560	BLUE	7025
WHITE	364	178	473	404	161	385	318	456	435	3174	WHITE	6340
Par	4	3	5	4	3	4	4	5	4	36	Par	72
Handicap	6	9	5	2	7	4	8	3	1			
RED	322	152	452	379	130	357	285	437	327	2841	RED	5810
Par	4	3	5	4	3	4	4	5	4	36	Par	72
Handicap	6	9	4	1	7	3	8	2	5			

Manager: Tom Brush   **Pro:** Randy Luberski, PGA   **Supt:** Fran Owsik
Architect: Hal Purdy 1976

TARA GREENS GOLF CENTER

PUBLIC

955 Somerset St., Somerset, NJ 08873   (732) 247-8284

Tara Greens is a regulation 9 hole course open 7 days a week all year. Tee time reservations are not required. A 9 hole "Pitch & Putt" is adjacent to it as well as a miniature golf course.

•**Driving Range**	Lockers
•**Practice Green**	Showers
•**Power Carts**	•**Food**
•**Pull Carts**	Clubhouse
•**Club Rental**	Outings
Soft Spikes	

Fees	Weekday	Weekend
Daily(18 holes) $15		$20
Sr(over65)	$8 (after 3PM)	
Power carts	$25	

Course Description: Maintained immaculately, Tara Greens is owned by the Cleary Chemical Co. and was originally built to test turf chemicals. The company continues to do so which helps the greens stay in excellent condition. The par 5 615 yard 7th is one of the longest holes in the state, it is a dogleg right with a big tree in the fairway. The course is flat and tree lined; some water is in play. The dogleg left par 4 6th is wooded and picturesque. The pitch & putt course has real greens. The full length driving range affords the golfer great practice opportunities.

Directions: Somerset County, #46 on West Central Map
NJTPKE to Exit 9, then take Rte. 18 North to Rte. 27 South towards Princeton. Go 3 & 1/2 miles south to club on right (Somerset St.)

Hole	1	2	3	4	5	6	7	8	9	Out	BLUE	Rating
BLUE												Slope
WHITE	213	238	417	455	352	465	615	247	137	3139		
Par	3	4	4	4	4	5	5	4	3	36	WHITE	Rating 70.8
Handicap	8	7	4	3	5	2	1	6	9			Slope 112
RED	203	228	400	440	342	460	515	237	130	2955		
Par	3	4	4	5	4	5	6	4	3	38	RED	Rating 74.0
Handicap	6	9	2	8	5	4	1	7	3			Slope 126
Hole	10	11	12	13	14	15	16	17	18	In		Totals
BLUE											BLUE	
WHITE											WHITE	3139
Par											Par	36
Handicap												
RED											RED	2955
Par											Par	38
Handicap												

Manager: John Christman   **Pro:** Brendan Boyle & Mike Bonetate, PGA
Supt: Robert Harris   **Built:** 1950s

TPC AT JASNA POLANA

8 Lawrenceville Rd., Princeton, NJ 08540   **(609) 688-0500**

The Tournament Player's Club (TPC) is an 18 hole course that opened in 1997. It is open 6 days a week all year. Guests play accompanied by a member. Tee time reservataions may be made up to 14 days. Corporate mbrs. 14-30 days.

- •Driving Range   •Lockers
- •Practice Green   •Showers
- •Power Carts   •Food
- •Pull Carts(elec)   •Clubhouse
- •Club Rental   •Outings
- Caddies   •Soft Spikes

Course Description: With its gently rolling terrain, natural creeks and mature hardwood trees, Jasna Polana's golf course as well as The Tour Player's Club is a welcome addition to the array of fine golf facilities in New Jersey. Gary Player, the architect here, is well known for creating golf courses that preserve and enhance the natural environment. The 230 acre property is designated exclusively for the 18 hole layout. The clubhouse utilizes the neo-classical country villa, Jasna Polana, (a replica of the Tolstoy mansion) the elegant home of the late Seward Johnson and his widow, Barbara.

Directions: Mercer County, #47 on West Central Map
NJTPKE to Exit #9; then take Rte. 1 South through Princeton to Province Line Rd. and turn right. Go past Rte. 206 (Lawrenceville Rd.) and turn right into main gate of Jasna Polana.

Hole	1	2	3	4	5	6	7	8	9	Out	BLUE	Rating 71.2
BLUE	378	127	480	304	361	427	558	193	441	3269		Slope 126
WHITE	359	101	474	277	351	395	508	162	414	3041		
Par	4	3	5	4	4	4	5	3	4	36	WHITE	Rating 68.8
Handicap	9	17	3	13	11	7	1	15	5			Slope 121
RED	267	53	401	198	309	290	402	115	188	2223		
Par	4	3	5	4	4	4	5	3	4	36	RED	Rating 65.3
Handicap	9	17	3	13	11	7	1	15	5			Slope 111
Hole	10	11	12	13	14	15	16	17	18	In		Totals
BLUE	414	152	517	411	380	419	293	165	515	3266	BLUE	6535
WHITE	400	135	480	364	325	356	281	128	494	2963	WHITE	6004
Par	4	3	5	4	4	4	4	3	5	36	Par	72
Handicap	10	18	4	6	12	8	14	16	2			
RED	242	115	345	291	221	267	182	95	437	2195	RED	4418
Par	4	3	5	4	4	4	4	3	5	36	Par	72
Handicap	10	18	4	6	12	8	14	16	2			

Manager: Billy Dettloff   **Pro:** Robert Dugger, PGA   **Supt:** Roger Stewart
Architect: Gary Player 1998

TRENTON COUNTRY CLUB

201 Sullivan Way, Trenton, NJ 08628   (609) 883-3800

Trenton Country Club is an 18 hole course open 6 days a week and closed for 3 weeks in the beginning of Jan. Guests play accompanied by a member. Tee time reservations are required on weekends.

•**Driving Range**	•**Lockers**
•**Practice Green**	•**Showers**
•**Power Carts**	•**Food**
Pull Carts	•**Clubhouse**
Club Rental	•**Outings**
•**Caddies**	•**Soft Spikes**

Course Description: A traditional course built in the late 19th century, Trenton has tight fairways and small, fast well bunkered greens. There are a number of tricky doglegs and blind shots on this relatively hilly course. Reasonable accuracy is needed due to the out of bounds on the right of 13 of the holes. The par 3 third, 195 yards from the whites is considered the signature hole; it is uphill with a sloped green. Renovations are being made in 1998 & 9 and there will be yardage added to some of the holes.

Directions: Mercer County, #48 on West Central Map
NJTPKE to Exit #9. Take Rte. 1 South and at Lawrenceville, take I-95/295 South; exit at Bear Tavern Rd. Follow exit south. Road becomes Sullivan Way; course is on right.

Hole	1	2	3	4	5	6	7	8	9	Out	BLUE	Rating 70.9
BLUE	286	450	212	448	196	315	452	366	475	3200		Slope 126
WHITE	275	441	195	419	182	303	440	355	461	3071		
Par	4	4	3	4	3	4	5	4	5	36	WHITE	Rating 70.0
Handicap	17	3	5	1	11	9	15	13	7			Slope 123
RED	266	433	178	408	148	284	429	305	447	2898		
Par	4	5	3	4	3	4	5	4	5	37	RED	Rating 71.9
Handicap	17	7	11	9	15	5	1	13	3			Slope 126
Hole	10	11	12	13	14	15	16	17	18	In		Totals
BLUE	162	437	565	150	422	114	351	529	392	3122	BLUE	6372
WHITE	152	429	560	134	407	102	344	521	382	3031	WHITE	6132
Par	3	4	5	3	4	3	4	5	4	35	Par	71
Handicap	16	2	6	14	4	18	12	8	10			
RED	132	420	555	110	353	86	304	455	315	2730	RED	5628
Par	3	4	5	3	4	3	4	5	4	35	Par	72
Handicap	14	10	2	16	8	18	4	6	12			

Manager: John Case   **Pro:** Dennis Milne, PGA   **Supt:** Tom Tuttle
Built: 1897

TWIN BROOKS COUNTRY CLUB

600 Mountain Blvd., Watchung, NJ 07060   (908) 561-8858

Twin Brooks is an 18 hole course open 6 days a week from March through December, Guests may play accompanied by a member. Tee time reservations are necessary on weekends.

•Driving Range	•Lockers
•Practice Green	•Showers
•Power Carts	•Food
Pull Carts	•Clubhouse
•Club Rental	•Outings
•Caddies	•Soft Spikes

Course Description: The Watchung Mountain setting at Twin Brooks provides its members with majestic views. The course is secluded so that no homes or roads are in sight. Hilly with rolling fairways, the layout features many uneven lies and small, fast difficult greens. The par 4 eighth has a green set on a peninsula surrounded on three sides by water. The unique par three 19th hole adds interest to many events here; it is used as an alternate hole or in some cases tournaments are played with a 19 hole format.

Directions: Somerset County, #49 on West Central Map
GSP to Exit #140A. Go west on Rte. 22 and take Mountain Ave. to end. Make a right onto Washington Valley Rd. Proceed until road becomes Mountain Blvd. Club is just after restaurant on left.

Hole	1	2	3	4	5	6	7	8	9	Out	BLUE	Rating 72.4
BLUE	370	450	490	135	520	365	435	365	210	3340		Slope 126
WHITE	360	420	475	120	505	355	410	355	185	3185		
Par	4	4	5	3	5	4	4	4	3	36	WHITE	Rating 71.0
Handicap	7	1	9	17	11	3	5	13	15			Slope 123
RED	290	400	405	110	485	300	385	285	135	2795		
Par	4	5	5	3	5	4	4	4	3	37	RED	Rating 73.9
Handicap	13	9	7	15	1	5	3	11	17			Slope 130
Hole	10	11	12	13	14	15	16	17	18	In		Totals
BLUE	350	195	420	145	380	320	510	380	580	3280	BLUE	6620
WHITE	335	170	385	135	375	300	500	355	530	3085	WHITE	6270
Par	4	3	4	3	4	4	5	4	5	36	Par	72
Handicap	8	14	6	18	2	16	12	10	4			
RED	330	150	330	125	365	290	450	310	445	2775	RED	5570
Par	4	3	4	3	5	4	5	4	5	37	Par	74
Handicap	4	16	6	18	8	14	10	12	2			

Manager: Jim Sampson   **Pro:** Ralph Romano, PGA   **Supt:** Tom Crump
Built: 1898

WARRENBROOK GOLF COURSE **PUBLIC**

500 Warrenville Rd., Warren Township, NJ 07060   **(908) 754-8402**

Warrenbrook is an 18 hole public course operated by Somerset County. It is open 7 days a week from April through November. Tee times may be made 7 days in advance for residents with ID. For $60/year non-res. have privilege to reserve tee times 5 days in advance. Reservation # is 231-1122.

Driving Range	Lockers
• **Practice Green**	Showers
• **Power Carts**	• **Food**
• **Pull Carts**	• **Clubhouse**
• **Club Rental**	• **Outings**
• **Soft Spikes**	

Fees	Weekday	Weekend
Res/ID	$12	$14
Sr/Jr	$7.50	$14
Non-res	$24	$28
Power carts $24		

Course Description: Originally 2 holes on the private estate of a golf enthusiast, Warrenbrook was subsequently increased to the present 18 holes and eventually purchased by Somerset County in 1978. It is very hilly, heavily wooded and gets quite busy. The fairways are tight with water affecting play on 3 holes. The signature third is the toughest; out of bounds lurks on the left. The contours provide plenty of uphill and downhill lies. The most picturesque hole is the 17th where a large pond confronts the golfer on the approach shot and out of bounds encroaches on the right.

Directions: Somerset County, #50 on West Central Map
NJTPKE or GSP to Rte. 78 West to Exit #36. Take King George Rd. South. At light, it becomes Bethel Rd. Continue and road becomes Warrenville Rd. Course is on left.

Hole	1	2	3	4	5	6	7	8	9	Out	BLUE	Rating 70.8
BLUE	378	369	407	186	561	213	365	473	145	3097		Slope 124
WHITE	355	349	391	165	558	199	355	455	125	2952		
Par	4	4	4	3	5	3	4	5	3	35	WHITE	Rating 69.5
Handicap	5	13	1	9	11	7	3	15	17			Slope 122
RED	305	298	315	152	449	170	345	407	85	2526		
Par	4	4	4	3	5	3	4	5	3	35	RED	Rating 96.2
Handicap	3	13	5	15	9	11	1	7	17			Slope 117
Hole	10	11	12	13	14	15	16	17	18	In		Totals
BLUE	393	364	174	406	326	522	345	376	369	3275	BLUE	6372
WHITE	371	350	157	390	311	510	331	355	347	3122	WHITE	6074
Par	4	4	3	4	4	5	4	4	4	36	Par	71
Handicap	8	6	10	2	16	14	12	4	18			
RED	321	280	130	334	260	407	287	304	246	2569	RED	5095
Par	4	4	3	4	4	4	4	4	4	35	Par	70
Handicap	10	12	16	4	18	8	14	2	6			

Manager: Joe Rios   **Supt:** Dave Richards
Architect: Hal Purdy 1966

UPPER SHORE REGION

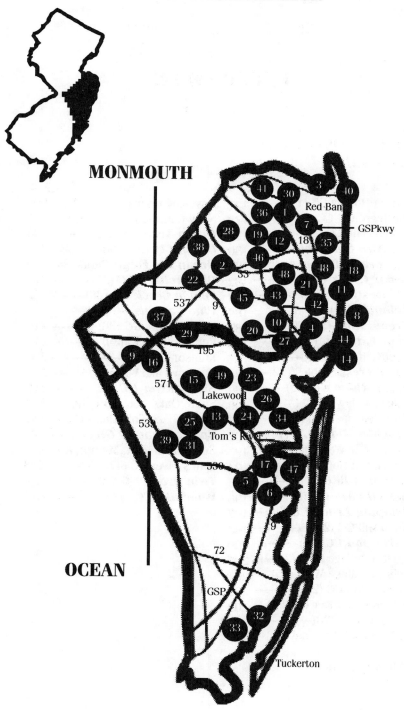

MONMOUTH

Red Bank

GSPkwy

537

195

571

Lakewood

533

Tom's River

530

72

GSP

OCEAN

Tuckerton

UPPER SHORE

Public Courses appear in
bold italics

*Military course

BAMM HOLLOW COUNTRY CLUB

215 Sunnyside Rd., Lincroft, NJ 07738

(732) 741-4774

Bamm Hollow is a 27 hole private course open 6 days a week all year. Guests play accompanied by a member. Tee time reservations are necessary on weekends. Pull carts are only permitted weekdays.

•**Driving Range**	•**Lockers**
•**Practice Green**	•**Showers**
•**Power Carts**	•**Food**
•**Pull Carts**	•**Clubhouse**
•**Club Rental**	•**Outings**
Caddies	Soft Spikes

Course Description: The three nines at Bamm Hollow offer a variety of playing combinations. The narrow, rolling fairways have changes in elevation that result in a number of blind shots challenging the golfer. On the signature 6th hole, a 90 degree dogleg left, a huge oak tree in the middle of the fairway must be negotiated; water in play adds to the difficulty. An LPGA tournament was played here in 1989. The score-card below shows the Blue and White nines.

Directions: Monmouth County, #1 on Upper Shore Map
GSP to Exit #114. Go right at first light onto Red Hill Road. Turn left at the next light onto Everett. Pass through 1 traffic light to Sunnyside Rd. and turn left to club 1/2 m. on the left.

Hole	1	2	3	4	5	6	7	8	9	Out	BLUE	Rating 72.7
BLUE	551	372	174	387	391	218	426	466	397	3382		Slope 127
WHITE	513	348	157	361	375	192	412	450	367	3175		
Par	5	4	3	4	4	3	4	5	4	36	WHITE	Rating 70.7
Handicap	3	5	9	2	4	8	1	7	6			Slope 123
RED	480	296	142	338	322	171	401	402	342	2896		
Par	5	4	3	4	4	3	5	5	4	37	RED	Rating 73.4
Handicap	1	7	9	2	4	8	3	6	5			Slope 121
Hole	10	11	12	13	14	15	16	17	18	In		Totals
BLUE	576	186	429	418	506	461	192	479	340	3687	BLUE	6669
WHITE	530	164	413	389	486	438	182	429	322	3354	WHITE	6529
Par	5	3	4	4	5	4	3	4	4	36	Par	72
Handicap	5	9	3	4	6	2	8	1	7			
RED	489	149	266	341	410	422	174	383	307	2961	RED	5857
Par	5	3	4	4	5	5	3	4	4	37	Par	74
Handicap	1	8	9	2	4	5	7	3	6			

Manager: Tom Yoshida   **Pro:** Bob Pedrazzi, PGA   **Supt:** Matt Dobbie
Architect: Hal Purdy 1959

BATTLEGROUND COUNTRY CLUB

100 Millhurst Rd., Tennent, NJ 07763   **(732) 462-7466**

Battleground is an 18 hole course open 6 days a week and closed for the months of Jan. and Feb. Guests play accompanied by a member. Reservations for tee times up to one week in advance.

```
• Driving Range    • Lockers
• Practice Green   • Showers
• Power Carts      • Food
  Pull Carts       • Clubhouse
• Club Rental      • Outings
  Caddies          • Soft Spikes
```

Course Description: Built on the site of the Battle of Monmouth, fought during the War of Independence, Battleground is on open country farmland with apple orchards adjoining Battlefield Park. Golfers may spot deer at dusk among the beautiful oak, pine, cedar and apple trees that line the fairways. Water is in play on several holes. Most greens are elevated and slope from back to front. The long par 5 signature sixth offers both a pond and a stream for challenge. The 7th requires a shot over a picturesque pond.

Directions: Monmouth County, #2 on Upper Shore Map
NJTpke to Exit 8. Proceed east on Rte.33 for approximately 9 miles to Millhurst Mills Rd. (Rte.527North). Go through light and use jughandle. Club is 1/2 mile on right.

Hole	1	2	3	4	5	6	7	8	9	Out	BLUE	Rating 73.8
BLUE	447	420	510	197	435	604	379	435	231	3658		Slope 129
WHITE	427	400	490	177	415	584	359	415	211	3478		
Par	4	4	5	3	4	5	4	4	3	36	WHITE	Rating 72.1
Handicap	3	13	9	17	7	1	11	5	15			Slope 125
RED	327	312	355	156	386	461	280	397	150	2824		
Par	4	4	5	3	4	5	4	4	3	36	RED	Rating 71.9
Handicap	5	13	7	15	1	3	9	11	17			Slope 121
Hole	10	11	12	13	14	15	16	17	18	In		Totals
BLUE	564	392	390	177	512	390	210	399	425	3459	BLUE	7117
WHITE	516	372	370	157	502	370	200	379	405	3271	WHITE	6749
Par	5	4	4	3	5	4	3	4	4	36	Par	72
Handicap	6	10	8	18	12	4	16	14	2			
RED	500	272	302	144	415	327	190	302	302	2754	RED	5578
Par	5	4	4	3	5	4	3	4	4	36	Par	72
Handicap	2	16	14	18	6	4	10	8	12			

Manager: Michael Rutkin   **Pro:** Dean Sklar, PGA   **Supt:** Gary Stedman
Architect: Hal Purdy 1961

BEACON HILL COUNTRY CLUB

Beacon Hill Rd., Atlantic Highlands, NJ 07716   **(732) 291-3344**

Beacon Hill is an 18 hole course open 6 days a week and closed in January. Guests play accompanied by a member. Tee time reservations are not necessary.

• **Driving Range**	• **Lockers**
• **Practice Green**	• **Showers**
• **Power Carts**	• **Food**
Pull Carts	• **Clubhouse**
Club Rental	• **Outings**
• **Caddies**	• **Soft Spikes**

Course Description: Although tricky and rather challenging, Beacon Hill is not very long. On clear days the views of the New York City skyline and Sandy Hook are spectacular. Featuring narrow fairways and small well-bunkered greens, water is in play on three holes. From the elevated tee on the par 5 5th, the best views are seen before hitting the difficult straight tee shot. This location has been the site of the Mid-Amateur Qualifyer and will host the NJ State Open qualifying round in 1999. Caddies are available if requested in advance.

Directions: Monmouth County, #3 on Upper Shore Map
GSP to Exit #117. Take Rte. 36East for 10 miles. Exit at Avenue D. Bear right to stop sign. Club is directly across the road.

Hole	1	2	3	4	5	6	7	8	9	Out	BLUE	Rating 70.2
BLUE	403	381	318	386	538	184	500	178	161	3049		Slope 124
WHITE	387	343	290	346	516	177	485	170	140	2854		
Par	4	4	4	4	5	3	5	3	3	35	WHITE	Rating 69.1
Handicap	5	3	15	1	11	13	7	9	17			Slope 123
RED	367	315	270	316	465	138	465	160	120	2616		
Par	4	4	4	4	5	3	5	3	3	35	RED	Rating 72.4
Handicap	5	7	11	3	9	15	1	13	17			Slope 123
Hole	10	11	12	13	14	15	16	17	18	In		Totals
BLUE	389	412	513	511	171	324	272	331	161	3084	BLUE	6133
WHITE	364	389	508	501	164	321	262	326	158	2993	WHITE	5847
Par	4	4	5	5	3	4	4	4	3	36	Par	71
Handicap	6	2	4	8	12	10	18	16	14			
RED	304	369	468	482	155	310	252	260	155	2755	RED	5371
Par	4	4	5	5	3	4	4	4	3	36	Par	71
Handicap	10	2	6	4	16	8	12	18	14			

Manager: John Murphy   **Pro:** Chuck Edwards, PGA   **Supt:** Michael Hocko
Architect: Seymour Dunn 1899

BEL-AIRE GOLF CLUB

PUBLIC

Route 34 & Allaire Rd., Allenwood, NJ 08720   (732) 449-6024

Bel-Aire is part of the Monmouth County Park System. The 27 holes here consist of one 18 hole executive and one 9 hole par 3 course. It is open to the public 7 days a week all year. Golfers play first come, first served. The driving range is for irons only.

•**Driving Range**	Lockers
•**Practice Green**	Showers
•**Power Carts**	•**Food**
•**Pull Carts**	•**Clubhouse**
•**Club Rental**	•**Outings**
•**Soft Spikes**	

Fees	Weekday	Weekend
Res/ID	$15	$19
Non-res	$24	$30
9 holes	$8	$9
Power carts $20		

Course Description: The 18 hole, par 60, executive layout has amply wide fairways and medium sized greens. Since purchased by Monmouth County, the courses have been upgraded to its standards. Water comes into play on 4 holes. For a short non-regulation layout, Bel-Aire can be quite interesting and somewhat challenging. The 9 hole course has no water and is easy to walk. This facility can be quite busy on weekends.

Directions: Monmouth County, #4 on Upper Shore Map
GSP to Exit 98. Follow signs to Rte. 34S and take it for 1/2 mile. Go left at circle and into Bel-aire parking lot.

Hole	1	2	3	4	5	6	7	8	9	Out	BLUE	Rating
BLUE												Slope
WHITE	141	116	157	275	118	335	110	298	138	1688		
Par	3	3	3	4	3	4	3	4	3	30	WHITE	Rating
Handicap	11	13	9	5	15	1	17	3	7			Slope
RED	101	116	115	255	118	290	110	255	138	1498		
Par	3	3	3	4	3	4	3	4	3	30	RED	Rating
Handicap	11	13	9	3	15	1	17	5	7			Slope

Hole	10	11	12	13	14	15	16	17	18	In		Totals
BLUE											BLUE	
WHITE	285	138	170	312	148	375	141	178	188	1935	WHITE	3623
Par	4	3	3	4	3	4	3	3	3	30	Par	60
Handicap	12	16	8	10	14	2	18	4	6			
RED	260	138	130	238	148	345	141	151	170	1721	RED	3219
Par	4	3	3	4	3	4	3	3	3	30	Par	60
Handicap	8	16	12	10	14	2	18	6	4			

Manager: Bill O'Shaughnessy   **Pro:** Alan Roberts, PGA   **Supt:** Rich Leyh
Architect: Mort Hansen 1964

BEY LEA GOLF COURSE

1536 Bay Ave., Toms River, NJ 08753   **(732) 349-0566**

Bey Lea is an 18 hole municipal course for Dover Township open to the public 7 days a week all year. Special rates for seniors, students. Memberships are available for residents (obtain ID card). Tee time reservations are necessary for weekends.

- **Driving Range**
- **Practice Green**
- **Power Carts**
- **Pull Carts**
- **Club Rental**
  Soft Spikes
- **Lockers**
- **Showers**
- **Food**
- **Clubhouse**
- **Outings**

Fees	Weekday	Weekend
Res/ID	$13	$15
Non-resNJ	$26	$30
Power carts $25		

Course Description: Bey Lea is a fairly open, well-maintained course with few hills. Water is in play on several holes and bunkers are placed along some of the fairways. The greens are large and undulating. The signature par 5 #18 is long and requires a shot over a picturesque lake. The 16th may result in an encounter with water which lurks on either side. If you join the private association, you may partake in tournaments every week. The course is very busy on summer mornings and on weekends.

Directions: Ocean County, #5 on Upper Shore Map
GSP to Exit 82. Take Rte.37 East for 2 traffic lights. Take jughandle to Hooper Ave. North (Rte.549). Proceed 6 lights to jughandle for Oak St. and into parking lot.

Hole	1	2	3	4	5	6	7	8	9	Out	BLUE	Rating 71.3
BLUE	370	490	377	170	455	342	553	203	383	3343		Slope 122
WHITE	345	469	354	150	430	322	530	173	366	3139		
Par	4	5	4	3	4	4	5	3	4	36	WHITE	Rating 69.3
Handicap	10	6	8	18	4	14	2	16	12			Slope 116
RED	320	419	331	130	410	298	509	146	351	2914		
Par	4	5	4	3	4	4	5	3	4	36	RED	Rating 72.2
Handicap	10	6	8	18	4	14	2	16	12			Slope 117
Hole	10	11	12	13	14	15	16	17	18	In		Totals
BLUE	397	336	207	362	434	516	390	187	505	3334	BLUE	6677
WHITE	375	314	182	344	412	490	368	142	485	3112	WHITE	6251
Par	4	4	3	4	4	5	4	3	5	36	Par	72
Handicap	9	13	15	11	7	3	5	17	1			
RED	353	291	159	322	391	465	332	134	432	2879	RED	5793
Par	4	4	3	4	4	5	4	3	5	36	Par	72
Handicap	9	13	15	11	7	3	5	17	1			

Manager: Gloria Pieretti   **Supt:** Gary Nokes
Architect: Hal Purdy 1969

CEDAR CREEK GOLF COURSE

PUBLIC

Tilton Blvd., Bayville, NJ 08721   **(732) 269-4460**

Cedar Creek is an 18 hole Berkeley Township course open 7 days a week all year. Annual memberships are available. Tee time reservations are not necessary.

Driving Range	Lockers
•**Practice Green**	Showers
•**Power Carts**	•**Food**
•**Pull Carts**	•**Clubhouse**
•**Club Rental**	•**Outings**
•**Soft Spikes**	

Fees	Weekday	Weekend
Res	$12	$14
Sr	$10	
Non-res	$23	$27
Power carts res.$20		
" " non-res $26		

Course Description: This well maintained and popular course draws players from Staten Island and Long Island as well as from New Jersey. The back nine can be quite challenging with water in play on holes 10, 12, 13 and 14. The par 5 18th is lined with pine trees, oaks and dogwood and has a beautiful view, making it the signature hole. A driving range is to be installed here.

Directions: Ocean County, #6 on Upper Shore Map
GSP to Exit 80. Go left onto Double Tree Rd. to end. At "T" make a left onto Pinewall-Keswick which becomes Forest Hills Parkway. Go past high school on right. Make a right onto Tilton Blvd. and go into Veteran's Park and Cedar Creek Golf Course.

Hole	1	2	3	4	5	6	7	8	9	Out	BLUE	Rating 70.5
BLUE	499	161	385	453	372	339	130	367	359	3065		Slope 120
WHITE	494	144	355	440	346	330	121	333	332	2895		
Par	5	3	4	5	4	4	3	4	4	36	WHITE	Rating 68.9
Handicap	6	18	4	16	8	12	14	10	2			Slope 117
RED	415	119	312	369	300	285	113	291	280	2484		
Par	5	3	4	5	4	4	3	4	4	36	RED	Rating 69.5
Handicap	6	18	4	16	8	12	14	10	2			Slope 118
Hole	10	11	12	13	14	15	16	17	18	In		Totals
BLUE	529	234	441	380	368	326	308	127	547	3260	BLUE	6325
WHITE	520	220	418	368	340	320	282	115	525	3108	WHITE	6003
Par	5	3	4	4	4	4	4	3	5	36	Par	72
Handicap	5	1	3	7	11	13	15	17	9			
RED	468	164	365	307	303	285	219	95	464	2670	RED	5154
Par	5	3	4	4	4	4	4	3	5	36	Par	72
Handicap	7	5	1	3	11	13	15	17	9			

Manager: Pat Wall   **Supt**: Dennis Parker
Architect: Nicholas Psiahas 1981

CHARLESTON SPRINGS GOLF COURSE

193 Sweetman's Lane, Millstone Twp., NJ 08535　(732) 409-7227

Charleston Springs is the newest golf facility for Monmouth County. 18 holes are ready now with another 18, clubhouse and driving range to begin construction in 1999. The North Course is open 7 days a week and will be closed in the winter. Residents obtain ID & reserve 7 days in adv. Non-res. 5 days.

- **Driving Range**
- **Practice Green**
- **Power Carts**
- **Pull Carts**
- **Club Rental**
- **Soft Spikes**

Lockers
Showers
- **Food**
- Clubhouse
- Outings

Fees	Weekday	Weekend
Res/ID	$30	$30
Non-res	$60	$60
Discounts for Sr & Jr.		
Power carts $29.68		

Course Description: Formerly a nursery, Charleston Springs is fairly flat with a few small rolling hills. It is built in an open links style using a wide variety of native and fescue grasses. The wind and some water are definite factors affecting play. The South layout will be more parkland style set in and retaining many more trees. Both courses will continue the high quality tradition that Monmouth County has set for its golf facilities. Ratings, slopes and handicaps are not yet available.

Directions: Monmouth County, #7 on Upper Shore Map
NJ Tpke to Exit 8. Proceed east on Rte. 33 to Rte. 527 South. For temporary entrance on Sweetman's Lane, make right at 4 way STOP to course ahead on left. Future entrance will be on Rte. 527 (Smithburg Rd.)

Hole	1	2	3	4	5	6	7	8	9	Out	BLUE	Rating
BLUE	200	408	531	439	436	495	203	358	412	3472		Slope
WHITE	170	361	473	398	397	469	175	327	341	3111		
Par	3	4	5	4	4	5	3	4	4	36	WHITE	Rating
Handicap												Slope
RED	111	292	425	321	328	382	131	256	290	2536		
Par											RED	Rating
Handicap												Slope

Hole	10	11	12	13	14	15	16	17	18	In		Totals
BLUE	165	418	427	521	170	396	430	564	455	3546	BLUE	7018
WHITE	131	379	355	469	149	358	360	521	403	3125	WHITE	6236
Par	3	4	4	5	3	4	4	5	4	36	Par	72
Handicap												
RED	94	309	314	402	96	289	312	448	343	2607	RED	5143
Par											Par	72
Handicap												

Manager: Bill O'Shaughnessy　**Pro:** Alan Roberts, PGA　**Supt:** Ron Luepke
Architect: Mark Mungeam 1998

COLONIAL TERRACE GOLF CLUB PUBLIC

1005 Wickapecko Drive, Wanamassa, NJ 07712   (732) 775-3636

Colonial Terrace is a 9 hole course open to the public 7 days a week all year. Tee time reservations are recommended on weekends.

Driving Range Practice Green •Power Carts •Pull Carts •Club Rental •Soft Spikes	Lockers Showers •Food •Clubhouse •Outings

Fees	**Weekday**	**Weekend**
Daily	$15	$18
Sr.	$11	
Power carts	$24/18	

Course Description: Colonial Terrace has recently refurbished its greens and tees. It is a regulation 9 hole course with different tees for the 2nd nine. The first hole is a drivable par 4. On the 3rd, a "lake" is in play; (environmentalists now consider this area marshland). The signature 463 yard par 4 2nd features woods and water surrounding the small green. Colonial Terrace is a good facility for iron practice and is easy to walk. A putting green is to be installed for 1999.

Directions: Monmouth County, #8 on Upper Shore Map
GSP to Exit #102. Bear right off the exit to Asbury Park traffic circle. Take Rte.35 North to Sunset Ave. (2nd light after circle) and turn right. At 2nd light, go right onto Wickapecko Drive; course is 1 and 1/2 blocks on right.

Hole	1	2	3	4	5	6	7	8	9	Out	BLUE	Rating
BLUE												Slope
WHITE	271	463	162	433	127	349	431	157	311	2704		
Par	4	4	3	5	3	4	5	3	4	35	WHITE	Rating
Handicap	7	1	5	4	9	2	3	8	6			Slope
RED	243	347	124	382	112	236	358	126	247	2175		
Par											RED	Rating
Handicap												Slope
Hole	10	11	12	13	14	15	16	17	18	In		Totals
BLUE											BLUE	
WHITE											WHITE	2704
Par											Par	35
Handicap												
RED											RED	2175
Par											Par	35
Handicap												

Manager: Consuelo Cesario   **Pro/Supt:** Lin Cesario
Built: 1925

CREAM RIDGE GOLF CLUB

PUBLIC

181 Route 539, Cream Ridge, NJ 08514   (609) 259-2849

Cream Ridge is an 18 hole semi-private club open 7 days a week all year. Tee times may be reserved up to one week in advance. Alternate phone # (800) 345-4957. Carts are mandatory until 2PM on weekends.

- **Driving Range**
- **Practice Green**
- **Power Carts**
- **Pull Carts**
- Club Rental
- **Soft Spikes**
- **Lockers**
- **Showers**
- **Food**
- **Clubhouse**
- **Outings**

Fees	M-Thurs	Fri-Sun
Daily	$25	$33
Twilight	$18	
Sr/Jr	$17	
Power carts $15pp		

Course Description: Golfers come from all over (Staten Island, Pa., Jersey Shore) to enjoy Cream Ridge believing that it is worth the trip. The course is well-maintained and features rolling hills, undulating mid-size greens and many water hazards. The signature par 5 18th demands strategy to deal with the double dogleg and the water that comes into play along one side as well as for the approach shot. There has been some redesign of the layout recently and the new clubhouse is a welcome addition.

Directions: Monmouth County, #9 on Upper Shore Map
NJTpke to Exit 7A. Take Rte.195E to Exit #7. Follow signs to Allentown. At first STOP sign, turn right onto Main St.(Rte.539S). Club is 4 miles ahead on right.

Hole	1	2	3	4	5	6	7	8	9	Out	BLUE	Rating 71.8
BLUE	530	165	263	162	385	403	414	426	580	3328		Slope 124
WHITE	520	138	258	145	343	307	408	401	573	3093		
Par	5	3	4	3	4	4	4	4	5	36	WHITE	Rating 69.5
Handicap	5	15	9	11	13	17	7	3	1			Slope 121
RED	432	128	250	116	308	295	337	317	433	2616		
Par	5	3	4	3	4	4	4	4	5	36	RED	Rating 69.6
Handicap	4	12	10	14	16	18	8	2	6			Slope 119
Hole	10	11	12	13	14	15	16	17	18	In		Totals
BLUE	418	396	340	180	440	367	331	191	500	3163	BLUE	6491
WHITE	352	380	334	172	430	362	316	154	488	2988	WHITE	6081
Par	4	4	4	3	4	4	4	3	5	35	Par	71
Handicap	6	12	18	8	2	10	16	14	4			
RED	332	334	297	151	321	328	293	145	333	2534	RED	5150
Par	4	4	4	3	4	4	4	3	4	34	Par	70
Handicap	3	11	15	13	7	5	17	9	1			

Manager: Bill Miscoski   **Pro:** Bill Marine, PGA   **Supt:** Ken Horner
Architect: Frank Miscoski 1958

CRUZ FARM COUNTRY CLUB
PUBLIC

55 Birdsall Rd., Farmingdale, NJ 07727   **(732) 938-3378**

Cruz Farm is an 18 hole course open 7 days a week, all year. Reserved tee times are not necessary.

Driving Range	Lockers
•**Practice Green**	Showers
•**Power Carts**	•**Food**
•**Pull Carts**	Clubhouse
Club Rental	•**Outings**
Soft Spikes	

Fees	Weekday	Weekend
Daily	$20	$24
Power carts	$28	

Course Description: Cruz Farm Country Club is a short, flat layout that is easy to walk. Many holes have water in play and the course is well bunkered. The medium sized greens are slow. Cruz Farm is quite busy in summer.

Directions: Monmouth County, #10 on Upper Shore Map
GSP to Exit 100A. Go west on Rte. 33 for 1 mile to circle. Proceed south on Rte. 34 for 2 lights. Turn right onto Belmar Blvd. and continue for 1 mile; turn left onto Birdsall Rd to club on left.

Hole	1	2	3	4	5	6	7	8	9	Out	BLUE	Rating
BLUE												Slope
WHITE	145	340	545	350	180	590	340	140	325	2955		
Par	3	4	5	4	3	5	4	3	4	35	WHITE	Rating
Handicap	18	12	8	4	6	2	10	16	14			Slope
RED												
Par											RED	Rating
Handicap												Slope
Hole	10	11	12	13	14	15	16	17	18	In		Totals
BLUE											BLUE	
WHITE	125	295	520	355	380	200	140	380	550	2945	WHITE	5900
Par	3	4	5	4	4	3	3	4	5	35	Par	70
Handicap	17	15	5	9	13	3	11	7	1			
RED											RED	
Par											Par	
Handicap												

Manager: Lee Cruz   **Supt:** Leo Silva
Architect: Evaristo Cruz 1979

DEAL GOLF CLUB

Roseld Ave., Deal, NJ 07723 **(732) 531-1190**

Deal is an 18 hole course open 6 days a week and closed in February. Guests play accompanied by a member. Tee time reservations are not necessary.

- **Driving Range**
- **Practice Green**
- **Power Carts**
- Pull Carts
- Club Rental
- **Caddies**
- **Lockers**
- **Showers**
- **Food**
- **Clubhouse**
- **Outings**
- **Soft Spikes**

Course Description: Deal Golf Club is old with narrow tree lined fairways and deep rough. Water is in play on several holes; three ponds confront the golfer. An errant shot on this course can land deep in the woods from which it is difficult to extricate oneself. The tee shot on the signature par 4 5th is out of a chute with water along the right side. The approach is daunting; the green is protected by a bunker and a creek. The course becomes even more challenging when a strong ocean wind is blowing. The clubhouse is beautiful and stately.

Directions: Monmouth County, #11 on Upper Shore Map
GSP to Exit 105. Go east for 2 miles to traffic circle and take Rte. 35S for about 3 miles to jughandle for Deal Rd. Continue on Deal to end and turn right onto Monmouth Rd. Turn left onto Roseld Ave. Club is ahead on right.

Hole	1	2	3	4	5	6	7	8	9	Out	BLUE	Rating
BLUE												Slope
WHITE	325	431	348	351	366	194	393	180	478	3066		
Par	4	4	4	4	4	3	4	3	5	35	WHITE	Rating 70.5
Handicap	15	1	11	7	3	13	5	17	9			Slope 126
RED	315	380	322	320	360	173	350	163	460	2843		
Par	4	5	4	4	5	3	4	3	5	37	RED	Rating 73.7
Handicap	17	7	11	3	5	13	9	15	1			Slope 128

Hole	10	11	12	13	14	15	16	17	18	In		Totals
BLUE											BLUE	
WHITE	355	332	554	139	478	413	408	388	170	3237	WHITE	6303
Par	4	4	5	3	5	4	4	4	3	36	Par	71
Handicap	12	10	2	18	8	6	4	14	16			
RED	343	320	472	118	427	402	375	372	160	2989	RED	5832
Par	4	4	5	3	5	5	4	4	3	37	Par	74
Handicap	14	12	2	18	8	6	4	10	16			

Manager: Jozsef de Kovacs   **Pro:** Dan Beveridge, PGA   **Supt:** Angelo Petraglia
Architects: Donald Ross, Lawrence Van Etten   **Estab:** 1898

DUE PROCESS STABLES

Route 537, Colt's Neck, NJ 07722   **(732) 542-0317**

Due Process Stables opened in 1996. It is an 18 hole course open 6 days a week and closed in winter. Guests play accompanied by a member. Tee times can be reserved 1 day in advance.

- **Driving Range**
- **Practice Green**
- **Power Carts**
- Pull Carts
- Club Rental
- **Caddies**

- **Lockers**
- **Showers**
- **Food**
- **Clubhouse**
- Outings
- **Soft Spikes**

Course Description: Formerly a working stable, Due Process was conceived of by Robert Brennan and designed in an equine motif by Johnny Miller and Gene Bates. The clubhouse is a converted barn with statues of racing horses all around. There are shamrocks on the entrance gates. The tees are designated as Derby, Preakness & Belmont, instead of the usual colors. The course features stacked sod bunkers, long fescue grass in the rough, considerable mounding and rolling terrain. Two holes have double fairways; some sections are in a links style. Opportunities abound for bump and run shots. Caddies are mandatory.

Directions: Monmouth County, #12 on Upper Shore Map
GSP to Exit 109, Lincroft. Make a right off the ramp to Rte. 520West. At 2nd light, turn left into Swimming River Road. Go for about 2 miles and bear right at fork onto Rte. 537West. Club entrance is at third driveway on left.

Hole	1	2	3	4	5	6	7	8	9	Out	BLUE	Rating 74.6
BLUE	417	458	435	158	529	403	182	508	336	3476		Slope 142
WHITE	360	416	384	150	503	336	175	480	362	3166		
Par	4	4	4	3	5	4	3	5	4	36	WHITE	Rating 72.1
Handicap	10	4	2	18	8	12	14	6	16			Slope 136
RED	347	351	357	134	479	319	142	435	338	2902		
Par	4	4	4	3	5	4	3	5	4	36	RED	Rating 70.0
Handicap	10	4	2	18	8	12	14	6	16			Slope 129
Hole	10	11	12	13	14	15	16	17	18	In		Totals
BLUE	437	209	540	451	398	216	413	427	521	3612	BLUE	7088
WHITE	407	182	524	423	363	179	385	402	496	3361	WHITE	6527
Par	4	3	5	4	4	3	4	4	5	36	Par	72
Handicap	3	15	5	1	13	17	7	9	11			
RED	376	364	450	302	127	435	387	141	344	2926	RED	5760
Par	4	3	5	4	4	3	4	4	5	36	Par	72
Handicap	3	15	5	1	13	17	7	9	11			

Manager: John Perrotta   **Pro:** Wayne Warms, PGA   **Supt:** John Wantz
Architect: Johnny Miller 1994

EAGLE RIDGE GOLF CLUB

PUBLIC

2 Augusta Blvd., Lakewood, NJ 08701   **(732) 901-4900**

Eagle Ridge is an 18 hole semi-private course opening the summer of 1999 & operating 7 days a week all year. Memberships are available. Special discounts for residents of the Fairways and the Meadows at Lake Ridge adult communities. Tee times 10 days for members, non members: 5 days.

- **Driving Range**
- **Practice Green**
- **Power Carts**
- Pull Carts
- **Club Rental**
- **Soft Spikes**
- **Lockers**
- **Showers**
- **Food**
- **Clubhouse**
- **Outings**

NEW

Fees	Weekday	Weekend
Daily	$30	$45
Power carts $15pp		

Course Description: Built on a former gravel mining pit, this new links style course will be a major attraction for the homeowners of the adult communities nearby. With considerable elevation changes, sloping fairways, natural grasses and scrub pines in the heavier rough, Eagle Ridge offers challenge and variety. Water is in play on 5 holes. The greens are contoured, some two-tiered. The signature par 5 5th has a pond confronting the golfer on the approach shot. Waste areas, sand and grass bunkers are encountered here along with elevated greens and tees. The magnificent clubhouse overlooks panoramic views of this unique property. Slopes, ratings and handicaps have not yet been determined.

Directions: Ocean County, #13 on Upper Shore Map
GSP to Exit 88. Take Rte. 70 West. Make a right onto Massachusetts Ave. At Cross St., turn left and course is on the left about 1 mile ahead.

Hole	1	2	3	4	5	6	7	8	9	Out	BLUE	Rating
BLUE	388	400	220	335	520	412	540	177	345	3337		Slope
WHITE	353	362	173	290	490	382	507	150	315	3022		
Par	4	4	3	4	5	4	5	3	4	36	WHITE	Rating
Handicap												Slope
RED	311	320	152	246	407	338	420	123	280	2597		
Par	4	4	3	4	5	4	5	3	4	36	RED	Rating
Handicap												Slope
Hole	10	11	12	13	14	15	16	17	18	In		Totals
BLUE	348	163	407	375	422	505	135	393	357	3105	BLUE	6442
WHITE	308	133	352	312	363	475	100	353	320	2716	WHITE	5738
Par	4	3	4	4	4	5	3	4	4	35	Par	71
Handicap												
RED	292	105	302	265	330	427	80	323	286	2410	RED	5007
Par	4	3	4	4	4	5	3	4	4	35	Par	71
Handicap												

Manager: Billy Casper Management   **Acting Dir. of Golf:** Mike Attara, PGA
Supt: Dennis Parker   **Architects:** Ault, Clark & Associates, Ltd. 1999

FAIRWAY MEWS GOLF CLUB

Warren Ave., Spring Lake Heights, NJ 07762   **(732) 449-8883**

Fairway Mews Golf & Racquet Club is an 18 hole executive course for residents of the adult community where it is located. It is open 6 days a week from Mar. 15th through Dec. 15th. Tee time reservations are advisable.

Driving Range	•Lockers
•Practice Green	•Showers
•Power Carts	Food
•Pull Carts	Clubhouse
Club Rental	Outings
Caddies	•Soft Spikes

Course Description: Fairway Mews is an executive layout, par 60 from the whites and playing to a par 64 from the Reds. Winding through the housing development, the course is narrow, flat and easy to walk. Most members own their golf carts. Water is in play on six holes. The fast greens are of medium size; some putts necessitate a careful read.

Directions: Monmouth County, #14 on Upper Shore Map
GSP to Exit 98. Take Rte. 34S about 1 mile to traffic circle. Proceed 3/4 around circle and go right on Allaire Rd. (towards Spring Lake). Go 2 miles and turn right onto Rte. 34S. Go 1 block and turn left onto Warren Ave. Club is 1 mile ahead on left.

Hole	1	2	3	4	5	6	7	8	9	Out	BLUE	Rating
BLUE												Slope
WHITE	142	180	238	307	166	160	157	150	300	1800		
Par	3	3	4	4	3	3	3	3	4	30	WHITE	Rating 57.2
Handicap	12	8	6	2	10	14	15	18	4			Slope 82
RED	134	140	201	263	157	133	146	141	285	1600		
Par	3	3	4	5	3	3	3	3	5	32	RED	Rating 57.7
Handicap	16	6	8	4	10	12	14	18	2			Slope 83
Hole	10	11	12	13	14	15	16	17	18	In		Totals
BLUE											BLUE	
WHITE	141	267	220	159	391	200	139	197	181	1895	WHITE	3695
Par	3	4	4	3	4	3	3	3	3	30	Par	60
Handicap	15	3	9	11	1	7	17	5	13			
RED	85	254	193	141	308	170	134	147	131	1563	RED	3163
Par	3	4	4	3	5	4	3	3	3	32	Par	64
Handicap	17	1	7	13	3	11	15	5	9			

Manager: Jane Balmer   **Pro:** Kevin Kenny, PGA   **Supt:** Joseph Beaudoin
Built: Late 1970s

FOUR SEASONS SPA & CC

1600 Spring Meadow Dr., Lakewood, NJ 08701   (732) 477-1668

Four Seasons Spa & Country Club contains a 9 hole executive course available to the residents of this adult community. It is open 6 days a week, closed Tues, from Mar. 15 to Dec. 15. Guests play accompanied by members.

Driving Range	Lockers
•**Practice Green**	Showers
•**Power Carts**	Food
•**Pull Carts**	Clubhouse
Club Rental	Outings
Caddies	•**Soft Spikes**

Course Description: This executive course has 6 par 3s and 3 par 4s. Many homes are situated on the left or right of every hole. The residents of this adult community are fortunate to have this attractive amenity along with the other activities offered here. Water is in play in a few places; the signature 4th hole where three quarters of the green is surrounded by water requires a well placed tee shot. The tees and greens are well conditioned. For variety, golfers play Blue for front and White for the second nine to make 18.

Directions: Ocean County, #15 on Upper Shore Map
GSP to Exit 88. Go east on Rte. 70 and make a right at first light, Shorrock Rd. Pass Lions Head Woods, another adult community, and turn right onto Four Seasons Drive into development. Make right onto Spring Meadow Drive to clubhouse.

Hole	1	2	3	4	5	6	7	8	9	Out	BLUE	Rating 29.8
BLUE	150	145	360	143	300	180	130	330	96	1834		Slope 98
WHITE	140	135	320	130	266	146	120	300	92	1649		
Par	3	3	4	3	4	3	3	4	3	30	WHITE	Rating 29.3
Handicap	8	7	2	3	4	5	6	1	9			Slope 100
RED	129	115	295	127	229	132	110	272	94	1503		
Par	3	3	4	3	4	3	3	4	3	30	RED	Rating 28.5
Handicap	8	7	2	3	4	5	6	1	9			Slope 91
Hole	10	11	12	13	14	15	16	17	18	In		Totals
BLUE											BLUE	1834
WHITE											WHITE	1639
Par											Par	30
Handicap												
RED											RED	1503
Par											Par	30
Handicap												

Pro: Art Robidoux, PGA   **Supt:** Harry Leonard
Architect: Tom Fazio 1997

GAMBLER RIDGE GOLF CLUB

PUBLIC

Burlington Path Rd., Cream Ridge, NJ 08514

(609) 758-3588

Gambler Ridge is an 18 hole course open 7 days a week all year. Tee times may be reserved 7 days in advance. Carts are required before 11 AM on weekends. Alternate phone # (800) 427-8463. Discounts available for seniors.

•Driving Range	Lockers
•Practice Green	Showers
•Power Carts	•Food
•Pull Carts	•Clubhouse
Club Rental	•Outings
•Soft Spikes	

Fees	Weekday	Weekend
Daily	$24	$32
after 11	$16	
Power carts	$7pp	$12pp

Course Description: Gambler Ridge is a course that is constantly being improved. It is a good challenge for the average golfer, fairly open with scattered trees. Built on a former farm deep in race horse country, it is relatively flat; the mid-sized greens are of bent grass and are fast. Water is in play on 12 holes. The par 3 12th requires a tee shot over two ponds.

Directions: Monmouth County, #16 on Upper Shore Map
NJTpke to Exit 7A. Take Rte. 195 East to Exit 16. At exit, make a right and go about 5 miles to the first light. Turn right onto Rte. 539 North. Go 2 miles to Burlington Path Rd. and turn right. Course is 1 mile ahead on the right.

Hole	1	2	3	4	5	6	7	8	9	Out	BLUE	Rating 70.2
BLUE	358	369	171	534	275	335	166	540	381	3129		Slope 119
WHITE	349	359	105	521	270	325	148	531	375	2983		
Par	4	4	3	5	4	4	3	5	4	36	WHITE	Rating 69.1
Handicap	16	8	12	2	18	10	14	4	6			Slope 116
RED	282	286	80	434	244	295	125	435	323	2504		
Par	4	4	3	5	4	4	3	5	4	36	RED	Rating 69.3
Handicap	16	8	12	2	18	10	14	4	6			Slope 115

Hole	10	11	12	13	14	15	16	17	18	In		Totals
BLUE	378	233	365	321	211	416	525	402	390	3241	BLUE	6370
WHITE	360	198	356	317	201	401	513	390	383	3119	WHITE	6102
Par	4	3	4	4	3	4	5	4	4	35	Par	71
Handicap	9	7	11	17	15	3	13	1	5			
RED	303	142	295	258	161	353	459	332	318	2621	RED	5125
Par	4	3	4	4	3	4	5	4	4	35	Par	71
Handicap	9	7	11	17	15	3	13	1	5			

Managers/Architects: Jason Nickelson, Brian Rockhill   **Supt:** Gary Cameron
Built: 1985

GREENBRIAR WOODLANDS

1 Kensington Circle, Toms River, NJ 08755   (732) 286-6889

Greenbriar is an 18 hole executive course. Residents of this adult community may take a yearly membership or may play on a daily basis. It is open 7 days a week and is closed for Jan & Feb. Reserved tee times are not necessary.

•**Driving Range**	Lockers
•**Practice Green**	Showers
•**Power Carts**	Food
•**Pull Carts**	•**Clubhouse**
•**Club Rental**	Outings
Caddies	Soft Spikes

Course Description: This lovely golf course may be found amidst the 1,000 housing units of Greenbriar Woodlands. The front nine is short consisting of all par 3s with the longest hole 120 yards. The more challenging back has longer par 3s and one par 4. The fairways are narrow and well bunkered. The small greens are elevated, hard and fast often sloping away from the pin. The most picturesque hole is the 18th; it features a pond to carry in front of the green. Golfers may play White/Blue on the front nine and Red/White on the back.

Directions: Ocean County, #17 on Upper Shore Map
GSP to Exit 83 (Seaside Heights). At the first jughandle, take Rte. 37E. Go to the next light and turn right onto Old Freehold Road. Continue until it becomes New Hampshire Ave. Make a right into Greenbriar Woodlands to the gatehouse and go straight ahead to clubhouse parking.

Hole	1	2	3	4	5	6	7	8	9	Out	BLUE	Rating 29.0
BLUE												Slope 91
WHITE	117	60	98	102	87	110	115	65	120	874		
Par	3	3	3	3	3	3	3	3	3	27	WHITE	Rating 29.2
Handicap	4	9	6	7	5	1	2	8	3			Slope 91
RED	152	95	143	145	403	94	196	135	172	1535		
Par	3	3	3	3	4	3	3	3	3	28	RED	Rating 29.2
Handicap	5	15	11	9	1	17	7	13	3			Slope 89

Hole	10	11	12	13	14	15	16	17	18	In		Totals
BLUE	131	110	121	167	381	111	182	146	156	1505	BLUE	1505
WHITE	117	60	98	102	87	110	115	65	120	874	WHITE	1748
Par	3	3	3	3	4	3	3	3	3	28	Par	55
Handicap	6	16	12	10	2	18	8	14	4			
RED											RED	1535
Par											Par	56
Handicap												

Pro: Mike Harris   **Supt:** Thomas McConnell
Architects: Smith Assoc. & Harry Harsin 1987

HOLLYWOOD GOLF CLUB

Roseld Avenue, Deal, NJ 07723   (732) 531-8950

Hollywood is an 18 hole course open 6 days a week between Mar 15 and Dec. 1. Guests play accompanied by a member. Tee time reservations are required for weekends.

- Driving Range
- Practice Green
- Power Carts
- Pull Carts
- Club Rental
- Caddies
- Lockers
- Showers
- Food
- Clubhouse
- Outings
- Soft Spikes

Course Description: Hollywood Golf Club has been rated as one of the top 8 courses in NJ by Golf Digest. With gently rolling terrain in a links style layout, accuracy off the tee is extremely important. The well-guarded, small greens are fast with some break. The bunkers and tees have recently been redesigned by Rees Jones. The signature par 3 4th is rated one of the best short par 3s in the world. Mounding and bunkering confront the golfer. Too short a shot and the ball rolls back off the green; over the target area and the ball rolls down a slope. The NJ State PGA was held here in 1998. With the recent work, the scorecard will be revised somewhat.

Directions: Monmouth County, #18 on Upper Shore Map
GSP to Exit 105. Proceed east on Rte. 36 to light (about 2 miles). Turn right onto Rte. 35S for about 3 miles to Deal Rd. (jughandle left). Go east on Deal Rd to end and turn right onto Monmouth Rd. Go 4 blocks to Roseld Ave. & turn right. Club is on right.

Hole	1	2	3	4	5	6	7	8	9	Out	BLUE	Rating 73.7
BLUE	419	359	456	149	392	391	539	392	384	3481		Slope 135
WHITE	404	347	394	143	351	366	523	360	369	3257		
Par	4	4	4	3	4	4	5	4	4	36	WHITE	Rating 72.1
Handicap	4	16	6	18	14	10	2	12	8			Slope 132
RED	388	335	342	130	330	321	463	341	335	2985		
Par	5	4	4	3	4	4	5	4	4	37	RED	Rating 73.9
Handicap	5	13	3	17	15	11	1	7	9			Slope 127

Hole	10	11	12	13	14	15	16	17	18	In		Totals
BLUE	512	382	452	315	378	167	459	230	396	3291	BLUE	6812
WHITE	491	375	432	310	352	158	454	210	392	3174	WHITE	6386
Par	5	4	4	4	4	3	5	3	4	36	Par	72
Handicap	7	3	1	13	9	17	15	11	5			
RED	407	307	418	275	314	133	390	183	354	2718	RED	5766
Par	5	4	5	4	4	3	5	3	4	37	Par	74
Handicap	8	10	2	16	12	18	4	14	6			

Manager: Angela O'Neill   **Pro:** Mike Killian, PGA   **Supt:** Jan Kasyjanski
Architects: Walter Travis 1898   **Redesign:** Dick Wilson, Rees Jones

HOMINY HILL GOLF COURSE

PUBLIC

92 Mercer Rd., Colt's Neck, NJ 07722   **(732) 462-9222**

Hominy Hill is an 18 hole Monmouth County course open 7 days a week from March 15 to Dec. 23. Residents may reserve up to 7 days in advance for $1.50, non residents 5 days $3 pp. Automated phone system (732) 758-8383.

• **Driving Range**	• **Lockers**
• **Practice Green**	• **Showers**
• **Power Carts**	• **Food**
• **Pull Carts**	• **Clubhouse**
• **Club Rental**	• **Outings**
• **Soft Spikes**	

Fees	Weekday	Weekend
Daily	$18.50	$23.50
Sr.	$13.50	
Non-res	$37	$47
Power carts $29.68		

Course Description: Originally built as a private golf course, Hominy Hill is long and well designed with many bunkers. Large contoured greens and long tees are prevalent here. The par 3 signature eleventh requires considerable carry over water to a sloping green. This highly reputed course is very popular and players from all over try to obtain the few starting times the county residents leave open. The US Women's Public Links Championship was played here in 1995.

Directions: Monmouth County, #19 on Upper Shore Map
GSP south to Exit 123. Take Rte. 9S to Rte. 18S to Rte.537East. The course is one mile on the right on Mercer Rd. **OR** NJTpke to Exit 7A. Then take Rte. 195E to Rte. 537E past Rte. 18 to course.

Hole	1	2	3	4	5	6	7	8	9	Out	BLUE	Rating 74.2
BLUE	426	396	211	542	341	406	195	435	513	3465		Slope 131
WHITE	390	328	181	498	312	374	175	390	475	3123		
Par	4	4	3	5	4	4	3	4	5	36	WHITE	Rating 71.5
Handicap	6	12	14	2	10	16	18	4	8			Slope 126
RED	356	298	141	458	288	337	130	366	430	2804		
Par	4	4	3	5	4	4	3	4	5	36	RED	Rating 73.6
Handicap	6	12	14	2	10	16	18	4	8			Slope 129

Hole	10	11	12	13	14	15	16	17	18	In		Totals
BLUE	458	207	441	393	535	397	209	537	417	3594	BLUE	7059
WHITE	430	176	419	370	504	375	188	501	384	3347	WHITE	6470
Par	4	3	4	4	5	4	3	5	4	36	Par	72
Handicap	11	13	5	15	1	17	9	3	7			
RED	397	123	378	320	473	344	160	464	331	2990	RED	5794
Par	4	3	4	4	5	4	3	5	4	36	Par	72
Handicap	11	13	5	15	1	17	9	3	7			

Manager: Howard Olt   **Pro**: Alan Roberts, PGA   **Supt**: Tim Mariner
Architect: Robert Trent Jones 1964

HOWELL PARK GOLF COURSE

PUBLIC

Preventorium Rd., Farmingdale, NJ 07727   (732) 939-4771

Howell Park is an 18 hole Monmouth County course open 7 days a week between Mar. 15 and Dec. 23. Residents with ID may reserve 7 days in advance @$1.50pp, non-res with ID, 5 days @ $3pp. Call 758-8383. Others walk on.

- •Driving Range
- •Practice Green
- •Power Carts
- •Pull Carts
- •Club Rental
- •Soft Spikes

Lockers

Showers

- •Food
- •Clubhouse

Outings

Fees	Weekday	Weekend
REs/ID	$18.50	$23.50
Sr.	$13.50	
Non-res	$37	$47
Power carts	$29.68	

Course Description: Howell Park is another exceptional facility for the fortunate Monmouth County residents to enjoy. Excellently maintained, the course presents an interesting challenge to the golfer. The medium to large sized greens are fast and have considerable break. Not much water is in play although some creeks run along the tree-lined fairways. The 8th hole was redesigned recently and has a "Pete Dye" look with 5 teeing areas. It plays 190-200 yards from the blue. With its outstanding reputation, this course gets very busy.

Directions: Monmouth County, #20 on Upper Shore Map
GSP to Exit 98. Take Rte. 195West to exit 31B. At light, take a left onto Rte. 524A (Squamgum-Yellowbrook Rd). Course is on left just before the high school.

Hole	1	2	3	4	5	6	7	8	9	Out	BLUE	Rating 73.0
BLUE	425	557	382	202	401	541	336	175	410	3429		Slope 126
WHITE	387	522	363	172	372	505	313	137	393	3164		
Par	4	5	4	3	4	5	4	3	4	36	WHITE	Rating 70.2
Handicap	11	1	13	15	9	3	7	17	5			Slope 120
RED	376	476	308	132	343	416	290	105	369	2815		
Par	4	5	4	3	4	5	4	3	4	36	RED	Rating 72.5
Handicap	11	1	13	15	9	3	7	17	5			Slope 125
Hole	10	11	12	13	14	15	16	17	18	In		Totals
BLUE	415	513	391	222	387	539	381	157	451	3456	BLUE	6916
WHITE	391	470	373	150	364	475	342	135	412	3112	WHITE	6302
Par	4	5	4	3	4	5	4	3	4	36	Par	72
Handicap	4	2	8	18	12	16	6	14	10			
RED	360	408	355	140	332	457	300	112	384	2878	RED	5725
Par	4	5	4	3	4	5	4	3	4	36	Par	72
Handicap	4	2	8	18	12	16	6	14	10			

Manager: Harold Cahoon   **Pro:** David Laudien, PGA   **Supt:** Bob Duncan
Architect: Frank Duane 1972

JUMPING BROOK GOLF & CC

210 Jumping Brook Rd., Neptune, NJ 07753   (732) 922-6140

Jumping Brook is an 18 hole semi-private course open to the public 7 days a week all year. Memberships are available. Tee time policy: 3 days in advance for weekdays, prior Wednesday for weekends.

- • **Driving Range**
- • **Practice Green**
- • **Power Carts**
- • **Pull Carts**
- • **Club Rental**
- • **Soft Spikes**

- • **Lockers**
- • **Showers**
- • **Food**
- • **Clubhouse**
- • **Outings**

Fees	Weekday	Weekend
Daily	$35	$42
Seniors	$25	
Power carts $34		

Course Description: Jumping Brook is hillier than most shore courses. Open, with severe small greens, it has a brook running through it that affects play on 4 holes. The front nine is more difficult than the back. The signature 4th, called Narrows, is a short, tight par 4 with trouble from tee to green; a stream on the left and water on the right are part of the difficulty. The NJ State Open was played here in the 1930s and the State PGA in 1951. A unique feature of this course is that you can see the entire layout from both the first tee and the clubhouse.

Directions: Monmouth County, #21 on Upper Shore Map
GSP South to Exit 100B. Take Rte. 33 east and at 2nd light make a left onto Jumping Brook Rd. to course 1 mile on the right.

Hole	1	2	3	4	5	6	7	8	9	Out	BLUE	Rating 72.2
BLUE	289	413	237	361	356	369	415	578	547	3565		Slope 124
WHITE	281	355	212	341	348	361	395	506	527	3326		
Par	4	4	3	4	4	4	4	5	5	37	WHITE	Rating 70.5
Handicap	15	9	17	7	11	13	5	1	3			Slope 121
RED	236	325	188	263	280	318	370	436	392	2808		
Par	4	4	3	4	4	4	4	5	5	37	RED	Rating 71.2
Handicap	13	5	17	15	7	9	11	1	3			Slope 118

Hole	10	11	12	13	14	15	16	17	18	In		Totals
BLUE	406	180	481	210	543	133	416	329	411	3109	BLUE	6674
WHITE	348	155	477	203	498	127	408	320	407	2943	WHITE	6269
Par	4	3	5	3	5	3	4	4	4	35	Par	72
Handicap	10	16	4	14	6	18	8	12	2			
RED	329	138	392	174	410	108	328	277	314	2470	RED	5278
Par	4	3	5	3	5	3	4	4	4	35	Par	72
Handicap	10	16	4	14	2	18	6	12	8			

Manager: Steve Catania   **Pro:** Daniel Hollis, PGA   **Supt:** Ed Mellor
Architect: Willard Wilkinson 1925

KNOB HILL GOLF CLUB

360 Route 33 West, Manalapan, NJ 07726   (732) 792-8118

An 18 hole course that has been open to the public on a limited basis, Knob Hill is open 6 days a week and closed in January. Temporarily, greens fees are $35 weekday and $50 weekends. Carts are $18pp. A clubhouse with all amenities is to be constructed.

Driving Range	•**Lockers**
Practice Green	•**Showers**
•**Power Carts**	•**Food**
Pull Carts	•**Clubhouse**
•**Club Rental**	•**Outings**
Caddies	•**Soft Spikes**

Course Description: The total redesign of the 140 acre layout at Knob Hill is one of the wonderful new courses in New Jersey. Great care has been taken to protect the environment by keeping the original trees intact. A completely automated double line irrigation system guarantees exceptional conditioning. The signature par 3 15th overlooks a horse farm with the pond behind the green adding to the scenic view. A variety of fine grass fairways, 15 ponds, lakes and elevation changes make this a very interesting golf course indeed.

Directions: Monmouth County, #22 on Upper Shore Map
NJTpke to Exit 8. Go east on Rte. 33 to Woodward Rd. and make U-turn. Club is on the right on Rte. 33 West.

Hole	1	2	3	4	5	6	7	8	9	Out	BLUE	Rating 72.0
BLUE	429	419	142	476	345	196	495	386	157	3045		Slope 126
WHITE	389	319	131	439	331	176	455	372	133	2745		
Par	4	4	3	4	4	3	5	4	3	34	WHITE	Rating 69.4
Handicap	11	9	13	1	7	15	3	5	17			Slope 124
RED	338	282	107	333	295	124	404	275	114	2272		
Par	4	4	3	4	4	3	5	4	3	34	RED	Rating 68.8
Handicap	11	9	13	1	7	15	3	5	17			Slope 121
Hole	10	11	12	13	14	15	16	17	18	In		Totals
BLUE	447	463	125	422	510	194	489	346	472	3468	BLUE	6513
WHITE	410	369	110	388	485	154	458	312	445	3131	WHITE	5876
Par	4	4	3	4	5	3	5	4	4	36	Par	70
Handicap	12	8	18	4	10	16	6	14	2			
RED	339	327	96	352	344	113	415	257	402	2645	RED	4917
Par	4	4	3	4	5	3	5	4	4	36	Par	70
Handicap	12	8	18	4	10	16	6	14	2			

Manager: Bob Elliot   **Pro:** Bill Johnson, PGA   **Supt:** Mike Kingo
Architect: Mark McCumber 1998

LAKEWOOD COUNTRY CLUB

45 Country Club Drive, Lakewood, NJ 08701   **(732) 364-8899**

Lakewood is an 18 hole semi-private course open 7 days a week all year. Memberships are available. Reservations for tee times up to 1 week in advance for weekends, for weekdays call 12 noon the day before.

- **Driving Range**
- **Practice Green**
- **Power Carts**
- **Pull Carts**
- **Club Rental**
- Soft Spikes
- **Lockers**
- **Showers**
- **Food**
- **Clubhouse**
- **Outings**

Fees	Weekday	Weekend
Daily	$22	$26
Twilight	$18	$20
Power carts $26/18, $16/9		

Course Description: Lakewood, nestled in the Pinelands of New Jersey, is a short, wooded course featuring small undulating greens. The signature par 3 15th has both a pond and a stream in play. The 16th has been redesigned as a par 5 of 512 yards. The front is flat and the back nine has elevated tees and greens. Holes 4-7 are being rebuilt over the winter. Interesting pictures of people dressed in old fashioned clothing decorate the clubhouse. Teddy Roosevelt and Babe Ruth played here earlier in this century. A new scorecard will soon be available to reflect the recent changes.

Directions: Ocean County, #23 on Upper Shore Map
GSP to Exit 91. Go straight thru light at end of ramp and proceed 1/2 mile to next light. Turn left onto Rte. 526West. Golf course is 6 miles on the left on Country Club Dr.

Hole	1	2	3	4	5	6	7	8	9	Out	BLUE	Rating 70.7
BLUE												Slope 118
WHITE	360	180	378	384	167	296	341	362	508	2976		
Par	4	3	4	4	3	4	4	4	5	35	WHITE	Rating 69.0
Handicap	16	12	8	3	10	18	14	4	6			Slope 116
RED												
Par	4	3	4	5	3	4	4	4	5	36	RED	Rating 71.0
Handicap												Slope 117

Hole	10	11	12	13	14	15	16	17	18	In		Totals
BLUE											BLUE	
WHITE	220	521	135	486	350	200	391	354	415	3272	WHITE	6248
Par	4	5	3	4	5	4	4	3	4	36	Par	71
Handicap	13	2	15	5	17	1	11	7	9			
RED											RED	
Par	4	5	4	5	5	3	4	4	5	39	Par	75
Handicap												

Manager: Michael Smith   **Pro:** Todd Toohey, PGA   **Supt:** Fran Owsik
Architect: Willie Dunn 1892

LEISURE VILLAGE EAST

1 Dumbarton Dr., Lakewood, NJ 08701   **(732) 477-7900**

Leisure Village East is a private residential adult community with a 9 hole executive golf course. It is open 7 days a week from April to the end of December. Reservations for tee times are not necessary.

Driving Range	Lockers
•**Practice Green**	Showers
Power Carts	Food
•**Pull Carts**	Clubhouse
Club Rental	Outings
Caddies	Soft Spikes

Course Description: This meticulously maintained course is generally flat with narrow fairways and undulating greens. The signature 117 yard 3rd hole, the longest on the course, is heavily bunkered and out of bounds on the left can catch a wayward shot. The 6th, considered the most picturesque, is deceptively bunkered and features a slightly elevated green that slopes toward the right.

Directions: Ocean County, #24 on Upper Shore Map
GSP to Exit 88. Take Rte. 70 East and go right on Shorrock Rd. Go one mile to Leisure Village community and to course on the right.

Hole	1	2	3	4	5	6	7	8	9	Out	BLUE	Rating
BLUE												Slope
WHITE	77	92	117	102	50	72	62	83	76	731		
Par	3	3	3	3	3	3	3	3	3	27	WHITE	Rating
Handicap	6	2	1	3	5	8	9	4	7			Slope
RED	72	87	102	95	45	67	55	77	70	670		
Par											RED	Rating
Handicap												Slope
Hole	10	11	12	13	14	15	16	17	18	In		Totals
BLUE											BLUE	
WHITE											WHITE	731
Par											Par	27
Handicap												
RED											RED	670
Par											Par	27
Handicap												

Manager: Rob Byrnes   **Supt:** Ken Mathis
Built: Leisure Technology 1960s

LEISURE VILLAGE WEST

1 Buckingham Drive, Lakehurst, NJ 08733   **(732) 657-9109**

Leisure Village West has 2 nine hole par 3 golf courses, the Pines and the Willows open 7 days a week all year, weather permitting. They are within a private residential adult community. Tee time reservations are not necessary.

Driving Range	Lockers
•**Practice Green**	Showers
Power Carts	Food
•**Pull Carts**	Clubhouse
Club Rental	Outings
Caddies	Soft Spikes

Course Description: There are homes on all sides of the holes here on both of these short, flat and walkable courses. No water confronts the golfer, but there are some bunkers to negotiate. Due to its short yardage, long hitters may opt to just use irons here. The longest hole is on the Willows course, 118 yards.

Directions: Ocean County, #25 on Upper Shore Map
GSP to Exit 88. Take Rte 70 West past Leisure Village West sign, then take the jughandle and stay straight on Buckingham to gatehouse.

Hole	1	2	3	4	5	6	7	8	9	Out	BLUE	Rating
BLUE												Slope
WHITE	60	97	118	75	103	63	80	57	70	723		
Par	3	3	3	3	3	3	3	3	3	27	WHITE	Rating
Handicap												Slope
RED												
Par											RED	Rating
Handicap												Slope
Hole	**10**	**11**	**12**	**13**	**14**	**15**	**16**	**17**	**18**	**In**		Totals
BLUE											BLUE	
WHITE	63	92	57	105	63	88	77	50	93	688	WILLOW	723
Par	3	3	3	3	3	3	3	3	3	27	Par	27
Handicap												
RED											PINES	688
Par											Par	27
Handicap												

Supt: Keith Fallon

LION'S HEAD COUNTRY CLUB

251 Lion's Head Blvd. S, Brick, NJ 08723   **(732) 477-7277**

Lion's Head, a private residential adult community, has a 9 hole executive course open 6 days a week from Mar. 15 to Dec. 30. Guests play accompanied by a member. Tee time reservations are not necessary.

Driving Range	Lockers
•**Practice Green**	Showers
Power Carts	Food
•**Pull Carts**	•**Clubhouse**
Club Rental	Outings
Caddies	•**Soft Spikes**

Course Description: Within this community of approximately 900 units is an easily walkable, flat course with a natural wildlife area in the center. In some cases, golfers need to use a boardwalk to go from one hole to another. The fairways are tree lined and a second set of tees may be used for a second nine. The oversized greens get faster as the day progresses. The signature par 4 5th is surrounded by trees adding to the scenic terrain. A stream crosses the ninth hole.

Directions: Ocean County, #26 on Upper Shore Map
GSP to Exit 88. Take Rte. 70East, turn right at light onto Shorrock Rd.(a winding road). At "T", turn left onto Beaverson Blvd. Make a right into Lionshead South Blvd. Club is on the right in the Lions Head community.

Hole	1	2	3	4	5	6	7	8	9	Out	BLUE	Rating
BLUE												Slope
WHITE	75	125	155	75	280	95	100	120	125	1150		
Par	3	3	3	3	4	3	3	3	3	28	WHITE	Rating
Handicap	8	4	2	9	1	7	6	5	3			Slope
RED												
Par											RED	Rating
Handicap												Slope
Hole	**10**	**11**	**12**	**13**	**14**	**15**	**16**	**17**	**18**	**In**		Totals
BLUE											BLUE	
WHITE	115	165	185	105	305	125	130	155	160	1445	WHITE	2595
Par	3	3	3	3	4	3	3	3	3	28	Par	56
Handicap	17	13	11	18	10	16	15	14	12			
RED											RED	
Par											Par	
Handicap												

Supt: H & L Landscaping   **Architect:** Hal Purdy 1963

MANASQUAN RIVER GOLF CLUB

Riverview Drive, Brielle, NJ 08730   (732) 528-9678

Manasquan River Golf club is an 18 hole course open 6 days a week, all year. Guests play accompanied by a member. Tee time reservations are not necessary.

> • **Driving Range**   • **Lockers**
> • **Practice Green**   • **Showers**
> • **Power Carts**   • **Food**
>   Pull Carts   • **Clubhouse**
> • **Club Rental**   • **Outings**
> • **Caddies**   • **Soft Spikes**

Course Description: The beautiful Manasquan River golf course is set in the woods with river views from many holes. Hillier than one would expect in this locale, water comes into play a great deal on the back nine. Being so near the river, wind is usually a factor; however, during most normal winters, the course is playable due to the moderate shore climate. The small greens are fast and undulating. The par 5 7th hole, known as Horizon, requires a daunting drive over a ravine to land in the fairway, a high point from which the ocean is visible.

Directions: Monmouth County, #27 on Upper Shore Map
GSP to Exit 98. Follow signs to Pt. Pleasant-Brielle and Rte. 34 South. At the 2nd traffic circle on Rte. 34, take Rte. 70 West for 1 mile to Riverview Drive and turn left. The club is on the left in about 1 mile.

Hole	1	2	3	4	5	6	7	8	9	Out	BLUE	Rating 72.5
BLUE	320	371	162	345	467	209	594	379	418	3265		Slope 128
WHITE	311	355	154	340	450	202	584	370	399	3165		
Par	4	4	3	4	5	3	5	4	4	36	WHITE	Rating 71.5
Handicap	15	3	17	11	9	13	1	5	7			Slope 126
RED	302	314	137	327	392	164	480	354	324	2794		
Par	4	4	3	4	5	3	5	4	4	36	RED	Rating 74.1
Handicap	13	3	17	9	7	15	1	5	11			Slope 129
Hole	10	11	12	13	14	15	16	17	18	In		Totals
BLUE	426	527	357	419	321	222	361	461	344	3438	BLUE	6703
WHITE	415	521	352	381	312	204	350	447	333	3315	WHITE	6480
Par	4	5	4	4	4	3	4	4	4	36	Par	72
Handicap	4	8	16	6	18	10	12	2	14			
RED	402	443	339	313	312	177	340	431	231	2988	RED	5782
Par	5	5	4	4	4	3	4	5	4	38	Par	74
Handicap	2	8	12	14	16	10	6	4	18			

Manager: Mark Moon   **Pro:** Brent Studer, PGA   **Supt:** Glenn Miller
Architect: Robert White 1922

MARLBORO COUNTRY CLUB

100 School Road East, Marlboro, NJ 07746   (732) 308-4600

Marlboro is an 18 hole executive course that is increasing its yardage to about 5600 yards, par 69. It is open 7 days a week, all year. Guests play accompanied by a member. Tee time reservations may be made in advance.

Driving Range	Lockers
•Practice Green	•Showers
•Power Carts	•Food
•Pull Carts	•Clubhouse
•Club Rental	•Outings
Caddies	•Soft Spikes

Course Description: Marlboro is in the midst of a major construction project. Twelve holes are to be redone and designed in a links style with rolling mounds and a variety of grasses. The 17th will be the signature, a par 3 out of a chute, featuring heavy mounds and fescue grass. There is a considerable amount of water to be found here and wind can affect play. The scorecard below is for the short course before the present lengthening and improvements scheduled to be completed by the end of 1999. A new clubhouse is to be built as well.

Directions: Monmouth County, #28 on Upper Shore Map
NJ Tpke to Exit #9. Follow signs and take Rte. 18 East over Rte. 9 to a left onto Rte. 79North. At first light, turn right onto School Rd. Club is ahead on right.

Hole	1	2	3	4	5	6	7	8	9	Out	BLUE	Rating
BLUE												Slope
WHITE	180	301	256	126	136	320	237	225	162	1943		
Par	3	4	4	3	3	4	4	4	3	32	WHITE	Rating 56.8
Handicap	11	5	7	17	15	1	3	9	13			Slope 88
RED	155	230	247	109	132	203	227	161	157	1621		
Par	3	4	4	3	3	4	4	4	3	32	RED	Rating 56.6
Handicap	11	5	7	17	15	1	3	9	13			Slope 85
Hole	10	11	12	13	14	15	16	17	18	In		Totals
BLUE											BLUE	
WHITE	333	145	138	132	93	113	161	79	288	1482	WHITE	3425
Par	4	3	3	3	3	3	3	3	4	29	Par	61
Handicap	2	6	12	14	16	10	8	18	4			
RED	313	111	130	123	82	107	140	70	190	1266	RED	2887
Par	4	3	3	3	3	3	3	3	4	29	Par	61
Handicap	2	6	12	14	16	10	8	18	4			

Manager/Pro: Bill Bodnar, PGA   **Supt:** Kerry Boyer
Architects: Harvey Holland 1970s **Redesign:** Stephen Kay 1999

METEDECONK NATIONAL

Hannah Hill Rd., Jackson, NJ 08527   **(732) 928-0111**

Metedeconk National Golf Club has 27 holes and is open 6 days a week from Mar. 15 to Dec. 1. Guests play accompanied by a member. Tee times may be made in advance.

- •**Driving Range**
- •**Practice Green**
- •**Power Carts**
- Pull Carts
- •**Club Rental**
- •**Caddies**
- •**Lockers**
- •**Showers**
- •**Food**
- •**Clubhouse**
- •**Outings**
- •**Soft Spikes**

Course Description: Metedeconk is hidden on a rolling piece of wooded property. Following the contours of the pinelands, each hole is distinct. The course could not be built today due to EPA regulations regarding wetlands. The layout features high fescue grass in the rough and small, fast well guarded greens. The very special signature hole, the 6th, crosses over the Metedeconk River and is a 150 yard carry from the blues. Opened in the summer of 1998, the 3rd nine is sculpted out of the woods and traverses natural wetlands. These nine, along with the original upgraded 18, are 27 of the most interesting and difficult in NJ. A stunning new clubhouse completes this elegant club. The scorecard below is for the front and the new third 9.

Directions: Ocean County, #29 on Upper Shore Map
NJTpke to Exit #7A. Take Rte. 195 East to Exit #21. Make a left turn at exit. Hannah Hill Rd. is 300 yards up on the right. Take this road through woods to club.

Hole	1	2	3	4	5	6	7	8	9	Out	BLUE	Rating 72.8
BLUE	392	195	551	397	505	176	386	408	406	3416		Slope 133
WHITE	362	170	517	364	465	156	364	387	370	3155		
Par	4	3	5	4	5	3	4	4	4	36	WHITE	Rating 70.4
Handicap	5	7	1	3	9	8	6	4	2			Slope 129
RED	316	124	467	288	416	124	304	318	316	2673		
Par	4	3	5	4	5	3	4	4	4	36	RED	Rating 72.2
Handicap	4	9	2	7	3	8	6	5	1			Slope 127
Hole	10	11	12	13	14	15	16	17	18	In		Totals
BLUE	369	392	534	404	169	502	165	410	419	3364	BLUE	6780
WHITE	347	363	500	387	140	467	152	366	377	3099	WHITE	6254
Par	4	4	5	4	3	5	3	4	4	36	Par	72
Handicap	8	4	1	3	7	6	9	5	2			
RED	329	339	467	320	91	435	92	339	341	2753	RED	5426
Par	4	4	5	4	3	5	3	4	4	36	Par	72
Handicap	7	6	3	5	8	4	9	2	1			

Manager: Michael Pollack   **Pro:** Bill Kriews, PGA   **Supt:** Steven Cadenelli
Architects: Robert Trent Jones 1988   Roger Rulewich 1998

NAVESINK COUNTRY CLUB

50 Luffburrow Lane, Middletown, NJ 07748   **(732) 842-3366**

Navesink is an 18 hole course open 6 days a week all year. Guests play accompanied by a member. Tee time reservations may be made one week in advance for weekends.

```
•Driving Range   •Lockers
•Practice Green  •Showers
•Power Carts     •Food
 Pull Carts      •Clubhouse
•Club Rental     •Outings
•Caddies         •Soft Spikes
```

Course Description: The drive on Navesink River Rd. is scenic with magnificent views of the hilly terrain, the Atlantic Ocean and nearby Sandy Hook. The course is kept in excellent condition and is known for its fast greens and uneven lies. Water in play on both the 5th and the 15th, two difficult par 5s, provides some of the challenge here. The NJ State Open has been held here twice as well as LPGA tournaments. There is a regulation ice hockey rink on the premises.

Directions: Monmouth County, #30 on Upper Shore Map
GSP to Exit 109. Turn left onto Rte. 520E & go under the Pkwy. Take jughandle onto Half Mile Rd. At end, turn right onto W. Front St. Turn left onto Hubbard Ave at light. Go 1 mi, passing school, to Navesink Rd, and turn right. Proceed, crossing Rte. 35, to Luffburrow Lane and turn left. Club is ahead on left.

Hole	1	2	3	4	5	6	7	8	9	Out	BLUE	Rating 72.3
BLUE	330	574	380	227	484	372	359	190	373	3289		Slope 126
WHITE	321	557	374	214	461	367	353	176	365	3188		
Par	4	5	4	3	5	4	4	3	4	36	WHITE	Rating 70.9
Handicap	13	3	11	15	1	5	7	17	9			Slope 124
RED	301	483	282	196	409	347	319	160	325	2822		
Par	4	5	4	3	5	4	4	3	4	36	RED	Rating 74.3
Handicap	11	3	13	15	1	5	7	17	9			Slope 128

Hole	10	11	12	13	14	15	16	17	18	In		Totals
BLUE	404	465	166	419	397	547	184	502	362	3447	BLUE	6736
WHITE	395	457	149	399	377	525	172	493	310	3277	WHITE	6465
Par	4	4	3	4	4	5	3	5	4	36	Par	72
Handicap	8	4	18	6	10	2	16	12	14			
RED	372	429	132	376	359	446	158	449	307	3028	RED	5850
Par	4	5	3	4	4	5	3	5	4	37	Par	73
Handicap	6	12	18	4	8	2	16	10	14			

Manager: Richard Mac Bain   **Pro:** Steve Sieg, PGA   **Supt:** Pat O'Neill
Architect: Hal Purdy 1963

NAVY GOLF COURSE

Lakehurst Naval Base, Lakehurst, NJ 08733   **(732) 323-7483**

Lakehurst has a 9 hole course open to the active duty military, Dept. of Defense employees and retired career military. It is open all year 7 days a week. Guests may play accompanied by members or at the discretion of the mgr. Tee time reservations on weekends and holidays April through September.

Driving Range	•Lockers
•Practice Green	•Showers
•Power Carts	•Food
•Pull Carts	•Clubhouse
•Club Rental	•Outings
Caddies	Soft Spikes

Course Description: Lakehurst is a short, resort type course. The rolling fairways are planted in rye, the easy to read greens are of bent grass. The many seniors that golf here find the course wide open and very playable. The signature par 4 ninth features an elevated tee, a dogleg right and a 70 yard long fairway bunker. There are different tee boxes for the second nine. The holes have been somewhat changed recently and the red tees were redone.

Directions: Ocean County, #31 on Upper Shore Map
GSP to Exit 88. Take Rte. 70 West to Rte. 547 North. Enter Lakehurst Naval Base and get pass at office to go through gate to golf course.

Hole	1	2	3	4	5	6	7	8	9	Out	BLUE	Rating 68.8
BLUE												Slope 116
WHITE	299	323	157	426	486	368	200	351	321	2923		
Par	4	4	3	4	5	4	3	4	4	35	WHITE	Rating 68.6
Handicap	17	7	13	1	5	11	15	3	9			Slope 116
RED	283	306	187	362	446	338	148	319	277	2628		
Par	4	4	3	4	5	4	3	4	4	35	RED	Rating 70.6
Handicap	15	9	11	1	3	7	17	5	13			Slope 119
Hole	10	11	12	13	14	15	16	17	18	In		Totals
BLUE											BLUE	
WHITE	321	332	200	529	520	384	158	292	334	3170	WHITE	6093
Par	4	4	3	5	5	4	3	4	4	36	Par	71
Handicap	18	12	8	2	6	14	16	4	10			
RED	290	313	176	352	446	342	151	323	282	2785	RED	5386
Par	4	4	3	5	5	4	3	4	4	36	Par	71
Handicap	14	10	6	8	2	12	16	4	18			

Manager: George Adamson
Built: 1956

OCEAN ACRES COUNTRY CLUB

Buccaneer Lane, Manahawkin, NJ 08050   (609) 597-9393

Ocean Acres is an 18 hole course open 7 days a week all year. Various membership plans are available. Reservations for tee times: 7 days in advance for members, 5 days for non-members.

Driving Range
- **Practice Green**
- **Power Carts**
- **Pull Carts**
- **Club Rental**
Soft Spikes

Lockers
Showers
- **Food**
- **Clubhouse**
- **Outings**

Fees	Weekday	Weekend
Daily	$45	$45
Fees include cart		
After 4 PM, reduced rates		

Course Description: The friendly atmosphere is quite pervasive at Ocean Acres, conveniently located just minutes off the GSP in Manahawkin. The front nine is comfortably open while the back is tight and wooded. The lakeview from the clubhouse is spectacular overlooking the signature par 3 10th. This hole requires a shot over a man made lake to an island green.

Directions: Ocean County, #32 on Upper Shore Map
GSP South to Exit 67 (Barnegat). Go right off the ramp onto Bay Ave. Make a left onto Lighthouse Dr. then left onto Buccaneer Lane to club. **OR** GSP North to Exit 63A to Rte. 72. Make a right onto Lighthouse, then right on Buccaneer to club.

Hole	1	2	3	4	5	6	7	8	9	Out	BLUE	Rating 70.8
BLUE	490	328	401	192	518	382	362	156	422	3251		Slope 124
WHITE	475	311	381	181	487	364	352	144	409	3104		
Par	5	4	4	3	5	4	4	3	4	36	WHITE	Rating 69.7
Handicap	8	14	4	16	2	12	10	18	6			Slope 118
RED	440	266	347	171	458	329	323	128	338	2820		
Par	5	4	4	3	5	4	4	3	4	36	RED	Rating 70.4
Handicap	8	14	4	16	2	12	10	18	6			Slope 117

Hole	10	11	12	13	14	15	16	17	18	In		Totals
BLUE	183	342	415	205	328	518	360	411	550	3312	BLUE	6563
WHITE	150	325	407	180	313	501	325	400	541	3142	WHITE	6246
Par	3	4	4	3	4	5	4	4	5	36	Par	72
Handicap	17	9	1	15	11	5	13	3	7			
RED	125	232	347	142	229	415	291	343	468	2592	RED	5412
Par	3	4	4	3	4	5	4	4	5	36	Par	72
Handicap	17	9	1	15	11	5	13	3	7			

Manager: Richard Taylor   **Pro:** Scott Brosman, PGA   **Supt:** Matt Szumski
Built: 1960s

OCEAN COUNTY AT ATLANTIS   PUBLIC

Country Club Boulevard, Tuckerton, NJ 08087   (699) 296-2444

This 18 hole Ocean County course is open to the public 7 days a week all year. Tee time reservations are necessary for play between 7AM -2PM up to 8 days in advance. Calll 6PM to 7PM. Walkons after 3 PM. Driving range is for irons only. Fees go up 5/1/99

•**Driving Range**	Lockers
•**Practice Green**	
•**Power Carts**	Showers
Pull Carts	•**Food**
•**Club Rental**	•**Clubhouse**
•**Soft Spikes**	•**Outings**

Fees	Weekday	Weekend
Res/ID	$16	$21
Non-res	$32	$38
Jr/Sr	$13	
Power carts	$24	

Course Description: Formerly a privately owned country club, Ocean County bought this course in 1989 and made improvements. Automatic sprinklers were installed, a modern clubhouse was built and the facility was generally upgraded. The par 3 6th is considered the most picturesque; from an elevated tee, the shot is over a lake. The 7th hole, a par 5, features a blind tee shot that necessitates intelligent club selection, too long and straight will end up in the woods. A daunting shot faces the golfer down the very narrow fairway.

Directions: Ocean County, #33 on Upper Shore Map
GSP to Exit 58. Take Rte. 539S (North Green St.) Make right on West Main Street (Rte. 9S). At fork, bear left and go 2 blocks to Radio Rd. & turn right. Follow signs to club.

Hole	1	2	3	4	5	6	7	8	9	Out	BLUE	Rating 73.6
BLUE	373	411	526	392	376	200	517	168	438	3401		Slope 134
WHITE	360	383	508	382	343	150	490	153	423	3192		
Par	4	4	5	4	4	3	5	3	4	36	WHITE	Rating 71.3
Handicap	15	5	3	9	11	13	7	17	1			Slope 129
RED	341	353	428	312	305	98	447	136	393	2813		
Par	4	4	5	4	4	3	5	3	4	36	RED	Rating 71.8
Handicap	13	9	2	11	7	17	4	15	1			Slope 124
Hole	10	11	12	13	14	15	16	17	18	In		Totals
BLUE	420	191	406	372	492	384	206	574	402	3447	BLUE	6848
WHITE	387	179	390	358	470	338	195	536	387	3240	WHITE	6432
Par	4	3	4	4	5	4	3	5	4	36	Par	72
Handicap	4	18	10	14	12	8	16	2	6			
RED	326	120	336	341	435	287	158	455	308	2766	RED	5579
Par	4	3	4	4	5	4	3	5	4	36	Par	72
Handicap	8	18	12	6	5	10	16	3	14			

Manager: Dan O'Connor   **Supt:** Barry Cox
Architect: George Fazio 1962

OCEAN COUNTY AT FORGE POND

Chambers Bridge Rd., Brick, NJ 08723   (732) 920-8899

Forge Pond is an 18 hole executive par 60 Ocean County course open all year and closed on Thursday afternoons. Tee time reservations may be made up to 1 week in advance.

Driving Range
- **Practice Green**
- **Power Carts**
- **Pull Carts**
- **Club Rental**
- **Soft Spikes**

Lockers
Showers
- **Food**
Clubhouse
Outings

Fees	Weekday	Weekend
Res/ID	$13	$15
Non-res	$22	$27
Sr	$9	
Power carts $18		

Course Description: A retiree haven, Forge Pond is a very busy course excellent for working on your game. It has narrow fairways and small greens. With only 6 par 4s and no par 5s, it is advisable to leave your woods at home unless you hit very straight. The signature par 3 12th requires a shot over with a beckoning bunker at the green.

Directions: Ocean County, #34 on Upper Shore Map
GSP to Exit 91. Bear left and follow road straight for 3 miles. Course is just past the library on the left.

Hole	1	2	3	4	5	6	7	8	9	Out	BLUE	Rating 59.4
BLUE	340	113	118	219	339	146	308	161	172	1916		Slope 98
WHITE	325	100	102	206	322	133	301	144	153	1786		
Par	4	3	3	3	4	3	4	3	3	30	WHITE	Rating 58.3
Handicap	3	16	18	8	5	12	1	13	10			Slope 95
RED	315	91	95	196	314	122	292	136	144	1705		
Par	4	3	3	3	4	3	4	3	3	30	RED	Rating 60.5
Handicap	3	16	18	8	5	12	1	13	10			Slope 97
Hole	10	11	12	13	14	15	16	17	18	In		Totals
BLUE	191	182	144	291	172	235	309	153	323	2000	BLUE	3916
WHITE	168	169	122	274	156	218	293	139	313	1852	WHITE	3638
Par	3	3	3	4	3	3	4	3	4	30	Par	60
Handicap	9	14	17	2	11	7	4	15	6			
RED	159	157	93	266	147	208	282	129	302	1743	RED	3448
Par	3	3	3	4	3	3	3	3	4	30	Par	60
Handicap	9	14	17	2	11	7	4	15	6			

Manager: Dan O'Connor   **Supt**: Ed Casteen
Architect: Hal Purdy 1990

OLD ORCHARD COUNTRY CLUB

PUBLIC

54 Monmouth Rd., Eatontown, NJ 07724   **(732) 542-7666**

Old Orchard is an 18 hole semi-private course open to the public 7 days a week all year. Memberships are available. For tee times, call in advance within the current month.

Driving Range
- **Practice Green**
- **Power Carts**
- **Pull Carts**
- **Club Rental**
- **Soft Spikes**

Lockers
Showers
- **Food**
- **Clubhouse**
- **Outings**

Fees	M-Thurs	Fri-Sun
Daily	$30	$35
After 4PM	$22	$25
Sr.	$20	
Power carts $16pp		

Course Description: Old Orchard is a mostly flat, wide open layout. The poana grass sloped greens are small and get fast in dry weather. A creek crosses 7 holes. The signature par 5 7th features an island green. This scenic course is well maintained. The distances from the forward tees have been made considerably longer. In recent years, there has been some reconstruction and the yardages have changed.

Directions: Monmouth County, #35 on Upper Shore Map
GSP to Exit #105. After toll, take Rte. 36East for 6 traffic lights to the jughandle for Rte. 71North (Monmouth Rd.). Course is on the left on Monmouth.

Hole	1	2	3	4	5	6	7	8	9	Out	BLUE	Rating 71.8
BLUE	441	497	158	423	404	205	480	345	392	3345		Slope 121
WHITE	421	457	143	397	390	175	450	325	372	3130		
Par	4	5	3	4	4	3	5	4	4	36	WHITE	Rating 69.8
Handicap	1	9	17	5	3	13	7	15	11			Slope 116
RED	400	442	438	387	375	455	440	250	360	2947		
Par	4	5	3	4	4	3	5	4	4	36	RED	Rating 73.0
Handicap	1	9	17	5	3	13	7	15	11			Slope 121

Hole	10	11	12	13	14	15	16	17	18	In		Totals
BLUE	442	420	435	360	170	360	365	195	532	3279	BLUE	6624
WHITE	425	390	390	320	140	348	350	175	500	3038	WHITE	6168
Par	5	4	4	4	3	4	4	3	5	36	Par	72
Handicap	8	4	2	14	18	16	10	12	6			
RED	420	375	375	265	122	346	335	155	470	2860	RED	5807
Par	5	4	4	4	3	4	4	3	5	36	Par	72
Handicap	8	4	2	14	18	16	10	12	6			

Manager/Pro: George Craig, PGA   **Supt:** Mark Krews
Architect: A. W. Tillinghast 1929

PEBBLE CREEK GOLF COURSE

40 Route 537East, Colt's Neck, NJ 07722   (732) 303-9090

Pebble Creek is a new 18 hole course open all year 7 days a week, weather permitting. Tee times may be made up to 5 days in advance. Carts are mandatory untill 1PM on Sat. & Sun.

Driving Range	
•**Practice Green**	Lockers
•**Power Carts**	Showers
•**Pull Carts**	•**Food**
•**Club Rental**	•**Clubhouse**
•**Soft Spikes**	•**Outings**

Fees	M-Thurs	Fri-Sun
Daily	$30	$40
Carts	$17pp	

Course Description: The picturesque natural atmosphere makes the recently opened Pebble Creek a welcome addition to New Jersey golf. Several holes are surrounded by mature woods; others are links type. Water is in play on six holes of the more difficult back nine. The greens are large, undulating and true. The par 4 16th, a 344 yard dogleg with water in play on both shots, has birdie potential. The cart paths are now totally paved and more trees are being planted.

Directions: Monmouth County, #36 on Upper Shore Map
GSP to Exit 109 (Lincroft). Go west on Rte. 520 to 2nd light and turn left onto Swimming River Rd. to the end. Turn right on Rte. 537West. Course is 3 and1/2 miles on the left.

Hole	1	2	3	4	5	6	7	8	9	Out	BLUE	Rating 69.3
BLUE	330	405	177	411	197	341	290	540	352	3043		Slope 116
WHITE	322	387	162	394	172	325	274	530	345	2911		
Par	4	4	3	4	3	4	4	5	4	35	WHITE	Rating 68.1
Handicap	9	5	17	3	15	7	13	1	11			Slope 114
RED	230	365	126	370	157	297	245	480	305	2575		
Par	4	4	3	4	3	4	4	5	4	35	RED	Rating 71.0
Handicap	9	5	17	3	15	7	13	1	11			Slope 119
Hole	10	11	12	13	14	15	16	17	18	In		Totals
BLUE	380	218	320	298	585	366	344	527	184	3222	BLUE	6265
WHITE	370	200	301	291	570	361	329	502	167	3091	WHITE	6002
Par	4	3	4	4	5	4	4	5	3	36	Par	71
Handicap	12	14	8	16	2	6	10	4	18			
RED	334	182	263	251	540	341	295	442	133	2761	RED	5356
Par	4	3	4	4	5	4	4	5	3	36	Par	71
Handicap	12	14	8	16	2	6	10	4	18			

Manager/Pro: David Melody, PGA   **Supt:** Rick Krok
Architect: Hal Purdy 1996

PINE BARRENS GOLF CLUB

540 S. Hope Chapel Rd., Jackson, NJ 08527   **(877) 746-3227**

Pine Barrens is a new course opening in the Spring of 1999. It is semi-private and open to the public all year 7 days a week. Weekday membership packages are available. The full service clubhouse is in construction as we go to press.

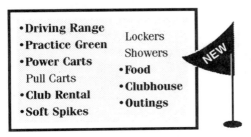

- **Driving Range**
- **Practice Green**
- **Power Carts**
- Pull Carts
- **Club Rental**
- **Soft Spikes**

Lockers
Showers
- **Food**
- **Clubhouse**
- **Outings**

Fees	Weekday	Weekend
Daily	$60	$90

Fees include cart

Course Description: Pine Barrens promises to be one of the finest new courses in New Jersey. Over 7100 yards from the championship tees, it features large waste bunkers, native grass vegetation in the rough and large undulating bent grass greens. It is a pinelands layout winding through the woods with 5 sets of tees. Water is in play on holes 10 and 18; on the latter a considerable carry is required off the tee. The course is in immaculate condition. An impressive double-ended practice facility with dual grass tees, target bunkers and greens will provide a chance for the golfer to warm up and learn.

Directions: Ocean County, #37 on Uppershore Map
GSP to Exit 98 & Rte. 195West or NJ Tpke to Exit 7A & Rte.195East. Get off at exit #21. Take Rte. 527 South and turn right to Rte. 547 East. Course is 3 miles on right.

Hole	1	2	3	4	5	6	7	8	9	Out	BLUE	Rating 72.8
BLUE	365	383	190	427	172	546	293	415	558	3313		Slope 128
WHITE	333	354	183	391	161	521	271	390	495	3099		
Par	4	4	3	4	3	5	4	4	5	36	WHITE	Rating 70.6
Handicap	12	16	6	2	14	10	18	8	4			Slope 124
RED	263	276	140	320	112	450	213	333	409	2516		
Par	4	4	3	4	3	5	4	4	5	36	RED	Rating 67.6
Handicap	12	16	6	2	14	10	18	8	4			Slope 112

Hole	10	11	12	13	14	15	16	17	18	In		Totals
BLUE	424	362	164	378	212	501	391	456	572	3460	BLUE	6773
WHITE	384	339	149	359	195	488	365	406	556	3241	WHITE	6340
Par	4	4	3	4	3	5	4	4	5	36	Par	72
Handicap	9	7	17	13	3	11	15	1	5			
RED	282	298	104	310	150	414	316	349	486	2709	RED	5225
Par	4	4	3	4	3	5	4	4	5	36	Par	72
Handicap	9	7	17	13	3	11	15	1	5			

Manager/Pro: Rudy Virga, PGA   **Supt:** Dave Giordano
Architect: Eric Bergstol 1999

PINE BROOK GOLF COURSE

PUBLIC

1 Covered Bridge Blvd., Englishtown, NJ 07726   (732) 536-7272

Pine Brook is an 18 hole Monmouth County executive course open 7 days a week. It closes Dec. 23 & reopens Mar. 15. With a county ID, automated tee times are available 7 days in advance, non ID 5 days. Walkons are allowed as well.

Driving Range
• **Practice Green**
• **Power Carts**
• **Pull Carts**
• **Club Rental**
• **Soft Spikes**

Lockers
Showers
Food
Clubhouse
Outings

Fees	Weekday	Weekend
Res/ID	$14	$16
Non-res	$28	$32
Sr.	$9.75	
Carts	$20	

Course Description: Excellently maintained, Pine Brook is a good place for iron practice. It is a flat, well shrubbed course with water occasionally in play. The signature par 3 9th has water surrounding the green. The par 4 16th can be quite interesting. This facility gets quite busy in season.

Directions: Monmouth County, #38 on Uppershore Map
GSP to Exit 123. Take Rte. 9 South and after the light for Union Hill Rd., watch carefully for Covered Bridge Blvd. and make right to course on right.

Hole	1	2	3	4	5	6	7	8	9	Out	BLUE	Rating
BLUE												Slope
WHITE	343	167	143	333	195	163	499	156	157	2156		
Par	4	3	3	4	3	3	5	3	3	31	WHITE	Rating 58.1
Handicap	1	13	17	9	7	11	5	15	3			Slope 90
RED	315	125	111	313	151	121	463	121	136	1856		
Par	4	3	3	4	3	3	5	3	3	31	RED	Rating 67.6
Handicap	1	13	17	9	7	11	5	15	3			Slope 112
Hole	10	11	12	13	14	15	16	17	18	In		Totals
BLUE											BLUE	
WHITE	150	194	333	347	154	134	380	158	192	2012	WHITE	4168
Par	3	3	4	4	3	3	4	3	3	30	Par	61
Handicap	14	4	8	10	16	18	6	12	2			
RED	112	157	288	275	117	92	266	105	153	1585	RED	3441
Par	3	3	4	4	3	3	4	3	3	30	Par	61
Handicap	14	4	8	10	16	18	6	12	2			

Manager: George Magerko   **Supt:** Diane Elwood

RENAISSANCE GOLF COURSE  PRIVATE

3 Renaissance Blvd. East, Lakehurst, NJ 08733   (732) 657-3703

Renaissance is a private adult community with a new 18 hole golf course open 6 days a week and closed Dec. through March. Guests play accompanied by a member. The residents can take an annual golf membership or walk on and pay as daily fee.

Driving Range   •Lockers
•Practice Green   •Showers
•Power Carts   •Food
•Pull Carts   •Clubhouse
•Club Rental   •Outings
Caddies   •Soft Spikes

Course Description: The first nine on this executive course has been completed with the remaining 9 to be built later. With 4-5 tees on each hole, some modest undulation and considerable water in play, Renaissance will be an interesting challenge for the golfing residents of this private country club community. Some of the homes have golf course views. The builders are Calton Homes. The scorecard below indicates totals for an 18 hole round.

Directions: Ocean County, #39 on Upper Shore Map
GSP to Exit 88. At bottom of exit ramp, turn right onto Rte. 70West. Go about 6 miles and turn right onto Rte. 571. North. Entrance is on the right.

Hole	1	2	3	4	5	6	7	8	9	Out	BLUE	Rating
BLUE	358	336	171	312	157	369	147	125	205	2162		Slope
WHITE	298	301	133	277	124	357	114	97	170	1851		
Par	4	4	3	4	3	4	3	3	3	31	WHITE	Rating
Handicap												Slope
RED	277	292	113	265	114	329	150	82	154	1732		
Par	4	4	3	4	3	4	3	3	3	31	RED	Rating
Handicap												Slope
Hole	10	11	12	13	14	15	16	17	18	In		Totals
BLUE											BLUE	4324
WHITE											WHITE	3702
Par											Par	62
Handicap												
RED											RED	3464
Par											Par	62
Handicap												

Pro: Art Robidoux, PGA   **Supt:** Management
Architect: J. Christopher Commins 1999

RUMSON COUNTRY CLUB

Rumson Rd., Rumson, NJ 07760   **(732) 842-2885**

Rumson is a private 18 hole course open 6 days a week all year, weather permitting. Guests play accompanied by a member. Tee time reservations are not necessary.

- •**Driving Range**   •**Lockers**
- •**Practice Green** •**Showers**
- •**Power Carts**   •**Food**
- •**Pull Carts**   •**Clubhouse**
- •**Club Rental**   •**Outings**
- •**Caddies**   •**Soft Spikes**

Course Description: Rumson is a typical seashore layout, flat and low lying with a moderate amount of water in play in the form of ponds or creeks. The Shrewsbury River can be seen from some areas of the course; the highest point is 6 feet above sea level. The most difficult hole is the par 4 7th, 433 yards from the blues. The landing area is guarded by bunkers for the tee shot; the 2nd shot, using a long iron or a fairway wood, is to a green protected in front by a pond.

Directions: Monmouth County, #40 on Upper Shore Map
GSP to Exit 109. Follow signs and take Rte. 520East. Continue to Broad St. and at end of road, turn left over RR tracks. Turn right onto Pinckney Rd. and then right onto Branch Ave. At light, turn left onto Rumson Rd. Club is ahead on right.

Hole	1	2	3	4	5	6	7	8	9	Out	BLUE	Rating 71.5
BLUE	399	551	145	493	433	388	433	408	396	3646		Slope 121
WHITE	389	503	134	463	421	377	425	358	385	3455		
Par	4	5	3	5	4	4	4	4	4	37	WHITE	Rating 70.1
Handicap	10	5	18	7	3	13	1	12	9			Slope 117
RED	339	460	117	436	375	339	400	329	320	3115		
Par	4	5	3	5	4	4	5	4	4	38	RED	Rating 72.8
Handicap	9	1	17	7	3	13	11	5	15			Slope 124
Hole	**10**	**11**	**12**	**13**	**14**	**15**	**16**	**17**	**18**	**In**		Totals
BLUE	299	400	443	380	163	429	307	180	370	2971	BLUE	6617
WHITE	283	381	434	364	146	417	301	169	352	2847	WHITE	6302
Par	4	4	4	4	3	4	4	3	4	34	Par	71
Handicap	16	6	2	8	17	4	14	15	11			
RED	267	317	401	332	113	409	273	147	308	2567	RED	5682
Par	4	4	5	4	3	5	4	3	4	34	Par	74
Handicap	16	4	8	2	18	10	12	14	6			

Pro: Don Brigham, PGA   **Supt:** Jim Cross
Architect: Herbert W. Barker 1908

SHADOW LAKE VILLAGE

1 Loch Arbor Way, Red Bank, NJ 07701   **(732) 842-9580**

Shadow Lake Village is an adult community that has a 9 hole par 3 golf course. It is open 6 and 1/2 days a week and closed in winter. Tee time reservations are not necessary.

Driving Range	Lockers
Practice Green	•**Showers**
Power Carts	Food
•**Pull Carts**	•**Clubhouse**
Club Rental	Outings
Caddies	•**Soft Spikes**

Course Description: Shadow Lake golf course is open only for residents of the adult community of 952 units. The mostly flat course is easy to walk. No water is in play. Power carts are available only for those with physical limitations. With three sets of tees, the golfers have the option of going around twice using different yardages.

Directions: Monmouth County, #41 on Upper Shore Map
GSP to Exit 114 (Holmdel-Middletown). Turn left at exit toward Middletown. Pass two traffic lights and turn right at Dwight. Pass a light and a school on the left. The road becomes Nut Swamp Rd. Go 1 and 1/2 miles to sign on right for Shadow Lake Village. The community has a security gate. An appointment is necessary to enter.

Hole	1	2	3	4	5	6	7	8	9	Out	BLUE	Rating
BLUE	191	188	133	130	164	193	141	123	175	1438		Slope
WHITE	186	176	127	124	161	183	137	113	171	1378		
Par	3	3	3	3	3	3	3	3	3	27	WHITE	Rating
Handicap	1	7	15	17	5	3	9	11	13			Slope
RED	161	161	122	115	143	121	122	105	167	1217		
Par	3	3	3	3	3	3	3	3	3	27	RED	Rating
Handicap	2	4	16	18	8	14	10	12	6			Slope
Hole	10	11	12	13	14	15	16	17	18	In		Totals
BLUE											BLUE	
WHITE											WHITE	
Par											Par	
Handicap												
RED											RED	
Par											Par	
Handicap												

Manager: Lisa Della Valle   **Supt:** Will Boyce
Built: 1972

SHARK RIVER GOLF COURSE

PUBLIC

320 Old Corlies Ave., Neptune, NJ 07753   (732) 922-4141

Shark River is an 18 hole Monmouth County course open to the public 7 days a week all year. Tee times for residents may be made 7 days in advance, others 5 days.

Driving Range	
Driving Range	Lockers
• **Practice Green**	Showers
• **Power Carts**	• **Food**
Pull Carts	• **Clubhouse**
• **Club Rental**	• Outings
• **Soft Spikes**	

Fees	Weekday	Weekend
Res/ID	$18	$21
Sr	$13.25	
Non-res	$36	$42
Carts	$27.56	

Course Description: Shark River was originally called Asbury Park Golf & CC and changed names in 1936. Rates were $1 weekdays, $2 weekends. Closed for a while, it reopened after World War II. Well maintained, it is an old style, fairly flat course with narrow fairways and greens that are medium sized and fast in summer. Many old trees and a few hills dot this well bunkered layout. The rough is of fescue grass; very little water is in play. The signature par 5 9th is a long, difficult double dogleg. There have been some minor changes to the yardages recently.

Directions: Monmouth County, #42 on Upper Shore Map
GSP to Exit 100B from north or south. Take Rte. 33 East for 4 lights. Then turn right on Green Grove Rd. Make left onto Old Corlies. Course is on right before Rte. 18 overpass.

Hole	1	2	3	4	5	6	7	8	9	Out	BLUE	Rating 68.9
BLUE	358	525	182	290	185	417	441	169	586	3153		Slope 112
WHITE	348	490	172	280	180	407	431	159	578	3045		
Par	4	5	3	4	3	4	4	3	5	35	WHITE	Rating 67.8
Handicap	12	9	13	14	6	5	4	8	1			Slope 110
RED	323	475	162	265	171	393	413	145	566	2913		
Par	4	5	3	4	3	4	4	3	5	35	RED	Rating 71.3
Handicap	12	9	13	14	6	5	4	8	1			Slope 116

Hole	10	11	12	13	14	15	16	17	18	In		Totals
BLUE	424	386	123	291	328	533	152	451	353	3041	BLUE	6194
WHITE	417	381	113	281	316	526	142	446	343	2965	WHITE	6010
Par	4	4	3	4	4	5	3	5	4	36	Par	71
Handicap	2	7	18	15	11	3	17	16	10			
RED	342	311	101	261	294	505	120	388	320	2642	RED	5555
Par	4	4	3	4	4	5	3	5	4	36	Par	71
Handicap	2	7	18	15	11	3	17	16	10			

Manager: Brian Corrigan   **Supt:** Gene Mack
Architect: Hal Purdy 1967

SHORE OAKS GOLF CLUB

20 Shore Oaks Dr., Farmingdale, NJ 07727   (732) 938-9696

Shore Oaks Golf Club is a private 18 hole course open 6 days a week and closed in Jan. and Feb. Guests play accompanied by a member. Tee time reservations are not necessary.

•**Driving Range** •**Lockers**
•**Practice Green** •**Showers**
•**Power Carts** •**Food**
Pull Carts •**Clubhouse**
Club Rental •**Outings**
•**Caddies** •**Soft Spikes**

Course Description: Shore Oaks Golf Club is the first designed by Johnny Miller and considered his signature effort. This generally flat, open course is well bunkered and has tricky artificial mounding to negotiate. Beautifully maintained and landscaped, there are hazards on 13 holes. Nearly all the holes are separated from each other giving it a links-style feel. The greens are relatively shallow making it a great test for iron play. The signature par 4 15th is picturesque, long and demanding; water is found left and short of the green. The 1992 State PGA was held here as well as the NJ State Amateur.

Directions: Monmouth County, #43 on Upper Shore Map
GSPSouth to Exit 100A or from south Exit 100B. Take Rte. 33 West to Rte. 547 South which merges with Asbury Ave. Take 1st right onto Shore Oaks Drive.

Hole	1	2	3	4	5	6	7	8	9	Out	BLUE	Rating 73.5
BLUE	427	351	558	412	192	391	456	167	557	3511		Slope 132
WHITE	365	310	520	368	141	353	386	135	515	3093		
Par	4	4	5	4	3	4	4	3	5	36	WHITE	Rating 71.6
Handicap	9	13	5	3	15	11	1	17	7			Slope 128
RED	365	310	363	280	141	302	352	118	445	2676		
Par	4	4	4	4	3	4	4	3	5	35	RED	Rating 71.2
Handicap	1	11	5	7	15	13	9	17	3			Slope 121
Hole	10	11	12	13	14	15	16	17	18	In		Totals
BLUE	422	171	438	397	399	453	207	494	427	3408	BLUE	6919
WHITE	377	138	364	342	315	396	157	461	376	2926	WHITE	6505
Par	4	3	4	4	4	4	3	5	4	35	Par	71
Handicap	8	16	6	14	10	2	18	12	4			
RED	413	110	364	342	315	339	157	416	320	2776	RED	5452
Par	5	3	4	4	4	4	3	5	4	36	Par	71
Handicap	8	18	6	12	14	4	16	2	10			

Manager: Joe Callahan   **Pro:** Lou Katsos, PGA   **Supt:** Mark Peterson
Architect: Johnny Miller 1990

SPRING LAKE GOLF CLUB

Warren Ave., Spring Lake, NJ 07762   **(732) 449-7185**

Spring Lake is an 18 hole course open 6 days a week all year. Guest play accompanied by a member. Tee time reservations are not necessary.

•**Driving Range**	•**Lockers**
•**Practice Green**	•**Showers**
•**Power Carts**	•**Food**
Pull Carts	•**Clubhouse**
Club Rental	•**Outings**
•**Caddies**	•**Soft Spikes**

Course Description: Spring Lake, an excellently maintained golf course, has interesting contours to intrigue the golfer. It is considered a pleasant test of golf requiring the use of every club in the bag. The long uphill par 5 3rd, with out of bounds on the right, usually playing into the wind, and a gully to get over on the approach to the plateau green, deserves to be the number one handicap hole. The NJ State Open has been played here in the past as well as the US Women's amateur. In 1998, Spring Lake again hosted the State Open.

Directions: Monmouth County, #44 on Upper Shore Map
GSP to Exit 98. Take Rte. 138East to Rte. 35South and make right turn. Go three lights and turn left onto Warren Ave. Club is ahead on right.

Hole	1	2	3	4	5	6	7	8	9	Out	BLUE	Rating 71.0
BLUE	408	392	542	345	311	218	354	136	476	3182		Slope 122
WHITE	399	384	534	339	301	214	341	125	465	3102		
Par	4	4	5	4	4	3	4	3	5	36	WHITE	Rating 70.1
Handicap	3	7	1	13	15	11	9	17	5			Slope 120
RED	337	330	484	288	212	165	302	123	440	2681		
Par	4	4	5	4	4	3	4	3	5	36	RED	Rating 72.3
Handicap	7	3	1	13	11	15	9	18	5			Slope 123
Hole	10	11	12	13	14	15	16	17	18	In		Totals
BLUE	162	334	536	462	330	387	196	402	373	3182	BLUE	6364
WHITE	155	319	527	442	320	376	189	389	359	3076	WHITE	6178
Par	3	4	5	5	4	4	3	4	4	36	Par	72
Handicap	18	14	2	10	12	6	16	4	8			
RED	142	286	477	422	294	364	183	354	341	2863	RED	5544
Par	3	4	5	5	4	4	3	4	4	36	Par	72
Handicap	17	14	2	10	12	4	16	6	8			

Manager: Hank Ver Heyden   **Pro:** Bill King, PGA   **Supt:** Bruce Peeples
Architects: George Thomas Jr. 1898 (Renovations A. W. Tillinghast)

SPRING MEADOW GOLF COURSE

PUBLIC

Atlantic Ave. Route 524, Wall Township, NJ 07719   (732) 449-0806

Spring Meadow is an 18 hole course open 7 days a week all year. It is the only facility owned by the State of New Jersey. Tee time reservations are not necessary.

- •Driving Range
- •Practice Green
- •Power Carts
- •Pull Carts
- •Club Rental
  - Soft Spikes
- •Lockers
- •Showers
- •Food
- •Clubhouse
- •Outings

Fees	Weekday	Weekend
Daily	$19.25	$22.50
Srs.	$9.75	
Power carts $25.97		

Course Description: A tributary of the Manasquan River runs through this golf course; water affects play on 5 holes. Adjacent to Allaire State Park, woods surround much of the property. From the the 14th tee, a beautiful view of the golf course can be seen. Spring Meadow is well maintained and has good drainage. It is a very popular and consequently busy facility with friendly and helpful personnel. About 70,000 rounds are played here each year.

Directions: Monmouth County, #45 on Upper Shore Map
GSP to Exit 98. Take Rte. 34 South. At jughandle make right onto Allenwood; take it to the end, then right onto Rte. 524 West (Atlantic Ave.). Course is 1 mile on left.

Hole	1	2	3	4	5	6	7	8	9	Out	BLUE	Rating
BLUE												Slope
WHITE	421	400	383	115	435	296	194	388	178	2810		
Par	5	4	4	3	4	4	3	5	3	35	WHITE	Rating 68.7
Handicap	14	2	4	18	6	12	8	10	16			Slope 118
RED	410	375	333	105	350	263	152	373	163	2524		
Par	5	5	4	3	5	4	3	5	3	37	RED	Rating 70.4
Handicap	4	6	10	18	8	12	14	2	16			Slope 120
Hole	10	11	12	13	14	15	16	17	18	In		Totals
BLUE											BLUE	
WHITE	426	471	135	452	385	296	168	469	341	3143	WHITE	5953
Par	4	5	3	5	4	4	3	5	4	37	Par	72
Handicap	1	5	17	7	13	11	15	3	9			
RED	410	434	125	442	365	208	148	391	263	2786	RED	5310
Par	5	5	3	5	5	4	3	5	4	39	Par	76
Handicap	3	7	17	1	13	5	11	9	15			

Manager/Supt: Ronald Faulseit
Built: 1920

SUN EAGLES at FORT MONMOUTH

Building 2067, Fort Monmouth, NJ 07703　　(732) 532-4307

Sun Eagles is an 18 hole course open to active duty personnel, 20 yr. retirees, civilian Fort employees GS 9 and above in rank, who may make tee time reservations. It is open all year, 6 days a week. Guests play accompanied by a member.

•Driving Range	•Lockers
•Practice Green	•Showers
•Power Carts	•Food
•Pull Carts	•Clubhouse
•Club Rental	•Outings
Caddies	•Soft Spikes

Course Description: Built originally for private use, this course was bought by the Fort in 1942 and is now called Sun Eagles at Fort Monmouth. Characteristic of a Tillinghast championship course, it has numerous treacherous bunkers and small, undulating greens. The demanding par 3 14th is well-bunkered and has beautiful views from both the tee and the slightly lower green. The 15th is a dogleg left and then another dogleg depending on the tee box location; it also features a bunker in mid fairway. A new pro shop opened in 1996. At this site was the first professional victory in 1935 for Byron Nelson who later won the NJ State Open when he was the assistant pro at Ridgewood Country Club.

Directions: Monmouth County, #46 on Upper Shore Map
GSP to Exit 105 (Eatontown). Take Hope Road and go north to 4th traffic light and make a right. Fort Monmouth is the 1st driveway on the right.

Hole	1	2	3	4	5	6	7	8	9	Out	BLUE	Rating 70.7
BLUE	365	212	460	433	350	260	113	392	437	3022		Slope 121
WHITE	338	169	428	411	333	237	110	374	421	2821		
Par	4	3	5	4	4	4	3	4	4	35	WHITE	Rating 69.2
Handicap	9	13	11	3	7	15	17	5	1			Slope 119
RED	317	147	400	370	319	215	85	330	403	2586		
Par	4	3	5	4	4	4	3	4	5	36	RED	Rating 71.4
Handicap	11	13	5	1	9	15	17	7	3			Slope 119
Hole	10	11	12	13	14	15	16	17	18	In		Totals
BLUE	365	470	355	378	204	575	341	165	509	3363	BLUE	6385
WHITE	343	453	336	357	196	558	323	144	490	3200	WHITE	6021
Par	4	5	4	4	3	5	4	3	5	37	Par	72
Handicap	12	18	16	6	4	2	10	8	14			
RED	259	410	311	307	170	489	293	120	440	2794	RED	5380
Par	4	5	4	4	3	5	4	3	5	37	Par	72
Handicap	14	6	8	10	12	2	18	16	4			

Manager/Pro: Gordon Digby, PGA　　　　**Supt:** Chip Dayton
Architect: A. W. Tillinghast 1926

TOMS RIVER COUNTRY CLUB

419 Washington St., Tom's River , NJ 08753   **(732) 349-8867**

Toms River CC is a 9 hole course open 7 days a week and closed in January. Guests play accompanied by a member. Tee time reservations are suggested. Overnight guests may play here for a daily fee.

Driving Range	**• Lockers**
• Practice Green	**• Showers**
• Power Carts	**• Food**
• Pull Carts	**• Clubhouse**
• Club Rental	**• Outings**
Caddies	**• Soft Spikes**

Course Description: The layout at Toms River was originally 18 holes. During the Depression, 9 holes were sold off. It became a member owned club in 1983. This picturesque course is noted for its small, elevated, fast greens that offer subtle breaks. The signature par 3 6th sits on the Toms River; its green is virtually an island. Some ditches on other holes confront the golfer. Players can watch the boats go by. The fairways have been narrowed in recent years and some tee boxes have been rebuilt and expanded. This work affects the yardages and will result in new ratings.

Directions: Ocean County, #47 on Upper Shore Map
GSP to Exit 81. Take Water St. East and turn left on Dock St. Make a right on Washington St. Club is ahead on right.

Hole	1	2	3	4	5	6	7	8	9	Out	BLUE	Rating
BLUE												Slope
WHITE	401	171	360	409	461	144	368	312	455	3081		
Par	4	3	4	4	5	3	4	4	5	36	WHITE	Rating 69.2
Handicap	3	15	11	1	7	17	5	13	9			Slope 113
RED	333	166	290	384	345	138	361	308	416	2741		
Par	4	3	4	4	5	3	4	4	5	36	RED	Rating 71.3
Handicap	13	15	11	1	7	17	3	9	5			Slope 117
Hole	10	11	12	13	14	15	16	17	18	In		Totals
BLUE											BLUE	3092
WHITE											WHITE	3014
Par											Par	36
Handicap												
RED											RED	2802
Par											Par	36
Handicap												

Manager/Supt: Ed McSeaman
Built: 1930s

TWIN BROOK GOLF CENTER

1251 Jumping Brook Rd., Tinton Falls, NJ 07724   (732) 922-1600

Twin Brook is a 9 hole regulation par 3 golf course open to the public 7 days a week all year. The golf center also has a driving range and a miniature golf course on the property. Tee time reservations are not necessary.

•Driving Range	Lockers
•Practice Green	Showers
Power Carts	Food
•Pull Carts	Clubhouse
•Club Rental	•Outings
•Soft Spikes	

Fees	Weekday	Weekend
9 holes	$12	$14
18 holes	$18	$20
Senior discount		

Course Description: Twin Brook is a fairly open, flat course with moderate size fairly slow greens giving the golfer a good place to practice one's game. A small pond is in play on the 6th and a ditch runs across holes #3, 4 and 5. A lake on the side of the ninth hole and its length make is the #1 handicap.

Directions: Monmouth County, #48 on Upper Shore Map
GSP to Exit 102. Stay right proceeding east on Asbury Ave. Turn right at 1st light. Twin Brook is on the right. From South: GSP to exit 100A. Go east on Rte. 66. Make a left at 1st light onto Jumping Brook Rd. Twin Brook is on the left.

Hole	1	2	3	4	5	6	7	8	9	Out	BLUE	Rating
BLUE	150	135	145	165	165	140	135	90	180	1305		Slope
WHITE	135	110	130	120	155	135	75	70	160	1090		
Par	3	3	3	3	3	3	3	3	3	27	WHITE	Rating
Handicap	7	6	8	3	2	4	5	9	1			Slope
RED	90	110	105	130	130	75	75	70	130	915		
Par	3	3	3	3	3	3	3	3	3	27	RED	Rating
Handicap	7	6	8	3	2	4	5	9	1			Slope

Hole	10	11	12	13	14	15	16	17	18	In		Totals
BLUE											BLUE	1305
WHITE											WHITE	1090
Par											Par	27
Handicap												
RED											RED	915
Par											Par	27
Handicap												

Manager: John Dinapoli   **Pro:** Timothy Stafford, PGA   **Supt:** John Cipriano
Architect: Harry Harsin 1992

WOODLAKE GOLF & COUNTRY CLUB

25 New Hampshire Ave., Lakewood, NJ 08701   (732) 370-1002

Woodlake is a semi-private course open to the public 7 days a week all year. Memberships are available. Members may reserve up to 7 days in advance, non-members 3 days. Carts are mandatory on weekends until 2PM.

- •Driving Range
- •Practice Green
- •Power Carts
- •Pull Carts
- •Club Rental
- •Soft Spikes

- •Lockers
- •Showers
- •Food
- •Clubhouse
- •Outings

Fees	M-Thurs	Fri-Sun
Daily	$32	$60/cart
After 2	$22	$32
Carts	$18pp	

Course Description: Woodlake is long and fairly flat with narrow fairways. Water comes into play on 12 holes. The medium size fast greens have severe undulations. The signature 16th is a difficult par 4; water can be encountered on the tee shot, along the fairway and on the approach shot as well. Although this is open to the public, it presents a private club atmosphere. The course recently changed ownership and is being improved and upgraded.

Directions: Ocean County, #49 on Upper Shore Map
GSP to Exit 91. Stay to the right at fork. Go straight for 3 lights to Rte. 88. Turn right and go right at light onto New Hampshire Ave. Go right to 2nd entrance on right.

Hole	1	2	3	4	5	6	7	8	9	Out	BLUE	Rating 72.5
BLUE	394	525	422	165	360	515	375	217	412	3385		Slope 126
WHITE	380	510	407	150	340	496	356	202	395	3236		
Par	4	5	4	3	4	5	4	3	4	36	WHITE	Rating 71.0
Handicap	10	8	2	18	14	6	12	16	4			Slope 124
RED	340	460	369	98	300	430	313	181	345	2836		
Par	4	5	5	3	4	5	4	3	4	37	RED	Rating 72.2
Handicap	8	2	16	18	14	4	12	10	6			Slope 120

Hole	10	11	12	13	14	15	16	17	18	In		Totals
BLUE	380	422	498	205	346	566	391	183	390	3381	BLUE	6766
WHITE	363	410	485	193	324	542	378	168	339	3202	WHITE	6438
Par	4	4	5	3	4	5	4	3	4	36	Par	72
Handicap	7	3	11	15	13	1	5	17	9			
RED	306	374	427	148	262	450	340	115	299	2721	RED	5557
Par	4	5	5	3	4	5	4	3	4	37	Par	74
Handicap	7	13	5	15	11	1	3	17	9			

Manager: Dave Birchill   **Pro:** Ken Pridgen, PGA   **Supt:** Gene Stiles
Architect: Edward Packard 1972

Golfer's Prayer: May the good Lord grant 'fore golfing days are done that I might just once score a legitimate "hole in one". (**Pine Brook**)

A golfer is someone who putts with great accuracy when his drive isn't working, and vice versa. (**Country Club of Salem**)

SOUTHWEST REGION

BURLINGTON

GLOUCESTER

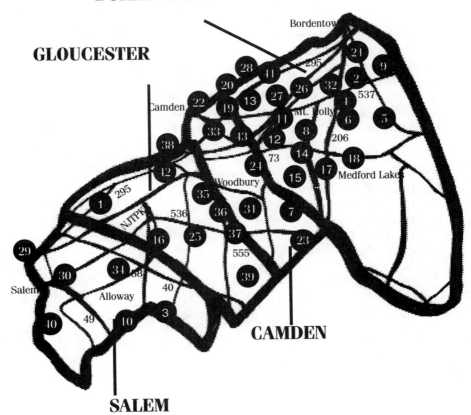

CAMDEN

SALEM

SOUTHWEST REGION

Public Courses appear in **bold italics**

*Military Course

BECKETT COUNTRY CLUB

PUBLIC

Old King's Highway, Swedesboro, NJ 08085   **(609) 467-4700**

Beckett is a 27 hole semi-private club open to the public 7 days a week, all year. Memberships are available. For weekend tee times: Members call 1 week in advance; non-members; the Monday prior.

- •Driving Range
- •Practice Green
- •Power Carts
- •Pull Carts
- •Club Rental
- •Soft Spikes
- •Lockers
- •Showers
- •Food
- •Clubhouse
- •Outings

Fees	Weekday	Weekend
Daily	$18	$22
Twi	$11	$17
Power carts $26		
Midweek Specials		

Course Description: The three nines that make up this 27 hole relatively hilly layout become progressively more difficult in the order of Red, White and Blue. The par 5 fifth on the Blue is heavily treed, boomerang shaped and the tee shot has water to carry. It is justifiably called the "monster hole." The Red nine offers the 5th hole over water with a dogleg left; the 6th has a severe dogleg right and the 8th is again a tee shot over water. There are special weekday packages including cart and lunch. Scorecard below is for Blue and Red nines.

Directions: Gloucester County, #1 on Southwest Map
Rte. 295 to Exit #10. At the top of the ramp going north, take a right; going south take a left. Proceed 4 & 1/2 miles and at the 3rd STOP go right onto Old Kings Highway. Course is 1.5 mi. on right. OR NJTPKE to Exit #2; get onto Rte. 322 W to Kings Hwy .(Rte, 620); follow to Swedesboro. Bear left then right to 2nd fork to club.

Hole	1	2	3	4	5	6	7	8	9	Out	BLUE	Rating 69.9
BLUE	513	173	386	157	488	472	348	342	377	3256		Slope 116
WHITE	502	162	375	146	477	371	337	331	366	3067		
Par	3	3	4	3	5	4	4	4	4	36	WHITE	Rating 69.0
Handicap	4	6	3	9	1	2	8	7	5			Slope 114
RED	500	152	365	116	467	361	327	321	356	2965		
Par	3	3	4	3	5	4	4	4	4	36	RED	Rating 72.3
Handicap	3	8	2	9	1	4	7	6	5			Slope 117

Hole	10	11	12	13	14	15	16	17	18	In		Totals
BLUE	498	199	338	387	313	465	378	358	226	3162	BLUE	6418
WHITE	488	189	328	377	303	455	368	348	216	3072	WHITE	6139
Par	5	3	4	4	4	5	4	4	3	36	Par	72
Handicap	1	8	3	5	6	9	7	2	4			
RED	488	150	318	367	286	373	278	259	206	2725	RED	5690
Par	5	3	4	4	4	5	4	4	3	36	Par	72
Handicap	1	9	6	5	7	2	3	4	8			

Manager/Pro: Steve DeVito, PGA   **Supt:** Wally Miller
Architects: Dick & Loretta Kidder 1964

BURLINGTON COUNTRY CLUB

Burrs Road, (Box 27), Mt. Holly, NJ 08060   **(609) 267-1887**

Burlington is an 18 hole course open 7 days a week all year. Guests play accompanied by a member. Tee time reservations are not necessary.

```
•Driving Range    •Lockers
•Practice Green   •Showers
•Power Carts      •Food
•Pull Carts       •Clubhouse
 Club Rental      •Outings
 Caddies          •Soft Spikes
```

Course Description: The traditionally styled and well maintained Burlington is a demanding course with narrow tree lined fairways and high rough. Out of bounds lurks on twelve holes; a meandering creek on the back nine may catch an errant shot. The small bent grass greens are firm and fast. The par 3 #12 signature hole with carry over water, has a Pete Dye type of bulkhead which is more modern looking than the rest of the course. Players may not use pull carts on Sat. or Sun. before 1 P.M,

Directions: Burlington County, #2 on Southwest Map
NJTPKE to Exit #5. Make a right onto Rte. 541 South. At first light, make a left onto Burrs Rd. Course is 1 mile ahead on left.

Hole	1	2	3	4	5	6	7	8	9	Out	BLUE	Rating 69.7
BLUE	420	215	396	501	115	392	480	413	432	3364		Slope 121
WHITE	409	203	383	461	106	376	461	408	399	3206		
Par	4	3	4	5	3	4	5	4	4	36	WHITE	Rating 68.4
Handicap	1	11	9	13	17	7	15	3	5			Slope 117
RED	335	165	340	432	98	310	425	399	311	2815		
Par	4	3	4	5	3	4	5	5	4	37	RED	Rating 70.3
Handicap	5	15	1	3	17	11	7	13	9			Slope 116
Hole	10	11	12	13	14	15	16	17	18	In		Totals
BLUE	143	333	177	412	371	379	361	350	318	2844	BLUE	6208
WHITE	135	320	141	398	365	358	355	344	280	2696	WHITE	5902
Par	3	4	3	4	4	4	4	4	4	34	Par	70
Handicap	18	14	6	2	10	4	12	16	8			
RED	127	304	78	354	356	293	334	336	247	2429	RED	5244
Par	3	4	3	4	4	4	4	4	4	34	Par	71
Handicap	16	14	18	2	4	10	6	12	8			

Pro: Mike Mack, PGA   **Supt:** Brian Minemiar
Architect: Alexander Findlay 1929

CENTERTON GOLF CLUB

540 Almond Rd., Centerton, NJ 08318 **(609) 358-2220**

Centerton is a semi-private course that is open to the public 7 days a week all year. Memberships are available. Tee times may be made 7 days in advance for members and 6 days for non-members.

- **Driving Range**
- **Practice Green**
- **Power Carts**
- **Pull Carts**
- **Club Rental**
- Soft Spikes

- **Lockers**
- **Showers**
- **Food**
- **Clubhouse**
- **Outings**

Fees	Weekday	Weekend
Daily	$33	$39
Twi(3PM)	$26	$33
Power carts included		

Course Description: Easily accessible from both Philadelphia and Atlantic City, Centerton is a challenging, enjoyable experience for both beginners and more advanced players. It is gently rolling and tree lined with large greens and no parallel fairways. Water is in play on three holes. The most difficult hole, the 430 yard 16th, is a dogleg left; its green is small andundulating. The 14th, designed in a links style, is open with some mounding.

Directions: Salem County, #3 on Southwest Map
NJTPKE to Exit #3. Then take Rte. 168 and make a right onto Rte. 573 and then to Rte. 55. Follow to Rte. 553 into Centerton then left on Rte. 540. Club is 1/2 mile on left.

Hole	1	2	3	4	5	6	7	8	9	Out	BLUE	Rating 69.2
BLUE	365	360	225	515	375	420	180	415	365	3220		Slope 120
WHITE	349	321	391	155	446	507	437	193	413	3212		
Par	4	4	3	5	4	4	3	4	4	35	WHITE	Rating 67.8
Handicap	6	16	4	14	8	10	18	2	12			Slope 117
RED	330	312	175	429	308	341	132	359	307	2693		
Par	4	4	3	5	4	4	3	4	4	35	RED	Rating 71.5
Handicap	6	16	14	4	10	12	18	2	8			Slope 120

Hole	10	11	12	13	14	15	16	17	18	In	Totals	
BLUE	400	585	170	420	535	330	440	175	450	3505	BLUE	6725
WHITE	350	565	155	405	485	320	430	165	420	3295	WHITE	6305
Par	4	5	3	4	5	4	4	3	4	36	Par	71
Handicap	9	5	15	7	17	13	1	11	3			
RED	289	518	135	338	400	261	358	130	405	2832	RED	5525
Par	4	5	3	4	5	4	4	3	5	37	Par	72
Handicap	2	16	14	18	6	4	10	8	12			

Manager: Greg Matteo   **Pro:** Bill Torlucci, PGA
Architect: Ed Carman 1962

DEERWOOD COUNTRY CLUB

PUBLIC

18 Deerwood Drive, Westampton, NJ 08060   (609) 265-1800

Deerwood is as 18 hole semi-private course open 7 days a week all year. Memberships are available. Tee times are required: may be made 24 hours in advance. Deerwood may be going private in the near future.

- **Driving Range**
- **Practice Green**
- **Power Carts**
- Pull Carts
- **Club Rental**
- **Soft Spikes**
- **Lockers**
- **Showers**
- **Food**
- **Clubhouse**
- **Outings**

Fees	Weekday	Weekend
Daily	$66	$76
Power carts included		

Course Description: Shot selection is critical at Deerwood which was constructed in a "Figure 8" pattern to provide a variety of wind and sun orientation. The golfers skill is tested on its five man made ponds, three tiered greens and naturally preserved hit overs. The par 4 465 yard fifth is known as the "there goes my score" hole. It has a tee shot over a pond and then goes uphill to a well trapped green. . The fourteenth plays longer than its 398 yards indicate with westerly winds and water confronting the golfer. The bent grass greens have been contoured to make putting them a challenge.

Directions: Burlington County, #4 on Southwest Map
NJTPKE to Exit #5. Go South on Rte. 541 then left at jughandle onto Woodlane Rd. (Rte. 630 East). Club is ahead on left.

Hole	1	2	3	4	5	6	7	8	9	Out	BLUE	Rating 69.4
BLUE	380	383	365	136	465	350	513	209	334	3135		Slope 126
WHITE	371	369	349	130	436	325	481	197	323	2981		
Par	4	4	4	3	4	4	5	3	4	35	WHITE	Rating 67.9
Handicap	7	11	9	17	1	13	5	3	15			Slope 124
RED	316	273	294	114	367	294	405	131	267	2461		
Par	4	4	4	3	4	4	5	3	4	35	RED	Rating 67.2
Handicap	7	11	9	17	1	13	5	3	15			Slope 111

Hole	10	11	12	13	14	15	16	17	18	In		Totals
BLUE	375	368	176	139	398	310	398	556	376	3096	BLUE	6231
WHITE	364	330	164	130	380	287	383	546	363	2947	WHITE	5928
Par	4	4	3	3	4	4	4	5	4	35	Par	70
Handicap	10	12	16	18	4	14	8	2	6			
RED	300	303	137	118	221	224	311	441	291	2346	RED	4807
Par	4	4	3	3	4	4	4	5	4	35	Par	70
Handicap	10	12	16	18	4	14	8	2	6			

Manager: Terry Mulligan   **Pro**: Greg Farrow, PGA   **Supt**: Joel Collura
Architects: Dick Alaimo, Jim Blaukovitch 1996

FALCON CREEK GOLF COURSE

McGuire Air Force Base, Wrightstown, NJ 08641   (609) 724-3330

Falcon Creek is an 18 hole course open to active duty military, career retirees, Dept. of Defense, reservists and their guests. It is open 7 days a week all year. Memberships are available. Tee times are necessary for weekends and holidays.

•Driving Range	•Lockers
•Practice Green	•Showers
•Power Carts	•Food
•Pull Carts	•Clubhouse
•Club Rental	•Outings
•Soft Spikes	

Fees	Weekday	Weekend
Daily	$10-$20*	
*Rates depend on rank		
Power carts $18/18		$9/9
Single cart $12		

Course Description: Relatilvely flat, Falcon Creek offers a good test of golf with as many as 52 bunkers clustered around the mid-sized bent grass greens. There are nine holes afffected by water. The signature thirteenth hole, the #1 handicap, is lined with trees and has a ditch running across it. The cart paths are asphalt.

Directions: Burlington County, #5 on Southwest Map
NJTPKE to Exit #7. Then take Rte. 206S briefly to Fort Dix Access Highway #68 to Rte. 537 East (Monmouth Rd.) Follow signs to McGuire Air Force Base and ask at gate for directions to golf course.

Hole	1	2	3	4	5	6	7	8	9	Out	BLUE	Rating 72.6
BLUE	320	145	527	349	280	429	239	378	550	3217		Slope 122
WHITE	300	140	507	339	275	409	185	368	535	3058		
Par	4	3	5	4	4	4	3	4	5	36	WHITE	Rating 70.6
Handicap	10	16	8	12	18	4	2	14	6			Slope 118
RED	280	135	343	329	270	320	242	348	429	2696		
Par	4	3	4	4	4	4	4	3	5	35	RED	Rating 70.7
Handicap	11	15	1	5	13	7	17	3	9			Slope 118
Hole	10	11	12	13	14	15	16	17	18	In		Totals
BLUE	437	162	468	430	419	596	200	402	498	3612	BLUE	6764
WHITE	407	126	448	410	399	586	188	382	478	3424	WHITE	6434
Par	4	3	4	4	4	5	3	4	5	36	Par	72
Handicap	11	17	5	1	3	7	9	13	15			
RED	261	122	428	390	369	443	160	283	458	2914	RED	5384
Par	4	3	5	4	4	5	3	4	5	37	Par	72
Handicap	14	16	6	12	10	2	18	8	4			

Manager: Val Mendoza   **Supt:** Glenn Morlack
Built: 1960s

FOUNTAIN GREEN GOLF COURSE

Fort Dix, NJ 08640   (609) 562-5443

Fountain Green is a private 18 hole course available for Dep't. of Defense employees with I.D., active military personnel & dependents & retired career military. It is open 7 days a week all year. Memberships are available. Tee time reservations are needed on weekends.

•Driving Range	•Lockers
•Practice Green	•Showers
•Power Carts	•Food
•Pull Carts	•Clubhouse
•Club Rental	•Outings
•Soft Spikes	

Fees	Weekday	Weekend
Daily w/ID	$10	$10
Twi	$7	
Guest	$20	$20
Power carts	$20	

Course Description: The regulation sized Fountain Green is short featuring small, very fast bent grass greens. It is a walkable layout with water affecting play on 3 holes. The tree lined fairways are somewhat hilly. Drainage here is excellent; even after a heavy rainfall, the course is playable. The maintenance is outstanding due to the talents of the superintendent, John Huda, who is himself a scratch golfer. It never gets crowded at Fountain Green because strict eligibility criteria are enforced.

Directions: Burlington County, #6 on Southwest Map
NJTPKE to Exit 7; then take Rte. 206 South to Rte. 68 East to end into Fort Dix. Go around circle and straight to clubhouse on left.

Hole	1	2	3	4	5	6	7	8	9	Out	BLUE	Rating 70.6
BLUE	505	413	114	430	313	550	373	423	218	3339		Slope 118
WHITE	485	397	104	313	302	535	357	413	210	3116		
Par	5	4	3	4	4	5	4	4	3	36	WHITE	Rating 68.7
Handicap	9	5	17	7	15	1	11	3	13			Slope 115
RED	423	380	87	245	292	401	339	404	201	2772		
Par	5	4	3	4	4	5	4	5	3	37	RED	Rating 71.8
Handicap	9	5	17	7	15	1	11	3	13			Slope 123
Hole	10	11	12	13	14	15	16	17	18	In		Totals
BLUE	400	388	356	219	401	311	210	295	470	3050	BLUE	6389
WHITE	383	378	334	176	380	301	200	284	437	2873	WHITE	5989
Par	4	4	4	3	4	4	3	4	4/5	34/35	Par	70/71
Handicap	4	6	10	14	2	16	8	18	12			
RED	361	368	311	115	364	291	187	272	425	2694	RED	5466
Par	4	4	4	3	4	4	3	4	5	35	Par	72
Handicap	4	6	10	14	2	16	8	18	12			

Manager: Joan Verna   **Pro:** Bill Lyons, PGA   **Supt:** John Huda
Built: 1st stage early 50s   2nd stage late 50s

FREEWAY GOLF COURSE

PUBLIC

1858 Sicklerville, Rd., Sicklerville, NJ 08081   **(609) 227-1115**

Freeway is an 18 hole semi-private course open to the public 7 days a week all year. Memberships are available. Tee time reservations are required for weekend play. Power carts are required on weekend mornings.

•Driving Range	•Lockers
•Practice Green	•Showers
•Power Carts	•Food
•Pull Carts	•Clubhouse
•Club Rental	•Outings
Soft Spikes	

Fees	Weekday	Weekend
Daily	$30	$40
Twi(3PM)	$25	$30
Sr(no cart)	$13	
Power Carts included		

Course Description: Freeway is a well maintained course that is flat and wide open on the front nine while the back is shorter and narrower. It is considered fairly easy; it is not formidable for low handicappers. Water affects play on four holes. The par 3 fourteenth signature hole is long, narrow and requires an accurate tee shot. Many golfers drive up from Philadelphia to play here making it quite busy in season. A new irrigation system is being installed and a new clubhouse is being built.

Directions: Camden County, #7 on Southwest Map
NJTPKE to Exit #3. Exit at Rte. 168 South; then to Rte. 42 South to Exit 168 North. At first light go right on Sicklerville Rd.; club is 2 miles on left.

Hole	1	2	3	4	5	6	7	8	9	Out	BLUE	Rating 71.0
BLUE	587	182	394	349	368	409	408	389	580	3666		Slope 121
WHITE	562	169	382	325	342	394	387	379	557	3497		
Par	5	3	4	4	4	4	4	4	5	37	WHITE	Rating 69.7
Handicap	2	7	8	11	12	5	6	9	1			Slope 119
RED	497	142	365	249	301	336	326	341	502	3059		
Par	5	3	5	4	4	5	4	4	5	39	RED	Rating 70.3
Handicap	2	7	9	11	12	5	6	9	1			Slope 118
Hole	10	11	12	13	14	15	16	17	18	In		Totals
BLUE	318	195	316	415	232	472	346	161	415	2870	BLUE	6536
WHITE	309	169	305	395	212	442	278	144	400	2654	WHITE	6151
Par	4	3	4	5	3	5	4	3	4	35	Par	72
Handicap	15	17	14	10	16	4	18	13	3			
RED	299	145	285	307	185	409	223	128	345	2336	RED	5395
Par	4	3	4	5	3	5	4	3	5	36	Par	75
Handicap	15	17	14	10	16	4	18	13	3			

Manager: Karlon Hickman   **Pro:** William Bishop, PGA   **Supt:** Dave Bird
Built: 1968

GOLDEN PHEASANT GOLF CLUB

PUBLIC

141 Country Club Dr. & Eayrestown Rd.,
Medford, NJ 08055

(609) 267-4276

Golden Pheasant is an 18 hole course open 7 days a week all year. Memberships are available. Tee time reservations are required for weekends & holidays in season.

Driving Range	• **Lockers**
• **Practice Green**	• **Showers**
• **Power Carts**	• **Food**
• **Pull Carts**	• **Clubhouse**
• **Club Rental**	• **Outings**
• **Soft Spikes**	

Fees	**Weekday**	**Weekend**
Daily	$33	$42
Sr (over 65) $26		
Twi rates available		
Power carts included		

Course Description: As one moves along the Golden Pheasant course, the holes become more challenging. Starting with open fairways, it progresses gradually to more demanding, rolling terrain and elevated greens. Other features that pique one's interest are the ravines, streams and valleys. The 450 yard par 4 fourth has a tough downhill approach shot to a small undulating green. This course is a pleasurable golf experience.

Directions: Burlington County, #8 on Southwest Map
NJTPKE to Exit #5, Mt. Holly. Take Rte. 541 South to Mt. Holly. Then take Mt. Holly bypass to Rte. 38 and turn left. Go right at 2nd light; Eayrestown Rd. As road dead ends, make a sharp right and then a quick left onto Country Club Drive to club on right.

Hole	1	2	3	4	5	6	7	8	9	Out	BLUE	Rating 68.1
BLUE	555	153	365	450	423	354	302	183	471	3256		Slope 119
WHITE	550	143	360	420	409	336	289	173	453	3133		
Par	5	3	4	4	4	4	4	3	5	36	WHITE	Rating 67.0
Handicap	3	11	5	1	7	17	13	9	15			Slope 116
RED	409	120	340	375	348	326	279	140	388	2725		
Par	5	3	4	4	4	4	4	3	5	36	RED	Rating 68.4
Handicap	3	11	5	1	7	17	13	9	15			Slope 114
Hole	10	11	12	13	14	15	16	17	18	In		Totals
BLUE	540	179	298	371	518	149	331	288	343	3017	BLUE	6273
WHITE	526	170	283	346	487	138	315	277	327	2869	WHITE	6002
Par	5	3	4	4	5	3	4	4	4	36	Par	72
Handicap	2	10	16	8	4	14	6	12	18			
RED	478	123	198	268	423	97	284	196	313	2380	RED	5105
Par	5	3	4	4	5	3	4	4	4	36	Par	72
Handicap	2	10	16	8	4	14	6	12	18			

Manager: Carmen Capri   **Supt:** Paul Capri
Architect: Richard Kidder 1964

HANOVER COUNTRY CLUB

133 Larrison Rd., Jacobstown, NJ 08562   **(609) 758-8301**

Hanover is an 18 hole public course open 7 days a week all year. Tee times may be made 1 week in advance for weekends. On weekdays, a sandwich is included with green fees.

• **Driving Range**	Lockers
• **Practice Green**	• **Showers**
• **Power Carts**	• **Food**
• **Pull Carts**	• **Clubhouse**
• **Club Rental**	• **Outings**
• **Soft Spikes**	

Fees	Weekday	Weekend
Daily	$35	$48
Sr w/cart	$26	
Power carts included		

Course Description: Hanover is a well groomed, fair course with tree lined fairways, large greens that hold well, and a hilly challenging back nine. Although a small creek runs through the entire course, water is actually in play on four holes. The signature eighteenth hole, a 620 yard par 5, has an elevated tee to an open fairway. The second shot is over water, or the less confident can lay up. The contoured green is not reachable in two.

Directions: Burlington County, #9 on Southwest Map
NJTPKE to Exit 7A. Take Rte. 195 East to Exit #16. Then take Rte. 537 West for 8 miles to Larrison Rd. Hanover CC is on the right.

Hole	1	2	3	4	5	6	7	8	9	Out	BLUE	Rating
BLUE	420	455	460	180	390	375	150	575	375	3380		Slope
WHITE	395	430	455	160	370	350	140	540	350	3190		
Par	4	4	4	3	4	4	3	5	4	35	WHITE	Rating 70.0
Handicap	6	2	4	16	12	10	18	8	14			Slope 120
RED	370	360	365	125	345	325	110	440	320	2760		
Par	4	4	4	3	4	4	3	5	4	35	RED	Rating
Handicap	4	8	6	16	10	12	18	2	14			Slope
Hole	10	11	12	13	14	15	16	17	18	In		Totals
BLUE	385	315	430	415	405	195	420	165	620	3340	BLUE	6720
WHITE	375	295	415	399	388	190	390	145	610	3202	WHITE	6392
Par	4	4	4	4	4	3	4	3	5	35	Par	70
Handicap	9	13	3	11	5	15	7	17	1			
RED	350	275	360	330	345	170	300	120	540	2790	RED	5550
Par	4	4	5	4	4	3	4	3	6	37	Par	72
Handicap	5	13	3	9	7	15	11	17	1			

Manager/Supt: John Limm   **Architect:** Robert Trent Jones 1960

HOLLY HILLS GOLF CLUB

PUBLIC

Friesburg Road, Alloway, NJ 08001

(609) 935-2412

Holly Hills is an 18 hole semi-private course open to the public 7 days a week all year. Memberships are available which include yearly green fees and preferred starting times. Tee times: 1 week in advance. Weekday specials: $26/greens, cart & lunch

• Driving Range	• Lockers
• Practice Green	• Showers
• Power Carts	• Food
Pull Carts	• Clubhouse
• Club Rental	• Outings
Soft Spikes	

Fees	Weekday	Weekend
Daily	$30	$40
Twi	$20	$30
9 holes	$15	$20
Power carts included		

Course Description: Not far from the Delaware River is Holly Hills, an appealing and well maintained golf course. Almost half of the holes are affected by water in the form of ponds and streams that cross the fairway. More bunkers and ponds have recently been added. It is a nature lover's delight with its rolling hills, variety of wildlife and rustic scenery. This course was rated #1 by the Courier-Post for publilc golf courses in 1994 & 95.

Directions: Salem County, #10 on Southwest Map
NJTPKE to Exit #2. Then take Rte. 322 East toward Mullica Hill. Turn right at Rte. 45 which becomes Rte. 77S. At traffic circle take Rte. 635W for 7 miles to Friesburg Rd. and turn right. Course is 1 mile on right.

Hole	1	2	3	4	5	6	7	8	9	Out	BLUE	Rating 71.4
BLUE	556	198	284	418	166	180	247	381	483	2913		Slope 124
WHITE	546	175	274	400	160	170	236	373	475	2809		
Par	5	3	4	4	3	3	4	4	5	35	WHITE	Rating 70.0
Handicap	7	5	17	1	13	11	15	3	9			Slope 123
RED	522	96	223	255	98	143	221	292	429	2279		
Par	5	3	4	4	3	3	4	4	5	35	RED	Rating 68.6
Handicap	1	17	15	9	7	13	11	5	3			Slope 118

Hole	10	11	12	13	14	15	16	17	18	In		Totals
BLUE	567	158	490	420	354	376	201	411	487	3464	BLUE	6377
WHITE	557	149	481	400	335	349	175	401	457	3304	WHITE	6113
Par	5	5	5	4	4	4	3	4	5	37	Par	72
Handicap	2	18	8	10	14	6	16	12	4			
RED	500	126	423	340	240	332	138	247	431	2777	RED	5056
Par	5	5	5	4	4	4	3	4	5	37	Par	72
Handicap	2	18	8	10	14	6	16	12	4			

Manager: Manuel Pataca   **Pro:** Mike Zack, PGA   **Supt:** Steve Marcus
Architect: Horace Smith 1970

INDIAN SPRING GOLF CLUB

S.Elmwood Rd. & Old Marlton Pike,
Marlton, NJ 08053

(609) 983-0222

Indian Spring is an 18 hole course open 7 days a week all year. Memberships are available with reduced rates for Evesham Township residents. Tee time reservations may be made 6 days in advance all week.

- •Driving Range
- •Practice Green
- •Power Carts
- •Pull Carts
- Club Rental
- •Soft Spikes
- •Lockers
- •Showers
- •Food
- •Clubhouse
- •Outings

Fees	Weekday	Weekend
Daily	$20	$24
Twi	$18	$20
Power carts	$24	

Course Description: Originally farmland, Indian Spring is relatively flat, walkable and quite busy. Water comes into play on a few holes in the form of creeks and ponds. The scorecard is helpful with yardages provided to the center of the green from strategic locations on the fairways. The par 3 sixth hole produces many holes-in-one. A new and beautiful clubhouse providing catering and a pro shop will be ready in April, 1999.

Directions: Burlington County, #11 on Southwest Map

NJTPKE to Exit #4. Take Rte. 73 South to Rte. 70 East (Olga's Diner). When Rte. 70 becomes 2 lanes from 4, at next set of lights, turn right onto Elmwood Rd. Club is 1/4 mile ahead.

Hole	1	2	3	4	5	6	7	8	9	Out	BLUE	Rating 68.9
BLUE	404	406	355	294	500	143	442	224	374	3142		Slope 113
WHITE	387	388	338	281	482	119	420	205	357	2977		
Par	4	4	4	4	5	3	4	3	4	35	WHITE	Rating 67.8
Handicap	7	5	9	13	1	17	3	11	15			Slope 111
RED	370	370	321	268	456	105	398	185	340	2813		
Par	4	4	4	4	5	3	4	3	4	35	RED	Rating 70.8
Handicap	7	5	9	13	1	17	3	11	15			Slope 116

Hole	10	11	12	13	14	15	16	17	18	In		Totals
BLUE	404	379	368	152	423	414	194	351	549	3234	BLUE	6376
WHITE	379	368	348	130	405	390	174	333	514	3041	WHITE	6018
Par	4	4	4	3	4	4	3	4	5	35	Par	70
Handicap	4	10	12	18	2	6	16	14	8			
RED	355	357	327	108	349	366	154	315	440	2771	RED	5584
Par	4	4	4	3	4	4	3	4	5	35	Par	70
Handicap	4	10	12	18	2	6	16	14	8			

Manager/Pro: David Quinn, PGA   **Supt:** Tim Rumbos
Architects: Burt Jaggard 1960s   **Redesign:** Ron Forsch 1998

KRESSON GOLF COURSE

298 Kresson-Gibbsboro Rd., Voorhees, NJ 08043   **(609) 435-3355**

Kresson is an 18 hole course open 7 days a week, all year. Tee time reservations are not necessary.

<table>
<tr><td>Driving Range</td><td rowspan="2">Lockers</td></tr>
<tr><td>•**Practice Green**</td></tr>
<tr><td>•**Power Carts**</td><td>Showers</td></tr>
<tr><td rowspan="2">•**Pull Carts**</td><td>•**Food**</td></tr>
<tr><td>Clubhouse</td></tr>
<tr><td>•**Club Rental**</td><td rowspan="2">Outings</td></tr>
<tr><td>Soft Spikes</td></tr>
</table>

Fees	Weekday	Weekend
Daily	$19	$23
Twi(after 3)	$15	$15
Sr	$17	
Power carts	$24	

Course Description: The well maintained Kresson is a relatively flat public course good for beginners and those wanting to practice iron shots. The greens have some bunkering and are relatively slow. Four ponds bring water into play on five holes. The front nine is longer than the back on this par 68 scenic course.

Directions: Camden County, #12 on Southwest Map
Rte. 295 to the Haddonfield exit. Then take Rte. 561 South (Haddonfield-Berlin Rd.) for 10 miles & turn left on Kresson-Gibbsboro Rd. Golf course is on the right.

Hole	1	2	3	4	5	6	7	8	9	Out	BLUE	Rating
BLUE												Slope
WHITE	253	300	480	105	122	210	500	250	485	2705		
Par	4	4	5	3	3	3	5	4	5	36	WHITE	Rating
Handicap												Slope
RED												
Par	4	4	5	3	3	4	5	4	5	37	RED	Rating
Handicap												Slope
Hole	10	11	12	13	14	15	16	17	18	In		Totals
BLUE											BLUE	
WHITE	120	260	360	175	160	220	340	160	300	2095	WHITE	4800
Par	3	4	4	3	3	4	4	3	4	32	Par	68
Handicap												
RED											RED	4800
Par	3	4	4	4	3	4	4	3	4	33	Par	70
Handicap												

Manager/Supt: John Aducat   **Built:** 1960s

LAUREL CREEK COUNTRY CLUB   **PRIVATE**

701 Moorestown-Centerton Rd., Mt. Laurel, NJ 08054   **(609) 234-7663**

Laurel Creek is an 18 hole course open all year 6 days a week.   Guests may play accompanied by a member. Tee time reservations are not necessary.

• **Driving Range**	• **Lockers**
• **Practice Green**	• **Showers**
• **Power Carts**	• **Food**
Pull Carts	• **Clubhouse**
Club Rental	• **Outings**
Caddies	Soft Spikes

Course Description: The excellently maintained Laurel Creek is considered a haven for the golf purist; Irish links type with tees, fairways and greens of bent grass. The course abounds with high fescue grass in the secondary roughs. There are 14 man-made lakes, many unique, special holes and five sets of tees. Laurel Creek is dotted with bunkers that can trap the unwary golfer. This layout was carved out of a defunct clay mining operation, a farm, and orchards. Great care was taken not to disturb the wetlands. There are many lovely homes built around the course and the clubhouse is impressive.

Directions: Burlington County, #13 on Southwest Map
NJTPKE to Exit #5 and turn left. Go 2 miles to Rte. 295 South to Exit #43 (Delran-Rancocas Woods). Bear right on exit ramp to Delran. At first light, turn left to Centerton Rd. Club is 1/2 mile up ahead.

Hole	1	2	3	4	5	6	7	8	9	Out	BLUE	Rating 72.7
BLUE	417	376	166	405	514	451	215	365	555	3464		Slope 132
WHITE	390	349	135	355	482	357	168	311	495	3042		
Par	4	4	3	4	5	4	3	4	5	36	WHITE	Rating 70.1
Handicap	6	16	18	14	4	2	12	8	10			Slope 126
RED	371	244	119	331	437	342	142	283	452	2721		
Par	4	4	3	4	5	4	3	4	5	36	RED	Rating 73.0
Handicap	2	18	16	12	4	8	14	10	6			Slope 128
Hole	10	11	12	13	14	15	16	17	18	In		Totals
BLUE	409	405	459	384	169	520	435	227	445	3453	BLUE	6917
WHITE	398	342	420	360	146	466	405	196	407	3140	WHITE	6182
Par	4	4	4	4	3	5	4	3	4	35	Par	71
Handicap	7	11	5	13	17	15	3	9	1			
RED	398	329	357	336	138	444	358	135	376	2871	RED	5592
Par	5	4	4	4	3	5	4	3	4	36	Par	72
Handicap	13	11	3	5	15	17	7	9	1			

Manager: Greg Dunham   **Pro**: John Tyrell, PGA   **Supt**: John Slade
Architect: Arnold Palmer 1990

LINKS GOLF CLUB

100 Majestic Way, Marlton, NJ 08053   **(609) 983-2000**

Links is an 18 hole private course open 7 days a week from March through December. Guests may play accompanied by a member. Tee time reservations are not necessary.

•**Driving Range**	•**Lockers**
•**Practice Green**	•**Showers**
•**Power Carts**	•**Food**
Pull Carts	•**Clubhouse**
Club Rental	Outings
Caddies	Soft Spikes

Course Description: Beautiful homes surround this little known golf course designed strictly for the dedicated golfer; it is not a typical country club. Most of its members come from Cherry Hill and Philadelphia and a few from the development. The layout is in the links style, particularly obvious on the back nine. The well groomed and narrow fairways make the golfer think about placement strategy on the way to the small greens. Driving areas are contoured and give way to lots of bunkers making this course one that demands accuracy and patience.

Directions: Burlington County, #14 on Southwest Map
NJTPKE to Exit #4. Take Rte. 73 South to Marlton Pkwy. and turn left. Follow to Crown Royal Pkwy. and turn right. Go 7/10 mile on left to Majestic Way and entrance.

Hole	1	2	3	4	5	6	7	8	9	Out	BLUE	Rating 70.7
BLUE	320	334	377	203	343	440	450	325	400	2892		Slope 131
WHITE	310	323	359	187	329	422	126	309	380	2745		
Par	4	4	4	3	4	4	3	4	4	34	WHITE	Rating 68.9
Handicap	15	9	5	11	7	1	17	13	3			Slope 126
RED	294	312	300	174	316	364	110	296	355	2521		
Par	4	4	4	3	4	4	3	4	4	34	RED	Rating 70.2
Handicap	15	9	5	11	7	1	17	13	3			Slope 125
Hole	10	11	12	13	14	15	16	17	18	In		Totals
BLUE	382	350	489	524	178	428	430	158	392	3331	BLUE	6223
WHITE	366	337	469	509	158	417	415	144	376	3191	WHITE	5936
Par	4	4	5	5	3	4	4	3	4	36	Par	70
Handicap	10	8	14	12	16	2	4	18	6			
RED	296	307	426	457	126	364	384	135	341	2836	RED	5357
Par	4	4	5	5	3	4	4	3	4	36	Par	70
Handicap	10	8	14	12	16	2	4	18	6			

Manager/Pro: Bob DeMarco, PGA   **Supt:** James Acheson
Architect: Frederick Hawtree 1971

242

LITTLE MILL COUNTRY CLUB

104 Borton's Rd., Marlton, NJ 08053   **(609) 767-0559**

Little Mill is a 27 hole course open 6 days a week all year. Guests play accompanied by a member. Tee time reservations are required on weekends and holidays in season.

- •Driving Range
- •Practice Green
- •Power Carts
- •Pull Carts
- •Club Rental
- Caddies

- •Lockers
- •Showers
- •Food
- •Clubhouse
- •Outings
- •Soft Spikes

Course Description: An abundance of trees can be found at Little Mill, a course cut out of a forest. The fairways are tree lined and relatively wide. There are 3 nines; Devil's Glen, Stoney Mt. and Little Mill and varying the combinations adds interest for golfers. Water comes into play on every nine. The signature par 3 eighth on the Stoney Mt. Blue nine, offers the highest elevation in Burlington County; 118 feet above sea level. On clear days, the amazing view goes as far as Philadelphia to the west and Atlantic City to the east. The scorecard below is for Little Mill and Stoney Mt. Power carts are required on weekends.

Directions: Burlington County, #15 on Southwest Map
NJTPKE to Exit #4. Take Rte. 73 South toward Atlantic City. Go left on Marlton Pkwy. to Hopewell Rd. and take it for 2 miles to club on right.

Hole	1	2	3	4	5	6	7	8	9	Out	BLUE	Rating 73.1
BLUE	307	164	436	510	456	419	564	218	411	3485		Slope 132
WHITE	287	148	410	490	440	399	542	198	385	3299		
Par	4	3	4	5	4	4	5	3	4	36	WHITE	Rating 71.6
Handicap	8	9	5	4	1	3	2	7	6			Slope 129
RED	242	117	312	390	334	344	415	145	313	2612		
Par	4	3	4	5	4	4	5	3	4	36	RED	Rating 71.9
Handicap	7	9	6	4	1	3	2	8	5			Slope 126

Hole	10	11	12	13	14	15	16	17	18	In		Totals
BLUE	514	377	383	391	161	514	372	159	419	3290	BLUE	6775
WHITE	494	364	371	378	141	502	360	143	400	3153	WHITE	6152
Par	5	4	4	4	3	5	4	3	4	36	Par	72
Handicap	2	7	6	5	9	1	4	8	3			
RED	429	329	317	325	124	416	306	143	419	2802	RED	5414
Par	5	4	4	4	3	5	4	3	5	37	Par	73
Handicap	2	6	7	4	8	1	3	9	5			

Managers: Bd. of Directors   **Pro:** Ken Peyre-Ferry, PGA   **Supt:** Doug Davis
Architect: Harry Wren 1967

MAPLE RIDGE GOLF CLUB

Woodbury-Glassboro Roads, Sewell, NJ 08080   (609) 468-3542

Maple Ridge is an 18 hole course open 7 days a week all year. Tee times may be reserved up to 1 week in advance.

Driving Range	•Lockers
•Practice Green	•Showers
•Power Carts	•Food
•Pull Carts	•Clubhouse
•Club Rental	•Outings
Soft Spikes	

Fees	Weekday	Weekend
Daily(Mon-Th)	$36	$45
Fri	$38	
Twi(3PM)	$22	$28
Power carts included		

Course Description: Tough, challenging and well maintained, Maple Ridge (formerly Eagle's Nest) is relatively flat on the front nine but very hilly, tree lined and narrow on the back offering many uneven lies. The par 3 16th is the signature hole requiring a tee shot over a big pond that features a little waterfall to a large sloping green. A creek meanders through the course making it interesting for the golfer on the par 5s, #7 and #15. A new irrigation system is being installed and the cart paths have been repaved.

Directions: Gloucester County, #16 on Southwest Map
Rte. 55 (accessible from the Atlantic City Xway or NJTPKE Exit #3) to Exit 53B. Take Rte. 553 for 1 & 1/2 miles; course on left.

Hole	1	2	3	4	5	6	7	8	9	Out	BLUE	Rating 71.3
BLUE	351	324	211	378	353	360	503	140	557	3177		Slope 130
WHITE	343	311	199	361	343	354	485	130	544	3070		
Par	4	4	3	4	4	4	5	3	5	36	WHITE	Rating 70.0
Handicap	11	16	15	13	12	8	2	18	3			Slope 128
RED	341	299	167	345	333	222	445	120	414	2686		
Par	4	4	3	4	4	4	5	3	5	36	RED	Rating 71.2
Handicap	9	13	7	5	11	17	3	15	1			Slope 125
Hole	10	11	12	13	14	15	16	17	18	In		Totals
BLUE	391	211	401	408	424	494	172	497	205	3203	BLUE	6380
WHITE	366	170	385	395	408	484	117	471	192	2988	WHITE	6058
Par	4	3	4	4	4	5	3	5	3	35	Par	71
Handicap	7	10	5	1	4	6	17	9	14			
RED	333	142	372	382	293	328	102	393	179	2524	RED	5210
Par	4	3	4	4	4	5	3	5	3	35	Par	71
Handicap	8	12	2	4	16	6	18	10	14			

Owners: Gotham Golf Partners   **Manager:** Dave O'Hara   **Supt:** John Hutchinson
Architects: William & David Gordon 1964

MEDFORD LAKES COUNTRY CLUB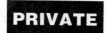

P.O.Box 600 Oak Dr., Medford Lakes, NJ 08055   **(609) 654-5109**

Medford Lakes is an 18 hole course open 6 days a week all year. Guests may play accompanied by a member. Tee time reservations are not necessary.

Driving Range	•**Lockers**
•**Practice Green**	•**Showers**
•**Power Carts**	•**Food**
•**Pull Carts**	•**Clubhouse**
Club Rental	•**Outings**
Caddies	•**Soft Spikes**

Course Description: Narrow wooded fairways are prevalent at Medford Lakes, a short tight course with bent grass greens. The front nine has two holes over water, while the back nine is surrounded by an abundance of water. The par 4 second hole is beautiful yet difficult requiring a shot over a large lake.

Directions: Burlington County, #17 on Southwest Map
NJTPKE to Exit #4 to Rte. 73 South to Rte. 70 East to Rte. 541South (Stokes Rd.) Go 3 miles to Settler's Inn & make a left on Tabernacle to course.

Hole	1	2	3	4	5	6	7	8	9	Out	BLUE	Rating
BLUE												Slope
WHITE	341	362	392	322	330	159	267	307	488	2968		
Par	4	4	4	4	4	3	4	4	5	36	WHITE	Rating 68.8
Handicap	11	1	3	9	5	15	17	13	7			Slope 121
RED	330	339	370	299	322	129	219	295	466	2769		
Par	4	4	4	4	4	3	4	4	5	36	RED	Rating 73.3
Handicap	11	1	3	9	7	15	17	13	5			Slope 125
Hole	10	11	12	13	14	15	16	17	18	In		Totals
BLUE											BLUE	
WHITE	305	162	361	316	497	416	163	403	512	3135	WHITE	6103
Par	4	3	4	4	5	5	3	4	5	36	Par	72
Handicap	12	18	4	14	8	2	16	6	10			
RED	297	141	344	302	482	403	148	382	498	2997	RED	5766
Par	4	3	4	4	5	4	3	4	5	37	Par	73
Handicap	14	18	8	12	2	10	16	4	6			

Manager: Dan Haskell **Pro:** Joe Schlindwein, PGA **Supt:** Gregg Armbruster
Architects: William Findlay (1st nine) 1929 Hal Purdy (back nine)

MEDFORD VILLAGE COUNTRY CLUB

Golf View Drive, Medford, NJ 08055   (609) 654-8211

Medford Village is an 18 hole private golf course open all year, 6 days a week. Guests may play accompanied by a member. Tee time reservations are not necessary.

- •**Driving Range**
- •**Practice Green**
- •**Power Carts**
- Pull Carts
- Club Rental
- Caddies
- •**Lockers**
- •**Showers**
- •**Food**
- •**Clubhouse**
- •**Outings**
- •**Soft Spikes**

Course Description: Designed with Pine Valley as an inspiration, Medford Village is heavily wooded; pine and oak trees encroach on the fairways. A long course (7100 from the blues), the fairways are tighter on the back nine and more open on the front. Constructed on property known as Sunny Jim's Farm, it originally was called Sunny Jim GC. The course is laid out so that no one can be hit by a stray shot from another hole. The #1 handicap for men is the first with water off the tee and again near the green. This club has hosted the South Jersey Open and other professional events.

Directions: Burlington County, #18 on Southwest Map
NJTPKE South to Exit #15. Turn right onto Rte. 541 S through Mt. Holly and Medford Circle (Rte.70.) Approx. 1mile after circle, go right onto Himmelein Rd. Then take the 2nd left onto Golf View Dr. Club is at end of street.

Hole	1	2	3	4	5	6	7	8	9	Out	BLUE	Rating 74.1
BLUE	420	415	536	230	545	166	380	375	440	3507		Slope 137
WHITE	402	411	490	205	485	150	360	350	408	3261		
Par	4	4	5	3	5	3	4	4	4	36	WHITE	Rating 71.7
Handicap	1	3	11	13	15	17	9	7	5			Slope 133
RED	320	335	342	140	412	96	305	285	367	2602		
Par	4	4	5	3	5	3	4	4	4	36	RED	Rating 69.9
Handicap	5	7	13	15	1	17	11	9	3			Slope 120
Hole	10	11	12	13	14	15	16	17	18	In		Totals
BLUE	590	215	415	400	550	385	213	385	440	3593	BLUE	7100
WHITE	520	163	397	340	510	362	200	355	395	3242	WHITE	6503
Par	5	3	4	4	5	4	3	4	3	36	Par	72
Handicap	6	18	4	2	12	10	14	16	8			
RED	473	130	301	272	413	302	130	304	305	2630	RED	5232
Par	5	3	4	4	5	4	3	4	3	36	Par	72
Handicap	2	18	6	8	4	12	16	14	10			

Manager: Larry Wizeman   **Pro:** Leo De Gisi, PGA   **Supt:** Bruce Rickert
Architect: William Gordon 1963

MERCHANTVILLE COUNTRY CLUB PRIVATE

Chapel Ave., Cherry Hill, NJ 08002   (609) 439-2513

Merchantville is a 9 hole private course open 6 days a week all year. Guests may play accompanied by a member. Reserved tee times are not necessary.

Driving Range	•Lockers
•Practice Green	•Showers
•Power Carts	•Food
•Pull Carts	•Clubhouse
•Club Rental	•Outings
Caddies	•Soft Spikes

Course Description: Built around an array of natural creeks, every hole has water at Merchantville CC, the fifth oldest club in the US. It is relatively flat and there is an interplay of crossovers to make the course interesting from a different perspective. The contoured fairways have plenty of rough increasing the difficulty. There are 6 square inches of land in Merchantville and the rest of the course is in Cherry Hill in order to preserve the liquor license, not available in dry Merchantville. The club pro here in the early nineteen hundreds, John McDermott, became the first American born golf professional to win the US Open, accomplishing this feat in 1910 and again in 1912.

Directions: Camden County, #19 on West Central Map
NJTPKE to Exit #4. Then take Rte. 73 North to Rte. 38 West. At Chapel Ave. make a right; club is on left.

Hole	1	2	3	4	5	6	7	8	9	Out	BLUE	Rating 70.3
BLUE	505	589	145	323	335	202	289	375	400	3163		Slope 135
WHITE	485	568	130	298	325	190	270	345	393	3004		
Par	5	5	3	4	4	3	4	4	4	36	WHITE	Rating 69.2
Handicap	7	4	9	6	1	2	8	5	3			Slope 132
RED	342	458	112	304	433	348	137	366	334	2834		
Par	4	5	3	4	5	4	3	4	4	36	RED	Rating 71.6
Handicap	7	1	9	6	2	5	8	4	3			Slope 123
Hole	10	11	12	13	14	15	16	17	18	In		Totals
BLUE											BLUE	6333
WHITE											WHITE	6031
Par											Par	72
Handicap												
RED											RED	5333
Par											Par	72
Handicap												

Dir. of Golf/Pro: Blaise S. Straka, PGA   **Supt:** Kent Rickenback
Built: 1892

MOORESTOWN FIELD CLUB

629 Chester Ave., Moorestown, NJ 08057   **(609) 235-2326**

Moorestown is a 9 hole course open all year, 7 days a week; (closes Mondays in Dec., Jan., and Feb.) Guests play accompanied by a member. Tee time reservations are not necessary. There is a long waiting list for membership.

- •**Driving Range**
- •**Practice Green**
- •**Power Carts**
- •**Pull Carts**
- •**Club Rental**
- Caddies
- •**Lockers**
- •**Showers**
- •**Food**
- •**Clubhouse**
- Outings
- •**Soft Spikes**

Course Description: The Field Club is an old style course; short, flat, straight and narrow with small well bunkered greens. The signature hole is the par 3 eighth; its green is virtually in the woods and is reached by hitting over a ditch. Different tees are used for the front and back nines to add interest. The engineers from Flexible Flyers (the well known sled company) built the original nine holes in 1910.

Directions: Burlington County, #20 on Southwest Map
NJTPKE to Exit 34. Then take Rte. 73 North to Kings Highway (Rte. 41) towards Moorestown where it becomes Main St. Make a left on Chester Ave. Club is 6 blocks up on the right.

Hole	1	2	3	4	5	6	7	8	9	Out	BLUE	Rating
BLUE												Slope
WHITE	313	311	323	148	457	412	510	143	360	2977		
Par	4	4	4	3	5	4	5	3	4	36	WHITE	Rating 68.3
Handicap	13	11	9	15	7	1	3	17	5			Slope 119
RED	313	311	323	148	457	412	510	143	360	2977		
Par	4	4	4	3	5	5	5	3	4	37	RED	Rating 74.1
Handicap	13	11	7	15	5	9	1	17	3			Slope 125
Hole	10	11	12	13	14	15	16	17	18	In		Totals
BLUE											BLUE	
WHITE											WHITE	6013
Par											Par	72
Handicap												
RED											RED	5851
Par											Par	73
Handicap												

Manager/Supt: John Carpinelli   **Pro:** Butch Schmehl, PGA
Established: 1892

OLDE YORK COUNTRY CLUB

228 Old York Rd., Columbus, NJ 08022   **(609) 298-0212**

Olde York is an 18 hole course open 6 days a week, all year. Guests may play accompanied by a member. Reserved tee times are recommended.

> • **Driving Range**   • **Lockers**
> • **Practice Green**   • **Showers**
> • **Power Carts**   • **Food**
> • **Pull Carts**   • **Clubhouse**
> • **Club Rental**   • **Outings**
> • **Caddies**   • **Soft Spikes**

Course Description: There are no less than 5 tees to a maximum of 9 tees at Olde York CC, which plays to a total of 6903 yards from the Blues. This accomodates golfers of varying proficiency and minimizes traffic. The course is heavily wooded with spectacular tee chutes; 5 of the holes are completely enclosed by woods. The fairways, tees & greens are bent grass; Kentucky Blue grass surrounds the 146 bunkers. Colorful fescue and native ornamental grass flank the out of play area. Stacked sod bunkers add to the traditional Scottish look. Designed by Gary Player, who considers this his signature course, it is world championship caliber. Golfers will notice the influence of Olde York's prior life as a stud farm by the attractive reminders of early history retained in the decorative setting.

Directions: Burlington County, #21 on Southwest Map
NJTPKE to Exit #7. Take Rte 206 S; after NJTPKE overpass, make 2nd U turn to Rte. 206 North. Take Old York Rd. on right. Go 3/4 mile to course on left.

Hole	1	2	3	4	5	6	7	8	9	Out	BLUE	Rating 73.0
BLUE	442	232	522	470	206	361	527	192	354	3306		Slope 138
WHITE	390	186	487	423	153	314	476	145	315	2889		
Par	4	3	5	4	3	4	5	3	4	35	WHITE	Rating 68.5
Handicap	3	13	9	1	5	15	7	17	11			Slope 122
RED	378	159	463	414	111	285	453	121	286	2670		
Par	4	3	5	5	3	4	5	3	4	36	RED	Rating 69.3
Handicap	3	13	9	1	5	15	7	17	11			Slope 122
Hole	10	11	12	13	14	15	16	17	18	In		Totals
BLUE	378	198	380	555	462	200	581	454	389	3597	BLUE	6903
WHITE	335	168	310	516	404	146	515	392	342	3128	WHITE	6017
Par	4	3	4	5	4	3	5	4	4	36	Par	71
Handicap	14	16	12	10	4	18	2	6	8			
RED	294	139	280	500	375	130	486	344	299	2847	RED	5517
Par	4	3	4	5	4	3	5	4	4	36	Par	72
Handicap	14	16	12	6	10	18	2	4	8			

Owners/Managers: Corinne & Ed Eget **Pro:** Doug Juhasz, PGA **Supt:** Mark Stallone
Architect: Gary Player 1994   (Orig. Estab. 1950)

PENNSAUKEN COUNTRY CLUB

3800 Haddonfield Rd., Pennsauken, NJ 08109   **(609) 662-4961**

Pennsauken is an 18 hole semi-private township owned course open 7 days a week, all year. Memberships are available. Tee times: call Wed. for weekdays and Mon. for weekends.

<table>
<tr><td>
Driving Range
•**Practice Green**
•**Power Carts**
•**Pull Carts**
•**Club Rental**
Soft Spikes
</td><td>
•**Lockers**
•**Showers**
•**Food**
•**Clubhouse**
•**Outings**
</td></tr>
</table>

Fees	Weekday	Weekend
Resident	$25	$25
Non-res	$27	$27
Sr/Twi	$23/22	$23/22
Power carts	$13pp	

Course Description: Excellently maintained and highly rated in Southern NJ, Pennsauken has benefitted in recent years from its renovations, including rebuilt tees and improved fairway contouring. A tunnel is under construction to avoid crossing over a road on the course. It is well bunkered with small bent grass greens; water is in play on nine holes. The front is open while the back is somewhat more difficult. The signature par 3 seventh is long measuring 216 yards from the white tees.

Directions: Camden County, #22 on Southwest Map
NJTPKE to Exit #4. Take Rte.73 North about 2 miles. Club is 1/4 mile past 3rd light. From Phila. Take Betsy Ross Br. onto Rte. 90 East for 1 mile to Rte. 644S. Proceed 1 & 1/2 mi. to club on left.

Hole	1	2	3	4	5	6	7	8	9	Out	BLUE	Rating 68.1
BLUE	325	353	156	397	319	341	240	526	388	3045		Slope 119
WHITE	309	344	142	387	301	323	216	510	386	2918		
Par	4	4	3	4	4	4	3	5	4	35	WHITE	Rating 66.6
Handicap	15	10	13	2	14	12	4	8	6			Slope 117
RED	304	306	111	317	290	302	189	433	278	2530		
Par	4	4	3	4	4	4	3	5	4	35	RED	Rating 67.9
Handicap	13	8	14	1	15	10	3	9	5			Slope 111

Hole	10	11	12	13	14	15	16	17	18	In		Totals
BLUE	471	127	336	339	485	113	392	283	415	2961	BLUE	5959
WHITE	461	117	326	313	469	98	379	271	397	2831	WHITE	5673
Par	4	3	4	4	5	3	4	4	4	35	Par	70
Handicap	1	16	11	9	7	18	5	17	3			
RED	320	88	300	294	401	85	288	254	300	2330	RED	4926
Par	4	3	4	4	5	3	4	4	4	35	Par	70
Handicap	6	16	11	4	2	18	12	17	7			

Manager/Supt: Robert Prickett   **Pro:** Quentin Griffith, PGA
Architect: Bob Prickett 1932

PINELANDS GOLF CLUB

887 S. Mays Landing Rd., Winslow, NJ 08037   (609) 561-8900

Pinelands is an 18 hole semi-private course halfway between Atlantic City and Philadelphia. It is open 7 days a week all year. Memberships are available. Tee times may be made 7 days in advance.

•Driving Range	•Lockers
•Practice Green	•Showers
•Power Carts	•Food
•Pull Carts	•Clubhouse
•Club Rental	•Outings
Soft Spikes	

Fees	Weekday	Weekend
Daily	$20	$24
Twi	$13	$17
Power carts $15pp		$26/dbl
Weekly specials available		

Course Description: Pinelands is a pretty course with tight tree lined fairways and small well maintained greens. The signature par 5 sixth hole, 581 yards from the blues, requires a third shot over water to a two tiered green. The par 3 sixteenth is fashioned after a hole at Augusta and features new landscaping of beautiful dogwoods and azaleas. The par 3s require great accuracy as the greens offer limited targets.

Directions: Camden County, #23 on Southwest Map
GSP or NJTPKE to Atlantic City Xpressway to Exit #28 (Hammonton.) Take Rte. 54 South. Make a right at 1st light onto Mays Landing Rd. (Rte. 561spur). Course is 4 miles on left.

Hole	1	2	3	4	5	6	7	8	9	Out	BLUE	Rating 69.7
BLUE	386	180	351	485	187	581	157	353	472	3152		Slope 114
WHITE	378	163	338	475	178	573	142	344	465	3056		
Par	4	3	4	5	3	5	3	4	5	36	WHITE	Rating 68.9
Handicap	3	13	9	17	11	1	15	5	7			Slope 113
RED	351	155	320	450	158	473	133	340	457	2837		
Par	4	3	4	5	3	5	3	4	5	36	RED	Rating 70.4
Handicap	3	17	11	7	13	1	15	5	9			Slope 119

Hole	10	11	12	13	14	15	16	17	18	In		Totals
BLUE	323	183	360	368	507	347	170	456	403	3117	BLUE	6224
WHITE	313	178	349	358	493	336	163	448	394	3032	WHITE	6033
Par	4	3	4	4	5	4	3	5	4	36	Par	72
Handicap	14	12	4	2	10	8	16	18	6			
RED	275	142	311	296	423	309	131	410	311	2608	RED	5375
Par	4	3	4	4	5	4	3	5	4	36	Par	72
Handicap	14	16	6	4	2	12	18	10	8			

Manager/Pro: Steve Wescott, PGA   **Supt:** Tom Mamrol
Architects: Brimfield Bros., Ralph Lespardi 1962

PINE VALLEY GOLF CLUB

Atlantic Ave., Pine Valley, NJ 08021   **(609) 783-9735**

Pine Valley is an 18 hole course open 6 days a week all year. Guests may play accompanied by a member. Tee time reservations are required.

- •Driving Range
- •Practice Green
- •Power Carts
- Pull Carts
- Club Rental
- •Caddies

- •Lockers
- •Showers
- •Food
- •Clubhouse
- Outings
- •Soft Spikes

Course Description: Chosen #1 in the world by Golf Digest year after year, Pine Valley deserves all its accolades. George Crump conceived the idea of this unique and tremendously difficult golf course. It is considered the ultimate in target golf as all the fairways and greens are surrounded by the sand & scrub characteristic of the NJ Pine Barrens. This irregular rough severely penalizes a wayward shot and makes intelligent, strategic club selection critical. The par 3 fifth, 226 yards over water, known as the hole "where only God can make a 3" has a heavily contoured plateau green with many bunkers. The par 3 tenth is rated the easiest on the scorecard, (more like the hardest at other courses) with a gaping right bunker luring the tee shot into trouble.

Directions: Camden County, #24 on Southwest Map
NJTPKE to Exit #4. Take Rte. 73 S past marker 19. At Franklin Ave. make a right; go to 3rd light. Go right onto Blackwood-Clementon Rd. & follow to amusement park. Make 1st left afte park to E. Atlantic Ave. to front gate of club.

Hole	1	2	3	4	5	6	7	8	9	Out	BLUE	Rating 74.1
BLUE	427	367	181	444	232	388	578	319	427	3363		Slope 153
WHITE	416	357	169	433	221	369	544	309	411	3229		
Par	4	4	3	4	3	4	5	4	4	35	WHITE	Rating 73.0
Handicap	3	9	17	5	11	13	1	15	7			Slope 150
RED												
Par											RED	Rating
Handicap												Slope

Hole	10	11	12	13	14	15	16	17	18	In		Totals
BLUE	146	392	344	448	184	591	433	338	428	3304	BLUE	6667
WHITE	137	379	340	445	168	570	423	335	410	3207	WHITE	6436
Par	3	4	5	4	3	5	4	4	4	35	Par	70
Handicap	18	10	14	4	16	2	8	12	6			
RED											RED	
Par											Par	
Handicap												

Manager/Pro: Charles Raudenbush, PGA   **Supt:** Rich Christian
Architects: George Crump & H.S. Colt 1914

PITMAN GOLF CLUB

501 Pitman Rd., Sewell, NJ 08080   (609) 589-6688

Pitman is an 18 hole course owned by Gloucester County and is open 7 days a week, all year. Tee time reservations are required 1 week in advance for weekends.

•**Driving Range**	•**Lockers**
•**Practice Green**	•**Showers**
•**Power Carts**	•**Food**
•**Pull Carts**	•**Clubhouse**
•**Club Rental**	Outings
Soft Spikes	

Fees	Weekday	Weekend
Res w/ID	$16	$21
Sr w/ID	$11	$18
Non-res	$24	$29
Power carts	$13pp	

Course Description: Appealing to all levels of golfers and very well maintained, Pitman is a scenic course that is convenient to Phila. and Camden. Relatively short, it has wide fairways and deep rough. The layout is constantly being upgraded with new bunkers and contour changes giving it more character. The signature par 4 429 yard eleventh, requires a well placed tee shot up a dogleg left fairway, then a shot over a ravine to an elevated green. Many consider this hole the most difficult although it is rated #2 handicap.

Directions: Gloucester County, #25 on Southwest Map
NJTPKE to Exit #3. Take Rte. 168 East (toward Atl. City) to Rte. 573 South and then a left onto Rte. 55 South to Exit 50B. Go to 1st light, turn right onto Lamb's Rd. for 1 mile to blinker & turn left. Course is 1/4 mile on right.

Hole	1	2	3	4	5	6	7	8	9	Out	BLUE	Rating 68.4
BLUE	329	346	528	204	296	382	422	138	383	3028		Slope 113
WHITE	302	328	497	186	268	356	398	122	373	2830		
Par	4	4	5	3	4	4	4	3	4	35	WHITE	Rating 66.4
Handicap	11	9	1	15	13	7	3	17	5			Slope 109
RED	263	268	425	143	222	317	335	103	349	2425		
Par	4	4	5	3	4	4	5	3	5	37	RED	Rating 67.9
Handicap	9	7	1	15	13	3	11	17	5			Slope 106
Hole	10	11	12	13	14	15	16	17	18	In		Totals
BLUE	386	429	338	421	129	432	415	158	389	3097	BLUE	6125
WHITE	328	408	321	404	110	409	388	128	368	2864	WHITE	5694
Par	4	4	4	4	3	5	4	3	4	35	Par	70
Handicap	12	2	14	4	18	10	6	16	8			
RED	310	336	300	359	95	377	348	98	294	2517	RED	4942
Par	4	4	4	5	3	5	4	3	4	36	Par	73
Handicap	12	2	6	10	16	4	8	18	14			

Manager/Pro: Orist Wells, PGA   **Supt:** Scott Hellerman
Architects: Alexander Findlay, James Chicwit 1926   **Renovation:** Brian Ault

RAMBLEWOOD COUNTRY CLUB

200 Country Club Pkwy., Mt. Laurel, NJ 08054   (609) 235-2119

Ramblewood is a 27 hole semi-private course open 7 days a week all year. Memberships are available. Tee time reservations may be made up to 1 week in advance.

Driving Range	• Lockers
• Practice Green	• Showers
• Power Carts	• Food
• Pull Carts	• Clubhouse
• Club Rental	• Outings
• Soft Spikes	

Fees	Weekday	Weekend
Daily	$43	$55
Twi(after 4)	$20	
Power carts included		

Description: Built on 220 lush acres with three distinct nines, Ramblewood is a public facility with a private style. The Blue course, where trees abound, is considered the most challenging although the shortest. The par 4 418 yard eighth on the Red nine is a difficult hole requiring a shot over a creek to a green on a hill with hazards on right and left. It has been known to cause more than a few broken clubs over the years. The fairly large sized greens, flanked by well positioned bunkers, have been rated as the best in South Jersey. The scorecard below is for Red/White.

Directions: Burlington County, #26 on Southwest Map
NJTPKE to Exit #4 to Rte. 73 south or Rte. 295 to Mt. Laurel exit (36A) to Rte. 73 S. Immediately after the intersection (Ramblewood Pkwy.) turn left onto Church Rd. for 1/2 mile to Country Club Pkwy. Turn left to club on left.

Hole	1	2	3	4	5	6	7	8	9	Out	BLUE	Rating 72.9
BLUE	380	367	549	485	250	490	391	418	161	3491		Slope 130
WHITE	375	354	526	457	176	464	382	409	144	3287		
Par	4	4	5	4	3	5	4	4	3	36	WHITE	Rating 71.3
Handicap	4	8	3	1	5	7	6	2	9			Slope 127
RED	352	345	439	439	122	415	369	354	131	2966		
Par	4	4	5	5	3	5	4	4	3	37	RED	Rating 72.7
Handicap	6	7	1	3	9	2	4	5	8			Slope 128
Hole	10	11	12	13	14	15	16	17	18	In		Totals
BLUE	390	384	200	513	400	210	537	386	372	3392	BLUE	6883
WHITE	384	353	168	503	385	196	502	365	355	3211	WHITE	6498
Par	4	4	3	5	4	3	5	4	4	36	Par	72
Handicap	3	9	7	2	1	8	6	5	4			
RED	279	323	132	457	374	152	423	292	343	2775	RED	5741
Par	4	4	3	5	5	3	5	4	4	37	Par	74
Handicap	3	6	8	1	4	9	2	7	5			

Manager/Pro: Sean Cooke, PGA   **Supt:** Jarry Jones
Architect: Edmund Ault 1960

RANCOCAS GOLF CLUB

Clubhouse Drive, Willingboro, NJ 08046   (609) 877-5344

Rancocas is an 18 hole semi-private course open to the public 7 days a week all year. Memberships are available. Tee times: members up to 8 days in advance; non-mbrs. 7 days.

• **Driving Range**   Lockers
• **Practice Green**   Showers
• **Power Carts**   • **Food**
• **Pull Carts**   • **Clubhouse**
• **Club Rental**   • **Outings**
Soft Spikes (sug)

Fees	Weekday	Weekend
Daily	$40w/ct	$50w/ct

PRICES ARE FOR 1998; WILL CHANGE FOR 1999; CALL AHEAD.

Course Description: Formerly a private club and still maintained in that style, Rancocas is considered one of the best public courses in NJ. With 100 bunkers throughout, the front is links style open to the wind while the back more wooded and tight. The par 4 320 yard 3rd hole is a dogleg left; the out of bounds requires a well placed tee shot to avoid going through the fairway. The fourth is a long par 4 to an elevated green. On the back nine, water affects play on 4 holes. The par 5 #13 is appropriately the #1 handicap needing accuracy off the tee; the 2nd shot is to an undulating severely sloped green. Rancocas continues to improve yearly as it matures.

Directions: Burlington County, #27 on Southwest Map
Rte. 295 To Beverly Rancocas Rd. (Exit 45B). Go west through Willingboro, left onto Country Club Rd., and make the 2nd left onto Clubhouse Dr.

Hole	1	2	3	4	5	6	7	8	9	Out	BLUE	Rating 72.7
BLUE	585	192	355	420	380	390	202	348	523	3395		Slope 130
WHITE	549	156	320	396	346	350	167	316	485	3085		
Par	5	3	4	4	4	4	3	4	5	36	WHITE	Rating 70.0
Handicap	2	18	14	4	8	10	16	12	6			Slope 124
RED	251	113	306	260	489	147	447	221	339	2573		
Par	5	3	4	5	4	4	3	4	5	37	RED	Rating 66.6
Handicap	2	18	14	4	8	10	16	12	6			Slope 116
Hole	10	11	12	13	14	15	16	17	18	In		Totals
BLUE	406	165	330	568	402	396	400	165	402	3234	BLUE	6629
WHITE	365	126	301	522	368	381	374	145	373	2955	WHITE	6040
Par	4	3	4	5	4	4	4	3	4	35	Par	72
Handicap	11	17	13	1	5	9	3	15	7			
RED	334	57	254	409	284	368	344	120	345	2515	RED	5284
Par	4	3	4	5	4	4	4	3	4	35	Par	72
Handicap	11	17	13	1	9	7	3	15	5			

Manager: Greg Mellors   **Pro:** Rob Martin, PGA   **Supt:** Adam Mis
Architect: Robert Trent Jones 1964

RIVERTON COUNTRY CLUB

Highland Ave., Riverton, NJ 08077   **(609) 829-1919**

Riverton is an 18 hole private course open 6 days a week all year. Guests may play accompanied by a member. Reserved tee times are not required.

- •Driving Range
- •Practice Green
- •Power Carts
- • Pull Carts
- •Club Rental
- •Caddies
- •Lockers
- •Showers
- •Food
- •Clubhouse
- •Outings
- •Soft Spikes

Course Description: Members of Riverton come predominantly from Moorestown and Cherry Hill although some are from other areas in New Jersey and Pa. as well. It is relatively busy with 375 memberships. Built by Donald Ross, the course offers a traditional layout with its multi-tiered well bunkered subtley breaking greens. Renovations were done a few years ago which improved the facility. Water affects play on four holes on the back nine. The 418 par 4 twelfth is the signature hole featuring a tee shot over water and a severely sloped green.

Directions: Burlington County, #28 on Southwest Map
NJTPKE to Exit #4. Take Rte. 73 North (toward Phila.) to Rte. 130 and turn right. After Cinnaminson Mall make a left onto Highland Ave. to club on right.

Hole	1	2	3	4	5	6	7	8	9	Out	BLUE	Rating 71.3
BLUE	364	386	418	364	356	208	525	331	491	3444		Slope 127
WHITE	354	379	384	353	342	197	510	319	480	3318		
Par	4	4	4	4	4	3	5	4	5	37	WHITE	Rating 70.2
Handicap	13	7	1	17	5	11	3	15	9			Slope 124
RED	274	373	341	323	332	156	458	311	423	2991		
Par	4	4	4	4	4	3	5	4	5	37	RED	Rating 73.3
Handicap	15	9	5	13	3	17	1	11	7			Slope 130
Hole	10	11	12	13	14	15	16	17	18	In		Totals
BLUE	428	173	432	398	207	417	162	475	355	3047	BLUE	6491
WHITE	409	142	418	389	186	405	156	466	346	2917	WHITE	6235
Par	4	3	4	4	3	4	3	5	4	34	Par	71
Handicap	6	18	4	8	12	2	16	10	14			
RED	391	118	368	379	136	394	124	448	337	2695	RED	5686
Par	5	3	4	4	3	5	3	5	4	36	Par	73
Handicap	8	18	4	2	16	12	14	6	10			

Manager: Jack Merget   **Pro:** Fred Philipps, PGA   **Supt:** Craig Roncace
Architect: Donald Ross 1900

SAKIMA COUNTRY CLUB

383 Shell Rd. Rte. 130 Carney's Pt., NJ 08069   **(609) 299-0201**

Sakima is a 9 hole course open all year 6 days a week. Guests may play accompanied by a member. Tee time reservations are not necessary.

- •Driving Range   •Lockers
- •Practice Green   •Showers
- •Power Carts   •Food
- Pull Carts   •Clubhouse
- •Club Rental   •Outings
- Caddies   •Soft Spikes

Course Description: Sakima is a deceptively difficult, tight, tree lined course with narrow fairways and small greens. A second round may be played changing the tees. There is no water on the course in the form of ponds or creeks but on the ninth and eighteenth, it is necessary to hit over drainage ditches. The signature par 3 third hole is long from the white tees and in the dead center of the course. It has a large back to front sloping green and with strategic pin placement can be quite challenging.

Directions: Salem County, #29 on Southwest Map
Rte. 295 South to Exit #4 (Penn's Grove.) Take Rte. 130 South and go 1 and 1/2 miles. Course is on left.

Hole	1	2	3	4	5	6	7	8	9	Out	BLUE	Rating
BLUE												Slope
WHITE	475	388	209	348	367	379	285	165	461	3077		
Par	5	4	3	4	4	4	4	3	5	36	WHITE	Rating 68.6
Handicap	9	1	7	13	3	5	17	15	11			Slope 115
RED	418	285	139	348	317	341	268	152	440	2708		
Par	5	4	3	4	4	4	4	3	5	36	RED	Rating 70.8
Handicap	1	13	17	7	9	5	11	15	3			Slope 116

Hole	10	11	12	13	14	15	16	17	18	In		Totals
BLUE											BLUE	
WHITE											WHITE	6150
Par											Par	72
Handicap												
RED											RED	5498
Par											Par	72
Handicap												

Manager/Pres: Lewis DiNicola   **Built:** 1898

COUNTRY CLUB OF SALEM

91 Country Club Lane, Salem, NJ 08079   (609) 935-1603

Salem is a 9 hole course open 7 days a week, all year. Guests play accompanied by a member. Tee time reservations are suggested on weekends.

Driving Range	Lockers
•**Practice Green**	Showers
•**Power Carts**	•**Food**
•**Pull Carts**	•**Clubhouse**
Club Rental	•**Outings**
Caddies	•**Soft Spikes**

Course Description: This small, friendly club is member-owned and professionally managed. The scenic views of the Delaware River are spectacular in all seasons; being near the water the golfers benefit from the exhilarating breezes. Salem has fast bent grass greens and is challenging for the scratch golfer as well as for the weekend duffer. The signature first hole, a 617 yard par 5 dogleg left, has a pond that comes into play. Water affects play on the second and seventh holes as well. Although it is 9 holes, alternate tees change the yardages adding interest to the second nine.

Directions: Salem County, #30 on Southwest Map
NJTPKE to Exit #1 (Pennsville). Take Rte. 49 East to Salem, over bridge to Chestnut St. Then turn right to club 3 miles ahead on right on Country Club Lane.

Hole	1	2	3	4	5	6	7	8	9	Out	BLUE	Rating
BLUE												Slope
WHITE	617	373	126	490	354	164	291	398	360	3173		
Par	5	4	3	5	4	3	4	4	4	36	WHITE	Rating 70.1
Handicap	1	8	18	12	3	16	14	4	7			Slope 116
RED	439	351	115	369	341	140	283	381	343	2762		
Par	5	4	3	4	4	3	4	5	4	36	RED	Rating 70.8
Handicap	8	6	18	1	4	16	13	12	3			Slope 120
Hole	10	11	12	13	14	15	16	17	18	In		Totals
BLUE											BLUE	
WHITE	451	363	187	480	369	150	299	386	370	3055	WHITE	6228
Par	5	4	3	5	4	3	4	4	4	36	Par	72
Handicap	10	9	11	13	2	17	15	5	6			
RED	400	360	126	408	292	153	240	307	353	2639	RED	5401
Par	5	4	3	5	4	3	4	4	4	36	Par	72
Handicap	9	5	17	11	10	15	14	7	2			

Manager: Lucille Goldey   **Supt:** Grayson Cole
Built: 1898

SCOTLAND RUN NATIONAL GC   **PUBLIC**

2626 Fries Mill Rd., Williamstown, NJ 08094   **(609) 863-3737**

Scotland Run is an 18 hole semi-private course opening in 1999, 7 days a week all year. Memberships will be available. Tee times may be made 14 days in advance for members and 5 days for non-members. Ratings and handicaps are not yet available.

- •**Driving Range**
- •**Practice Green**
- •**Power Carts**
- Pull Carts
- •**Club Rental**
- •**Soft Spikes**

- •**Lockers**
- •**Showers**
- •**Food**
- •**Clubhouse**
- •**Outings**

NEW

Fees	Weekday	Weekend
Approximately $50 - $75		

Course Description: A truly unique experience will be presented to golfers at Scotland Run. Being built on a former sand quarry and carved out of the landscape with a backdrop of cliffs and an expansive waste area, the course offers breathtaking views. It has 5 sets of tees on a 6600 yard layout encompassing 200 acres of winding fairways, naturally blue ponds and elevation rises not characteristic of the flatlands of Southern NJ. Stephen Kay's design will make an unusual golfing experience giving players a host of different shots in a variety of settings. The architect is known for creating Harbor Pines & Blue Heron Pines, as well as renovating over 100 courses.

Directions: Gloucester County, #31 on Southwest Map
From Phila. take the W.Whitman Bridge to Rte. 42 South; continue & at 5th light go right to Fries Mill Rd. (Rte.655). Course is 2 miles on left. From Trenton & North, take 295 South to Rte.42 South & follow as above.

Hole	1	2	3	4	5	6	7	8	9	Out	BLUE	Rating
BLUE	495	445	375	155	455	310	350	365	195	3145		Slope
WHITE	480	420	355	145	435	300	340	350	185	3010		
Par	5	4	4	3	4	4	4	4	3	35	WHITE	Rating
Handicap												Slope
RED	405	358	285	100	367	238	287	280	135	2455		
Par	5	4	4	3	4	4	4	4	3	35	RED	Rating
Handicap												Slope
Hole	**10**	**11**	**12**	**13**	**14**	**15**	**16**	**17**	**18**	**In**		Totals
BLUE	510	365	435	195	310	165	385	460	495	332 0	BLUE	6465
WHITE	490	340	400	170	285	150	370	435	480	3120	WHITE	6130
Par	5	4	4	3	4	3	4	4	5	36	Par	71
Handicap												
RED	425	300	315	120	250	130	315	330	405	2590	RED	5045
Par	5	4	4	3	4	3	4	4	5	36	Par	71
Handicap												

Owner: Chip Ottinger   **Manager:** John Igoe   **Supt:** Andrew Franks
Architect: Stephen Kay 1999

SPRINGFIELD GOLF CENTER

Jacksonville-Mt. Holly Rd. Mt. Holly, NJ 08060   **(609) 267-8440**

Springfield is an 18 hole semi-private par 68 course open to the public 7 days a week all year. Memberships are available. Tee time reservations are required on weekends. There is miniature golf and a chip & putt on the premises.

•**Driving Range**	Lockers
•**Practice Green**	Showers
•**Power Carts**	•**Food**
•**Pull Carts**	•**Clubhouse**
•**Club Rental**	•**Outings**
Soft Spikes	

Fees	Weekday	Weekend
Daily	$15	$18
Twi(3PM)	$12	$15
Power carts	$22	(mandatory
til 12 on weekends)		

Course Description: Fairly short, flat and open, Springfield has water in play on several holes. The front nine is more difficult than the back which has wider fairways and fewer hazards. A tee shot through a chute and over water on the par 5 signature #5 is followed by more water to the left and a drainage creek to the right. The facility draws many players from local senior residence communities who appreciate the easily walkable terrain.

Directions: Burlington County, #32 on Southwest Map
NJTPKE to Exit #7. Take Rte. 206 South to Rte. 630 West and then a right on Rte. 628 which is Jacksonville-Mt. Holly Rd. Course is on left.

Hole	1	2	3	4	5	6	7	8	9	Out	BLUE	Rating 66.6
BLUE	350	370	375	186	570	150	350	130	351	2832		Slope
WHITE	340	360	365	157	560	140	340	123	345	2730		
Par	4	4	4	3	5	3	4	3	4	34	WHITE	Rating 65.7
Handicap	9	5	3	13	1	15	11	17	7			Slope
RED	320	310	355	126	440	125	317	112	331	2436		
Par	4	4	4	3	5	3	4	3	4	34	RED	Rating 68.0
Handicap	9	5	3	13	1	15	11	17	7			Slope
Hole	10	11	12	13	14	15	16	17	18	In		Totals
BLUE	380	200	370	200	585	360	395	190	360	3040	BLUE	5872
WHITE	370	192	360	195	578	350	388	182	350	2965	WHITE	5695
Par	4	3	4	3	5	4	4	3	4	34	Par	68
Handicap	10	16	6	14	2	12	4	18	8			
RED	350	92	352	180	485	340	376	136	335	2646	RED	5082
Par	4	3	4	3	5	4	4	3	4	34	Par	68
Handicap	10	16	6	14	2	12	4	18	8			

Manager: Jodi Lehman   **Supt**: Ernst Yelencsice
Architect: Garrett Renn 1965

TAVISTOCK COUNTRY CLUB

Tavistock Lane, Haddonfield, NJ 08033   **(609) 429-1827**

Tavistock is an 18 hole course open all year 6 days a week. Guests play accompanied by a member. Tee time reservations are recommended on weekends.

- •**Driving Range**   •**Lockers**
- •**Practice Green**   •**Showers**
- •**Power Carts**   •**Food**
- Pull Carts   •**Clubhouse**
- •**Club Rental**   •**Outings**
- •**Caddies**   •**Soft Spikes**

Course Description: Alexander Findlay built 300 courses on the east coast and according to his grandsons, he believed Tavistock was the best work he had ever done. A variety of 28 different trees were planted on the property enhancing the beauty of the course. The twelfth hole is guarded by a buttonwood tree that golfers must avoid. The signature par 4 fourteenth hole has a lake parallel to the fairway beautified with azalea, rhododendron and dogwood plantings. Tavistick's greens are undulating which makes positioning of the approach shot critical.

Directions: Camden County, #33 on Southwest Map
Rte. 295 South to Exit #30, Warwick Rd. Make a left at the STOP; go 800 yards to club. If traveling north, exit on Rte. 295 at Exit 29B and follow as above.

Hole	1	2	3	4	5	6	7	8	9	Out	BLUE	Rating 72.7
BLUE	354	535	403	146	523	392	341	189	362	3245		Slope 134
WHITE	323	518	378	166	444	532	194	486	408	3364		
Par	4	5	4	3	5	4	4	3	4	36	WHITE	Rating 71.4
Handicap	13	9	7	17	3	1	11	15	5			Slope 131
RED	287	455	352	122	424	326	278	152	315	2711		
Par	4	5	4	3	5	4	4	3	4	36	RED	Rating 67.1
Handicap	11	3	5	17	1	9	13	15	7			Slope 121
Hole	10	11	12	13	14	15	16	17	18	In		Totals
BLUE	345	391	398	166	444	532	194	486	408	3364	BLUE	6609
WHITE	334	388	389	148	414	518	168	479	389	3227	WHITE	6321
Par	4	4	4	3	4	5	3	5	4	36	Par	72
Handicap	16	10	6	18	2	4	14	12	8			
RED	312	371	368	123	328	460	127	411	341	2841	RED	5552
Par	4	4	4	3	4	5	3	5	4	36	Par	72
Handicap	14	12	6	18	10	2	16	4	8			

Manager: George Wolf   **Pro**: Charles Genter, PGA   **Supt**: Thomas Grimac
Architect: Alexander Findlay 1921

TOWN & COUNTRY GOLF LINKS

197 East Ave., Woodstown, NJ 08098   (609) 769-8333

Town and Country will open in the summer of 1999. It will be open to the public 7 days a week all year. Memberships are available with tee time reservations up to 14 days in advance. Non-members, 7 days. The amenities listed include the clubhouse which will be completed in 2001.

- •Driving Range
- •Practice Green
- •Power Carts
- •Pull Carts
- •Club Rental
- •Soft Spikes

- •Lockers
- •Showers
- •Food
- •Clubhouse
- •Outings

NEW

Fees	Weekday	Weekend
Daily	$34	$55/cart

Twilight rates TBA
Power carts $12pp
Carts required on weekends

Course Description: Town & Country is a links style course playing about 6500 yards from the back tees and about 5200 from the forward tees. The slope is expected to be about 128, but official ratings, slopes and handicaps are not yet determined. The exact scorecard yardages are also unavailable at press time. Thirteen holes are bordered with water. The 13th will be the signature featuring an island green.

Directions: Salem County, #34 on Southwest Map
NJTpke to Exit 1. Then go east about 15 minutes on Rte. 40 to Woodstown. Course is on the left. From the Jersey Shore area, take Rte. 40 West to Woodstown. Course is on the right.

Manager/Dir. of Golf: Joe Callahan, PGA   **Supt:** Dave Colson
Architect: Carl Gaskill 1999

VALLEYBROOK GOLF CLUB

PUBLIC

200 Golfview Dr., Blackwood, NJ 08012   (609) 227-3171

Valleybrook is an 18 hole semi-private course open to the public 7 days a week all year.
Memberships are available. Tee times: members 2 weeks, non-members 1 week.

- **Driving Range**   Lockers
- **Practice Green**   Showers
- **Power Carts**   • **Food**
- **Pull Carts**   • **Clubhouse**
- **Club Rental**   • **Outings**
- **Soft Spikes**

Fees	Weekday	Weekend
Daily	$29	$39
Fri	$35	
Power carts included		
Discounts available		

Course Description: The well maintained Valleybrook combines flat and open terrain
with hills, valleys and some narrow tree lined fairways. The bent grass greens are
undulating and in very good condition. The challenges are presented by the water in
play on ten holes, the many bunkers and mounds, and the numerous out of bounds.

Directions: Gloucester County, #35 on Southwest Map
NJTPKE to Exit #3. Then take Rte. 168 East to Rte. 42 South to Blackwood-Clementon
exit (#534). Turn right off ramp 1/2 mile to Little Gloucester Rd. Turn left on Golfview
Dr. for 1 mile; club on left. From Phila.: Rte. 42 South & follow as above.

Hole	1	2	3	4	5	6	7	8	9	Out	BLUE	Rating 70.6
BLUE	488	322	177	342	186	296	347	479	411	3048		Slope 125
WHITE	482	318	167	337	182	293	342	475	406	3002		
Par	5	4	3	4	3	4	4	5	4	36	WHITE	Rating 70.0
Handicap	16	12	6	10	8	14	2	18	4			Slope 124
RED	452	277	132	312	140	257	301	428	328	2627		
Par	5	4	3	4	3	4	4	5	4	36	RED	Rating 69.1
Handicap	2	12	18	10	14	16	8	4	6			Slope 120
Hole	10	11	12	13	14	15	16	17	18	In		Totals
BLUE	385	487	217	324	176	326	328	341	501	3085	BLUE	6314
WHITE	380	482	197	319	170	316	321	336	487	3008	WHITE	6179
Par	4	5	3	4	3	4	4	4	5	36	Par	72
Handicap	3	9	1	15	13	11	7	17	5			
RED	336	441	173	291	128	271	301	319	432	2692	RED	5518
Par	4	5	3	4	3	4	4	4	5	36	Par	72
Handicap	5	3	15	11	17	13	9	7	1			

Manager/Supt: James Asher   **Pro:** Ed Kramer, PGA
Architects: David Beakley 1960   **Redesign:** Hal Purdy 1990

WASHINGTON TOWNSHIP GOLF CLUB

Fries Mill Rd., Turnersville, NJ 08012   **(609) 227-1435**

Washington Township is a 9 hole executive course run by the Department of Parks & Recreation. It is open 7 days a week all year. Tee time reservations are not necessary. Memberships are available.

Driving Range	Lockers
•**Practice Green**	Showers
Power Carts	Food
•**Pull Carts**	Clubhouse
•**Club Rental**	Outings
Soft Spikes	

Fees	Weekday	Weekend
Daily Mbr	$7	$9
Sr/Jr	$5	$7
Non Mbr	$8	$10

Course Description: This municipal course is very well maintained with low rolling hills and no natural water. On some holes, accuracy is essential. The 155 yard par 3 sixth is out of a chute and over a ditch to a small green. There are other ditches to traverse on holes 6, 7 and 9. Washington Township Golf Course is suitable for walkers.

Directions: Gloucester County, #36 on Southwest Map
From Phila: Walt Whitman Bridge & go South on Rte. 42 to split in road, then take Black Horse Pike bearing right. Before the 5th light, bear right onto Fries Mill Rd. Course is 3/4 mile on right. (NJTPKE to Exit #3 to Rte. 168 S to Rte. 42 & follow as above).

Hole	1	2	3	4	5	6	7	8	9	Out	BLUE	Rating
BLUE												Slope
WHITE	99	151	134	101	128	155	74	161	248	1251		
Par	3	3	3	3	3	3	3	3	4	28	WHITE	Rating
Handicap	8	5	6	7	4	1	9	2	3			Slope
RED	99	151	134	101	128	155	74	161	248	1251		
Par	3	4	3	3	3	4	3	4	5	32	RED	Rating
Handicap	6	9	2	8	5	4	1	7	3			Slope

Hole	10	11	12	13	14	15	16	17	18	In		Totals
BLUE											BLUE	
WHITE											WHITE	1252
Par											Par	28
Handicap												
RED											RED	1251
Par											Par	32
Handicap												

Manager/Supt: Wendell Beakley   **Architect:** Tom Fazio 1960s

WEDGEWOOD COUNTRY CLUB PUBLIC

200 Hurffville Rd., Turnersville, NJ 08012 (609) 227-5522

Wedgewood is an 18 hole course open 7 days a week all year. Reserved tee times are suggested for weekends. Power carts are mandatory weekdays till 1PM and weekends & holidays till 2PM.

Driving Range
- Practice Green
- Power Carts
- Pull Carts
- Club Rental
- Soft Spikes
- Lockers
- Showers
- Food
- Clubhouse
- Outings

Fees	Weekday	Weekend
Daily	$50	$60
Power carts included		

Course Description: Completely renovated, Wedgewood is long, narrow and challenging. The improvements include new bent grass tees, fairways and greens. The signature and most difficult hole is the par 4 #13 where too long a tee shot can land in one of two ponds on the fairway. The drive should be about 210 yards and straight, followed by a second shot over water to a wide but short well bunkered green. When Wedgewood was used as a qualifying course for the PGA, the 18th hole was so difficult that the pros didn't tee off from the blues. There are 4 sets of tees here including Black.

Directions: Gloucester County, #37 on Southwest Map
NJTPKE to Exit #13. Take Rte. 168 East (Black Horse Pike) to Wilson Rd. (approx. 5 miles.) Make a right and club is up ahead.

Hole	1	2	3	4	5	6	7	8	9	Out	BLUE	Rating 72.5
BLUE	424	522	371	150	539	378	392	188	383	3347		Slope 130
WHITE	380	500	349	138	531	365	379	178	359	3179		
Par	4	5	4	3	5	4	4	3	4	36	WHITE	Rating 70.4
Handicap	2	8	4	18	14	12	10	15	6			Slope 126
RED	328	430	332	126	396	330	318	122	320	2702		
Par	4	5	4	3	5	4	4	3	4	36	RED	Rating 72.1
Handicap	7	3	15	17	1	11	5	13	9			Slope 127
Hole	10	11	12	13	14	15	16	17	18	In		Totals
BLUE	381	551	188	421	367	408	181	486	388	3371	BLUE	6718
WHITE	365	524	178	411	355	375	163	464	342	3177	WHITE	6356
Par	4	5	3	4	4	4	3	5	4	36	Par	72
Handicap	3	9	13	1	17	11	18	7	5			
RED	346	457	171	404	257	341	150	400	326	2852	RED	5554
Par	4	5	3	4	4	4	3	5	4	36	Par	72
Handicap	6	8	10	2	14	4	18	12	16			

Manager/Pro: Mike Tucci, PGA   **Supt:** Marty Musho
Architect: Gary Wren 1964

WESTWOOD GOLF CLUB

PUBLIC

850 Kings Highway, Woodbury, NJ 08096   (609) 845-2000

Westwood is an 18 hole course open 7 days a week all year. Memberships are available. Tee time reservations are required on weekends and holidays; members get preferred times.

Driving Range
- **Practice Green**
- **Power Carts**
- **Pull Carts**
- **Club Rental**
- **Soft Spikes**

- **Lockers**
- **Showers**
- **Food**
- **Clubhouse**
- **Outings**

Fees	Weekday	Weekend
Daily	$23	$28
9 holes/4PM	$11.50	$13.50
Power carts	$15/pp	

Course Description: This pleasantly challenging course is in excellent shape and quite hilly for this part of Southern New Jersey. The fairways are narrow and the greens are large. The par 3 11th signature hole is extremely picturesque especially in Spring when 1,000 daffodils, crab apple and dogwood plantings blossom. Westwood Golf Club is well worth the price.

Directions: Gloucester County, #38 on Southwest Map
NJTPKE to Exit #2 (Swedesboro/Rte. 322). Take 322 West. At light at Rte. 551 make a right turn onto 551 North. Club is 8 miles on the right (across from Wawa).

Hole	1	2	3	4	5	6	7	8	9	Out	BLUE	Rating
BLUE												Slope
WHITE	450	274	517	303	128	417	359	323	210	2981		
Par	5	4	5	4	3	4	4	4	3	36	WHITE	Rating 68.2
Handicap	7	15	3	11	17	1	5	9	13			Slope 116
RED	415	252	442	279	103	297	324	288	126	2526		
Par	5	4	5	4	3	4	4	4	3	36	RED	Rating 69.1
Handicap	1	15	3	9	17	11	5	7	13			Slope 114

Hole	10	11	12	13	14	15	16	17	18	In		Totals
BLUE											BLUE	
WHITE	360	190	383	180	390	325	442	374	343	2987	WHITE	5968
Par	4	3	4	3	4	4	5	4	4	35	Par	71
Handicap	12	14	4	18	2	16	10	8	6			
RED	315	172	305	148	352	280	419	352	313	2656	RED	5182
Par	4	3	4	3	5	4	5	4	4	36	Par	72
Handicap	16	12	14	18	6	8	2	4	10			

Owners/Managers: Janet & Ken Vogt   **Supt:** Charles Hund
Architect: Horace Smith   **Built:** 1962

WHITE OAKS COUNTRY CLUB PUBLIC

2951 Dutch Mill Rd., Newfield, NJ 08344 (609) 694-5585

White Oaks is scheduled to open in August of 1999. It will be open to the public 7 days a week all year. Memberships are available. Members may make tee time reservations 7 days in advance, non-members fewer days, still to be decided at press time.

Driving Range
- Practice Green
- Power Carts
- Pull Carts
- Club Rental
- Soft Spikes
- Lockers
- Showers
- Food
- Clubhouse
- Outings

NEW

Fees	Weekday	Weekend
Daily	$25	$30

Power carts $13pp

Course Description: White Oaks is situated on gently rolling terrain and cut out of the woods. A large lake affects play on the first hole and must be carried on the approach shot to the 9th green. Trees encroach the narrow fairways and most greens are bunkered. The course has large sand waste areas dotted with shrubs. The par 5 7th hole may be the longest in South Jersey when extended to a possible 630 yards. Asphalt cart paths are provided throughout; a state of the art irrigation system will help maintain the course. The actual scorecard is not yet available. The yardages below are approximate.

Directions: Gloucester County, #39 on Southwest Map

From Phila. area, take Rte. 55 to Rte. 40 East. Proceed 4 miles and make right onto Dutch Mill Rd. for 4.5 miles to club. From Jersey Shore area, take Rte. 40 West to Newfield and make right onto Dutch Mill Rd. 4.5 miles to club.

Hole	1	2	3	4	5	6	7	8	9	Out	BLUE	Rating
BLUE	370	300	425	200	350	415	615	170	350	3195		Slope
WHITE												
Par	4	4	4	3	4	4	5	3	4	35	WHITE	Rating
Handicap												Slope
RED												
Par	4	4	4	3	4	4	5	3	4	35	RED	Rating
Handicap												Slope

Hole	10	11	12	13	14	15	16	17	18	In		Totals
BLUE	525	425	150	380	320	335	300	350	360	3135	BLUE	6330
WHITE											WHITE	
Par	5	4	3	4	4	4	4	4	4	36	Par	71
Handicap												
RED											RED	
Par	5	4	3	4	4	4	4	4	4	36	Par	71
Handicap												

Manager: Billy Casper Golf Management **Supt:** Kenneth Van Fleet
Architect: Casper Management 1999

WILD OAKS GOLF CLUB

75 Wild Oaks Drive, Salem, NJ 08079   **(609) 935-0705**

Wild Oaks is a 27 hole privately owned course open to the public 7 days a week all year. Tee time reservations are necessary on weekends and holidays; may be made 1 week in advance.

•**Driving Range**	Lockers
•**Practice Green**	Showers
•**Power Carts**	•**Food**
•**Pull Carts**	•**Clubhouse**
•**Club Rental**	•**Outings**
•**Soft Spikes**	

Fees	Weekday	Weekend
Daily	$24	$36
Twi(3PM)	$17	$22
Power carts included		

Course Description: At Wild Oaks there are 3 separate nines which may be played in a variety of combinations. On the longest, Willow Oaks, the first hole, a 431 yard par 4, is a wooded sharp dogleg left with a tree in the middle of the fairway and water in play. White Cedar is generally straight, wide open and is the easiest of the three nines. Pin Oaks is narrow with small greens that necessitate accurate approach shots. Wild Oaks attracts players from Phila. and parts of NJ and Del. The scorecard below is for Willow Oaks and White Cedar.

Directions: Salem County, #40 on Southwest Map
Rte. 295 South to Exit 1C. Then take Rte. 49 through Salem to Quinton to traffic light (only light in town.) Make the 2nd right after light to club. OR: NJTPKE to Exit #1 to Hook Rd. (Rte. 551) to Rte. 49 through Salem & follow as above.

Hole	1	2	3	4	5	6	7	8	9	Out	BLUE	Rating 72.1
BLUE	431	461	429	169	397	412	566	190	372	3427		Slope 126
WHITE	416	448	417	155	377	394	550	175	360	3292		
Par	4	5	4	3	4	4	5	3	4	36	WHITE	Rating 71.0
Handicap	1	9	3	8	6	4	2	7	5			Slope 124
RED	352	383	336	141	304	324	398	159	276	2673		
Par	4	5	4	3	4	4	5	3	4	36	RED	Rating 71.4
Handicap	1	2	7	9	4	5	6	3	8			Slope 118
Hole	10	11	12	13	14	15	16	17	18	In		Totals
BLUE	543	417	381	183	375	151	396	393	460	3299	BLUE	6726
WHITE	523	400	365	168	361	144	377	380	445	3163	WHITE	6455
Par	5	4	4	3	4	3	4	4	5	36	Par	72
Handicap	2	1	6	7	5	9	3	4	8			
RED	452	334	297	155	253	125	328	325	380	2649	RED	5322
Par	5	4	4	3	4	3	4	4	5	36	Par	72
Handicap	3	6	7	4	9	8	2	1	5			

Manager: Mark Ludes   **Supt:** Dave Hunt

WILLOW BROOK COUNTRY CLUB PUBLIC

4310 Bridgeboro Rd., Moorestown, NJ 08057   **(609) 461-0131**

Willow Brook is a semi-private 18 hole course open to the public 7 days a week all year. There are full, weekday and social memberships available. Members have preferred tee times: (Monday for the following week.) A variety of specials are available.

•**Driving Range**	•**Lockers**
•**Practice Green**	•**Showers**
•**Power Carts**	•**Food**
•**Pull Carts**	•**Clubhouse**
•**Club Rental**	•**Outings**
•**Soft Spikes**	

Fees	Weekday	Weekend
Daily	$24	$33
Twi(3PM)	$16.50	$19.50
Power carts	$26	

Course Description: Well maintained, Willow Brook is constantly being upgraded. It is moderately hilly, relatively wide open and the bent grass greens are well bunkered. Water affects play on five holes. The 418 yard par 4 18th is a challenging dogleg with a stream in front and a large lake near the green presenting a daunting approach shot.

Directions: Burlington County, #41 on Southwest Map
NJTPKE to Exit # 4. Then take Rte. 73 North to Rte. 130 North to Rte. 613 East. Proceed 2 miles and club is on left. OR: Rte. 130 South to 613 East and follow as above.

Hole	1	2	3	4	5	6	7	8	9	Out	BLUE	Rating 71.2
BLUE	324	377	546	350	199	400	169	490	378	3233		Slope 125
WHITE	313	365	530	340	184	374	157	469	363	3095		
Par	4	4	5	4	3	4	3	5	4	36	WHITE	Rating 69.9
Handicap	17	7	1	11	5	3	13	15	9			Slope 118
RED	253	253	434	239	155	319	153	409	281	2496		
Par	4	4	5	4	3	4	3	5	4	36	RED	Rating 68.3
Handicap	17	7	1	11	5	3	13	15	9			Slope 110

Hole	10	11	12	13	14	15	16	17	18	In		Totals
BLUE	378	399	160	503	156	530	362	349	418	3255	BLUE	6488
WHITE	368	391	149	493	127	500	352	341	388	3109	WHITE	6204
Par	4	4	3	5	3	5	4	4	4	36	Par	72
Handicap	10	6	18	8	14	4	12	16	2			
RED	269	335	320	154	290	404	163	422	257	2614	RED	5518
Par	4	4	3	5	3	5	4	4	4	36	Par	72
Handicap	10	6	18	8	14	4	12	16	2			

Manager: Edward Klumpp, Jr.   **Pro:** Brian Feld, PGA   **Supt:** Tim McBrearty
Architect: William Gordon, 1967

WOODBURY COUNTRY CLUB

467 Cooper St., Woodbury, NJ 08096   **(609) 848-5000**

Woodbury is a 9 hole privatae course open 7 days a week all year. Guests may play accompanied by a member. Tee time reservations are not necessary.

Driving Range	•Lockers
•Practice Green	•Showers
•Power Carts	•Food
•Pull Carts	•Clubhouse
Club Rental	•Outings
Caddies	•Soft Spikes

Course Description: Chartered in 1897, Woodbury is one of the oldest clubs in New Jersey. It is very well maintained and was redesigned several years ago with new tees, greens and bunkers. The generally flat course has narrow fairways with mature trees lining them.   To add to its challenge, there are double greens and differing tee placements, as indicated on the scorecard below. The par 3 fourteenth signature hole is 189 yards requiring a tee shot over a picturesque lake.

Directions: Gloucester County, #42 on Southwest Map
NJTPKE to Exit #3. Then take Rte.168 (Black Horse Pike.) Make a left onto Rte. 573 and then right onto Rte. 544 which ends at Cooper St. Make a right onto Cooper to club. OR: Rte. 295 to Exit 25A to Rte. 47 South. At Cooper St. turn right to club.

Hole	1	2	3	4	5	6	7	8	9	Out	BLUE	Rating
BLUE												Slope
WHITE	366	310	200	481	160	367	365	445	372	3066		
Par	4	4	3	3	3	4	4	4	4	35	WHITE	Rating 69.7
Handicap	5	15	3	7	17	11	9	1	13			Slope 124
RED	332	251	196	466	135	358	357	420	366	2881		
Par	4	4	3	3	3	4	4	5	4	36	RED	Rating 73.3
Handicap	11	15	13	1	17	7	5	3	9			Slope 125
Hole	**10**	**11**	**12**	**13**	**14**	**15**	**16**	**17**	**18**	**In**		Totals
BLUE											BLUE	
WHITE	361	277	157	467	189	363	357	420	369	2960	WHITE	6026
Par	4	4	3	5	3	4	4	4	4	35	Par	70
Handicap	10	18	16	12	14	8	4	2	6			
RED	332	280	153	466	137	358	357	358	365	2806	RED	5687
Par	4	4	3	5	3	4	4	4	4	35	Par	71
Handicap	10	14	16	2	18	6	4	12	8			

Manager: Trevor Lacy   **Pro:** John Borrell, PGA   **Supt:** Charles Clarke
Architects: Geoffrey Cornish   (Orig. design H. Clark 1897)

WOODCREST COUNTRY CLUB

Evesham-Berlin Rd., Cherry Hill, NJ 08003   **(609) 439-2513**

Woodcrest is an 18 hole course open from March through December, 6 days a week. Guests may play accompanied by a member. Tee time reservations are necessary on weekends.

•**Driving Range**	•**Lockers**
•**Practice Green**	•**Showers**
•**Power Carts**	•**Food**
Pull Carts	•**Clubhouse**
Club Rental	•**Outings**
•**Caddies**	•**Soft Spikes**

Course Description: Well maintained, Woodcrest Country Club can be justifiably proud of both the condition of its greens and fairways, and of the difficulty of the course (140 slope from the white tees). The course has a very narrow layout and small greens. On the par 4 third signature hole "The Oaks", the golfer is confronted by water and a large tree on the right. The ninth called "Long John" is a 538 yard par 5 from the white tees with water in play off the tee, very thick rough and a lake to carry on the approach shot.

Directions: Camden County, #43 on Southwest Map
Rte. 295 North (Cherry Hill area) and take Exit #32 (Haddonfield-Gibbsboro). Turn right onto Rte. 561. At 5th traffic light turn left onto Evesham Rd. Club is 500 ft. ahead on left.

Hole	1	2	3	4	5	6	7	8	9	Out	BLUE	Rating 71.5
BLUE	361	511	443	187	430	348	409	177	547	3413		Slope 142
WHITE	347	489	425	178	425	338	363	154	538	3257		
Par	4	5	4	3	4	4	4	3	5	36	WHITE	Rating 70.8
Handicap	13	9	1	7	5	17	11	15	3			Slope 140
RED	334	434	378	124	416	299	347	140	427	2899		
Par	4	5	5	3	5	4	4	3	5	38	RED	Rating 72.4
Handicap	9	5	1	11	13	15	7	17	3			Slope 123
Hole	10	11	12	13	14	15	16	17	18	In		Totals
BLUE	405	521	175	505	154	320	211	429	362	3082	BLUE	6495
WHITE	385	511	163	494	146	312	203	408	360	2982	WHITE	6239
Par	4	5	3	5	3	4	3	4	4	35	Par	71
Handicap	4	8	12	2	16	18	10	6	14			
RED	317	474	144	415	133	255	176	379	355	2648	RED	5547
Par	4	5	3	5	3	4	3	5	4	36	Par	74
Handicap	4	8	12	2	16	18	10	14	6			

Pro: Dick Smith, Jr., PGA   **Supt:** Patrick Lucas
Architects: H. Toomey & William Flynn 1929

Time spent playing golf is not deducted from one's lifespan. (**Fairway Valley**)

Golf means going into God's out-of-doors, getting close to nature, fresh air, exercise, a sweeping away of the mental cobwebs, genuine recreation of the tired tissues.

(**St. Andrew's, Scotland**)

LOWER SHORE REGION

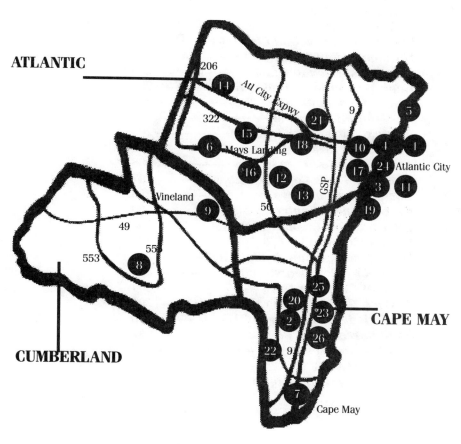

ATLANTIC

206

14

Atl City Expwy

322

21

9

5

15

18

6 Mays Landing

10

4

1

16

12

17

24 Atlantic City

13

GSP

3

11

Vineland

9

19

56

49

55

553

8

25

20

23

CAPE MAY

2

26

CUMBERLAND

22

9

7

Cape May

273

LOWER SHORE REGION

Public Courses appear in *bold italics*

ATLANTIC CITY COUNTRY CLUB

Jackson & Leo Fraser Rd., Northfield, NJ 08225   **(609) 641-7575**

Atlantic City CC is an 18 hole course now owned by Hilton and only available to guests of the AC Hilton or Bally's. It is open 7 days a week all year. Reservations are only made in conjunction with the hotels.

• **Driving Range**	• **Lockers**
• **Practice Green**	• **Showers**
• **Power Carts**	• **Food**
Pull Carts	• **Clubhouse**
• **Club Rental**	• **Outings**
• **Caddies**	• **Soft Spikes**

Course Description: Extensive renovations are being made at this club as the result of the new ownership. It is a well-maintained seaside course in the temperate climate of the Jersey Shore. The wind will always be a factor here. Atlantic City CC is famous among golf aficionados because the word "birdie" was first used here to indicate a hole played in one under par. According to A. W. Tillinghast, this coinage occurred in 1903 when a player exclaimed as a second shot on the par 5 12th came to rest on the green, "that's a bird of a shot". Thus this popular golf term was born at the Jersey shore. The scorecard below shows the yardages prior to the aforementioned work now in progress.

Directions: Atlantic County, #1 on Lower Shore Map
GSP to Exit 36, Tilton Rd. Take Tilton (Rte. 563) for 7 lights and then make left onto Shore Rd. Club is 1 mile ahead on the right. From Phila. take AC Xpressway to GSP and exit at #36. Follow as above.

Hole	1	2	3	4	5	6	7	8	9	Out	BLUE	Rating
BLUE	464	443	375	133	403	575	467	187	442	3489		Slope
WHITE	442	421	360	121	364	510	425	168	420	3231		
Par	4	4	4	3	4	5	4	3	4	35	WHITE	Rating 70.8
Handicap	1	5	13	17	11	9	7	15	3			Slope
RED	417	369	308	102	332	462	408	132	405	2935		
Par	5	5	4	3	4	5	5	3	5	39	RED	Rating 71.8
Handicap	5	9	13	17	11	1	7	15	3			Slope

Hole	10	11	12	13	14	15	16	17	18	In		Totals
BLUE	423	217	407	135	493	393	407	174	515	3164	BLUE	6653
WHITE	412	170	377	126	483	363	352	150	488	2921	WHITE	6152
Par	4	3	4	3	5	4	4	3	5	35	Par	70
Handicap	2	14	6	18	4	10	12	16	8			
RED	374	160	358	116	422	340	330	139	446	2685	RED	5620
Par	4	3	4	3	5	4	4	3	5	35	Par	74
Handicap	4	14	8	18	2	10	12	16	6			

Manager: Denise Petrino   **Pro:** Billy Ziobro, PGA   **Supt:** Jeff Kent
Architect: John Reed 1897

AVALON GOLF CLUB

1510 Route 9, Cape May Courthouse, NJ 08210   (609) 465-GOLF

Avalon is a semi-private 18 hole course open to the public 7 days a week all year. Tee times may be reserved up to 2 weeks in advance. Memberships are encouraged. Off season, discounted fees available.

• Driving Range	• Lockers
• Practice Green	• Showers
• Power Carts	• Food
• Pull Carts	• Clubhouse
• Club Rental	• Outings
Soft Spikes	

Fees	Weekday	Weekend
Daily	$73	$73
Twilight specials		
Prices include cart		
Walking permitted off season		

Course Description: The public loves to play at this scenic bayside course. Warmer here than in northern New Jersey, it is not as hard frozen in the winter. Amidst the pines and oaks, views of the bay can be seen. The course is basically flat; the variable wind is a factor. With six natural lakes, water comes into play on many holes. The greens are well groomed and beautiful.

Directions: Cape May County, #2 on Lower Shore Map
GSP to Exit 13. Go right at exit to Rte. 9 South and make a left at light. Golf course is about 1 mile ahead on the left.

Hole	1	2	3	4	5	6	7	8	9	Out	BLUE	Rating 70.7
BLUE	392	338	177	540	207	408	521	368	355	3306		Slope 122
WHITE	372	302	161	529	160	393	497	348	305	3067		
Par	4	4	3	5	3	4	5	4	4	36	WHITE	Rating 68.4
Handicap	7	15	9	1	11	3	5	13	17			Slope 117
RED	265	279	146	404	129	318	380	328	287	2536		
Par	4	4	3	5	3	4	5	4	4	36	RED	Rating 67.0
Handicap	7	15	9	1	11	3	5	13	17			Slope 111
Hole	10	11	12	13	14	15	16	17	18	In		Totals
BLUE	351	163	478	350	528	145	418	166	420	3019	BLUE	6325
WHITE	319	140	465	339	473	133	404	151	405	2829	WHITE	5896
Par	4	3	5	4	5	3	4	3	4	35	Par	71
Handicap	14	18	12	4	8	16	2	10	6			
RED	301	128	381	328	369	111	390	86	294	2388	RED	4694
Par	4	3	5	4	5	3	4	3	4	35	Par	71
Handicap	14	18	12	4	8	16	2	10	6			

Managers: Russell Buckingham, Stanley Casper   **Pro:** Ted Wenner, PGA
Supt: Mike Robinson   **Architect:** Bob Hendricks 1971

B L ENGLAND GOLF COURSE

Route 9 P.O. Box 844, Beesley's Point, NJ 08215   **(609) 390-0472**

B L England is a regulation 9 hole course open to the public 7 days a week all year. Golfers may call ahead for tee times.

Driving Range	Lockers
•**Practice Green**	Showers
•**Power Carts**	•**Food**
•**Pull Carts**	•**Clubhouse**
•**Club Rental**	Outings
•**Soft Spikes**	

Fees	Weekday	Weekend
Daily	$30	$30
Power carts	$10pp	

Course Description: B L England is a flat well maintained course with tree-lined fairways and lightning fast greens. Great Egg Harbor Bay can be seen from the clubhouse. Water is in play on 4 holes. The par 4 4th is a dogleg right with a tee shot out of a chute; trees and water make the hole difficult. The signature 6th hole is a par 3 with an elevated, small, well-bunkered green. Breezes from the bay keep the course cool and comfortable in summer.

Directions: Cape May County, #3 on Lower Shore Map
GSP to Exit 25. Make a right onto Rte. 9 North. Access to the course is on a road just before the Tuckahoe Inn. Go left at signs for Atlantic Electric (power plant). Do not go over bridge on Rte. 9 North.

Hole	1	2	3	4	5	6	7	8	9	Out	BLUE	Rating
BLUE												Slope
WHITE	271	143	320	331	457	99	341	205	311	2478		
Par	4	3	4	4	5	3	4	3	4	34	WHITE	Rating 63.7
Handicap	13	15	7	3	1	17	11	5	9			Slope 100
RED	252	126	296	313	385	81	322	135	235	2145		
Par	4	3	4	4	5	3	4	3	4	34	RED	Rating 63.3
Handicap	9	13	7	3	1	17	5	15	11			Slope 97
Hole	10	11	12	13	14	15	16	17	18	In		Totals
BLUE											BLUE	
WHITE											WHITE	4956
Par											Par	68
Handicap												
RED											RED	4290
Par											Par	68
Handicap												

Manager: Terry Smick   **Pro:** Ralph Carson, PGA   **Supt:** Jim Waniak
Built: Atlantic Electric Co. 1961

BLUE HERON PINES GOLF CLUB

PUBLIC

550 W. Country Club Dr., Cologne, NJ 08213 — (609) 965-GOLF

Blue Heron Pines has one 18 hole course open 7 days a week all year. Memberships are available. Tee times may be made up to 5 days in advance.

- •Driving Range
- •Practice Green
- •Power Carts
- Pull Carts
- •Club Rental
- •Soft Spikes
- •Lockers
- •Showers
- •Food
- •Clubhouse
- •Outings

Fees	Weekday	Weekend
May-Oct 14	$89	$125
Oct15-Nov.3	$66	$71
Dec 1-Mar 16	$51	$51
Call for new rates for 1999.		

Course Description: With a contemporary clubhouse that looks like a fine private club, Blue Heron Pines is worth a visit. The flat well maintained course has lush rye grass fairways and lots of woods that narrow the landing area. The greens are large with the back nine more of a challenge than the front; the bunkering throughout can be deceptive. The 11th and 14th holes are designed to be like Pine Valley, the 12th like Pinehurst. Other holes bring to mind Beth Page Black and Oyster Harbor on Cape Cod. A 2nd 18 hole course is in construction, designed by architect, Steve Smyers, and should be ready for play in 2000.

Directions: Atlantic County, #4 on Lower Shore Map
GSP to Exit 44. Take a right at top of exit onto Rte. 575 South (Pomona Rd.) for approx. 5 miles. Turn right onto Rte.563 (Tilton Rd.) and then in about 1 mi. a left into club.

Hole	1	2	3	4	5	6	7	8	9	Out	BLUE	Rating 73.0
BLUE	315	180	533	183	413	412	323	575	387	3321		Slope 136
WHITE	290	150	485	160	390	366	283	520	347	2991		
Par	4	3	5	3	4	4	4	5	4	36	WHITE	Rating 70.1
Handicap	17	13	3	7	5	9	15	1	11			Slope 128
RED	221	119	369	138	348	284	225	443	308	2455		
Par	4	3	5	3	4	4	4	5	4	36	RED	Rating 68.4
Handicap	17	11	5	15	3	9	13	1	7			Slope 116

Hole	10	11	12	13	14	15	16	17	18	In		Totals
BLUE	395	135	415	374	518	421	218	451	529	3456	BLUE	6777
WHITE	367	114	386	342	483	383	176	401	471	3123	WHITE	6114
Par	4	3	4	4	5	4	3	4	5	36	Par	72
Handicap	8	18	16	14	2	6	10	4	12			
RED	315	90	330	305	358	321	132	342	405	2598	RED	5053
Par	4	3	4	4	5	4	3	4	5	36	Par	72
Handicap	12	18	10	14	2	6	16	4	8			

Manager: Rick Schlingmann   **Pro:** Jason Lamp, PGA   **Supt:** Clark Weld
Architects: Stephen Kay 1993 Steve Smyers 2000

BRIGANTINE GOLF LINKS

PUBLIC

Roosevelt Blvd. & The Bay, Brigantine, NJ 08203   (609) 266-1388

Brigantine is an 18 hole course open to the public 7 days a week all year. Memberships are available. Tee times may be made up to 7 days in advance for members, 5 days for daily fee golfers.

Driving Range
- **Practice Green**
- **Power Carts**
- **Pull Carts**
- **Club Rental**
- **Soft Spikes**

Lockers
Showers
- **Food**
- **Clubhouse**
- **Outings**

Fees	Weekday	Weekend
Daily	$50	$60
Twilight	$30	
Reduced fees for Fall, Winter & Spring		

Course Description: Brigantine is a long Scottish links style course built in the early part of the 20th century. The golfer plays near water, over water and surrounded by the bay. Consequently, the prevailing winds affect play. The bent grass greens are beautifully maintained. The picturesque 15th hole is a relatively lengthy par 3 over a lake. Since the course was opened, there has been considerable housing built around some of the holes. It is very close to Atlantic City. Walkers are allowed, but bring your own pull cart.

Directions: Atlantic County, #5 on Lower Shore Map
GSP to Atlantic City Exit 40. Follow Rte. 30 East to Huron Ave & turn left at light. Road becomes Brigantine Blvd. Go over bridge and continue. Make a left at the Clipper Ship Motel and follow Roosevelt Blvd. to clubhouse.

Hole	1	2	3	4	5	6	7	8	9	Out	BLUE	Rating 71.9
BLUE	510	370	205	380	410	545	155	370	380	3325		Slope 123
WHITE	488	310	186	365	395	534	146	359	370	3097		
Par	5	4	3	4	4	5	3	4	4	36	WHITE	Rating 70.1
Handicap	14	16	4	12	2	6	18	10	8			Slope 121
RED	440	250	135	320	380	440	140	310	320	2735		
Par	5	4	3	4	5	5	3	4	4	37	RED	Rating 71.2
Handicap	4	16	8	12	6	2	18	14	10			Slope 123

Hole	10	11	12	13	14	15	16	17	18	In		Totals
BLUE	530	330	190	360	410	175	360	425	465	3245	BLUE	6570
WHITE	515	310	160	344	370	160	339	410	450	3059	WHITE	6156
Par	5	4	3	4	4	3	4	4	5	36	Par	72
Handicap	3	13	15	5	9	7	11	1	17			
RED	430	300	150	300	350	120	315	360	400	2725	RED	5460
Par	5	4	3	4	4	3	4	4	5	36	Par	73
Handicap	1	13	11	9	7	17	15	3	5			

Manager: Patricia Vanderstine   **Pro:** Frank Reiser, PGA   **Supt:** Matt Weaver
Architect: John Van Kleek 1927

BUENA VISTA COUNTRY CLUB   PUBLIC

Route 40, Box 507, Buena, NJ 08310   (609) 697-3733

Buena vista is an 18 hole semi-private course open to the public 7 days a week all year. Memberships are available. Members can reserve tee times up to 7 days in advance, daily fee 5 days. Carts are mandatory June 6 thru Sep. weekdays until 1PM.

- •Driving Range
- •Practice Green
- •Power Carts
- •Pull Carts
- •Club Rental
- •Soft Spikes
- •Lockers
- •Showers
- •Food
- •Clubhouse
- •Outings

Fees	Weekday	Weekend
Daily	$41	$48
After 1PM	$27	
After 4PM		$20
Fees include cart		

Course Description: Buena Vista is a Carolina style course, woodsy, generously bunkered, and relatively narrow. Well maintained with not much water in play, the most interesting hole is the par 5 10th. A 200 yard bunker runs along the left of this dogleg left; more sand protects the elevated and undulating green. On the 8th, a lengthy par 3, the slightly elevated green is well guarded, yet forgiving. The 13th is a double dogleg par 5.

Directions: Atlantic County, #6 on Lower Shore Map
From Phil. area or GSP to Atlantic City Xpressway to Exit 28. Take Rte. 54S. Proceed 8 mi. and make a left onto Rte. 40 East. Go 1 and 1/2 miles to club on left.

Hole	1	2	3	4	5	6	7	8	9	Out	BLUE	Rating 71.8
BLUE	372	440	538	423	203	379	536	244	406	3540		Slope 127
WHITE	351	411	511	403	185	359	517	223	379	3339		
Par	4	4	5	4	3	4	5	3	4	36	WHITE	Rating 70.2
Handicap	17	1	5	3	13	11	7	15	9			Slope 124
RED	317	336	442	338	160	328	441	148	346	2856		
Par	4	4	5	4	3	4	5	3	4	36	RED	Rating 72.6
Handicap	13	3	5	1	15	11	9	17	7			Slope 124
Hole	10	11	12	13	14	15	16	17	18	In		Totals
BLUE	502	375	173	522	367	392	393	192	413	3329	BLUE	6869
WHITE	486	345	152	489	343	372	368	169	359	3083	WHITE	6422
Par	5	4	3	5	4	4	4	3	4	36	Par	72
Handicap	2	12	16	4	8	10	14	18	6			
RED	447	314	113	427	321	350	345	149	329	2795	RED	5651
Par	5	4	3	5	4	4	4	3	4	36	Par	72
Handicap	2	12	16	6	4	14	10	18	8			

Manager: Eric Brandt   **Pro:** Kevin Cotter, PGA   **Supt:** Ben Dunn
Architect: William Gordon 1957

CAPE MAY NATIONAL GOLF CLUB

PUBLIC

Route 9 & Florence Ave., Cape May, NJ 08204   (609) 884-1563

Cape May National is an 18 hole semi-private course open to the public 7 days a week all year. Memberships are available. Fees vary according to season. Reservations for tee times may be made up to 7 days in advance. For special packages. (888) CAPETRIP.

•**Driving Range**	•**Lockers**
•**Practice Green**	•**Showers**
•**Power Carts**	•**Food**
•**Pull Carts**	•**Clubhouse**
•**Club Rental**	•**Outings**
•**Soft Spikes**	

Fees	Weekday	Weekend
Daily	$50 to $78 in season	
Twilight reduced		
Fees include cart		
Golf packages available.		

Course Description: At Cape May National the well maintained tees, fairways and greens are of bent grass. In the heart of the course is a 50 acre nature preserve. Each hole is distinctive with fast, undulating greens, some 2 and 3 tiered. After the golfer chooses one of the multiple sets of tees, the well marked cart paths help him wend his way through the wetlands. The beautiful and challenging 18th, rated one of the best closing holes in NJ, offers water alongside on the left and a large sloped green half surrounded by water. Cape May itself is a popular tourist attraction; after a round of golf at this outstanding course, continue further south to see this town of Victorian charm.

Directions: Cape May County, #7 on Lower Shore Map
GSP to Exit 4A. Follow road to 2nd light. Turn left onto Rte. 9. Club is 2 miles south on the left.

Hole	1	2	3	4	5	6	7	8	9	Out	BLUE	Rating 71.5
BLUE	367	457	186	544	411	195	502	202	312	3176		Slope 132
WHITE	358	448	121	521	370	161	491	192	287	2949		
Par	4	4	3	5	4	3	5	3	4	35	WHITE	Rating 69.4
Handicap	11	3	13	1	7	17	5	15	9			Slope 123
RED	301	321	100	335	284	109	418	149	245	2262		
Par	4	4	3	5	4	3	5	3	4	35	RED	Rating 68.8
Handicap	7	5	17	3	9	13	1	15	11			Slope 115

Hole	10	11	12	13	14	15	16	17	18	In		Totals
BLUE	499	409	341	187	520	443	425	165	427	3416	BLUE	6592
WHITE	488	361	318	153	491	421	399	125	378	3134	WHITE	6083
Par	5	4	4	3	5	4	4	3	4	36	Par	71
Handicap	6	12	14	16	2	8	10	18	4			
RED	386	275	234	93	378	353	339	91	295	2449	RED	4711
Par	5	4	4	3	5	4	4	3	4	36	Par	71
Handicap	2	12	14	18	4	8	10	16	6			

Dir. of Guest Services: Allison Maund   **Pro:** David C. Smith, Jr. PGA
Architects: Carl Litten & Robert Mullock 1991

COHANZICK COUNTRY CLUB

PUBLIC

Box 64, Bridgeton-Fairton Rd., Fairton, NJ 08320   (609) 455-2127

Cohanzick is an 18 hole course open to the public 7 days a week all year. Various membership plans are available. The golfer's weekday special for two includes greens fee, cart and lunch, $45. Tee time reservations are advisable for weekends.

- •Driving Range
- •Practice Green
- •Power Carts
- •Pull Carts
- •Club Rental
- Soft Spikes

- •Lockers
- •Showers
- •Food
- •Clubhouse
- •Outings

Fees	Weekday	Weekend
Daily	$16	$20
Power carts	$12pp	

Course Description: This spare rustic golf course is hilly compared to others in south Jersey. Golfers encounter natural ponds and inlets as well as turtles, deer and herons as they make their way through this tight layout. The 15th hole overlooks the Cohansey River. The excellent drainage allows play shortly after rainfall. Trouble awaits an errant shot on the par 3 6th, a hole that straddles a craggy overgrown ravine. In the immediate vicinity, there is access to fishing, hunting, boating, water-skiing and tubing on the river.

Directions: Cumberland County, #8 on Lower Shore Map
NJTpke to Exit #2. Follow signs to Rte. 322 to Rte. 77 South through Bridgeton to club. GSP to Exit 36. Go west on Rte. 40 to Rte. 552W to Rte. 553S. Make right onto Bridgeton-Fairton Rd. to club on left.

Hole	1	2	3	4	5	6	7	8	9	Out	BLUE	Rating 70.2
BLUE	415	345	173	394	533	175	474	384	390	3283		Slope 123
WHITE	405	335	163	384	508	150	464	334	375	3118		
Par	4	4	3	4	5	3	5	4	5	36	WHITE	Rating 69.1
Handicap	3	7	11	1	13	9	15	17	5			Slope 120
RED	395	325	127	374	463	137	454	266	330	2871		
Par	4	4	3	4	5	3	5	4	5	36	RED	Rating 70.5
Handicap	3	7	15	1	11	13	9	17	5			Slope 120
Hole	10	11	12	13	14	15	16	17	18	In		Totals
BLUE	143	549	313	293	391	190	167	416	540	3002	BLUE	6285
WHITE	135	539	303	283	381	164	150	406	530	2891	WHITE	6009
Par	3	5	4	4	4	3	3	4	5	35	Par	71
Handicap	12	14	8	18	4	10	16	2	6			
RED	118	516	246	260	366	150	145	382	416	2599	RED	5470
Par	3	5	4	4	4	3	3	4	5	35	Par	71
Handicap	14	4	10	18	2	8	16	12	6			

Manager: Jeff Pellegrini   **Supt:** Pete Adams
Architect: Alexander Findley 1917

EASTLYN GOLF COURSE

4049 Italia Ave., Vineland, NJ 08361   **(609) 691-5558**

Eastlyn is an 18 hole executive course open to the public 7 days a week all year. Memberships are available. Tee time reservations are not necessary.

•**Driving Range**	Lockers
•**Practice Green**	Showers
•**Power Carts**	•**Food**
• **Pull Carts**	•**Clubhouse**
•**Club Rental**	•**Outings**
Soft Spikes	

Fees	Weekday	Weekend
Daily	$16	$18
Twilight rates available		
Power carts $14		

Course Description: Meticulously maintained, Eastlyn is narrow with an abundance of diverse plants, trees and shrubs. Twelve holes offer natural water hazards; the par 3 10th is protected by water on two sides, a bunker and a slope-away provide additional challenge. The short dogleg par 4 7th also can prove difficult. The longest par 4, the 18th, is where the stronger hitters may use their drivers. This property, formerly acres of swampland, is still a haven for owls, orioles, bullfrogs, bass and other wildlife.

Directions: Cumberland County, #9 on Lower Shore Map
NJTpke to Exit #3. Take Rte.55 to Exit 26. Bear left & then 1st right onto Lincoln Ave. Follow to 2nd light & turn right onto Dante. At STOP, make left onto Panther Ave. for 1 block and then left onto Italia Ave..

Hole	1	2	3	4	5	6	7	8	9	Out	BLUE	Rating
BLUE			·									Slope
WHITE	135	149	136	217	160	249	285	265	165	1761		
Par	3	3	3	4	3	4	4	4	3	31	WHITE	Rating
Handicap												Slope
RED	130	139	126	210	155	240	275	255	155	1685		
Par	3	3	3	4	3	4	4	4	3	31	RED	Rating
Handicap												Slope

Hole	10	11	12	13	14	15	16	17	18	In		Totals
BLUE											BLUE	
WHITE	195	215	142	175	140	169	205	143	323	1707	WHITE	3468
Par	4	4	3	3	3	3	4	3	4		Par	62
Handicap												
RED	190	185	137	165	130	160	200	135	318	1620	RED	3305
Par	4	4	3	3	3	3	4	3	4		Par	62
Handicap												

Manager: Dana Wasil   **Pro:** Frank Carman, PGA   **Supt/Owner:** Tom Galbiati
Architect: Francis Galbiati 1964

GALLOWAY NATIONAL GOLF CLUB

270 S. New York Rd., Absecon, NJ 08201   **(609) 748-1000**

Galloway National is an 18 hole championship course open 6 days a week all year. Guests may play accompanied by a member. Reserved tee times are not necessary.

•**Driving Range**	•**Lockers**
•**Practice Green**	•**Showers**
•**Power Carts**	•**Food**
Pull Carts	•**Clubhouse**
•**Club Rental**	•**Outings**
•**Caddies**	•**Soft Spikes**

Course Description: At Galloway, the members come to play serious golf, not swim or play tennis. Overlooking Reeds Bay, the course is lined with bunkers and scrub pines. The layout follows the contours of the natural terrain. The beautiful par 3 5th faces Reeds Bay and golf club selection is critical due to prevailing winds and the salt marsh hugging the green. The par 5 6th begins with a tee shot that crosses a quarry and climbs a hill to the left. The second shot must be carefully placed to set up for the approach to the undulating and slightly crowned green. Galloway is an outstanding recent additon to fine golfing in New Jersey.

Directions: Atlantic County, #10 on Lower Shore Map
GSP to Exit 48. Take Rte. 9 South toward Absecon. The club is on the left about 5 miles ahead on Rte. 9.

Hole	1	2	3	4	5	6	7	8	9	Out	BLUE	Rating 73.8
BLUE	400	146	375	446	189	548	390	196	539	3229		Slope 142
WHITE	366	138	336	415	175	520	357	170	504	2981		
Par	4	3	4	4	3	5	4	3	5	35	WHITE	Rating 71.2
Handicap	5	15	17	1	13	3	11	9	7			Slope 138
RED												
Par											RED	Rating
Handicap												Slope
Hole	10	11	12	13	14	15	16	17	18	In		Totals
BLUE	475	501	375	470	219	409	532	249	426	3656	BLUE	6885
WHITE	409	481	356	449	190	390	493	212	408	3388	WHITE	6369
Par	4	5	4	4	3	4	5	3	4	36	Par	71
Handicap	6	18	16	2	14	10	8	12	4			
RED											RED	
Par											Par	
Handicap												

Manager/Pro: Jim Mancill, PGA   **Supt:** Eric Cadenelli
Architect: Tom Fazio 1994

GREATE BAY GOLF CLUB

901 Mays Landing Rd., Somers Point, NJ 08244   **(609) 927-0066**

Greate Bay is an 18 hole course open to the public 7 days a week all year. Memberships are available at various rates. Tee time reservations may be made 10 days in advance for members, 3 days for others.

- **Driving Range**
- **Practice Green**
- **Power Carts**
- **Pull Carts**
- **Club Rental**
- Soft Spikes
- **Lockers**
- **Showers**
- **Food**
- **Clubhouse**
- **Outings**

Fees	Weekday	Weekend
Daily	$95	$95
After 2PM	$60	$60

Reduced rates off season
Fees include cart

Course Description: The afternoon bay breeze is refreshing in summer and pleasant at other times at this well maintained course. The many bunkers pose a challenge as does water on the 12th and 13th holes, the signature holes. The long dogleg par 4 has a three tiered green. Many holes have been rebuilt recently and new tee boxes constructed as well as new waste areas installed. There is a country club atmosphere at Greate Bay as memberships are encouraged. Only members may play in championship tournaments and events. This club is only minutes away from Atlantic City. Carts are mandatory.

Directions: Atlantic County, #11 on Lower Shore Map
GSP to Exit 30. At 1st light, go right onto Rte. 9 South to Somers Point. At 2nd light make left onto Mays Landing Rd. Club is on the left.

Hole	1	2	3	4	5	6	7	8	9	Out	BLUE	Rating 72.0
BLUE	381	439	126	386	408	548	426	421	216	3351		Slope 127
WHITE	364	414	120	358	389	537	409	406	183	3180		
Par	4	4	3	4	4	5	4	4	3	35	WHITE	Rating 70.0
Handicap	9	13	5	17	11	3	1	15	7			Slope 124
RED	309	346	97	320	326	466	368	325	133	2690		
Par	4	4	3	4	4	5	4	4	3	35	RED	Rating 71.9
Handicap	9	13	5	17	11	3	1	15	7			Slope 122
Hole	10	11	12	13	14	15	16	17	18	In		Totals
BLUE	424	423	410	185	387	549	151	423	402	3354	BLUE	6705
WHITE	396	402	364	164	374	535	129	386	385	3135	WHITE	6315
Par	4	4	4	3	4	5	3	4	4	35	Par	70
Handicap	4	8	18	2	16	14	6	10	12			
RED	326	331	316	135	299	441	111	355	345	2659	RED	5349
Par	4	4	4	3	4	5	3	4	4	35	Par	70
Handicap	4	8	18	2	16	14	6	10	12			

Manager: Tim McGlaughlin   **Pro:** John Appleget, PGA   **Supt:** Chris Lynch
Architects: Willie Park, Jr. 1921 George Fazio 1971

GREEN TREE GOLF COURSE

PUBLIC

1030 Somers Pt.-Mays Landing Rd.,
Egg Harbor Twp., NJ 08234

(609) 267-8440

Green Tree is an 18 hole Atlantic County course open 7 days a week all year. Tee time reservations may be made 7 days in advance. Memberships are available for both county and non-county residents.

- **Driving Range**
- **Practice Green**
- **Power Carts**
- **Pull Carts**
- **Club Rental**
  Soft Spikes
- **Lockers**
- **Showers**
- **Food**
  Clubhouse
- **Outings**

Fees	Weekday	Weekend
Daily(res)	$10	$13
Non.res.	$20	$26
Twi(3PM)	$8	$10
Power carts $10pp		

Course Description: Purchased from a private owner in the early nineties, Green Tree is the only Atlantic County owned course. It is well maintained despite becoming quite crowded in season. The scorecard is very helpful with its depictions of each hole and an overall layout scheme as well. Water comes into play on nearly every hole on the back nine. The challenging par 4 8th needs the approach shot to carry over a water hazard lurking in front of the contoured green.

Directions: Atlantic County, #12 on Lower Shore Map
From North: GSP to Exit #36. Then take Rte. 322/Rte.40 to Rte. 50 South. Make a left onto Rte. 559S (*Somers Pt., Mays Landing Rd.) Course is 4 miles on left. OR From South: GSP to Exit #29 or Rte. 9N to Rte. 559N.* Course is about 10 mi. on right.

Hole	1	2	3	4	5	6	7	8	9	Out	BLUE	Rating
BLUE												Slope
WHITE	449	349	596	119	256	263	163	401	413	3009		
Par	4	4	5	3	4	4	3	4	4	35	WHITE	Rating 66.6
Handicap	3	7	1	17	13	11	15	2	5			Slope 110
RED	409	309	434	95	229	240	120	372	328	2536		
Par	5	4	5	3	4	4	3	5	4	37	RED	Rating 65.5
Handicap	3	7	1	17	13	11	15	2	5			Slope 109
Hole	10	11	12	13	14	15	16	17	18	In		Totals
BLUE											BLUE	
WHITE	165	319	275	240	397	181	312	326	485	2700	WHITE	5709
Par	3	4	4	4	4	3	4	4	5	35	Par	70
Handicap	18	8	12	14	4	16	10	6	9			
RED	118	257	251	219	375	119	254	251	424	2268	RED	4804
Par	3	4	4	4	5	3	4	4	5	36	Par	73
Handicap	18	8	12	14	4	16	10	6	9			

Manager: John Lamey   **Supt:** Bob Miller
Architect: Horace Smith 1968

HAMILTON TRAILS COUNTRY CLUB ▪ PUBLIC

620 Harbor Rd., Mays Landing, NJ 08330   (609) 641-6824

Hamilton Trails is a 9 hole regulation course open 7 days a week all year. Tee time reservations are not necesssary.

- **Driving Range**
- **Practice Green**
- **Power Carts**
- **Pull Carts**
- **Club Rental**
- **Soft Spikes**

Lockers
Showers
Food
- **Clubhouse**
Outings

Fees	Weekday	Weekend
Daily	$10	$12
Power carts	$12	$12

Course Description: This nine hole course is easy to walk. The golfer encounters many interesting ditches and ponds throughout the layout. The tree lined open fairways are flat and the large bent grass greens are fast and well bunkered. Hamilton Trails is close to Atlantic City making it a convenient place to play golf.

Directions: Atlantic County, #13 on Lower Shore Map
GSP to Exit #36. Take Rte. 563 (Tilton Rd.) West to Rte. 40. Go left on Rte. 40 (Black Horse Pike) to English Creek Rd. and turn left. Turn right onto Ocean Heights Ave. for 1.7 miles to Harbor Rd. Club is on right.

Hole	1	2	3	4	5	6	7	8	9	Out	BLUE	Rating 69.4
BLUE	405	390	520	410	170	345	370	465	190	3265		Slope 123
WHITE	395	370	495	395	160	325	350	445	160	3095		
Par	4	4	5	4	3	4	4	5	3	36	WHITE	Rating 67.3
Handicap	3	15	7	1	13	11	9	17	5			Slope 120
RED	380	310	470	380	115	320	335	340	145	2795		
Par	4	4	5	4	3	4	4	4	3	35	RED	Rating 66.0
Handicap	6	9	2	8	5	4	1	7	3			Slope 119

Hole	10	11	12	13	14	15	16	17	18	In		Totals
BLUE											BLUE	6530
WHITE											WHITE	6190
Par											Par	72
Handicap												
RED											RED	5590
Par											Par	70
Handicap												

Manager: Tim McGlaughlin   **Pro:** Devon Peterson, PGA   **Supt:** Chris Lynch
Architect: Bill Sholtko 1983

HAMMONTON COUNTRY CLUB **PUBLIC**

420 Boyer Ave., Hammonton, NJ 08037   **(609) 561-5504**

Hammonton is a recently expanded 18 hole course open 7 days a week all year. Tee time reservations may be made up to 7 days in advance.

• **Driving Range**   Lockers
• **Practice Green**   Showers
• **Power Carts**   • **Food**
• **Pull Carts**   • **Clubhouse**
• **Club Rental**   • **Outings**
• **Soft Spikes**

Fees	Weekday	Weekend
Daily	$25	$35
Fees include cart		

Weekday special for 2, $40 includes cart, fee & lunch

Course Description: This former 12 hole course has been expanded recently to a full 18 holes. Its rustic and park-like setting lead to an interesting golf experience. Originally, its name was Frog Rock and it was known for its rolling hills and tight fairways. The par 3 13th requires a well struck tee shot to carry over water. The greens are Penn Cross bent grass.

Directions: Atlantic County, #14 on Lower Shore Map
Atl. City Xpressway OR GSP to ACXwy. to Hammonton Exit. Take Rte. 54 North to Rte. 30. Watch for a sign saying "entering Hammonton". Pass a Chrysler dealership. As you make the curve, turn right onto Rte. 561. Keep straight & after STOP, club is on right.

Hole	1	2	3	4	5	6	7	8	9	Out	BLUE	Rating
BLUE	383	505	345	135	370	195	400	515	195	3043		Slope
WHITE	360	455	335	120	320	170	340	480	130	2710		
Par	4	5	4	3	4	3	4	5	3	35	WHITE	Rating
Handicap	1	7	11	17	9	13	5	3	15			Slope
RED	291	380	280	120	305	140	305	440	113	2374		
Par	4	5	4	3	4	3	4	5	3	35	RED	Rating
Handicap	1	7	11	17	9	13	5	3	15			Slope

Hole	10	11	12	13	14	15	16	17	18	In		Totals
BLUE	368	325	353	178	318	188	331	480	435	2976	BLUE	6019
WHITE	350	310	305	150	305	145	315	465	400	2745	WHITE	5455
Par	4	4	4	3	4	3	4	5	4	35	Par	70
Handicap	6	8	12	16	4	18	14	10	2			
RED	315	290	280	95	290	120	285	410	340	2425	RED	4799
Par	4	4	4	3	4	3	4	5	4	35	Par	70
Handicap	6	8	12	16	4	18	14	10	2			

Manager: Ernie Merighi   **Pro:** Don Larcher, PGA   **Supt:** Jack Montecalvo
Built: 1970s

HARBOR PINES COUNTRY CLUB

3071 Ocean Hts. Ave., Egg Harbor Twp., NJ 08215   (609) 927-0006

Harbor Pines is an 18 hole course open to the public 7 days a week all year. Memberships, both corporate and associate, are available. For tee times, dial extension 10, up to 10 days in advance for members, 7 days for daily fee golfers.

- **Driving Range**
- **Practice Green**
- **Power Carts**
- Pull Carts
- **Club Rental**
- **Soft Spikes**

- **Lockers**
- **Showers**
- **Food**
- **Clubhouse**
- **Outings**

Fees	M-Thurs	Fri-Sun
Daily	$89	$115
Seasonal specials		
Fees include cart		

Course Description: Recently opened Harbor Pines CC is a relatively flat, well conditioned layout that takes advantage of the surrounding beauty and landscape to provide an interesting experience for all levels of golfers. The parkland setting, strategically placed bunkers, wide fairway corridors, large, fast greens and well mown rough are features of this highly rated course. The par 4 9th fairway, sloping on both sides, has water on the left and woods on the right. The property is in the midst of an upscale real estate development. Within the comtemporary clubhouse is the well stocked Pro Shop.

Directions: Atlantic County, #15 on Lower Shore Map
GSP to Exit 30. At first major intersection, turn left onto Rte. 9 North. At the 5th light, turn left onto Ocean Heights Ave. Go about 1 and 1/2 miles to club on left.

Hole	1	2	3	4	5	6	7	8	9	Out	BLUE	Rating 70.7
BLUE	480	360	153	395	422	364	502	190	435	3301		Slope 125
WHITE	465	340	143	370	402	345	474	170	419	3128		
Par	5	4	3	4	4	4	5	3	4	36	WHITE	Rating 69.1
Handicap	15	9	17	5	3	7	13	11	1			Slope 122
RED	412	271	123	296	360	263	418	137	367	2626		
Par	5	4	3	4	4	4	5	3	4	36	RED	Rating 68.8
Handicap	9	11	17	7	1	13	5	15	3			Slope 118

Hole	10	11	12	13	14	15	16	17	18	In		Totals
BLUE	530	172	333	383	325	158	385	437	479	3202	BLUE	6503
WHITE	511	162	291	351	315	150	367	409	458	3014	WHITE	6142
Par	5	3	4	4	4	3	4	4	5	36	Par	72
Handicap	8	10	14	6	16	18	4	2	12			
RED	419	130	233	296	252	108	298	335	402	2473	RED	5099
Par	5	3	4	4	4	3	4	4	5	36	Par	72
Handicap	4	16	14	8	12	18	6	2	10			

Manager: Maurice Lepine   **Pro:** Mike Carson, PGA   **Supt:** Rick Broome
Architect: Stephen Kay 1996

LATONA GOLF & COUNTRY CLUB ███ PUBLIC ███

Oak & Cumberland Rds., Buena, NJ 08310   **(609) 692-8149**

Latona is a 9 hole public course open 7 days a week all year. Tee time reservations are not necessary.

Driving Range	Lockers
•**Practice Green**	Showers
•**Power Carts**	•**Food**
•**Pull Carts**	Clubhouse
•**Club Rental**	•**Outings**
Soft Spikes	

Fees	**Weekday**	**Weekend**
Daily	$13	$16
Twi(5PM)	$11	$13
Power carts $14pp		

Course Description: This well maintained 9 hole course is built on wide open terrain with very little water in play. The greens have subtle breaks and are hard to read; some say it has the "best greens in South Jersey." It is family operated and has a country-type friendly atmosphere.

Directions: Atlantic County, #16 on Lower Shore Map
Atlantic City Expressway West from the GSP or East from Phila.-Camden area (reached by NJTPKE) to Exit #28. Then take Rte. 54 South to Rte. 557 in Buena. Turn left and road becomes Cumberland Ave. Club is on right on Oak Rd.

Hole	1	2	3	4	5	6	7	8	9	Out	BLUE	Rating
BLUE												Slope
WHITE	360	480	390	185	330	155	440	495	225	3060		
Par	4	5	4	3	4	3	4	5	3	35	WHITE	Rating 70.6
Handicap	9	5	3	13	15	17	1	7	11			Slope 122
RED												
Par											RED	Rating
Handicap												Slope
Hole	10	11	12	13	14	15	16	17	18	In		Totals
BLUE											BLUE	
WHITE	370	490	400	195	340	165	450	505	235	3150	WHITE	6210
Par	4	5	4	3	4	3	4	5	3	35	Par	70
Handicap	10	6	4	14	16	18	2	8	12			
RED											RED	
Par											Par	
Handicap												

Manager: Joyce De Klerk   **Supt:** Nick Levari, Jr.
Architect: Garret Renn 1963

LINWOOD COUNTRY CLUB

800 Shore Rd., Linwood, NJ 08221   (609) 927-7374

Linwood is an 18 hole course open 7 days a week all year. Guests play accompanied by a member. Tee time reservations are necessary on weekends.

- •Driving Range
- •Practice Green
- •Power Carts
- Pull Carts
- •Club Rental
- •Caddies
- •Lockers
- •Showers
- •Food
- •Clubhouse
- Outings
- •Soft Spikes

Course Description: Excellent views of the bay prevail at the well maintained Linwood CC. So near the water, the wind is a major factor here. Golfers find the small greens difficult to putt and the breaks hard to read. The signature par 5 twelfth hole, 518 yards from the blues, has a lake running through the lay up area and is dominated by wind in your face. Stephen Kay has done some redesign recently to upgrade the course and produce a more links style feeling with additional bunkers and waste areas.

Directions: Atlantic County, #17 on Lower Shore Map
GSP to Exit #36. Take Rte. 40 East (Black Horse Pike) to Rte. 585 (becomes Shore Rd.) Go right on Rte. 585 to club on left. From Atl. Cty. Xway: exit at Rte. 585 and go South to club.

Hole	1	2	3	4	5	6	7	8	9	Out	BLUE	Rating 68.5
BLUE	348	363	167	421	357	171	377	205	531	2940		Slope 120
WHITE	333	323	127	387	328	164	360	198	505	2725		
Par	4	4	3	4	4	3	4	3	5	34	WHITE	Rating 67.4
Handicap	11	5	17	1	13	15	7	9	3			Slope 115
RED	319	314	114	280	312	157	289	121	409	2315		
Par	4	4	3	4	4	3	4	3	5	34	RED	Rating 69.6
Handicap	5	7	17	11	3	13	9	15	1			Slope 119
Hole	10	11	12	13	14	15	16	17	18	In		Totals
BLUE	366	365	518	345	389	404	173	532	376	3468	BLUE	6408
WHITE	355	325	433	333	370	346	164	463	362	3151	WHITE	5876
Par	4	4	5	4	4	4	3	5	4	37	Par	72
Handicap	10	18	6	8	2	14	12	4	16			
RED	345	264	407	319	351	333	151	414	348	2932	RED	5247
Par	4	4	5	4	4	4	3	5	4	37	Par	71
Handicap	8	16	4	14	6	12	18	2	10			

Manager: Bill Coulter   **Pro:** Jeff Lefevre, PGA   **Supt:** Alan Beck
Built: 1920s

MAYS LANDING COUNTRY CLUB

Cates Rd. & McKee Ave., McKee City, NJ 08232   (609) 641-4411

Mays Landing is an 18 hole semi-private course open to the public 7 days a week all year. Fees vary according to season and early-bird specials are available. Tee time reservations may be made up to 7 days in advance.

• Driving Range	• Lockers
• Practice Green	• Showers
• Power Carts	• Food
• Pull Carts	• Clubhouse
• Club Rental	• Outings
• Soft Spikes	

Fees	Weekday	Weekend
Daily	$50/cart	$60/cart
After 1PM	$25	
After 2PM		$25
Power carts $14pp		

Course Description: Mays Landing is a well designed and maintained course that wends its way through the Jersey Pinelands. The many trees encroach from the rough to produce narrow fairways. Water is in play on seven holes. The medium size greens are rather fast. One of the more interesting holes is the lengthy par 4 13th, featuring a long waste bunker on one side and a somewhat elevated green. Mays Landing is near the Atlantic City Airport, where private planes often land, so that those passengers who are golfers can play very conveniently at this club.

Directions: Atlantic County, #18 on Lower Shore Map
GSP to AC XPressway to Exit #9. Turn left at top of exit. Go approx. 2 miles & at STOP turn right onto Rte. 322. Turn right immediately after Canal's Liquor Store onto McKeeAve. Follow road approx. 1/4 mile to club on right.

Hole	1	2	3	4	5	6	7	8	9	Out	BLUE	Rating 71.3
BLUE	570	207	426	331	516	431	363	183	365	3392		Slope 120
WHITE	544	188	379	301	500	421	356	164	346	3199		
Par	5	3	4	4	5	4	4	3	4	36	WHITE	Rating 69.6
Handicap	3	11	7	17	5	1	9	15	13			Slope 117
RED	487	132	336	264	464	350	325	132	293	2783		
Par	5	3	4	4	5	4	4	3	4	36	RED	Rating 70.2
Handicap	1	15	5	11	7	3	9	17	13			Slope 117
Hole	10	11	12	13	14	15	16	17	18	In		Totals
BLUE	392	501	180	434	354	220	373	541	412	3407	BLUE	6799
WHITE	376	482	154	385	337	172	357	527	388	3178	WHITE	6377
Par	4	5	3	4	4	3	4	5	4	36	Par	72
Handicap	10	16	18	2	12	14	8	4	6			
RED	322	386	116	376	295	123	294	426	288	2626	RED	5409
Par	4	4	3	4	4	3	4	5	4	35	Par	71
Handicap	10	4	18	2	14	16	8	6	12			

Manager: Sean Donnelly   **Pro:** Bob Herman, PGA   **Supt:** Jeff Allen
Architect: Leo Fraser 1962

OCEAN CITY GOLF COURSE

PUBLIC

Bay Ave. & 26th St., Ocean City, NJ 08226   **(609) 399-1315**

Ocean City is a 12 hole municipal course operated by the Ocean City Dep't. of Publlic Works. It is open 7 days a week all year. Tee time reservations are not necessary.

Driving Range	Lockers
•**Practice Green**	Showers
Power Carts	•**Food**
•**Pull Carts**	Clubhouse
•**Club Rental**	Outings
Soft Spikes	

Fees	Weekday	Weekend
Daily	$9	$9
Sr/Jr	$7.50	$7.50

Course Description: The warm and friendly atmosphere at this golf facility is a welcome attraction. Adjacent to an airport from which you can literally walk to the first tee, golfers who fly can really enjoy this unique feature at this well maintained course. Ocean City is recommended for beginners, seniors and for those who want to practice their game at an inexpensive twelve hole layout. Due to environmental restrictions, no more holes may be built.

Directions: Cape May County, #19 on Lower Shore Map
GSP to Exit #30. Follow signs to Rte. 52 (Laurel Ave.) Take bridge across bay to Ocean City and make a right onto Bay Ave. to 26th St. to club on right. From South: GSPNorth to Exit 25 toward Ocean City. At 1st light, go left onto Bay Ave. for 8 blocks to course.

Hole	1	2	3	4	5	6	7	8	9	Out	BLUE	Rating
BLUE												Slope
WHITE	70	145	135	115	140	105	135	180	165			
Par	3	3	3	3	3	3	3	3	3	27	WHITE	Rating
Handicap	12	7	9	10	8	11	6	1	3			Slope
RED												
Par											RED	Rating
Handicap												Slope

Hole	10	11	12	13	14	15	16	17	18	In		Totals
BLUE											BLUE	
WHITE	230	155	175								WHITE	1750
Par	4	3	3								Par	37
Handicap	5	4	2									
RED											RED	
Par											Par	
Handicap												

Club Manager: Bill DeAngelis   **Built:** 1962

THE PINES AT CLERMONT

358 Kings Highway, Clermont, NJ 08210 **(609) 624-0100**

The Pines is a 9 hole executive course officially opening in 1999. It is open 7 days a week all year. Limited memberships are available. Tee times are up to 7 days in advance for members and 3 days for daily players.

Driving Range	Lockers		Fees	9 holes	18 holes
• **Practice Green**	Showers		6/15 -9/15	$30	$50
• **Power Carts**	• **Food**		9/16-12/1	$20	$30
• **Pull Carts**	• **Clubhouse**		12/2-3/14	$10	$15
• **Club Rental**	• **Outings**		3/15-6/14	$20	$30
• **Soft Spikes**			Power carts extra		

Course Description: The Pines at Clermont is a wonderful new addition to Southern New Jersey golf. The course is easily walkable and excellent for short game practice. With bent grass tree-lined fairways, tees and greens, the waste bunkers and water in view make this an intelligently conceived and peacefully comfortable venue for a quiet golf getaway. There is beauty in the signature loop of holes 5, 6 and 7 around the lake; the layout is mature looking and well groomed. The relatively small greens and pot bunkers add to the challenge here.

Directions: Cape May County, #20 on Lower Shore Map
GSP to Exit 17. From ramp, turn left and then left onto Rte. 9South. Go 1 mile to Academy Rd. and turn right. Go 1 mile to STOP. Course is 50 yards ahead on the left.

Hole	1	2	3	4	5	6	7	8	9	Out	BLUE	Rating
BLUE												Slope
WHITE	356	124	400	324	185	153	131	270	132	2085		
Par	4	3	4	4	3	3	3	4	3	31	WHITE	Rating
Handicap	6	9	1	3	2	4	7	5	8			Slope
RED	323	114	387	306	162	149	111	253	116	1921		
Par											RED	Rating
Handicap												Slope
Hole	10	11	12	13	14	15	16	17	18	In		Totals
BLUE											BLUE	
WHITE											WHITE	2085
Par											Par	31
Handicap												
RED											RED	1921
Par											Par	31
Handicap												

Manager/Dir. of Golf: Adele Montecalvo, LPGA   **Supt:** Steve Malikowski
Architects: Steve Malikowski, Vince Orlando 1999

POMONA GOLF & COUNTRY CLUB

Moss Mill Rd. & Odessa Ave., Pomona, NJ 08240   (609) 965-3232

Pomona is an executive 9 hole semi-private course open 7 days a week all year. Memberships are available. Tee time reservations are not necessary.

•**Driving Range**	Lockers
Practice Green	Showers
•**Power Carts**	•**Food**
•**Pull Carts**	
•**Club Rental**	•**Clubhouse**
Soft Spikes	Outings

Fees	Weekday	Weekend
Daily	$12	$14
Power carts for members only		

Course Description: Pomona is a family owned and managed facility. It is a flat, wooded course not far from bustling Atlantic City. Water hazards come into play on three holes. The fairways are tree lined and there are bunkers on every hole. The bent grass greens are elevated. Accuracy with irons is a must to score well here. The friendly atmosphere and reasonable rates make it very appealing.

Directions: Atlantic County, #21 on Lower Shore Map
GSP to mile marker #41. Follow Hospital signs past Stockton State College to Rte. 561 and make a right. Watch for house with white picket fence. Turn right onto Odessa Ave. & go 1 & 1/2 miles to course.

Hole	1	2	3	4	5	6	7	8	9	Out	BLUE	Rating
BLUE												Slope
WHITE	295	150	295	290	290	275	126	365	340	2426		
Par	4	3	4	4	4	4	3	4	4	34	WHITE	Rating 62.5
Handicap												Slope
RED												
Par	4	3	5	4	5	4	3	5	5	38	RED	Rating
Handicap												Slope
Hole	10	11	12	13	14	15	16	17	18	In		Totals
BLUE											BLUE	
WHITE	295	150	295	290	290	275	126	365	340	2426	WHITE	4852
Par	4	3	4	4	4	4	3	4	4	34	Par	68
Handicap												
RED											RED	
Par	4	3	5	4	5	4	3	5	5	38	Par	76
Handicap												

Managers: Andrea Truitt & Pam Grenda   **Supt:** Bruce Ritchie
Built: 1940s

PONDERLODGE GOLF COURSE

7 Shawmount Ave., Villas, NJ 08251   **(609) 886-8065**

Ponderlodge is an 18 hole semi-private course open to the public 7 days a week all year. Memberships are available. Tee time resesrvations can be made up to 2 weeks in advance.

Driving Range	•**Lockers**
•**Practice Green**	•**Showers**
•**Power Carts**	•**Food**
•**Pull Carts**	•**Clubhouse**
•**Club Rental**	•**Outings**
•**Soft Spikes**	

Fees	Weekday	Weekend
Daily	$44	$48
After 1:30PM	$35	
Power carts	$12pp	

Course Description: At the end of a long, shaded, tree lined entrance road lies the golf course and the private Ponderlodge Conference Center. The wooded course is rather tight, scenic and interesting. Each hole has its own character with water in play on many of them. The long, narrow par 5 seventh is the signature hole and justifiably the #1 handicap. Formerly an estate owned by William Former of Schmidts's Brewery, horses are still stabled on the premises. It is close to Cape May Airport. Nine holes were added in 1992 when the course was redone. This short course is in the process of a major renovation. Scorecard below is for 1998 yardages and ratings.

Directions: Cape May County, #22 on Lower Shore Map
GSP to Exit #4A (Rio Grande) to Rte. 47 North. Cross over Rte. 9 and turn left at Fulling Rd. Turn left onto Bayshore Rd. Club entrance is 1 mile on the right side just past Bayshore Village.

Hole	1	2	3	4	5	6	7	8	9	Out	BLUE	Rating 69.6
BLUE	329	143	363	326	506	216	537	301	425	3149		Slope 120
WHITE	302	137	358	321	504	211	532	296	420	3081		
Par	4	3	4	4	5	3	5	4	4	36	WHITE	Rating 69.1
Handicap	11	17	7	9	3	15	1	13	5			Slope 119
RED	251	113	306	260	489	147	447	221	339	2573		
Par	4	3	4	4	5	3	5	4	4	36	RED	Rating 68.6
Handicap	11	17	7	9	3	15	1	13	5			Slope 117

Hole	10	11	12	13	14	15	16	17	18	In		Totals
BLUE	365	188	312	315	321	487	347	418	149	2902	BLUE	6051
WHITE	360	183	307	310	316	482	342	413	144	2857	WHITE	5938
Par	4	3	4	4	4	5	4	4	3	35	Par	71
Handicap	6	16	14	12	10	2	8	4	18			
RED	299	128	234	235	218	402	289	337	119	2261	RED	4770
Par	4	3	4	4	4	5	4	4	3	35	Par	71
Handicap	6	16	14	12	10	2	8	4	18			

Manager: Tony Funari **Dir. of Golf:** Joseph Farina
Supts: Herbie Phillip & John Thompson **Architect:** Tony Funari 1977

SAND BARRENS GOLF CLUB

PUBLIC

1765 Route 9 North, Swainton, NJ 08210   (609) 465-3555

Sand Barrens is an 18 hole semi-private course open 7 days a week all year. A third nine is under construction to be opened in the Spring of 1999. Memberships are available with discounted rates and preferred reservation privileges. Tee time reservations may be made up to 7 days in advance.

- **Driving Range**
- **Practice Green**
- **Power Carts**
- Pull Carts
- **Club Rental**
- **Soft Spikes**

Lockers
Showers
- **Food**
Clubhouse
- **Outings**

NEW

Fees	Weekday	Weekend
Daily	$85	$85
9holes 4PM	$40	$40
Sept-Nov	$69	$69
Dec-Mar	$39	$39
Power carts included		

Course Description: The new more densely treed nine being built as we go to press will be mixed in to make the layout change. The scorecard below is for the original 18. Sand Barrens has wide gently rolling fairways and large relatively fast contoured greens, all of bent grass. The course has been created out of vast pine and oak forests; the environment has been treated with respect leaving wetlands, native grasses and bayberry vegetation in the rough. Unique are huge waste areas of sand in play on every hole where the golfer may ground his club. The yardage from the "Pro" tees is 6902 and there are longer tees of 5857 as an option for ladies. This beautifully maintained course has been rated highly by several prestigious golf magazines and deservedly so.

Directions: Cape May County, #23 on Lower Shore Map
GSP to Exit 13 (Avalon). Go right to Rte. 9 and turn right. Go north for about a mile to course on left.

Hole	1	2	3	4	5	6	7	8	9	Out	BLUE	Rating 71.1
BLUE	385	395	389	355	150	557	430	562	183	3406		Slope 130
WHITE	355	377	365	345	140	539	416	545	171	3253		
Par	4	4	4	4	3	5	4	5	3	36	WHITE	Rating 69.7
Handicap	7	9	11	15	17	3	5	1	13			Slope 128
RED	266	282	273	255	90	425	308	479	85	2463		
Par	4	4	4	4	3	5	4	5	3	36	RED	Rating 68.9
Handicap	7	9	11	15	17	3	5	1	13			Slope 119

Hole	10	11	12	13	14	15	16	17	18	In		Totals
BLUE	375	548	165	379	285	425	353	179	500	3209	BLUE	6615
WHITE	362	530	141	356	276	409	329	163	485	3051	WHITE	6304
Par	4	5	3	4	4	4	4	3	5	36	Par	72
Handicap	8	4	18	6	16	2	12	14	10			
RED	250	448	113	279	210	308	254	105	387	2354	RED	4817
Par	4	5	3	4	4	4	4	3	5	36	Par	72
Handicap	8	4	18	6	16	2	12	14	10			

Manager: Mike Gaffney   **Dir. of Golf:** E. Alden Richards, PGA   **Supt:** Tim Christ
Architects: Dr. Michael Hurdzdan, Dana Fry 1997

SEAVIEW GOLF RESORT

PUBLIC

401 South New York Rd., Absecon, NJ 08201   **(609) 652-1800**

Seaview is a golf resort with two separate 18 hole courses that are open to the public and to hotel guests 7 days a week all year. Tee times may be made up to 30 days in advance for hotel guests; 1 week for non-guests.

- **Driving Range**
- **Practice Green**
- **Power Carts**
- Pull Carts
- **Club Rental**
- **Soft Spikes**
- **Lockers**
- **Showers**
- **Food**
- **Clubhouse**
- **Outings**

Fees	Weekday	Weekend
4/30-10/10	$110	$135
10/10-10/31	$99	$99
11/1-12/31	$49	$59
Power carts included		

Course Description: The legendary Bay course, designed by Donald Ross in a "Scottish links" style was completed in 1913. With 89 bunkers in a picturesque wind-swept setting, it features wide open mounded fairways and greens that are open in front to allow "bump & run" approach shots. The 1931 Pines course was updated in 1957 by William Gordon. Cut out of the NJ Pinelands, it has pine tree lined fairways, splashy rhododendra, large and steep bunkers and fast, undulating elevated greens. The PGA Championship was held here in 1942, & the Shop Rite LPGA Classic is now being held here again. Scorecard below is for the Bay Course.

Directions: Atlantic County, #24 on Lower Shore Map
GSP to Exit #48. Go South on Rte. 9 for 9 & 1/2 miles. Seaview Resort is on right.

Hole	1	2	3	4	5	6	7	8	9	Out	BLUE	Rating 70.7
BLUE	357	434	484	360	301	393	190	319	425	3253		Slope 122
WHITE	345	421	464	347	292	380	180	302	401	3131		
Par	4	4	5	4	4	4	3	4	4	36	WHITE	Rating 69.5
Handicap	9	1	7	11	15	5	17	13	3			Slope 120
RED	293	341	394	290	255	319	110	288	325	2615		
Par	4	4	5	4	4	4	3	4	4	36	RED	Rating 68.4
Handicap	9	1	7	11	15	5	17	13	3			Slope 114
Hole	10	11	12	13	14	15	16	17	18	In		Totals
BLUE	419	204	377	115	230	320	476	352	501	2994	BLUE	6247
WHITE	403	193	366	104	221	311	463	337	482	2880	WHITE	6011
Par	4	3	4	3	3	4	5	4	5	35	Par	71
Handicap	2	16	8	18	14	12	6	10	4			
RED	322	150	294	92	179	275	411	272	408	2402	RED	5017
Par	4	3	4	3	3	4	5	4	5	35	Par	71
Handicap	2	16	8	18	14	12	6	10	4			

Director of Golf: Rob Bartley   **Pro:** Mike Rushing, PGA   **Supt:** John O'Connor
Architects: Donald Ross 1913 Bay, Flynn & Toomey 1929 Pines

STONE HARBOR GOLF CLUB

905 Rte. 9 North, Cape May Courthouse, NJ 08210   **(609) 465-9270**

Stone Harbor is an 18 hole course open 7 days a week all year. Associate members pay cart & green fees in addition to their dues. Guests may play accompanied by a member. Members may request tee times up to 2 weeks in advance.

•**Driving Range**	•**Lockers**
•**Practice Green**	•**Showers**
•**Power Carts**	•**Food**
Pull Carts	•**Clubhouse**
•**Club Rental**	•**Outings**
•**Caddies**	•**Soft Spikes**

Course Description: The slope rating of 143 from the championship tees indicates how difficult the beautiful Stone Harbor course can be. Some consider it comparable to and as demanding as the famed Pine Valley. The well groomed fairways and fast greens are dotted with bunkers of unusual configurations. With water coming into play on well over half of the holes, the picturesque hilly course offers a multitude of photo opportunities. The par 4 6th hole features an island fairway with a green guarded by more water. Golfers encounter water on the par 3 7th hole everywhere but the tee and oval shaped putting surface which is surrounded by grass banks. Five sets of tees give variety to the course.

Directions: Cape May County, #25 on Lower Shore Map
GSP to Exit #13 and follow road to Rte. 9 South. Course is ahead on right.

Hole	1	2	3	4	5	6	7	8	9	Out	BLUE	Rating 74.0
BLUE	398	419	557	174	509	435	182	419	423	3516		Slope 143
WHITE	379	384	536	161	499	406	148	402	392	3307		
Par	4	4	5	3	5	4	3	4	4	36	WHITE	Rating 72.4
Handicap	17	3	7	15	13	1	11	9	5			Slope 123
RED	319	328	476	107	429	338	84	327	300	2708		
Par	4	4	5	3	5	5	3	4	4	37	RED	Rating 72.4
Handicap	17	3	1	15	13	5	11	9	7			Slope 123
Hole	10	11	12	13	14	15	16	17	18	In		Totals
BLUE	354	505	183	427	470	387	517	167	409	3419	BLUE	6935
WHITE	339	494	170	385	456	354	490	161	389	3238	WHITE	6545
Par	4	5	3	4	4	4	5	3	4	36	Par	72
Handicap	16	10	14	12	2	8	6	18	4			
RED	264	410	133	334	410	304	376	135	291	2657	RED	5365
Par	4	5	3	4	5	4	5	3	4	37	Par	74
Handicap	16	10	14	12	4	8	6	18	2			

Manager/ Pro: Harry Bittner, PGA   **Supt:** Ken Thompson
Architect: Desmond Muirhead 1987

WILDWOOD GOLF & CC

Golf Club Rd., Cape May Courthouse, NJ 08210   (609) 465-7823

Wildwood is an 18 hole course open 7 days a week all year. Courtesy is extended on weekdays to members of other clubs & guests of members; weekends are reserved for members of other clubs in the Phila. area only. Reserved tee times are advisable.

- •Driving Range •Lockers
- •Practice Green •Showers
- •Power Carts •Food
- •Pull Carts •Clubhouse
- •Club Rental •Outings
- Caddies •Soft Spikes

Course Description: The traditional links style Wildwood in Cape May County is a well groomed layout that surrenders to the breezes of the shore area affecting play much of the time. The course has several small lakes and mounds and is relatively flat with a short, tight back nine. There are bent grass fairways and greens; the latter are small and well bunkered. The par 3 scenic seventh is considered the signature hole; it is short and interesting yet requires a shot over water. The course is open to the public off season; call for dates.

Directions: Cape May County, #26 on Lower Shore Map
GSP to Exit #9. At light, turn left and make 1st right onto Golf Club Rd. Club on left.

Hole	1	2	3	4	5	6	7	8	9	Out	BLUE	Rating
BLUE												Slope
WHITE	425	463	335	364	387	331	161	358	355	3179		
Par	4	5	4	4	4	4	3	4	4	36	WHITE	Rating 71.1
Handicap	6	2	10	14	4	16	18	8	12			Slope 124
RED	366	362	335	329	387	301	122	315	320	2837		
Par	4	5	4	4	5	4	3	4	4	37	RED	Rating 72.3
Handicap	3	1	9	11	7	15	17	5	13			Slope 122
Hole	10	11	12	13	14	15	16	17	18	In		Totals
BLUE											BLUE	
WHITE	384	390	213	410	345	508	140	397	378	3165	WHITE	6344
Par	4	4	3	4	4	5	3	4	4	35	Par	71
Handicap	5	9	15	1	13	3	17	7	11			
RED	369	355	152	330	311	353	113	354	343	2680	RED	5517
Par	5	4	3	4	4	5	3	4	4	36	Par	73
Handicap	6	2	16	10	14	12	18	4	8			

Manager: Robert Keating   **Dir. of Golf:** Stacy Bunker   **Supt:** Khlar Holthouse
Architects: Stiles and Van Kleek 1916

COMING ATTRACTIONS

Rumors abound regarding the building of more golf courses. Although detailed information is not available, **as a service to our readers,** we decided to alert you to what we hear on the grapevine.

Some of the **New Courses** still on the drawing board or in early stages of construction.

Atlantic County

Twisted Dunes in Egg Harbor Twonship

Renault in Egg Harbor Township

Salem County

Running Deer in Elmer

Ocean County

Sea Oaks

Cumberland County

New course in **Vineland**

See page 316 for special supplement offer

Golf is a game in which you put a ball 1 and 1/2 inches in diameter on a ball 8,000 miles in diameter and you try to hit the little ball without hitting the big ball.

A golfer may be careful with his money in other matters but never minds spending a small fortune on clubs, balls, lessons, fees and therapy (when his game drives him to the brink of a nervous breakdown).

(**Country Club of Salem**)

INDEX

Key: Names of golf clubs or golf courses are in **bold**.

Names of architects are in *italics*.

Towns indexed are locations of the courses.

Head golf pros are listed.

Findlay, Alexander 125,230, 253,261,282
Findlay, William 245
Finger, Joe 158
Flanders 62
Flanders Valley 62
Flemington 134, 143
Flood, Val 46
Florham Park 55,82
Flynn, William 166 ,271, 298
Forest Hill 105
Forsch, Ron 239
Forsgate 137
Fort Dix 234
Fort Monmouth 222
Foster, Robert 39
Fountain Green 234
Four Seasons 191
Fox Hollow 138
Francis Byrne 106
Franklin 52,92
Franklin Lakes 28
Franklin Township 1165
Fraser, Leo 292
Fredon Township 51
Freeway 235
Fry, Dana 297
Funari, Tony A296
Galbiati, Francis 283
Gallagher, Mickie 111
Galloping Hill 107
Galloway GC 284
Gambler Ridge 192
Gaskill, Carl 262
Genter, Charles 261

Giuliano, Mark 59
Glen Ridge 108
Glen Ridge CC 108
Glenwild Greens 25
Glenwood CC 139
Glenz, Dave 50, 52, 56
Glenz, Dave 52
Golden Pheasant 236
Gordon & Gordon 78
Gordon, William 142,153,244, 246,269,280
Granger, Rod 126
Great Gorge 63
Greate Bay 285
Green Brook 109
Green Knoll 142
Green Pond 64
Green Tree 286
Green, Harold 66
Greenacres 140
Greenbriar Woodlands 193
Greenbriar at Whittingham 141
Hackensack GC 26
Hackettstown 75, 79
Haddonfield 261
Hainesville 66
Hamburg 50,56
Hamilton Trails 287
Hammonton 288
Hammonton CC 288
Handwerg, John Jr. 37
Hanover CC 237
Hansen, Mort 180
Harbor Pines 289
Harkers Hollow 65

SPECIAL UPDATE

In 2000, a special supplement will be available with the latest details on the "new" courses and coming attractions.

Purchasers of this book may obtain this update for the nominal cost of $3.00 to cover shipping and handling.

We may be reached by phone, fax or on-line. See the last page of this book for ordering information.

Notes & Comments

Notes & Comments

*Quality products for women who play
or just enjoy the sport of Golf.*

Apparel and accessories for the Woman Golfer

To see our merchandise, place an order or request a brochure,
We invite you to visit our web site at: WWW.Chixwstix.com

Or call us at: 973-669-0977
Fax: 973-669-1296
Email: Chixwstixp@AOL.COM

Wholly owned and operated by Women Golfers

Chix with Stix Productions, Inc.

*43 Sicomac Road
North Haledon, NJ 07508*

We accept Master Card, Visa, and American Express

ORDERING INFORMATION

Telephone: (201) 569-6605
(201) 461-7960
Fax# (201) 569-6949

By Mail: **Weathervane Press**
44 Bliss Avenue
Tenafly, NJ 07670

THE GARDEN STATE GOLF GUIDE
Send check or money order for $15.95 plus tax,
shipping and handling.

THE GREATER NEW YORK GOLF GUIDE
Send check or money order for $18.95 plus tax,
shipping and handling.

NJ Sales tax; Add 6% per book
NY Sales tax: Add 8.25% per book
Shipping and handling: $3.00 per book.

TO **ORDER** and **PAY** by Charge Card, visit us on-line
at www.chixwstix.com and click on **Golf Guides** or
Weathervane Press

For quantity orders, please call Weathervane Press at
telephone numbers above.